D0915962

DISCARD

Exploring Competency Based Education

Edited by

W. Robert Houston

University of Houston

McCutchan Publishing Corporation
2526 Grove Street
Berkeley, California 94704

© 1974 by the Board of Regents of the University of Houston
All rights reserved
Library of Congress Catalog Card no. 74-76532
ISBN 0-8211-0752-6
Manufactured in the United States of America

Copyright is claimed until May 31, 1979. Thereafter all
portions of this work covered by this copyright will be
in the public domain.

This work was developed under a grant from the U.S. Office of
Education, Department of Health, Education, and Welfare. However,
the opinions and other content do not necessarily reflect the
position or policy of the Agency, and no official endorsement
should be inferred.

Dedicated to
Elizabeth Houston

Compassionate,
Competent,
and
Committed to a better life for everyone.

Contents

Contributing Authors

THEODORE E. ANDREWS
  Director, Multi-State Consortium on Performance Based
    Teacher Education
  Division of Teacher Education and Certification
  New York State Education Department

FRANK H. BLACKINGTON III
  Director, The Honors College
  Michigan State University

HARRY S. BROUDY
  Professor of Philosophy of Education
  University of Illinois

ARTHUR W. COMBS
  Professor of Education
  University of Florida

JAMES M. COOPER
  Associate Dean, College of Education
  University of Houston

M. VERE DeVAULT
Professor of Curriculum and Instruction
University of Wisconsin

DONNA DOLINSKY
Assistant Professor of Education
University of Toledo

WILLIAM H. DRUMMOND
Professor of Education
University of Florida

SANDRA FELDMAN
Assistant to the President
United Federation of Teachers, New York

HORACE C. HARTSELL
Director, Instructional Development Services
University of Texas Dental School

PATRICIA HEFFERNAN-CABRERA
Chairman, Program for TESOL/Bilingual
Director, Teacher Corps
University of Southern California

W. ROBERT HOUSTON
Associate Dean, College of Education
University of Houston

ROBERT B. HOWSAM
Dean, College of Education
University of Houston

BRUCE JOYCE
Professor, Teachers College
Columbia University

PATRICIA M. KAY
Director, Competency Based Teacher Education Project
City University of New York

SUZANNE M. KINZER
  Assistant Professor, Department of Childhood Education
  University of Florida

HERBERT F. LaGRONE
  Dean, School of Education
  Texas Christian University

FREDERICK J. McDONALD
  Senior Research Psychologist
  Educational Testing Service

ANN G. OLMSTED
  Professor, Medical Education and Education
  Michigan State University

DAVID A. POTTER
  Associate Research Psychologist
  Educational Testing Service

BENJAMIN ROSNER
  Dean, College of Education
  Temple University

THOMAS J. QUIRK
  Associate Professor of Psychology and Education
  Principia College

H. DEL SCHALOCK
  Research Professor, Teaching Research
  Division of the Oregon State System of Higher Education

ALLEN A. SCHMIEDER
  Chief, Operations Coordination
  National Center for the Improvement of Educational Systems
  United States Office of Education

JAMES P. STEFFENSON
  Director of Planning and Development
  Teacher Corps, United States Office of Education

ELVIRA R. TARR
> Associate Professor of Education and Assistant Dean
> of Students
> Brooklyn Branch of City University of New York

ADELE K. THOMAS
> Research Assistant, Office of Teacher Education
> City University of New York

RICHARD L. TURNER
> Associate Dean for Research and Development
> Indiana University

SANDY A. WALL
> Professor of Education
> Texas Christian University

WILFORD A. WEBER
> Associate Professor of Education
> University of Houston

MARSHA WEIL
> Director of Elementary Preservice Progress in Childhood
> Education
> Teachers College
> Columbia University

RICHARD WOLLIN
> Dean, School of Education
> Southwest Minnesota State College

Foreword

The experience of the reform movements in education over the past two decades has underlined the importance of high-quality training of educational personnel. One major national effort to provide a plan for that improvement is given careful review by the contributors to this collection of essays on competency based education.

The development of and the dialogue on a competency-oriented system within the teacher education community have at least two reasonably distinguishable sources. The first is associated with the impact of the separate as well as collective efforts of the many faculties across the nation to improve their efforts in the preparation of elementary and secondary teachers. The other, of no greater magnitude but of probably more clearly identifiable impact, is that of the Office of Education through its support of such programs and projects as Teacher Corps, the Bureau of Educational Personnel Development Task Force 72, the Multi-State Consortium of Performance Based Teacher Education, and the Elementary Teacher Education Models project.

The latter activity—the Models Project—is generally identified as providing the early literature associated with competency based teacher education, while the National Center for Improvement of

Educational Systems and Teacher Corps are viewed as being the OE programs most persistently involved with the exploration of CBTE as a system through which the restructuring of teacher education might take place.

The major impetus for CBTE may be traced back to late 1967 when the Bureau of Research within the Office of Education issued a request for proposals to support the development of "Educational Specifications for a Comprehensive Undergraduate and Inservice Teacher Education Teachers." The problem to which the design of the models was addressed was stated as follows:

Because of the key role that the teacher plays in facilitating learning, particularly with young children, he/she must have the most up-to-date theoretical and substantial knowledge and professional skills to perform successfully. To date, research and development activities have generated new knowledge, materials, and methodologies with great potential for improving the effectiveness and efficiency of the teaching-learning process. If funds are made available, institutions should be able at this time to completely restructure their teacher education programs to include the best of what is now known and available.

The request for proposals indicated that a system analysis approach should be used in developing the specifications of the models. It was further stated that "the program initiated . . . is designed to enable ready development into operating programs and full implementation by other institutions that train teachers."

In supporting this project, it was agreed that the OE's strategy should be to: (1) support the redesign of teacher training programs rather than individual investigators or the development of program pieces or subsystems; (2) encourage alternative conceptual designs for the training of elementary teachers; (3) design a strategy that would identify and utilize the extant high-quality nationwide talent in developing a diverse but limited number of conceptual models for training elementary teachers; and (4) support program development that would be generalizable and "transportable." Each model would include a behavioral description of important teaching competencies and the relationship of these competencies to the educational milieu in which the teacher would perform. The models would include specifications for training systems designed to prepare the teacher to demonstrate these competencies. Assessment procedures for both individual competencies asked prior to school experience and the teacher performance in an instructional setting were to be specified.

The charge included the design of management systems and procedures for developing and implementing the model within a school of education and cooperating local education agencies.

Following the initial research activities, the Office of Education engaged in planned and organized effort to disseminate the products of the development phase. Specifications for implementation contracts were distributed nationally. Presentations were made at numerous national professional meetings. Media presentations were prepared. Conferences were held in cooperation with the American Association of Colleges for Teacher Education. The nation's leadership in teacher education became involved in a dialogue about competency based systems. By 1970 the CBTE processes and procedures for developing systematic teacher training had become well-known throughout the teacher education community at the college and school level.

At the same time, OE units involved in teacher training, and particularly Teacher Corps, began to review the potential of a competency based program, since the procedures then available were inadequate for Teacher Corps purposes. Although the original Teacher Corps guidelines included several features that promised improvement of teacher training—e.g., the involvement of parents and community members—these did not suffice to overcome problems caused by the vagueness of training goals or imprecise training methods.

Hence the decision: To fulfill its mission, Teacher Corps also had to engage in program improvement in teacher education. It then turned to the components of the "models" of teacher training as a major source of ideas, procedures, and carefully planned systems. Local project staffs were familiarized with the models, induced to begin their own competency oriented training, and involved in a general staff-development and technical assistance effort that influenced all local Teacher Corps sites. Because of the discernible improvement in intern training, Teacher Corps has continued to support site development of competency based components.

The final, or developmental, phase of the original models project was never initiated, and thus the plans for the implementation of a variety of systems models based on those designs have not come to fruition. However, over the past seven years the products of the project have continued to exert considerable influence on the teacher education community in this country and even to some extent abroad. Much of this impact, it would seem, has come from the close relationship between the emerging CBTE leadership and the original designers of the models.

The individuals invited to contribute statements for this publication represent an array of viewpoints and the collection of essays should make a significant contribution to the growing library of materials on competency based teacher education. They suggest a number of issues: the importance of CBTE for the inservice as well as preservice programs, the potential of shared decision-making for the development of teacher education, and the reconciliation of possible conflicts between systems theory and humanism are among the many major questions raised. The collection should be of considerable assistance as a reference tool for a large community, including those persons involved with the review and improvement of state licensing procedures as well as those concerned with anticipated and current developments in teacher education at the school and university levels.

James P. Steffenson
Teacher Corps
U.S. Office of Education

Preface

The ebb and flow of educational thought has been shaped by and has in turn spawned a series of educational movements and trends. Each movement has reflected a general societal climate, technological advances, research, innovations, and the dreams of educators. As each movement has matured, it has come under increasingly close scrutiny by educators and the general public. Operationalized programs never quite achieve the idealized models. Critics point out basic structural flaws in the model and inherent weaknesses in the operational programs. The ensuing debate between advocates and critics causes both to focus more clearly on basic issues, and from the analysis is derived a more viable educational enterprise. Of such is progress.

Competency based education as a movement has gained high visibility during the past five years. As with most movements, it reflects a general cultural trend as well as specific educational goals. Initiated by educators, supported by grants from federal, private, and state sources, and encouraged by state education agencies and others searching for a means to accountability or their own brand of Shangri-la, CBE has rapidly gained both advocates and critics. Because of its prominence in American teacher education during the early seventies, it is a movement whose basic tenets should be analyzed from a theoretical perspective, an extensive series of micro and macro research studies, and its program models assessed.

The authors of the various chapters in this book have attempted to put into perspective the issues that surround competency based education. Each speculates on a basic position, reflects on the alternatives, and analyzes the potential for the movement. The purpose of the volume is to stimulate discussion, analysis, and, through such study, to gain a deeper understanding of CBE; from such efforts is derived the increased power of the movement for improving education.

The first of five parts explores the basic meaning of competency based education. Chapter 1 presents several definitions, while in the second chapter McDonald traces the psychological and theoretical bases for CBE. In chapter 3, Andrews speculates on several misconceptions about the movement. In the next two chapters, DeVault and Heffernan-Cabrera explore individualized and humanized education, two closely aligned concepts which CBE has been credited by some with fostering and by others with thwarting. DeVault delineates a research model for studying individualized instruction.

Part 2 appraises the basic concepts of competency based education. Chapter 6 reports on a debate between philosopher Harry Broudy and CBE advocates Drummond and Rosner. Their insightful comments and discussion provide a balanced view of several basic issues. In chapter 7 Tarr emphasizes philosophic inconsistencies in the definitions and descriptions of CBE. Feldman takes the practical view of a teacher unionist, supporting the basic concept of competency based education but opposing the movement as a basis for certification. Blackington and Olmsted raise sociological issues about the potential effectiveness of formal schooling in general and competency based education in particular.

In Part 3 several models for identifying competencies are described. Weil reports on a process derived from alternative models of teaching. In the following chapter, LaGrone and Wall describe a model of professionalism that could form the basis for identifying competencies. A third approach is described by Thomas and Kay. They used a task analysis of teaching and the judgments of classroom teachers and supervisors in specifying competencies. Results of their study are reported in this chapter. Combs and Kinzer describe an alternative approach to CBTE that is based on Combs's theories and research.

A major problem in competency based programs is the design of assessment and evaluation systems—both for student achievement and program effectiveness. In chapters 14 and 15 Joyce and Schalock speculate on several issues in assessment and describe some potential procedures for designing an assessment system. In the following chapter, Quirk, arguing from a psychometric viewpoint, projects several critical problems inherent in measuring competencies. Turner then suggests a model for assessing performances, while Kay analyzes techniques appropriate for measuring specific performances. According to some educators, assessment by pupils is the most valid competency measurement; Weber speculates on this and suggests some ways in which pupils can contribute to teacher assessment. Finally, Potter suggests a research strategy that is sorely needed to build a viable base for CBE.

Perhaps one of the most important potential contributions of CBE is in its inherent capacity to bring about institutional as well as programmatic change. In chapter 21, several propositions related to institutional change are projected. In the following chapter, Hartsell describes the roles assumed by the faculty of a dental school as they developed a competency based program. Wollin then considers the change processes employed in a small state-supported college. And finally, Dolinsky emphasizes that students in CBE programs can play an active role in program design and development.

The number of papers, modules, books, and research studies in CBE has increased rapidly during the past year. Schmieder has surveyed the literature widely, listing and indexing over 700 entries in an extensive bibliography.

Compiling a book as comprehensive and pervasive as this one requires the efforts of many people. Most obvious are the contributions of the chapter authors who shared so freely of their thoughts and papers. Several chapters were presented originally at professional meetings, others were private papers circulated only among close professional colleagues, while several were written specifically for this book.

National Teacher Corps supported this publication to stimulate further exploration and to refine CBE concepts. Dr. William Smith, director of Teacher Corps, has encouraged educational innovations, particularly those which promise more effective education for youth from low-income families. As a teacher and school administrator, then as director of the Urban-Renewal Program and Career Opportunities Program, and as associate commissioner of the U.S. Office of Education, he has maintained the vision of improved education and articulated this through innovative and effective programs.

Perhaps more than any other person James Steffenson has fostered and sparked the continued development of CBE. In 1968, he monitored for USOE the design of nine models of elementary teacher preparation. In subsequent years, he has supported efforts to analyze, prototype, test, and disseminate CBE ideas. As chief of Program Development for Teacher Corps, he has encouraged experimentation in CBE and vigorously supported efforts to improve the education of minorities. To William Smith and James Steffenson, the authors are particularly grateful for their support and encouragement in this endeavor.

Karl Massanari, associate director for the American Association of Colleges for Teacher Education, not only stimulated the editor and provided a number of useful suggestions related to the manuscript, but also provided the written transcript of the panel discussion which formed the basis for chapter 6.

Preliminary editing of manuscripts was completed by Sheila Ford at the University of Houston, who also standardized and checked bibliographic entries. Linda Rageh served as copy editor, making many excellent recommendations for improving the manuscript. Cammie Carlson, Joy Stefan, and Cheryl Johnson typed and proofed the manuscript. Finally, John McCutchan coordinated production schedule, editorial efforts, a contractual agreement, and stimulated authors at appropriate moments in an effort to publish this book on a stringent time schedule.

Part 1
The Essence of the Approach

1. Competency Based Education

W. Robert Houston

EXTENSIVENESS OF MOVEMENT

The movement toward competency based or performance based education now permeates every aspect of American education. In particular, the education of professionals is being revamped through this movement. By fall 1972, seventeen states had devised teacher certification procedures based on the CBE/PBE concept.[1] Washington and New York have been studying the concept for several years, with the fourth or fifth drafts of certification plans being studied by professionals. These states and Texas have defined a *process* approach to certification; an educational consortium, minimally composed of schools, colleges, and the organized profession, is responsible for program development. For these states, the procedures by which each consortium identifies its competencies and specifies its programs are used as selection criteria. On the other hand, New Jersey and Pennsylvania have undertaken the specific identification of required competencies. While recognizing the thin knowledge base undergirding any particular competency, these two states have relied on the professionals within their states for an initial list of required competencies. Florida has invested over a million dollars each year in projects like the Catalog of Competencies at Florida State University, Middle School CBTE Project at the University of Florida, Module Bank at Miami, and a resource distribution center through the Panhandle Educational Cooperative in Chipley, Florida. The Texas Education Agency has sponsored more than twenty-five conferences for teacher educators; the Texas Teacher Center Project supports five institutions in the design process and seventeen change agents. Arizona has focused on recertification, placing responsibility on local schools to identify competencies.

Of 783 teacher education institutions responding to the 1972 AACTE survey, 125 indicated that their programs "for the most part" could be characterized as competency based, while another 366 indicated that they "are now in the developmental stage and plan to establish a PBTE program."[2] In a follow-up study, seventy-five of these institutions indicated that they had 123 separate CBTE programs with nearly 25,000 students. Nearly all had both CBTE and traditional programs, while 71 percent had operated CBTE programs less than two years.[3] Several, including Southwest Minnesota State, Florida International, University of Toledo, and University of Houston, have committed their total program to the concept.

The National Teacher Corps requires its projects to be competency based. State University of New York at Buffalo, Kansas State College at Emporia, San Diego State College, and Western North Carolina have attracted national attention through their project efforts. Career education and other programs funded by the U.S. Office of Education and the National Institute of Education are designing programs using the CBE format.

Several national committees and commissions have been formed to study or to coordinate various aspects of the movement. The Committee on Performance Based Teacher Education[4] has published a dozen monographs on CBE/PBE and has sponsored a number of regional and national study conferences. The Multi-State Consortium on Performance Based Teacher Education[5] works primarily through the state education departments of nine states. It publishes monographs and a periodic newsletter, and also sponsors conferences on special topics. While the consortium focuses primarily on problems of certification, it has published several papers on program design.

The National Consortium of CBE Centers[6] is composed of representatives of eight institutions which have been designing programs for several years. The consortium has published two books and several papers; member institutions develop exemplary programs or experimental efforts related to CBE. The National Commission for Performance Based Education[7] is concerned primarily with research and development. It works with institutions and states in the design and implementation of research that will increase the knowledge base.

Programs are being designed and syllabi rewritten in elementary and secondary schools to reflect the national competency movement. Programs in mathematics, reading, social studies, and science have been implemented; textbooks—or at least their teachers' guides—include behavioral objectives and some procedures for individualizing instruction.

Other professions are also turning to a competency approach. Physicians in Illinois, Michigan, and Texas are being trained through competency based programs. The program of The University of Texas Dental School is described in chapter 22. Nursing, allied health programs, pilot licensing, and other training for paraprofessionals are focusing on CBE. Engineers, electricians, plumbers, and computer programmers are engaged in competency based programs. Only a cursory glance at education today is required to note the prevalence of the movement. It appears to be an idea whose time has come; for this reason it should be carefully examined. That is the purpose of this volume.

A CULTURALLY BASED MOVEMENT

Competency based education has evolved as part of a culturally based movement. Two forces in American society today have contributed to the development of CBE. The first is the emphasis on *accountability*. Football coaches, plumbers, teachers, physicians, etc., are expected by those who receive their services to be responsible and accountable for their actions. They are not only expected to be knowledgeable in their fields, but to employ that knowledge successfully in practice as well. People have always been judged by the success of their professional efforts, but the current emphasis on measurement and the increased precision of measuring tools make accountability more obvious.

The press for accountability derives from the commercial and industrial sector of society. With increasing budgets and restricted funds, society is pressing educators to relate systems input (dollars, personnel, buildings, resources) to systems output (increased student achievement related to goals of society). While noting the complexity of the task, educators have instituted a number of practices that lead toward fiscal, programmatic, and managerial accountability. Accountability is reflected in the current emphasis on objectives, which in turn direct fiscal, programmatic, and managerial efforts. Management by objectives (MBO) programs and PPBS (planning, programming, budgeting systems) for fiscal responsibility grow from the same cultural press as does competency based education.

The second force shaping educational directions is the need for *personalization*. This need reflects current societal changes so comprehensive that Alvin Toffler described them as "the roaring current of change, a current so powerful today that it overturns institutions, shifts our values, and shrivels our roots."[8] Permanence and stability are less characteristic of man's life-style than ever before.

With fewer demands on the work force to produce foodstuffs, population patterns in the United States have shifted to increasing concentrations of people in urban areas. Toffler calls ours a transient society. One family in four moves each year. Products are made to be discarded—paper napkins, paper swimming suits, disposable drink bottles, even motels, which often are built with a life expectancy of ten years. Television brings into the home instant communication on the gore of war and accidents, the corruption of government, rackets, and labor, and the combat of the football field. Day-old news is discarded like Kleenex. But the mind retains the impression of a world of violence depersonalized through TV's cathode-ray tube.

Urban areas pack people together yet leave few opportunities for real interaction or interdependence. Job specialization contributes to lack of personalization: each worker deals with a small part of the whole and knows little about the job or aspirations of his fellow workers. When several men gather in a social setting, the conversation usually concerns not their vocations but some neutral subject—a common denominator that all can understand, appreciate, and be verbally knowledgeable about: typically, sports.

Toffler charges that schools are dehumanizing institutions modeled after factories, preparing students for industrial life. Schools are run by the clock, not by the sun, they are crowded and noisy, supervisors (teachers) evaluate the efforts of students, and students compete with each other. In such a setting, students easily become objects rather than persons. Vance Packard succinctly documents that we are in danger of becoming *A Nation of Strangers.*

Yet the human spirit cries out for individuality, for freedom, for independence, for recognition. Today's youth culture reflects this need for individual attention. The need for individualized and personalized treatment has strong roots in the American culture.

COMPETENCY BASED EDUCATION

From these two perceived needs—accountability and personalization—has come the movement referred to as competency based or performance based education. CBE and PBE refer to the same movement and will be used interchangeably in this volume. Advocates of performance based terminology refer to the way in which the learner demonstrates knowledges and skills. Demonstration is "observable" (objectives are to *write, do, describe*); avoided are "nonobservable" verbs, such as *understand, perceive.* Further, the emphasis on performance reminds us that knowledge alone is inadequate; knowledge must be employed in overt action.

Competency based education emphasizes a minimum standard for effective performance; it adds criterion levels, value orientations, and quality to the definition. Advocates of CBE define five types of objectives. In *cognitive based objectives,* the participant is expected to demonstrate knowledge and intellectual abilities and skills. In *performance based objectives,* the participant is required to *do* something rather than simply to *know* something. While contingent on knowledge, performance based objectives put the emphasis on observable action. In *consequence based objectives,* the participant is required to bring about change in others: a prospective teacher's ability to teach is assessed by examining the achievements of students he instructs. In CBE, greater emphasis is placed on performance based and consequence based objectives than on cognitive based objectives. For example, what teachers know about teaching seems less important than their ability to teach and to bring about change in children.[9]

Two other types of objectives are usually included in the competency based programs. Objectives in the *affective* domain are embedded in all other classes of objectives but tend to resist the specific description expected of the first three types. Affective objectives are vital in a competency based program.

The fifth type, *exploratory objectives,* does not completely fit within the classification of objectives, since the definition of desired outcomes in learners is defaulted. The outcomes are not precisely defined; rather, activities that hold promise for significant learning are specified. Characteristic of exploratory objectives is a high degree of randomness in what may be encountered. Further, the idiosyncratic dispositions of the learner largely influence the actual learning outcomes of the experience. Competency based programs do not depend on exploratory objectives; such objectives are employed in program areas where precise outcomes cannot as yet be explicated.

Advocates of PBE terminology also see consequence objectives as the ultimate test of the individual's effectiveness, but point out that there are many intervening factors which are often uncontrollable by the person demonstrating competence. For example, teachers are held accountable for the learning outcomes of their students, yet they have little or no control over many of the relevant factors influencing that learning (e.g., student ability, interest, motivation, availability of resources). PBE advocates stress that our present understanding of these variables and our inability to control them adequately in field settings preclude consequence objectives as realistic requirements. They contend that since performance objectives are the major guidelines for programs, the identifier—PBE—should be used since it is more descriptive than CBE.

While a case can be made for either CBE or PBE, both provide needed foci for understanding the movement—one emphasizing *objectives* and the other *criteria*. Both press for educational programs that go beyond knowledge for its own sake and emphasize performance and consequences of actions. Exploration of the meanings implied by "competency" and "performance" provides a useful process through which the central core and parameters of CBE/PBE are identified and employed to improve education.

DEFINING THE MOVEMENT

A number of definitions of competency based education have been written during the past few years. Several are included below for comparison and analysis.

The most widely quoted and accepted definition was suggested by Stanley Elam in *Performance Based Teacher Education: What Is the State of the Art?* In August 1971, the AACTE committee sponsored a conference in which a group of experts discussed salient aspects of CBE/PBE. Elam prepared a perceptive report on their deliberations, and included three levels of descriptors in his definition of CBE/PBE: (1) essential elements; (2) implied characteristics; and (3) related or desirable characteristics. The essential elements must all be included in a program for it to be defined as CBE/PBE. These are listed below:

(1) Competencies (knowledge, skills, behaviors) to be demonstrated by the student are
- Derived from explicit conceptions of teacher roles;
- Stated so as to make possible assessment of a student's behavior in relation to specific competencies; and
- Made public in advance.
(2) Criteria to be employed in assessing competencies are
- Based upon, and in harmony with, specified competencies;
- Explicit in stating expected levels of mastery under specified conditions; and
- Made public in advance.
(3) Assessment of the student's competency
- Uses his performance as the primary source of evidence;
- Takes into account evidence of the student's knowledge relevant to planning for, analyzing, interpreting, or evaluating situations or behavior; and
- Strives for objectivity.
(4) The student's rate of progress through the program is determined by demonstrated competency rather than by time or course completion.
(5) The instructional program is intended to facilitate the development and evaluation of the student's achievement of competencies specified.[10]

Several other characteristics seem to be *implied* in the list of essential elements and are often found in competency based programs:
(1) Instruction is individualized and personalized.
(2) The learning experience of the individual is guided by feedback.

(3) The program as a whole is systemic.

(4) The emphasis is on exit, not on entrance, requirements.

(5) Instruction is modularized.

(6) The student is held accountable for performance, completing the preparation program when, and only when, he demonstrates the competencies that have been identified as requisite for a particular professional role.

Less central than the essential elements and implied characteristics are several other related and desirable characteristics:

(1) The program is field centered.

(2) There is a broad base for decision-making (including such groups as college/university faculty, students, and public school personnel).

(3) The materials and experiences focus on concepts, skills, knowledges, which can be learned in a specific instructional setting.

(4) Both the teachers and the students are designers of the instructional system.

(5) [The program] includes a research component and is open and regenerative.

(6) Preparation is career continuous.

(7) Role integration takes place as the prospective teacher gains an increasingly comprehensive perception of teaching problems.[11]

Houston and Howsam, after defining competence and CBE and discussing its implications, summarize their position in this way:

Competency based instruction is a simple, straightforward concept with the following central characteristics: (a) specification of learner objectives in behavioral terms; (b) specification of the means for determining whether performance meets the indicated criterion levels; (c) provision for one or more modes of instruction pertinent to the objectives, through which the learning activities may take place; (d) public sharing of the objectives, criteria, means of assessment, and alternative activities; (e) assessment of the learning experience in terms of competency criteria; and (f) placement on the learner of the accountability for meeting the criteria. Other concepts and procedures—such as modularized packaging, the systems approach, educational technology, and guidance and management support—are employed as means in implementing the competency based commitment. For the most part, these contributory concepts are related to individualization.[12]

Cooper and Weber define competency based teacher education in a succinct passage:

A competency based teacher education program specifies the competencies to be demonstrated by the student, makes explicit the criteria to be applied in assessing the student's competencies, and holds the student accountable for meeting those criteria. While at first glance this definition appears to depict a rather harsh, almost mechanistic process, nothing could be further from the truth. The competencies referred to are attitudes, understandings, skills, and behaviors that facilitate intellectual, social, emotional, and physical growth in children. The student is held responsible for demonstrating these competencies, because they are necessary to teaching effectiveness. He may, however, help to determine either the competencies to be acquired, or the setting in which the competencies are to be demonstrated, or both.[13]

Johnson defined CBE by comparing the characteristics of common programs and CBE programs:[14]

Characteristics of CBE Programs	*Characteristics of Common Programs*
The main indicator of the student's achievement is his ability to do the job for which he is preparing effectively and efficiently.	The main indicators of the student's achievement are his knowledge of the subject and his ability to tell how the job for which he is preparing may be done effectively and efficiently.
Once a student has demonstrated his ability to do the job for which he is preparing, he may do it when he has completed his preparation. Time is not a factor. He may finish earlier than others or take more time than usual if need be the case.	The student operates within specified time limits such as academic years, semesters, and quarters. Class hour requirements are generally adhered to.
The criterion of success is demonstrating one's ability to do the job. Mastery criteria are used to determine how well the student performs. He must satisfy these criteria if he is to be considered competent.	The criteria of success are letter grades which indicate the extent to which the student knows the required subject matter.
There is little concern for entrance requirements. The student starts where he is. If he is not ready, he is helped to become ready.	Entrance requirements are important concerns. If he is not ready he cannot be admitted.
Flexible scheduling of learning activities is essential to provide for individual differences among students. This allows for year round educational opportunities and numerous possible times for enrollment.	Students are scheduled for instruction into fairly rigid blocks of time. The academic year and infrequent mass registration are standard practices.
There are no fixed rules as to how, when, or where learning is to be accomplished.	On-campus classroom teaching is the most common approach to instruction. Lengthy on-campus required attendance is standard.
Opportunities are provided to acquire competencies in practical field experiences or on-the-job.	Practical field experiences are limited.

The issue of minimum competencies continually arises, particularly in debates on certification requirements. Is there a set of competencies that should be demonstrated by all effective teachers? If so, might these competencies be learned, or are they personal characteristics? Do equally effective teachers demonstrate a set of competencies to varying extents, i.e., do they have different competency profiles? Speculation on these questions and related issues may help clarify the concept of competency itself.

CONSIDER THE FIDDLE

When one analyzes the performance of a violin soloist at the symphony, certain skills become apparent. He must be able to read music, properly handle the bow, tune the instrument, and have a certain stage presence. So must the beginner at the seventh grade concert. The differences are in the criteria that are acceptable for an adequate performance. What is more than adequate in one instance is not acceptable in another. The seventh grader may be as skilled as the professional in many aspects of the performance; he may properly hold the bow and read music, but he may not be able to coordinate these in the total program.

The parallel in teaching is obvious. The prospective teacher may perform adequately in asking higher order questions, establishing set induction, and writing criterion-referenced objectives, but he may not be able to integrate these skills and employ them appropriately in given circumstances. Beginning teachers may be judged competent and show promise for further development, but three or five years later that same level of competence would be inadequate. This implies that the profession should define a series of competency requirements that might increase in complexity and scope as the teacher gains experience. Such criteria could also form one basis for differentiated school staffing.

Personal styles of demonstrating required competencies lead to different but often equally effective teaching strategies, just as violinists interpret music in a variety of ways. Indeed, the more competent the violinist, the more likely he is to extend the interpretation and not play the music precisely as written. Jascha Heifitz and Yehudi Menuhin can play the same composition, but each interprets it differently—yet both are acclaimed as virtuosos. So it is with teachers;

master teachers perform in differing styles. Our own research indicates that some teaching virtuosos are child focusers, some task focusers, some pragmatists.[15] One is concerned primarily with how children feel; the second emphasizes completion of tasks and projects; the third considers situation variables in making decisions. The teacher-stance study, the research of Bruce Joyce, and common sense indicate that effective teachers employ a variety of styles. Two hypotheses would logically follow: (1) While a competency core may exist, *the varied teacher personalities, styles, and stances preclude definition of a single set of requirements for all teachers*; and (2) *the more a person is proficient as a teacher, the more likely his professional style is to be unique.*

Again using the analogy of the violinist, the lowest level of performance demonstration was at the single skill level (correctly holding the bow, reading music, asking higher order questions). When these were combined into a performance, and if the individual met stipulated criteria appropriate to the objectives of that performance (seventh grade orchestra or New York Philharmonic, concert or practice), he was judged competent. Thus competence is *situational* (contextual).

A parallel might be drawn between measurement and evaluation. One measures a performance but evaluates competence. In assessing a violinist, a diver, or a teacher's verbal interaction with children, rating scales, tests, observations, or other instruments may be employed; they describe *what is*. Evaluation of those data considers the adequacy of measured phenomena within a context and value orientation.

Competence is also demonstrated over a period of time; a single performance does not indicate competence. A teacher's typical performance may be of such quality as to be judged "competent," but occasionally he may have poor performances. Competent athletes, speakers, or musicians all have "off days"; so do competent teachers.

Teacher education programs are concerned more with competence than with individual performance, although some judgments are necessary in assessing competence. Further, a program of teacher development is goal (or goals) oriented, and it lasts an entire lifetime. A professional seldom attains his goals because as he develops his goals change and evolve. Each individual, as the Spanish philosopher Santayana reminds us, chooses his own personal star toward which he strives.

COMPETENCY BASED OR PROFICIENCY DIRECTED?

When quality of performance is considered, two concepts aid in clarifying the issues: competency and proficiency. These two terms are defined by the *American Heritage Dictionary of the English Language* as follows:

Competent. 1. Properly or well-qualified; capable. 2. Adequate for the purpose; suitable, sufficient. 3. Legally qualified or fit; admissible.

Proficient. Performing in a given art, skill, or branch of learning with expert correctness and facility. Proficiency implies a high degree of competence through training.

Perhaps we should refer to certification as competency based and to teacher education as proficiency directed. In the former, we are considering a base, a legal standard that tends to protect society from incompetents. Proficiency, on the other hand, more nearly describes the scope, objectives, and structure of teacher education programs. Teacher education seeks to aid prospective and inservice teachers in meeting minimum certification standards, but it goes far beyond this; it encourages teachers and the profession to seek maximum expertise. Further, while competency may refer to minimum standards below which no one is acceptable, proficiency can be multidimensional —reflecting the varied needs of task focusers, child focusers, and pragmatists; of varied instructional assignments; and of urban or suburban environments.

SUMMARY

The CBE movement has gained such momentum during the past few years that it has the potential for reshaping American education, particularly teacher education. The extensiveness of the efforts sometimes cloud the need for theoretical constructs, for clarity of conceptualization, and for research. It also cloaks the vast differences in quality among programs. Some CBE programs have become creative efforts that are harbingers of more effective preparation of professionals. Others are only warmed-over programs with little changed but the name. They assume that using the terminology of the movement will automatically lead to greater effectiveness, or at least intellectual respectability. Not so!

CBE offers the opportunity to reconceptualize professional education, to make it more relevant in a rapidly changing culture. Simply translating current courses into modules and course objectives into behavioral terminology short-circuits the process and undermines a potentially powerful movement.

NOTES FOR CHAPTER 1

1. From a survey conducted by the American Association of Colleges for Teacher Education, fall 1972, and reported in Allen A. Schmieder, *Competency Based Education: The State of the Scene* (Washington, D.C.: AACTE, 1973), pp. 10-13.

2. Schmieder, *Competency Based Education: The State of the Scene.*

3. Susan S. Sherwin, *Performance-Based Teacher Education: Results of a Recent Survey* (Princeton, N.J.: Educational Testing Service, 1973), pp. 5-7.

4. The AACTE committee is directed by Karl Massanari; for information, write to AACTE, One Dupont Circle, Washington, D.C. 20036.

5. The director of the consortium, Theodore Andrews, can furnish information on consortium activities and resources. Write him at the New York State Education Department Division of Certification and Teacher Education, Twin Towers, Albany, New York 12224.

6. Norman Dodl, Florida State University, Tallahassee 32306, coordinates consortium efforts.

7. Frederick McDonald, Educational Testing Service, Princeton, New Jersey 08549, directs the commission's efforts.

8. Alvin Toffler, *Future Shock* (New York: Random House, 1970).

9. Richard Turner has conceptualized objectives in six domains. These are described by Benjamin Rosner in chapter 6 and included in an assessment model proposed by Turner in chapter 17.

10. Stanley Elam, *Performance Based Teacher Education: What Is the State of the Art?* (Washington, D.C.: AACTE, 1971), p. 67.

11. Ibid., pp. 7-11.

12. W. Robert Houston and Robert B. Howsam, *Competency Based Teacher Education: Progress, Problems, and Prospects* (Chicago: Science Research Associates, 1972), pp. 5-6.

13. James M. Cooper and Wilford A. Weber, "A Competency Based Systems Approach to Teacher Education," in *Competency Based Teacher Education*, vol. 2, *A Systems Approach to Program Design*, by James M. Cooper, Wilford A. Weber, and Charles E. Johnson (Berkeley: McCutchan Publishing Corp., 1973).

14. Charles E. Johnson, "Competency Based and Common Teacher Education Programs Compared" (Athens: University of Georgia, College of Education, Competency Based Education Center, 1972), pp. 7-10.

15. Other teaching stances include time servers, contented conformists, ambivalents, and alienated. For a report of the research, see Ann G. Olmsted, Frank Blackington III, and W. Robert Houston, "Stances Teachers Take: A Basis for Selective Admission," *Phi Delta Kappan* 55, no. 5 (January 1974).

2. The Rationale for Competency Based Programs

Frederick J. McDonald

The roots of competency based teacher education concepts are in training psychology, which in turn has its roots in behavioral psychology[1] —the aspects of social learning theory that are concerned with modeling and imitative behavior[2] —and in systems analysis strategies for the development of effective man-machine systems.[3] During the late fifties and the early sixties, first programmed learning and then computer-based instruction were developed as practical applications of these ideas. In the same period the portable videotape camera and recorder were invented, and were quickly adapted in teacher education as feedback devices to apply reinforcement principles and as an inexpensive way of providing models of teaching performances to apply social learning theory principles.[4] These applications of principles solidly founded in research demonstrated that these principles could be applied with significant practical benefits, and also provided experience in how to apply the principles.

These origins account for three characteristics of practically all competency based programs: (1) the organization of what is to be learned into interdependent components; (2) the precise specification of what is to be learned; (3) the provision of feedback during learning sequences. A fourth characteristic may be found in programs whose developers attempt to apply what has been learned about modeling and imitative behavior; in such programs models of the performances to be learned are inserted into the learning sequences.

Although these are the source of the concepts used in developing competency based programs, they do not justify the design of any one program over another nor do they prove that competency based programs necessarily produce better teachers. Any justifications must rest on empirical evidence that each program is achieving the desired goals of teacher education, and the array of competency based programs must stand on the evidence that their products are superior in important ways to the products of other types of programs.

THE CRITERIA FOR A RATIONALE FOR COMPETENCY BASED PROGRAMS

A program of teacher training is effective if it produces teachers with certain desired characteristics, the most important being that teachers are able to influence the learning of their students in significant ways. The ultimate justification of any program is the evidence that its teachers can and do help children learn.

The effectiveness of a program, however, can be assessed only after it has been designed and put into operation. A new program needs to argue for its potential effectiveness. The most reasonable argument is one that demonstrates that the program's design incorporates principles which when applied in other circumstances have produced results analogous to those desired for the program being developed. A more direct approach would apply research on the teacher training process to the design being developed. The latter source in teacher education, however, is meager; the developer of programs of teacher education must rely on analogies between learning to be a teacher and learning other skills.

We are all aware of the difficulties in drawing analogies, and one must be acutely sensitive to these difficulties in a field where so little is known about the nature of the processes to be engaged in teaching, and how the skills for engaging in them are learned. Joyce's analysis of models of teaching amply illustrates how many different analogies may be drawn between teaching and other interactive processes.[5] A program developer using Joyce could select his or her preferred model of the instructional process and develop a training program to produce teachers who had the skills to implement this model in practice. An eclectic developer might select several different models as the basis for designing a training program. While these ways of conceptualizing a model on which to build a competency based program are to be recommended, we cannot ignore the problem of the bases for choices made. Should we not have criteria for the choice of these analogies which comprise the rationale for the design of a teacher education program?

A distinction needs to be made before suggesting such criteria: the distinction between the nature of teaching itself and the nature of the processes by which teaching skill is acquired. The former pertains *to what* is to be learned, the latter *to how* it is learned. There are two points of view on this distinction. One is that the teacher ought to be taught in the same way he or she is to teach. The other is that training is mediated by variables that may not be manipulated in the processes the trainee is to create and manage.

According to the first viewpoint, a teacher who is to stimulate inquiry learning in his or her students should learn to teach by being taught in the same way he or she will subsequently teach. Thus, a prospective teacher would learn inquiry teaching by inquiring about inquiry teaching. He would discover inquiry style, thus internalizing his understanding of the inquiry process.

The second point of view is that the processes of teaching inquiry skills may be learned by quite different processes. Those who hold this view argue that the skills required to elicit inquiry processes may be learned by practicing the appropriate performances, and receiving feedback on the effectiveness of these performances.

Strong commitment to either of these two views seems unjustified at the present time. It seems reasonable that a teacher must understand the nature of the processes in which he proposes to engage students. It seems equally reasonable that how he learns to engage students in these processes may require different processes than those in which he will actually engage his students. If the designer is choosing one of the two positions, he or she must make a strong argument for the position chosen. The first criterion for evaluating the rationale for a training program ought to be, therefore, the solidness of its justification for the *learning* processes in which it engages its students. The case for the training design is an argument that the learning model explicit in the design is likely to produce teachers with the desired competencies.

Recall that this justification will be an analogy, which here is a set of inferences of two kinds. First, an analogy is made between the teaching skill or performance or process to be learned and some other kind of learning. The second analogy is a set of inferences about the similarities of conditions or variables that affect both kinds of learning.

The first kind of inference is speculative. The designer is saying that the kind of skill to be learned by the teacher is like some other kind of skill. Two examples will illustrate the difficulties in drawing this kind of analogy:

(1) "Skill" generally means proficiency in a performance. Its defining characteristics are typically minimal error in performance, ability to anticipate errors, ability to correct errors. However, as the skill becomes more complex these characteristics become more difficult to describe operationally, particularly when the skill is supposed to produce effects on other people. A skillful lathe operator produces a piece of metal that conforms exactly to specifications within tolerable limits of deviancy. His performance in producing this object is marked by few and correctable errors; he may also produce it more quickly than less skillful operators. A concert pianist may also produce an error-free performance, but we expect this performance to have other qualities. His interpretation of the piece is a factor in evaluating his skillfulness, and is reacted to and judged by those who hear him play.

(2) The research on teaching behavior has frequently indicated that if teachers provide positive feedback in the form of approval consistently and substantially, students' learning will be affected positively and significantly.[6] Such findings appear to be consistent with the research on positive reinforcement. Is this seeming consistency sufficient grounds for generalizing the research on "positive reinforcement" to "feedback to students," or "approval," or "positive appraisal"?—the category names used frequently in describing reinforcing acts of teachers.

The largest portion of the research literature on positive reinforcement, however, lies in studies in which rats or chimpanzees are given reinforcers for powerful drives. Straightforward application of these principles in human training programs has not always proved effective. Further, positive approval given to students "works" for reasons that are neither obvious or clear; probably *not* because this approval satiates an innate drive that periodically requires satiation.

This example is instructive because it suggests the requirements for analogizing between teacher behavior and other behaviors. The research literature on learning—in this example the effects of providing positive reinforcers—may provide a paradigm of a performance, which is a structure to which analogies may be drawn. Providing positive reinforcement, for example, is a set of events with two characteristics: (1) what is provided by the reinforcing agent must be "desired" or "wanted" by the recipient of the reinforcing action, or "beneficial" to him; (2) the act of providing a reinforcer must be contingent on a response that is to be modified or acquired.

Once the paradigm is described in terms of its generic features, analogizing proceeds with less risk. "Approval" is a reinforcing event because students generally "desire" it; thus, the necessary condition for creating the reinforcement paradigm is present. Hence, to analogize between reinforcement paradigms and the rewarding behaviors of teachers, it is necessary to find analogues between how a teacher may administer "approval" and how reinforcing events are administered in other contexts where they have been shown to affect learning. Given that such analogues may be created (and they have been), it is reasonable to generalize the literature on reinforcement to a class of events or performances in teaching.

The above is a somewhat extended didactic on analogizing. It suggests that a paradigmatic analysis of two domains of performance may reveal similarities. To the degree that this analysis reveals similarities, the research on one domain of performance may be generalized, with some risk to the other. The more precise the thinking in analyzing similarities between domains of performance, the more persuasive the rationale generalized from one domain to another.

A brief interpolation on economy in thinking may be useful at this point. We are, in this presentation, providing a rationale for competency based teacher education. We are about to say that such a rationale exists by way of a complex set of inferences about the

WHITWORTH COLLEGE LIBRARY
SPOKANE, WASH.

similarities of teaching to other performances about which we have more knowledge and more incisive understanding. We cannot claim that a foundation in research on teaching directs, leads, or supports unequivocally the competency based teacher education movement. We must resort to derivative modes of support. Hence, we are preoccupied with and concerned about how we draw support for and how we may make strong heuristic arguments for the concepts, themes, and motifs of the competency based movement in teacher education.

In making analogies there are numerous models of learning and human development from which to choose. A model ought to subsume as many characteristics of the process being modeled as possible. A comprehensive model is an economic device for heuristic thinking. The conceptualizer applies the same set of ideas consistently when he or she uses such a model. He tests the model in many different ways. The application of the design is more likely to be consistent.

To this point, we have been describing the general logic of the rationale that can be provided for competency based teacher education. Given that this rationale is essentially a set of analogies, what other characteristics ought it to have?

Four other criteria are relevant to evaluating rationales derived by analogizing of the kind described above. One is that the model used in the analogy must account for the key features of the phenomena to which the model is being applied. Teaching skills, for example, are a composite of discrete but interdependent skills; there is no reason to believe they are a gestalt of some type. Secondly, there is reason to believe that they are acquired incrementally. The trainee, for example, typically has few of these skills, but acquires more of them with training. A model of the teacher training process, therefore, must be keyed to these characteristics.

A third criterion for evaluating the power of a model or an analogy to be used in designing a teacher training program is that it should account for the most critical aspect of the phenomena being studied or manipulated—whether this phenomenon is essentially dynamic or static. Bridge-building profits from the use of static models; engine design, from the use of dynamic models.

A fourth criterion is that the model or analogy relate to whether the phenomena of interest is homeostatic or evolutionary. States of health are examples of homeostatic phenomena; they are steady-states in which countervailing forces are balanced. Evolutionary phenomena change in their nature as a way of adapting to the forces that act on them, i.e,, they change by coping.

The implication of stating the above criteria for evaluating a rationale for the design of a teacher training program is that the designer or conceptualizer faces three kinds of tasks. (1) He must decide on the critical features of the process of acquiring teaching skills—is it dynamic or static; is it homeostatic or evolutionary? (2) Are the components of teaching skill discrete and independent or interdependent? (3) Having answered these questions, the designer must select models of the skills that fit their critical characteristics, and models of the training process that are relevant to the answers he has given to the questions above.

The rationale for the design is therefore an explication of the decisions made and the arguments for making these choices. It also includes arguments for the selection of the models of the skills and a model of the training process.

These arguments are heuristic in character. The criterion of the validity of these heuristic arguments is the effects of the program that has been designed. If it meets its stated criteria, the models have been a useful device for understanding the phenomena.

THE RATIONALE FOR COMPETENCY BASED TEACHER EDUCATION

No one disagrees that a conception of the nature of teaching is a prerequisite to designing a teacher training program. But many individuals seem to be confused about the difference between the nature of teaching and the nature of the acquisition process by which teaching competence is learned.

The nature of teaching is determined by what the child to be taught is to learn and how he or she best may learn it. The nature of the acquisition process by which teaching competence is acquired is determined by what the teacher is to learn and how he or she may best learn it. The rationale for competency based teacher education pertains to the latter. The former determines its content.

The Characteristics of Teaching Competence

Teaching acts are observable performances. In principle these performances are linked to situations that vary in terms of the purposes of the teaching, the materials and media of instruction, the characteristics of the children being taught, and their responses in specific situations.

Such performances have two components: (1) a behavioral component and (2) a cognitive component. The behavioral component is a set of observable actions. The cognitive component is a combination of perceptions, interpretations, and decisions. Skill in both components is required to produce a competent performance.

The critical question usually asked is what performances are required for effective teaching? Much of the discussion of competency based teacher education revolves around the answers to this question.

Such answers ought to derive from conceptions of what is to be learned and how this learning might be facilitated. A variety of models of the teaching-learning process are available to describe the relations between teaching performances and various kinds of student learning. They may be used to describe the content of a teacher training program.

We are not concerned here with the choice among these models, other than to remind the reader of our earlier comments about the processes of making analogies. The important conclusion to be drawn is that no one model adequately describes all the kinds of learning to be mediated by teaching; while there may be performances common among the models, each appears to include unique performances or unique combinations of performances. Teaching competence, therefore, is defined in terms of a variety of performances. Some of these are subsets of others. To acquire teaching performances one must learn both the discrete performances and their combinations.

Teaching competence means possessing a set of performances on which the teacher can draw as situations vary. The complexity of the teaching situations a teacher faces strongly suggests that a teacher must continually adapt performances to situations.

The specificity of the performance is not its most critical characteristic. The designers of competency based programs have urged that performances be described as specifically as possible. This recommendation urges a useful heuristic which stimulates designers to focus on the characteristics of a performance and on the assessment of competence. It is also an antidote against the prevailing tendency to describe teaching acts in vague terms.

The critical descriptors of a performance are: (1) the actions to be taken; (2) the data needed to take the action; (3) the decisions to be made to initiate and carry out the actions; (4) the information to be processed as the actions are taken; (5) its intended effects and their indicators. These descriptors should be specific enough so that the actions to be taken are clearly indicated, the information to be gathered and the decisions to be made are concrete and readily identifiable, and the effects can be observed.

The critical characteristics of the performance are its links to the situations in which it is to be used. Such a description takes into account its effects and the conditions under which they are likely to be achieved.

The critical characteristic of a set of performances is their interdependency. Some performances subsume others. Some performances must be linked in sequences if their effects are to be achieved.

Thus, teaching acts are complexes of performances whose components and interdependencies are identifiable. The total set of performances required is sufficiently large that it is unlikely that the set can be learned as a totality. It seems likely, therefore, that the most useful models for describing the acquisition of teaching skill are those which account for the acquisition of discrete actions and clusters of actions and their combinations and integrations.

At the beginning of this chapter we stated that two of the characteristics of competency based programs were the organization of what is to be learned into components and precise specification of what is to be learned. The first characteristic reflects what we currently know about teaching performance: it is a behavioral and cognitive repertoire that is drawn upon to create and adapt to a wide variety of instructional purposes and means, and students. The precise specification of the competence is a heuristic device for being clear about what is to be done in teaching and under what conditions.

Thus, the rationale for competency based programs is rooted in the nature of teaching acts. The arguments about the behavioristic character of the movement are beside the point. A behavioral description of performance is necessary if we are to design a program that educates effective teachers. But it is not sufficient.

CHARACTERISTICS OF THE PROCESS OF ACQUIRING TEACHING SKILLS

As we pointed out earlier, the assumptions we make about the processes of acquiring teaching competence are not the same as those that we make about how it is acquired. When we look at the latter process, we are thinking about the teacher trainee as a learner. How does he or she acquire these performances and how does he or she learn to use these performances?

It will be useful to consider and make assumptions about the basic characteristics of this process. An obvious fact is that few if any persons have available all the performances required to be effective when they begin a training program. Training stimulates a growth process in which performances are progressively acquired and integrated.

Acquiring teaching competence is a dynamic process. The trainee does not move through a set of predetermined stages. What is learned at any one moment in time interacts with what was previously learned to create temporarily a new state of acquisition. Each of these successive states integrates prior with current learning. Each act of learning is an adaptation to a particular teaching situation.

It is probably true that some teachers do not grow in this way. The argument here is that acquiring competence in teaching requires that they do. Such growth requires that the teacher-learner be placed in a variety of situations and that he or she receive continuous feedback on performance.

This latter requirement is essential if a dynamic growth process is to be stimulated. Thus, competency based programs typically build feedback procedures into their designs. (Feedback procedures may or may not be reinforcement procedures.)

Another significant characteristic of the acquisition process is that it should stimulate autonomous evolutionary processes, or the processes by which teaching competence becomes adaptive. Such autonomous growth processes are best described as "learning-how-to-learn" processes rather than as coping mechanisms that enable the teacher to adapt homeostatically to each new situation. Autonomous growth processes are necessary for the evolution of teaching competence over time.

We are arguing here that the acquisition of teaching competence requires that the training program stimulate dynamic growth and the potential for evolutionary growth.

Do competency based programs have these characteristics? They do to the degree that they apply the basic learning model of such programs. Unfortunately, this model has not been explicated frequently enough and many assume that it is a reinforcement model, an error in judgment easily avoided if one recalls that designers of these programs advocate a systems approach to design.

THE LEARNING MODEL OF COMPETENCY BASED PROGRAMS

The learning model of competency based programs is a *cybernetic* model. Its simplest form appears in Figure 2:1. The learner is the input into the system. He or she is placed in teaching situations in which teaching performances are enacted. The output is the set of performances that are used in this situation, on which continuous feedback is given so that they are effective in the situation.

Figure 2:1. The Cybernetic Model of a Competency-Based Program

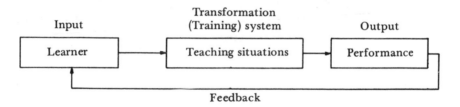

The modular design of competency based programs is a technological device for implementing this model. There are many performances to be learned; each one, or combinations of them, is the basis for designing a cybernetic system for their acquisition. The design of the modules usually includes a first phase where the simpler skills are acquired; subsequent phases are to learn more complex skills and combinations of skills.

Given that teaching performances have behavioral and cognitive components, it is useful to think of the teacher-trainee as an information-processing organism. This model implies that what the trainee learns is a function of his encoding processes—his perceptions and interpretations, the situations to which he is exposed, and the kinds of feedback he receives.

The training system must take into account the potential interactions between the trainees' encoding system and the situations to which he is exposed that determine the characteristics of the feedback he ought to receive. Thus, modules may be adapted to the characteristics of the trainee or they may be built to modify the trainee's processing systems.

The overall design of the modular system is the means by which dynamic growth is stimulated. This growth is stimulated by the variety and complexity of teaching situations to which the trainee is exposed and by the complexity of performances that are required of him.

It should be apparent that feedback depends on what aspects of performance are being modified at any point in time. In some cases a simple reinforcement paradigm will be useful. In other cases, analytic processes will have to be stimulated so that interpretations and decisions may be affected. No assumptions need be made about the most effective kinds of feedback. Finding them is an empirical problem.

Autonomous growth processes are stimulated in a competency based program in two ways: (1) by stimulating information-gathering and -interpreting processes, and (2) by teaching procedures for providing feedback to oneself. These processes can be learned in special modules designed to teach them and can be made part of the performance learning of each module.

Analogies in the Learning Model

The first analogy is between the learner and information processing organisms. The key features of this analogy are that modifying the learner's encoding of information is a necessary condition for affecting his behavioral performances, and that such encoding processes may themselves be influenced by feedback.

The second analogy is between the processes by which the trainees learn about the effects of their performances and feedback processes. This analogy assumes that information on effects is likely to lead to modifications in performance.

These analogies seem strong. They are more likely to be productive than a "black box" model of the learner because they do not ignore highly salient ways of responding available to the trainee. They also require feedback processes as an essential component of their applications.

CONCLUSION

This analysis of the rationale for competency based programs has attempted to distinguish between the rationale for the content of such programs and that for their design. The rationale for the content derives from a philosophy of education—a philosophy of what children should be educated for—and from models of the teaching-learning process. Both of these sources are diverse. But a competency based program ought to be built from a philosophy of education. Choosing models of the teaching-learning process is perhaps best if it is eclectic.

But, in these two respects competency based programs are no different than any other program. Competency based training is not necessarily associated with any one philosophy or any model of teaching and learning.

The rationale for competency based programs derives from concepts about the nature of what is to be learned—teaching competence—and from a model of a system most likely to enhance this acquisition.

Teaching competence means having available a diverse set of performances adaptable to a wide range of teaching situations. These performances are integratable in a variety of combinations. Some are simple; others are complex.

The learning of these performances requires learning the simple performances, the complex performances, and all their combinations and interrelations. The training sequence must provide for all these acquisitions. It makes sense, therefore, to organize the training sequences so that simpler skills can be learned efficiently and so that they may be integrated into combinations.

An array of performances to be learned may be sequenced in any number of ways. It is an empirical question as to which sequences are effective. The least risky design for the first generation of programs seems to be to order performances from simple to complex.

The basic learning model for designing the training system is a cybernetic one. This model conceptualizes the trainee as an information processor whose information processing skills and habits must be taken into account in designing a particular set of training events. It also requires a feedback process that will have different features depending on the information-procession characteristics of the trainee and the characteristics of the performance being learned.

This model sets the structure of the competency based system. A particular module, while it has this general structure, may apply a specific learning model within it. The rationale for such an application is specific to what is being learned and its value rests on the strength of the analogy implicit in the application.

It may come as a surprise to some readers that competency based programs rest on such a broad-gauged model, but developers have long recognized that their problem is one of designing a program of training for teaching competence. It is not a problem of diminishing teaching competence to fit a preferred learning model. The cybernetic model is a heuristic device for designing programs that embrace the richness of the concept of teaching competence.

NOTES FOR CHAPTER 2

1. R. Glaser, ed., *Training Research and Education* (Pittsburgh: University of Pittsburgh Press, 1962).

2. A. Bandura and R. P. Walters, *Social Learning and Personality Development* (New York: Holt, Rinehart & Winston, 1962); A. Bandura, *Principles of Behavior Modification* (New York: Holt, Rinehart & Winston, 1969).

3. M. Gagné, *Psychological Principles in System Development* (New York: Holt, Rinehart & Winston, 1962).

4. F. J. McDonald and D. W. Allen, "Training Effects of Feedback and Modeling on Teaching Performance," U.S. Office of Education Project no. OE 6-10-078 (Stanford, Calif.: Stanford University, 1967).

5. Bruce Joyce and Marsha Weil, *Models of Teaching* (Englewood Cliffs, N.J.: Prentice-Hall, 1972).

6. B. Rosenshine, *Teaching Behaviours and Student Achievement* (London, England: National Foundation for Educational Research, 1971).

3. What We Know and What We Don't Know

Theodore E. Andrews

People who know only a little about performance education often make dangerous leaps in their assumptions. They believe that

(1) A list exists which includes the basic competencies all teachers should possess and be able to demonstrate;

(2) Techniques exist to evaluate objectively whether or not a candidate actually has these competencies;

(3) Research has shown which teacher competencies are related to children's learning; and

(4) Developing a competency system of preparation and evaluation is a relatively simple task and not likely to be more expensive than present systems.

All these assumptions are false.

Before any state makes a commitment to competency education, it should prepare a description (a management plan) of how each of these four statements will be handled in that state.

Opinions and prejudices are abundant, but the best way to approach each issue is to ask the classic performance question: "What evidence will you accept?"

Examining each of the statements will more clearly illustrate what we know and what we don't know.

(1) *A list exists that includes the basic competencies that all teachers should possess and be able to demonstrate.*

What *does* exist are lists of competencies. The best resource now available is the *Catalog of Teacher Competencies,* which resulted from an intensive search of the literature and a year's review and revision by educators throughout the United States.[1] Well over one thousand competencies are included. However, no attempt is made to indicate which competencies are most, or even more, appropriate. The purpose of the catalog is described in the introduction: "The catalog should provide users with an array of competency statements from which descriptions of teachers can be built."[2]

The difficulty of preparing a list of basic competencies revolves around both a human and a philosophical problem. The human problem is that of obtaining consensus about an area of extreme controversy. According to Peter Airasian, selecting the competencies is the most crucial issue in competency education: "I would argue that the most powerful individuals are those who frame the competencies to be attained. These are the individuals who explicitly define what is a good teacher."

States have varied in their approaches to the selection of competencies. Some states have pushed that decision out to local and/or regional consortia; others have established a state list of required competencies.

The philosophical problem is whether any competency is so broad that all teachers should possess it. If schools and teacher roles are changing and if local systems make extremely different demands on their teachers, is it possible to establish competencies that are needed by *all* teachers? If that is true, are educators with a competency approach not again risking the creation of an irrelevant system?

Some people have been attracted to the competency movement because they see it as a way to describe the unique strengths and weaknesses of each teacher. The goal is not to hold all teachers to the demonstration of required competencies, but the creation of a system that would allow teachers to do what they do best and at the same time facilitate the restructuring of the public schools to give children greater opportunities to learn.

(2) *Techniques exist to evaluate objectively whether or not a teacher actually has these competencies.*

This is simply not true. Much of the enthusiasm for performance education results from the accountability thrust permeating all aspects of our society. People believe that objective evaluation of a prospective teacher (and/or inservice teacher) will reveal whether the person possesses the competency and whether the program is meeting its objectives. The assumption is valid, but no evidence is now available to indicate that assessment techniques are sophisticated enough to validate any program. If the reader doubts this conclusion, he should look at the performance programs and modules presently in use.

Florida funded the development of the *Annotated Listing of Competency Based Modules,* another excellent resource. The Florida Center for Teacher Training Materials set only three criteria for the inclusion of materials:

(1) Performance objectives are stated in explicit terms.

(2) Instructional activities or resources are specified for the attainment of the stated objectives.

(3) Evaluation indicators are linked to stated objectives.

The center reviewed thousands of modules and in its first catalog found only 288 that met the three criteria. (Note the word "linked" in the third criterion—no one was asked to validate the evaluation system.)

Many people are using behavioral objectives to develop performance programs. In most cases the activity of the teacher or the student is described in detail. However, far too often the evaluation consists of one person's subjective judgment about whether or not the person being evaluated demonstrated the competency, usually on a rating scale of 1 to 3, 1 to 5, or 1, 2, . . . , 9, 10. In some instances several raters evaluate the performance, but the evaluation is still subjective.

One should not be overly critical of such approaches. They are a significant improvement over previous rating scales, which had no performance criteria and were totally subjective: e.g., "Friendly— 1-10." However, such systems are not truly objective (philosophers would argue that nothing is). It is essential, however, that those making policy decisions recognize the limitations that exist in the assessment area.

While some modules do possess objective evaluation systems, no one would maintain that an entire program can now be evaluated objectively. The most difficult evaluation problems occur in the affective area. At best we are using indicators rather than absolutes for measuring effectiveness. Does the fact that a teacher calls on minority children as often as nonminority children prove the person is not prejudiced? This is not an atypical example of an indicator. One might compare the best evaluation systems in competency programs to an iceberg: The most visible part may well be using modules with objectives and criteria, but the greatest part lies submerged; the areas that truly make a difference are not so easily measured yet are really the foundation for the entire program.

Another difficult problem involves the issue of whether the desired performance is totally discrete (it either exists or it does not) or whether it is subject to qualification (ten times in twelve attempts). How one feels about this issue can vastly change the nature of the assessment program. Researchers have shown us that consistency of performance is exceptionally difficult to predict. Therefore, the demonstration of a discrete performance does not assure anyone that the performance can or will be duplicated when appropriate. Setting cut-off levels (e.g., seven out of ten times, with 80 percent effectiveness, or three out of four) is even more misleading. The measure is very accurate; however, the criteria level established is unrelated to any validation that, for example, three out of four is ultimately any more meaningful in terms of student learning (or predictability) than two out of four.

(3) *Research has shown which teacher competencies are related to children's learning.*

Some evidence is beginning to appear linking certain teacher behavior to student learning. Researchers Barak Rosenshine and Norma Furst have indicated that eleven variables appear to be worth beginning to train teachers for: clarity, variability, enthusiasm, task oriented and/or businesslike, student opportunity to learn criterion material, teacher indirectness, criticism, use of structuring comments, types of questions, probing, and level of difficulty of instruction. The best results were obtained on the first five variables.

But even Rosenshine and Furst indicate that much research needs to be done to completely validate these characteristics. Beyond this, research tells us nothing. Actually, what is reported is more disturbing than nothing.

James Popham completed a study that compared student learning in classes instructed by students prepared in a teacher education program with learning in students selected at random. He found that there were no measurable differences in learning.

If a state takes the position that the ultimate test of a teacher's effectiveness is student learning, then deciding which competencies are related to student learning is the overriding task. Many knowledgeable people accept the logic of that position but still reject it. Not only is there no positive evidence that *any* competency is related to student learning, but there is also no way to control the many human factors that influence the student, before or during the time that he is in class. Such critics also maintain that the ultimate goals of education are not revealed in whether the student can pass a cognitive exam but in the decisions he makes as an adult many years later.

Another problem is related. The competencies needed for effective teaching may not exist separately; the successful teacher may be the one who can utilize a variety of skills within a short time. Effectiveness is really the unique combination of competencies, not the capability to demonstrate each singularly. Many people believe that competencies are situationally specific, that is, in a given class on a given day certain competencies may be highly related to student learning, while on different days and/or with different students the same competencies may be irrelevant.

(4) *Developing a competency system of preparation and evaluation is a relatively simple task and is not likely to be more expensive than present systems.*

The complexity of developing a competency based program will be described later in this book. The cost factors are no less complex to determine.

Competency based teacher education programs will cost more money. No one argues too much about that. But how much more money will be needed? Bruce Joyce did a cost analysis for one state, and estimated that the development of one program would be between five and six million dollars—one program at one institution. Joyce is assuming that the program is totally competency based, and that the appropriate technological support is available. He estimates that the cost of turning the whole country's programs around is easily 100 million dollars and will probably take twenty years.

Herbert Hite, who did a similar analysis for another state, saw a rise of 150 percent in program costs as compared with traditional programs. In both estimates a significant amount of the cost appears as faculty time necessary to develop the program.

Neither Joyce nor Hite is trying to paint a totally negative picture. The costs are manageable, but only through careful development. Joyce recommends borrowing and sharing the work that others have done, while Hite proposes a different faculty load ratio that will provide the needed resources.[3]

In conclusion what we *do* know is:

(1) Competency statements are available for review and consideration.

(2) Objective evaluation is not yet perfected.

(3) Research relating student learning to teacher competencies still needs to be done.

(4) Developing a competency system is a complex and costly task.

NOTES FOR CHAPTER 3

1. Norman Dodl et al., *A Catalog of Teacher Competencies* (Tallahassee: Florida State University, November 1971).
2. Ibid.
3. Theodore Andrews, *Assessment* (Albany, N.Y.: Multi-State Consortium on Performance Based Education, 1973).

4. Individualizing Instruction in CBTE

M. Vere DeVault

Two assumptions provide direction for the position presented in this chapter. The first assumption is that an essential ingredient of competency based teacher education is individualized instruction. This assumption is specifically identified because, although most persons working in CBTE ascribe individualization as a useful or desirable characteristic, not all believe it to be essential.

The second assumption is that planning for and implementing individualized instruction both in CBTE and in school programs are significantly handicapped by our inability to communicate clearly what we mean by individualized instruction.

The need for improved communication is apparent as soon as we begin sharing our experiences at meetings and through professional journals. Individualization means all things to all people. We frequently read into comments by others ideas that have meaning for us and from which we are able to extend our own ideas or generate new ones. These new ideas become a part of our own set of beliefs about

Figure 4:1. Descriptor for

INSTRUCTION

AIMS

OBJECTIVES

	Skills and Concepts	Interests and Attitudes	Constructions	Interpersonal Relations
Same for All Information Used				
Differentiated for Groups Information Used				
Differentiated for Individuals Information Used				

Planning Sessions
Held / Scheduled Regularly

LEARNER ASSESSMENT PROCEDURES

	Skills and Concepts	Interests and Attitudes	Constructions	Interpersonal Relations
Testing pre				
mid				
post				
Conferences				
Products				
Other Observations				

Planning Sessions
Held / Scheduled Regularly

PROGRAM CONTEXT

Functioning Program / Ideal Program

PROGRAM CHARACTERISTICS				SOURCE OF DATA
Subject Matter	mathematics	reading	teacher education	Instructor
Grade Equivalents	P K 1 2 3 4 5 6 7 8 9 10 11 12 13 14 15 16			Learners
Production Agency	local schools	educational agency	commercial agency	Administrators Supervisors
Packaging	modules	text	multi-texts	tests	Developers
Learner Arrangement	alone	fixed groups	changing groups	Materials
Learner Time	unscheduled	scheduled fixed	scheduled flexible	Other
Space Arrangement	open	multiple rooms	single room	
Staff Arrangement	teacher	teacher group	specialist(s)	aide(s)	

SEQUENCE

o	o	o	o	o	o	o	o
o	o	o	o	o	o	o	o
o	o	o	o	o	o	o	o
o	o	o	o	o	o	o	o
o	o	o	o	o	o	o	o

Linear   Branched   Network   Nonspecified

Planning Sessions
Held / Scheduled Regularly

PROGRAM PATTERN

Activity   Test   Other Assessment   Recorded Assessment   Decision   Other Information Used

MEDIA

	Reading Materials	Audio-Visual Materials	Manipu-lative Materials	No Media
Percent of Instructional Time	Variety	Variety	Variety	Variety
Who Determines Information Used				

Planning Sessions
Held / Scheduled Regularly

Individualized Instruction

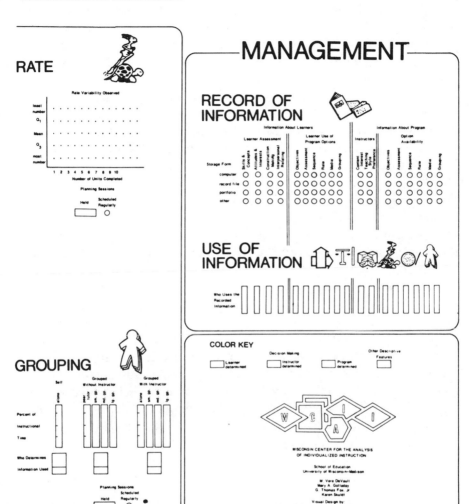

individualization. In this sense it can be seen that lack of clear, concise communication is not always a handicap and, in some instances, is a source of productive thought. This kind of "talking past" each other, however, is detrimental to progress when one is seriously interested in adopting or adapting successful procedures under way in one location to the context of their own. In this case, clear communication is essential.

As essential as communication is between one institution and another, it is of even greater importance that we come to communicate better within our own institutions. The improvement of communication among staff members in planning a given CBTE program is the focus of this chapter.

CBTE is essentially a process. Products evolve along the way and through use are accepted, revised, or rejected as experience seems to indicate. No CBTE program comes into existence full-blown. To those in positions of responsibility for planning CBTE, it is essential that one's vision encompass both short-term and long-range images of the program to be designed.

In a project funded by the National Institute of Education, my colleagues[1] and I spent a number of months observing individualized programs of instruction and developing an instrument through which these programs can be concisely described. Out of this experience came the identification of a number of components with which all program developers must contend as they design individualized programs, including CBTE. A number of questions associated with each of these components must be considered sooner or later as one plans and implements an individualized program. Several specific questions are discussed here as illustrative of the many we have provided for in our instrument (see Figure 4:1).

DESCRIPTOR FOR THE ANALYSIS OF INDIVIDUALIZED INSTRUCTION

The Descriptor provides for the consideration of several specific components of an individualized instructional program. Programs vary in the extent to which their natures may be characterized by variety of emphasis across these several components. While one program reported to be individualized provides for individualization through an emphasis on variation in *sequence,* another places the emphasis on *rate*; another emphasizes both; and yet another varies on neither. The components recognized on the Descriptor include: *objectives, assessment, sequence, rate, media, grouping,* and *management.*

A detailed description of each component is not the purpose here. Two components, *sequence* and *media,* will be discussed to provide the reader with a general understanding of the way in which the Descriptor functions to answer questions about the specific nature of a given individualized program.

Considering first the sequence of modules or units of study, a specific individualized program can be represented by any one of a number of patterns (Figure 4:2). Given these four alternative sequence patterns, one may decide that initially a linear network will be used; as more instructional materials are developed or as more is learned about students' progress while using the materials, a network procedure may be expected to evolve. One may begin, of course, with the more complicated network at the outset. We suggest that (1) planners need to give consideration to the question of sequence—it should not be allowed to just happen—and (2) once a decision (or decisions) has been made, this decision needs to be clearly understood by all involved in planning, developing, and implementing the program.

Associated with program sequence is another kind of question that relates to the determination of how, within a given learning environment, decisions about sequence will be made for specific learners. In a linear-sequenced program, decisions about what the student will study next are embedded within the program. In any of the other sequence patterns, however, decisions may be embedded in the program where assessment results determine assignment of next study or may be in the hands of the learner, the instructor, or both. Plans to accommodate appropriate decision makers within learning environments will depend on the faculty's position on the feasibility of putting decisions about learner options in the hands of the learner. Early discussion of such decisions and the early determination of program position facilitate clear communication among those involved in program development.

Figure 4:3 shows examples of *sequence* patterns reported for two CBTE programs that were part of a field-test study conducted during the spring of 1973. In the linear sequence shown, decisions about

Figure 4:2. Alternative Sequence Patterns

Linear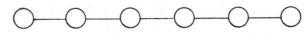

Branched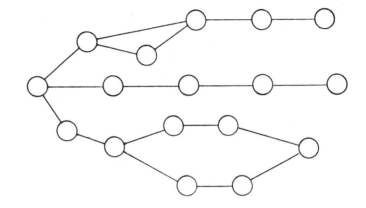

Network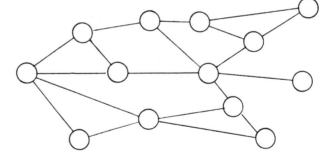

Nonspecified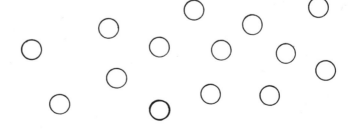

Figure 4:3. Examples of Sequence Patterns

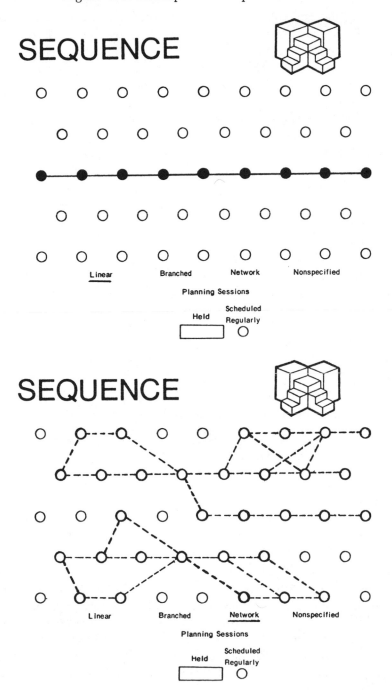

that sequence are embedded in the teacher education curriculum. In the network sequence decisions were shared by learners and instructors.

The *media* component responds to several kinds of questions. As shown in Figure 4:3, we have come to consider a number of questions to be crucial as one plans for *media* in the individualized portions of the CBTE program. Media types are divided into four classifications: (1) reading materials, (2) audiovisual materials, (3) manipulation materials, and (4) no media. (The last classification is included to show that portion of time when the learner is without media— usually with an instructor or a peer group.) The chart provides for a display of the percent of instructional time the learner experiences each of the several media settings. Also of importance in relation to *media* is our concern for who determines its use. Is its use determined simply by the nature of the available program materials, do learners make the choice, or do instructors decide when use is to be made of a specific media? Additionally, the chart provides for evidence of the use of information provided by the learner assessment and the management system that supports the program.

Figure 4:4 shows examples of *media* use for each of two CBTE programs observed during spring 1973. The first reports a heavy emphasis on reading and no-media activities, and the second includes a greater distribution of instructional time among reading, audiovisual materials, manipulatives, and no-media activities.

USING THE DESCRIPTOR

This review of the two components *sequence* and *media* used to characterize the individualized nature of CBTE programs was provided to illustrate how the Descriptor communicates information about instruction. The Descriptor provides a useful way of coding (1) the administrator's view of the program he supports; (2) how faculty planners and developers view the program; and finally (3) how the instructors working within the program view its functioning. As decision-makers, faculty are responsible for determining answers to each of these questions about their own program. The position taken here is that they want a beginning point description of the program they have, a description of the program as it is envisioned at some distant point (we will not call it an end point), and perhaps one or more intermediate point descriptions.

Figure 4:4. Examples of Media Use

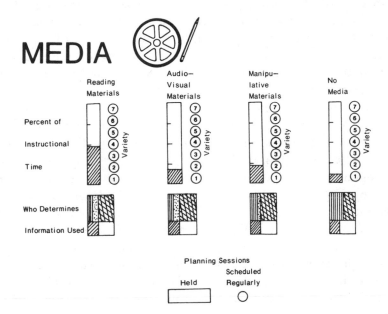

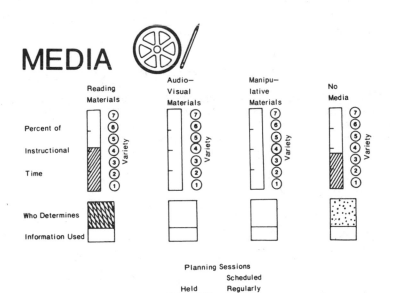

A final word about four individualizing strategies will indicate the manner in which program planning assists in providing consistency across components. *Variety* is a strategy characteristic of each component. Extensive variety in one may be associated with variety in others so that a program may be identified as high or low in this strategy. *Decision-making* by the learner is another strategy that cuts across all components and may help in communicating the extent to which a program may be characterized as emphasizing the learner as decision-maker. *Personalization* is another strategy that cuts across most of the components. In this strategy one may view an individualized program as one that emphasizes learner involvement with others —peers or instructors—as opposed to an emphasis on independent study. Finally, the manner in which *Management* serves each component of the program is a strategy that may have greater or lesser significance in the planning of any given program.

Although reports from faculty and staff in programs that have been described with the use of the Descriptor indicate that clearer communication has resulted, it is still too early to report on the impact of this improved communication on program development. There is ample evidence, however, that the Descriptor has demonstrated its utility in the improvement of communication about programmatic features of individualized instruction in CBTE.

NOTE FOR CHAPTER 4

1. M. Vere DeVault, Mary A. Golladay, G. Thomas Fox, Jr., and Karen Skuldt, *Descriptor for Individualized Instruction: Development Procedures and Results*, and *User's Manual: Descriptor for Individualized Instruction* (Madison: Wisconsin Center for the Analysis of Individualized Instruction, School of Education, University of Wisconsin at Madison, September 1973).

5. The Potential for Humanistic Endeavor

Patricia Heffernan-Cabrera

THE BOX THING

(The Tradition Dilemma)

See our boxes? Aren't they neat?
I can tell you about every nook and cranny
   . . . in every box.

This one is for emotions: small and tidy.
That one for intelligence: larger with
      logical corners. . . .

Just look. They are so straight, tidy,
      beautiful and ever so rational.

I'm not sure how they got that way,
      but there they are.
I like them. Besides they are good for us
      All. Good for all of us. . . .

Oh, my God! I'm having strange feelings!
What shall I do? They must fit in the emotion box.
But, they are running over. I can't stop them.
What do I do? Do I do?

Intelligence can be improved by man—ridiculous!
That isn't even logical. Intelligence is a God-given capacity.
Some of us have a lot; others have very little.
Why that notion doesn't even fit into the logic box;
It doesn't even exist, exist! . . .

Boxes, boxes, boxes, boxes . . . boxes everywhere,
And nothing seems to fit in any of them.
Oh, my God! What have I done to deserve this punishment?
You know what the boxes are for, don't you? . . .

You aren't playing tricks on me like the rest, are you, God?
There is no doubt in my mind about our boxes, no
        doubt . . . is there God?
God? . . . the boxes? . . . all the boxes? . . . . . some of the
        boxes? . . . . a few? . . . . [1]

This is the Gordian Knot of humanistic endeavor and competency based education.

The advocacy of humanistic philosophy within teacher education is in itself an emerging movement. So is the advocacy of competency based education. Due to the nature of systems, e.g., flow charts, PERT-ing, the writing of criterion-referenced behaviorally stated objectives with feedback and recycling, competency based education programming would seem to be antithetical to humanistic philosophy. But is it?

There is another intricacy to compound deliberations. Political modes of the day speak to the democratic process, with all members of society freely participating in that process, regardless of race, color or creed. And it is readily admitted that those who hold the power to mold and shape our society are those who mold and shape the children in the public schools, by both leading and modeling behaviors. Therefore if one speaks to a program of teacher training that is based on the assumption that the acts of teaching and learning can be reduced to a system of knowledges, skills, and performances which are evaluated like an industrial model in a normative way, and demands accomplishment of a minimum set of criterion referenced performances, one must realize that the goals of a greater society cannot be attained.

Although the prestatement of behavioral objectives and the establishment of a *minimal* level of performance are anathema to humanists, the critical element is really *evaluation*. Heavy reliance on a quantitative approach seems to negate the value of human experience. Otto Krash points this out when he states that education viewed in the light of John Dewey's belief in the moral purposes of education[2] and Silberman's hope for a lovely education for each child is almost certainly unmeasurable. Yet is it any less important and should it not be dealt with merely because it cannot be quantified? It would seem then that a program dealing with holistic development of a teacher must concern itself with qualitative evidence as well.

The nature of evaluation works against the self-determining nature of free man, i.e., to be "evaluated" is more often to have to *prove* that one can, rather than to have it *accepted* that one can. The insistence on proof seems to emerge out of the old "man is born evil" idea—in essence, that man is unable to "see" himself for himself and to analyze honestly what he does for himself.

Yet if teacher competencies are clearly stated and performances are clearly described, as the proponents of the competency based model insist, can a teacher not know for himself when he has attained a competency? Must he always have to prove that he "can," and if so does the act of "proving it" to another lend any more credence to his competency?

Clearly, the most important facet of self-determination is the ability to make decisions for oneself, and a great part of control over one's destiny must include the power to evaluate one's own behavior. "If teachers are allowed to practice such self-determination, even in matters of evaluation, can it not be assumed that children will be allowed to be self-evaluating, thereby developing into responsible adults capable of being self-determining?"[3]

If a program is to promote self-determination as a consequence of teacher impact on children, it seems evident that the program has to allow for self-determination on the part of the teacher candidate.

Who is this person—the teacher candidate? He is a blend of existential humanism, or humanistic existentialism, with a new consciousness of *Being*. That is not an intellectual attainment but a "new view, a new attitude, a new Gestalt. . . . Man is not simply a creature who exists but rather, he exists HERE, he is located, situated and embodied HERE where he stands . . . no matter where [he] may be."[4] He is a mutation of a technological society, with faith in mankind and the infinite possibilities for human dignity and power. Such is the personal philosophy of the Be-ing of the teacher-to-be. He is relevant because he is self-defining and self-actualizing.[5]

Among Abraham Maslow's fourteen statements about self-actualizing people, the ones most relevant to the incongruence between a tightly defined competencies based/performances based program and humanistic beings in such a program are those concerned with:

Interpersonal relations: Self-actualizing people have deep interpersonal relations with others.

The democratic character structure: The self-actualizing person does not discriminate on the basis of class, education, race, or color. He is humble in his recognition of what he knows in comparison with what could be known and is ready to learn from anyone. He respects all people as potential contributors to his knowledge, but also just because they are human beings.

Means and ends: Self-actualizing persons are highly ethical. They clearly distinguish between means and ends and subordinate means to ends.

Creativeness: All of Maslow's subjects were judged to be creative, each in his own way. The creativity involved here is not the special talent creativeness. It is a creativeness potentially inherent in everyone, but usually suffocated by acculturation. It is a fresh, naive, direct way of looking at things.[6]

These attributes describe self-actualizers, the humanists who are entering teaching today—the *users* of a technocratic society. To pump them into teacher training programs in which they perform without voice or self-determination is to obtrude into their personal philosophy as well as into the function of education in society.

At the August 1971 Invitation Conference on Performance Based Teacher Education, sponsored by the American Association of Colleges for Teacher Education, a definition of competency based teacher education was developed. The language noted that PBTE/CBTE is characterized by certain *essential elements,* i.e., the competencies (knowledge, skills, and behaviors) to be demonstrated; the criteria to be used to assess those competencies; the assessment of the student's competency; progress determined by demonstrated competency; and an instructional program intended to facilitate the achievement of the stipulated competencies. If the program is competency based and also field centered (referring to the active involvement of other education agencies in decision making re the teacher education process), the definition of elements is expanded to include other *related elements,* such as emphasis on exit rather than entrance, on achievement, on field centeredness, on modularization, and on formative feedback to the student. Some *desirable elements* were nominated, e.g., open system; negotiation of instruction goals by faculty and students; faculty and students as codesigners of the instructional system; and the role of the teacher as an enabler of learning.

Herein lies the problem. CBE seems to be weighted toward the competencies to be attained and the criteria to be used in evaluation. The *intent* seems to be to "box" human behavior.

If one accepts literally the definition sponsored by AACTE as the design structure for a CBE program, one would indeed be in conflict with humanistic philosophy. However, a review and restructuring of that definition can allow for humanistic endeavor in teacher education under the rubric of CBE.

For the professor of education to remove the mysticism from his curriculum, to "unbox" the behavior of his class, to unbell the curve, to make transparent his expectations of achievement, to allow the learner freedom of choice as well as the opportunity to participate is in keeping with humanistic endeavors. In other words, CBE can be an organizer for humanists.

The humanistic concerns can be accommodated if one reorders the seeming priorities as stated in the most widely used definition of CBE. The value-loaded words "essential," "related," and "associated" should be eliminated, and the defining process should include:

(1) Descriptors of the nature of the *system,* e.g., publicly stated competencies, assessment criteria to be used, modularization, field centeredness, etc.

(2) Descriptors of the nature of the *process,* i.e., the participative management of the learner's progress through that system.

We propose that a CBTE program that would be congruent with the Be-ings who will participate in it will be grounded in the following principles:

(1) Humanism as an affirmative philosophy in support of concern for "all men" is an undergirding force for any teacher education program, recognizing that learning to teach involves more than just cognitive development—that man is a self-reflecting art form.

(2) Fundamental to this humanistic effort is the belief that teach-

ing is a process made up of several interrelated strategies that grow from the multiple roles a teacher assumes in daily interaction with children.

(3) A competency based curriculum is a transparent curriculum, i.e., terminal objectives are made public and the learner knows exactly what he will be doing and the criterion by which he will be evaluated.

(4) In addition to transparency in the curriculum, the learner assumes the management of his own destiny. He participates in the decision making process by

    (a) Designing instructional activities to achieve successful completion of enabling objectives, or

    (b) Making choices if optional instruction activities are given.

(5) Basic to the humanistic approach is recognizing the need for a systemic approach that is consistent. Modules within the system exhibit these characteristics:

    (a) Although in an implied sequence, the components actually compose a matrix, each part of which is interdependent with other parts in an integrated process, but each of which can also stand alone.

    (b) Each module generates from a terminal objective, which is public and is evaluated by stated criteria.

    (c) Preassessment is so designed that the participant can self-diagnose his ability to perform the terminal behavior. If he self-diagnoses that he is ready to meet the terminal objective, he moves directly to compliance. Should the terminal objective not be met, he recycles back through the module until he can perform the terminal objective. Other self-diagnostic devices in the preassessment are tied to individual enabling objectives, so the participant can easily determine his strengths and weaknesses in relation to the terminal objective. In this manner, each module provides for multiple routes to exit, for recycling, and for making participant choices.

    (d) Each module is so constructed that maximum use is made of a feedback system, so that a participant knows at what level of competence he is performing as he meets each enabling objective en route to achieving the terminal objective. Further, because he can select and/or design his own instructional activities, allowance is made for his participation in generating new activities as well as validating or negating others.

(e) Finally, each module is so designed and executed that the participant knows at the beginning all the information he needs to achieve the terminal objective.

(6) In summary, evaluation is a *self*-evaluative process with performance as the measure. The burden of proof is willingly carried by the learner, and he presents that proof as part of his self-actualizing process.[7]

NOTES FOR CHAPTER 5

1. Nelson Haggerson, "The Box Thing," *Leadership AASCD Review* (fall 1972): 4.

2. Otto Krash, "The Narrative Character of Teacher Education," unpublished paper (November 1972), p. 2.

3. Patricia Cabrera and William Tikunoff, "Mother, I Can Do It Myself!" paper to be published in AERA Monograph for 1973, pp. 1-2.

4. Thomas Hannah, *Bodies in Revolt* (New York: Holt, Rinehart & Winston, 1970), pp. 91-93.

5. Patricia Cabrera, "Teacher Education: Humanized, Personalized and Competencies Based," Ph.D. thesis, chapter 1.

6. Abraham Maslow, "Self Actualizing People: A Study of Psychological Health," *The Self: Exploration in Personal Growth* (New York: Harper & Row, 1956), pp. 26-27.

7. Patricia Cabrera and William Tikunoff, "A Proposal to Teacher Corps for Preservice-Inservice Teacher Education," unpublished paper (1973), pp. 24-27.

Part 2
Critics' and
Advocates' Appraisal

6. Three Perspectives on CBE: A Panel Discussion

Harry S. Broudy
William H. Drummond
Robert B. Howsam
Benjamin Rosner

INTRODUCTION

Robert B. Howsam

One of the most significant developments of recent years in teacher education is the competency or performance based teacher education movement, a movement that has been developing very rapidly with active participation in the process by the AACTE and a number of other institutions. As with all movements, it has those who support, those who doubt, and those who oppose.

The papers in this chapter include the salient remarks of a panel at the combined session of the American Association of Colleges for Teacher Education and the Society of Professors of Education, February 22, 1973. Professor Harry S. Broudy critiqued the concept of CBTE and its attending implementations. Professors Drummond and Rosner then reacted to his remarks, and a general discussion followed. Dr. Howsam chaired the panel. Appreciation is expressed to Dr. Karl Massanari and the AACTE Committee on Performance Based Teacher Education for providing a transcript of proceedings.

This panel discussion is an attempt to bring into the open as many as possible of the fundamental issues that exist in the application of this movement to teacher education. Many of us are aware of John Gardner's comments about the unloving critics and the uncritical lovers, and some of us are aware that others have put together a third category—the critical lovers.

The attempt today is to give all of us a chance to expose the benefits, the doubts, and the opposition to the movement of competency based teacher education. I am sure we all welcome this opportunity. Those who favor CBTE are as much frightened by their friends as they are by their enemies, and they are particularly concerned about casual acquaintances of the movement who may well cause it to go in directions that were never intended. The highest level of understanding seems important to all of us, on whichever side we stand.

The panel purposely has been formed to represent divergent points of view; the panelists are asked to express themselves openly, as briefly as possible, but nonetheless to the extent that an adequate portrayal of their views is set forth.

WHY OPPOSE CBTE?[1]

Harry S. Broudy

It may puzzle some of you that anyone with a sound heart and a clear head would criticize CBTE/PBTE proposals, the latest enthusiasm among educationists. Who in all conscience can be against competence, and who does not prefer competence in the classroom to As and Bs on a report card? Who, in other words, does not prefer performance to a *promise* of performance?

Is it any wonder then that resistance to CBTE/PBTE pressures is dismissed as misunderstanding, knocking down straw men, and defensiveness of the status quo, not to speak of just plain wrong-headedness? It seems appropriate, therefore, to ask why the criticism persists and is becoming more intense.

There are at least four hypotheses that might account for the opposition:

(1) CBTE/PBTE—and I shall use these words almost interchangeably, although I think there are some differences—threatens those in

teacher education (chiefly professors of education) who are in favor of incompetence.

(2) It threatens those in teacher education who are afraid to have their "products" tested and take refuge in untestable objectives and promises, or do not want their graduates tested in the real classroom, especially in the tough classroom of the inner city.

(3) It disturbs those in teacher education who believe that CBTE/PBTE doctrines, taken strictly and seriously, will lead to apprentice or technician programs.

(4) It disturbs those who see in the denigration of theory a threat to the college of education as a professional school.

Let us examine these hypotheses in order.

(1) Nobody, as far as I know, is in favor of basing a program of teacher education on incompetence, so if CBTE is saying anything significant, it must be saying that it offers teacher education based on a kind of competence different from that found in conventional programs. What then are the "right" competencies for a teacher?

How is this issue to be decided? By research, if possible. Well, how possible is it? According to the staff report of the Advisory Commission on Intergovernmental Relations, studies—twenty-four studies done very recently—have identified a lengthy list of teacher characteristics as associated with pupil achievement. Among these variables are the percentage of teachers in the upper salary quartile (Benson), teacher's experience (Michelson and O'Neill), teacher's undergraduate institution (Michelson), teacher's verbal ability (Bowles, Guthrie, and Jencks), or percent of teachers with M.A. degrees (Perl). And I have only listed some of them.

The lists of characteristics of "good" teachers are without end, and the end of the search for more is nowhere in sight. Indeed, if we insisted on the competence and performance criteria for educational research on this topic, how well would it come off?

This approach to evaluating teaching ability—by looking for characteristics—has soaked up so much effort and money with so little success that by now the researchers should be asking themselves whether this is the question they should be asking. I for one remain depressed by the number of alternative analyses of the teaching act (including my own) that vie for attention without any way of deciding among them. If, as so many of these analyses insist, the teaching act "takes into account" the inner states of pupils, cultural impacts, and personal histories, the prospect of research giving us a definitive and credible anatomy of teaching is no brighter today than it was when researchers began chasing this hare down the road fifty years ago. Operant conditioning, neuropharmacology, neurosurgery, and genetic management offer the greatest promise for the kind of behavior control that our efficiency lads dream about. But one man's dream can be another man's nightmare. If that is the kind of control we want, we should say so.

Another way of settling the issue of what are the right competencies in teaching is to argue from some consensus about what teaching is or ought to be, but this is a controversial matter. It becomes even more controversial insofar as the "good" teacher is defined as one who can bring about "good" learning. However, consensus, or at least high reliability, in judging even so complex a phenomenon as teaching, is not impossible if "experts" using the same criteria do the evaluating. If superintendents or principals qualify as experts, why don't they judge, hire, fire, promote, and demote? Either they are not experts, or they are not so recognized, or they can't agree on the criteria, or they are afraid to act on their judgments.

The remedy for this lack of consensus, lack of courage, or lack of expertise, we are told, is the *consensus gentium*. Thus, the way to make everybody an expert is to split up the teaching act into performances so small and so easily recognizable that evaluation is reduced to noting and counting. This is like doing away with expert winetasters by giving the layman a manual for judging wines.

You recall that in the 1960s the great aim was to produce a teacher-proof curriculum. What we are undergoing now is an attempt to provide an expert-proof method of evaluating teachers.

For such a manual only behaviorally observable competencies or objectives that can be stated in clear terms are suitable. Others that are not are to be regarded as obfuscating and protective of incompetence. For example, doing fractions is a permissible objective; appreciating the quantitative aspects of experience might not be. This brings us to the second hypothesis—that those who have doubts about CBTE/PBTE are afraid of losing the protection that vagueness of objectives affords them.

(2) How tenable are these doubts? Leaving to one side the matter of motives, can one make a case for educational outcomes in general

and for the objectives of teacher education in particular that are not statable in terms of publicly observable behavior?

First, is it really the case that CBTE/PBTE promoters mean to exclude all nonbehavioral objectives? Or do they mean by behavioral something broader than publicly observable, overt behavior? It is difficult to generalize on the numerous lists of objectives, competencies, and performances that are flooding the market. Some are as broad as "ability to conduct a meaningful discussion," and some are as narrow as "being able to adjust an opaque projector." The broader the objective, the more difficult it is to make it testable. This is so because the broader an objective the greater the variety of acts that can be used to attain it. However, the narrower the objective is, the more valid is the criticism that CBTE unduly impoverishes the teaching encounter. One of my colleagues, Ralph Smith, has suggested that PBTE is the acronym for poverty based teacher education.

There is much to be said for making instructional outcomes as precise as possible and for measuring these outcomes as accurately as possible. But the converse is not true, viz, that only that which has been specified and measured has been learned—even at the end of an instructional episode. It certainly runs counter to common sense to believe that life outcomes of schooling can be specified in advance and tested on demand, and that if they are not, they are not worth aiming at. If CBTE/PBTE means this, it ought to say so.

Let us now turn to the hypothesis that the skeptics of CBTE/PBTE do not want their teacher education programs tested by performance in the real classroom. No doubt there are some teacher educators who entertain such fears, and perhaps all those who teach in professional schools ought to. The reason for this lies in the very nature of a professional school, which aims at *preparational* competence rather than at *operational/performatory* competence.

All preparatory competence can claim is that if Teacher T has met the requirements of Program P, it is reasonable to expect that T will perform well in *typical* teaching tasks X, Y, Z. One recognizes that other variables may intervene to frustrate this expectation, especially since every real performance is particular and does not replicate the training task.

If this is all that CBTE/PBTE intends to claim for its programs, it too must rely heavily on transfer from principles, rules, and typical training classes. If the thrust is to be significant, CBTE must reject reliance on courses, credits, and grades as predictors of performance competence. "Performance based" must mean the opposite of "promise based."

What preparational competence is not promise based—or is this a contradiction in terms? The apprentice training program can qualify as a performance program rather than a promise program. In apprentice training, the learner does the real thing all the time. He may do it differently as the master corrects him, but he works with the master on real tasks. He learns by operant conditioning with the master controlling the reinforcement schedule.

Do CBTE/PBTE advocates propose an apprentice program carried on in the schools themselves? Again, it is hard to generalize. Some programs sound as if they do; others want a theory-practice program but to have it all take place in the real classroom. Programs must therefore be judged as to where on the continuum of preparation-performance competence they fall. But if the word *performance* is to have any polemical significance, it must contrast sharply with *promise*. For all teacher education programs are promises to perform in the classroom.

(3) How seriously do CBTE/PBTE programs propose to advocate an apprentice program? How seriously they intend to do this determines how tenable the third and perhaps the fourth hypotheses are.

The primary argument seems to be that any overt performance, especially if broken down into small segments, can be performed to some acceptable criterion of correctness by imitation, practice, and correction. This can be accomplished without the practitioner understanding why the performance is appropriate, at least initially.

I once had a mother-in-law whose son was a practicing physician. She treated his patients when he wasn't in. She didn't go to medical school; she had no license, no credentials. She treated hundreds of patients. How? Well, she did what the son did; she dispensed blue pills, green pills, Band-Aids, etc. If the person could stagger into the office, there was something she could do. Many of her performances could not be distinguished from the performances of her son. Any overt performance, unless it takes a great talent, e.g., imitating Caruso, can be imitated. In other words, theory, which alone provides explanation and understanding, is not necessary for a correct performance. To put it differently, although there may be a rationale of correct performance, the individual performer need not be aware of it, nor does knowledge of it guarantee a correct performance. The question is, how broad a perspective of the educational process shall the teacher use to control the performance?

If teaching can be reduced to a set of imitative performances, two modes of training immediately become possible to supplant conventional programs that contain large segments of theory, principles, and the like. One is the apprentice program; the other is a technical training kind of program in which practice of procedures according to rules constitutes the totality or at least the bulk of the instruction. The advantages of the latter possibility are not insignificant. First, it would downgrade the scholastic aptitude requirements for entry into the program, for scholastic aptitude is aptitude for theory. Secondly, the program could be carried on in postsecondary institutions other than four-year colleges. And, finally, as paraprofessionals, teachers would not command or expect a "professional" salary.

Given the potential of educational technology, the tax revolts, teacher strikes, and kindred phenomena, CBTE/PBTE offers a tempting rationale for transforming the teaching population into a very large cadre of paraprofessionals more or less directed and supervised by a very small cadre of specialists.

(4) Are fears well founded that the future of colleges of education may be jeopardized if the CBTE/PBTE movement flourishes?

Yes, if the baccalaureate teacher education program is its mainstay. If a college of education depends heavily on turning out large numbers of classroom teachers, this may be the end of that program. For if the majority of beginning teachers can be trained in public schools or in two-year postsecondary technical institutions, colleges of education will be accused of overqualifying the product formally while at the same time underqualifying him practically. The fear is not so well grounded if there are to be specialists needing a truly professional preparation and if the study of education can be justified on grounds other than that of teaching it to beginning teachers.

Let there be no misunderstanding. Nobody in American teacher education is unduly impressed by its success, including myself. Nobody denies that certain aspects of teaching can be taught as prespecified techniques. The question is whether teaching as a whole can be so taught without serious distortion of what the culture implicitly expects from the school as an institution and from instructional personnel. The current complaints about the failure of many children to learn the three Rs do not mean that the parents of these children are or ought to be content with literacy alone. The countercomplaints that the schools are ignoring the social forces that make some children woefully unready even for literacy must not be taken as mere countercultural militance. Fundamentally, both are demands for an opportunity to participate fully in the culture. Such demands can neither be understood nor served by a teaching staff made up entirely of technically competent paraprofessionals.

A system, no matter how sophisticated its self-regulating mechanisms are, is no more than a machine as long as the highest control panel is external to it. A human system, no matter how well defined its regulatory mechanisms, has the ultimate control panel within itself. These ultimate norms are themselves the product of imagination and are never finished mechanisms.[2]

The culture is demanding a far higher level of professional competence than ever before, yet the response of colleges of education has been neither technical nor professional; at best it must be called pseudoprofessional. The proportion of hours devoted to general studies and to the subject matter fields of instruction has been increased, but this prescription, so heartily endorsed by the Council for Basic Education in the early 1960s, has not helped to solve the problem. These do not supply the behavioral and humanistic theory directed specifically toward the problems of schooling in general and of teaching in particular, and without such theory the college of education has no future as a professional school. Embryonic and inchoate as this theory presently is, the attempts to eliminate it from teacher education curricula, to discourage its development by specialists, to bypass study of it by direct experience could lead to the bankruptcy of professional teacher education.

CBTE/PBTE programs, if consistent, should be arguing that such theoretical understandings can be reduced to overt performances or that they are unnecessary. I believe that the first option is based on a serious mistake about the nature of knowledge, the second on a serious error as to what are the culture demands of teachers. One can, of course, evade this dilemma by labeling the theoretical components of the conventional program as performances whether or not they can be reduced to overt observable behaviors. In this way one gains the political benefits of CBTE/PBTE with little risk. This is transubstantiation by semantic incantation.

Under the pressure and threats of certification boards and the United States Office of Education, not to mention the death wishes of certain educationists, such semantic incantations may become a way of institutional life. If using the right words will relieve the pressure, win certification and grants, then the right words will be forthcoming—by the yard, at so much a yard. As to performance, that remains to be seen.

RESPONSE TO DR. BROUDY'S CRITIQUE

William H. Drummond

When I first read Professor Broudy's critique, I really did not like it. I felt then and still feel that Professor Broudy defined performance based teacher education the way he wanted to, not the way the Committee on Performance Based Teacher Education of AACTE defined it; then, using his own definition he proceeded to criticize performance based teacher education. Admittedly, the Committee on PBTE may not have built an adequate context for writing about or defining performance based teacher education into this first document. A committee of independent thinkers, I rationalize, has a hard enough time coming to agreement on key concepts, much less the philosophical or theoretical propositions from which these concepts have grown. But irrespective of the adequacy or inadequacy of the monograph, I felt that Professor Broudy should have devoted more time and energy to what was written in "The State of the Art" paper and far less to what he thought was *implied* by what was written.

Professor Broudy indicated clearly what he thought were the assumptions underlying performance based teacher education:

(1) The teaching act is the sum of performances into which it is analyzed.
(2) The performance unit is a matter of indifference, i.e., the number and character of the performance units can vary from one program to another.
(3) The criterion for the "product" is demonstrated competence in the selected set of training performances.[3]

Using these assumptions, Dr. Broudy imputes a variety of characteristics of PBTE and is able to build a very convincing case. In the nonphilosophical world, this is known as "gotcha."

Several questions and comments come to mind. First, where did he get the idea that those advocating performance based teacher education believe that all aspects of teaching (or of specific teaching acts or episodes) are the sum of the described and observable parts? The Elam paper[4] didn't imply this; frankly, I was glad that Broudy did not take much time in his critique to talk about it.

Secondly, where did Dr. Broudy get the notion that the performance unit—whatever that means—is a matter of indifference? Again, the Elam article doesn't use this language. Does Broudy mean that whenever an action is analyzed into parts for purposes of observation, each part becomes a performance unit? Does he mean that any unit so created can be treated with indifference—that therefore *any* performance unit can be treated with indifference? If one counts things or acts or people, is he then ipso facto indifferent to them? At this point I feel like breaking into song, "It Ain't Necessarily So."

I am reminded of a little family custom that started when our kids were small but which we continue even though the kids are grown and gone. Whenever we drive over one of those counting mechanisms the highway department stretches across roads, one of us in the car usually speaks up in a loud voice, "One!" That may sound a bit silly, but over the years the event has taken on special meaning for us—a declaration that we in the car are one and that we consider ourselves important. I suppose to Dr. Broudy our family traveling past a counting point is a matter of indifference—but of indifference to whom?

These questions and responses follow: Who is interested in a teaching act, no matter how analyzed? The student? Of course. The teacher? You'd better believe it. The teacher educator? Yes, indeed! The principal? He or she ought to be. The parents? Most of the time. And what language, other than operational language, should these people use to communicate their interest? One might ask, "Do all of these people care whether or not a teacher who intends to use heuristic processes pauses after he or she asks a question?" I guess the average parent wouldn't understand the question, but to the teacher who is trying to improve his skills in heuristic methods and to the teacher educator who is trying to help, the pause is important. Even the length of the pause is important, up to a point.

Teaching, like many other important human functions, is a transactional process. But according to most PBTE advocates, teaching "is purposeful and role associated."[5] If one wishes to obtain knowledge about teaching, a good approach is to analyze what seems to occur in teaching situations based on role and purpose. Using this analysis as a data-gathering system, one can provide data to the person who wants the knowledge, attending to what the teacher and student intended to do (using Dr. Broudy's term, promised); what the teacher did or did not do; what the student did or did not do; and what if anything happened as a consequence.

My third concern is: Must one use dualisms when thinking about teaching? Maybe I can tell you my difficulty with dualistic thinking if I tell you what happened to me last week as I was getting ready for this program.

It was late in the evening and I had just reread Dr. Broudy's critique and had made a handful of notes about what he had said when I decided I was tired and went to bed. I had a dream about myself and the new bird feeder that had just been put up in my backyard. In my dream, I was down at Johnson & Ferris—a local nursery and garden store in Gainesville. One of the clerks came up to me and asked in kind of a friendly way if he could help me and I replied that I wanted to buy some birdseed. He said, "Okay, what kind do you want?" I replied, "Oh, you know, some pretty *good* birdseed. You see, I have a new bird feeder. I guess I would buy whatever you recommend."

"Well," he said, "It just isn't that simple! *I* need to know more about how *you* look at birds and bird feeding before I can recommend anything."

I remember in the dream I shifted my weight a little bit at that point; I was getting edgy. He continued, "Some people view birds as creatures of habit, that is, they believe that birds move from place to place for food in a regular routine, returning to the same place about the same time every day. Others view birds in relation to their feeding habits as being goal directed, that is that birds go where they see the food. Depending on how you view birds and bird feeding, I will recommend a different kind of birdseed," he concluded.

I mumbled something about song birds and bird watching underneath my breath; I was not about to raise old bird issues right there. I screwed up my courage and asked if I could look at both kinds. Secretly I had decided that I was going to buy both and mix them myself.

As I read him, Dr. Broudy distrusts inductive analysis as a basis for theory building. Deductive analysis, on the other hand, is of a higher order and is therefore preferred. Because the PBTE statement did not deal with a priori theory or indicate that theory has to precede practice, advocates of PBTE, according to Dr. Broudy, are not concerned with theory or art. In my opinion such a position is not justified.

Before I close, let me concede to Professor Broudy and to you that there is much to be critical of in performance based teacher education if one looks without charity at some of the attempts being made to implement it. Some program developers are not attending to a necessary context for the teaching of pedagogical skills. They are not providing an appropriate rationale, nor are they generating the necessary personal motivation for the learning of skills. I think this is shortsighted.

Some people seem to feel there is something magical in the individualization of instruction, but most of us know that magic occurs when people interact and undergo and share an experience together. More of the focus of learning units or modules probably should be designed for small group work. Certainly, it has become clear that people who are beginning to develop performance based teacher education models need to clarify their own motives and values before they begin to structure new worlds for other people.

We obviously do not have the necessary technology and assessment instruments to go whole hog on performance based teacher education. There are too many people jumping on the bandwagon without doing their theoretical and political homework. I would agree that what we need is gradualism in the implementation of this movement.

I want to thank Professor Broudy for taking a whack at performance based teacher education. I also want to say that despite what Dr. Broudy has said, the ideas presented in the "State of the Art" paper are still pretty good, and I invite each of you to confront them yourself.

RESPONSE TO DR. BROUDY'S CRITIQUE

Benjamin Rosner

I am personally grateful that we have in Professor Broudy an erudite and clear-thinking critic of competency based teacher education.

I share the point of view that Bill Drummond expressed in closing, that we seem somehow to be plunging forward at a mad pace toward some rather unknown or some not too clear goals. I think that Professor Broudy's critique will serve a useful purpose, for it will give us some pause and enable us to assess much more clearly where it is we are going and why.

I am going to attempt to present to you some of my own thoughts on the power of competency based teacher education, and I hope to respond to some of the criticism explicit and implied in Professor Broudy's statement.

There is no question but that teacher education today is on the defensive. As a dean of teacher education, I have a leadership role—a role that I share with many colleagues—and those of you who have responsibilities for teacher education on your campuses share this leadership role with me. To lead, however, is to assume an obligation; and it seems to me that one of our obligations is to come face to face with the question, "What evidence do we have to convince the public and our students that teacher preparation merits their continued support?"

Criticisms of teacher education confront us day after day. Preservice students protest that the contemporary teacher education curriculum is inadequate—that it does not offer the power to cope with the problems they confront in the schools.

Inservice teachers tell us that they cannot remember what it was that we taught them that somehow made a difference in their professional lives. School administrators tell us that they have to reteach the students we send to them. State officials tell us that our programs are not cost effective and that we do not have the power within the teacher education curriculum to make a difference in the operation of the public schools. Community groups decry our inability to improve the quality of instruction. We are confronted daily with the evidence that hundreds of thousands of children in cities—and in suburbs—fail to achieve the basic skills of reading and arithmetic.

I grant you that some of this criticism may be unfair. Students are not in a position to criticize our program when they do not really know whether what we are offering them today will make a difference tomorrow. I grant you that inservice teachers may be passing the buck of failure—they may be blaming us because they see every day the evidence of their own inability to make a difference. I grant you that school administrators may be passing the buck, that government officials at the local, state, and federal levels may be passing the buck, and that the community at large may be unwilling to recognize the serious problems in society that are presenting the schools with instructional problems that may be impossible to solve.

But somehow the buck always seems to stop with me, and I suspect the buck always seems to stop with you. The problem I confront, and I assume the problem you confront, is to generate the evidence that investment in teacher education makes a difference in the quality of instruction.

When I was working with a committee to assist a U.S. Office of Education task force, headed by Allen Schmieder, to examine the federal investment in a variety of programs in teacher education and to formulate a plan that would make some sense out of it, the first question our committee had to address was, "What evidence can we identify to justify continuing investments in teacher education?" To put it another way, "How do we assess the effectiveness of a teacher education program?"

Richard Turner synthesized the committee's deliberations and suggested that there were six criterion levels by which to appraise the effectiveness of teacher education. These criterion levels defined a continuum of confidence in predictions of teacher effectiveness against criteria of pupil change.

The first criterion level, one that was perhaps the most remote from the ultimate criterion of effective teacher behavior, was the criterion of knowledge. That is, if we could demonstrate that prospective or inservice teachers possessed certain knowledge, we would then be able to predict that they would be more effective as teachers than if they failed to possess that knowledge.

The second criterion level, somewhat closer to the criterion of pupil change, was the student's demonstration of mastery of teacher behavior under simulated conditions—not conditions in the real school, nor with school-age pupils.

The third criterion level pushed the degree of confidence higher by asking for evidence of mastery under microteaching or miniteaching situations with small groups of school-age pupils.

At the fourth level, the student, or prospective teacher, would demonstrate behaviors in the real world of the classroom or in other instructional settings in which teachers are expected to function.

These behaviors would be integrated teaching sequences that characterized the total observable teaching act.

At the fifth level we would expect to find evidence that a teacher was able to produce short-term changes in pupil behavior.

Finally, at the sixth level, we argued that the teacher's behavior produced changes in pupil performance over long periods of time. The question we were compelled to put to ourselves was, "What is the most appropriate level of evidence regarding the effectiveness of a teacher education program?" We argued that the most appropriate level was the level at which teachers display integrated, highly complex instructional behavior under actual classroom conditions. We did not argue that the appropriate criterion level was demonstrated change in pupil performance, but rather that it was observable change in teacher behavior.

The problem then was to analyze the relationship between criteria of teacher education effectiveness and criteria of school effectiveness. We argued that studies of the relationship between teacher behavior and effective school operations would validate the teacher education curriculum. What we needed, therefore, was a procedure that would enable us to test hypotheses about teacher behavior against criteria of school effectiveness.

One of the major difficulties of teacher behavior research has been that we have been unable to observe teacher behavior that was stable over sufficiently long periods of time to permit conclusions about the relationship between what teachers do and the results they obtain. We felt that competency based teacher education would require the preparation of teachers who possessed specific knowledges and skills to a certain level of mastery, so that we could expect observable, stable teacher behavior that permitted study to determine whether or not that behavior made a difference in pupil performance.

PBTE or CBTE is, then, an approach to the identification of a powerful teacher education curriculum—the knowledges, skills, and predispositions that are associated with criteria of pupil change or other criteria of effective school operations. It is an approach to the preparation of teachers who demonstrate mastery of a teacher education curriculum under actual classroom conditions, so that we can ultimately study relationships between patterns of teacher behavior and criteria of school effectiveness. It is an approach to teacher education that links teacher preparation to school operations in a re-search-and-evaluation context.

PBTE does not emphasize pedagogical skill to the detriment of theory or knowledge. The performance based teacher education movement probably gives much greater visibility to the roles of theory and of concepts in the interpretation of teacher and pupil behavior than more traditional approaches that have not examined the role of knowledge as critically. As a matter of fact, we have on this AACTE program a number of sessions devoted to instructional materials intended to assist teachers to acquire the concepts by which they will observe and interpret pupil, teacher, or teacher-pupil behavior.

Performance based teacher education does fractionate the teaching act, but every teacher education curriculum fractionates the teaching act. The difference between performance based teacher education and more traditional teacher education programs is that PBTE publicly recognizes this assumption. It makes very explicit the fact that we are looking at teacher behavior and that we are trying to analyze it. We do not pretend that the whole is equal to the sum of the parts. There will be much that we will miss. But it is a virtue of performance based teacher education that it publicly acknowledges the fact that the teacher education curriculum fractionates teaching. Current teacher education programs do not make explicit their fractionation of the total teaching act.

The question is not whether PBTE fractionates teacher behavior, but whether there are more useful degrees of fractionation, more useful degrees of discreteness by which to approach the preparation of teachers.

It is argued that performance based teacher education will tend to emphasize those things that we can do, and it will deemphasize in an obvious way those things we cannot do. We have spent much time arguing that what we can do is so limited that we dare not do it. I would like to see teacher education do the things it *can* do and then get on with the task of learning to do the things we presently cannot do. At this point I personally would be very satisfied with some limited successes.

DISCUSSION

DR. BROUDY: I would like to express my relief that the trauma of reading my material did not really affect Professor Drummond very seriously. I do not think he even intended to read that critique very seriously, and I must say to both Professor Drummond and to Dean Rosner that I did use the words "taken seriously and strictly." If PBTE is not taken seriously or strictly, then there is no sense to the whole movement because we are all for good teaching, we are all for theory and practice, we are all for defining and clarifying our common goals. This PBTE movement, however, was promoted as a polemic against conventional programs and against the institutions that have those programs.

Now, if all PBTE means is that we are going to do what we have been doing, but do it a little better, let's spend the money on doing it a little better and less on the promotion. Let us stop taking up the thousands of hours of teachers' time trying to spin yards of objectives out of their standard courses of study.

I think Dean Rosner gave the thing away when he talked about the six levels of criteria. Number 3, I recall, is "demonstrate behavior" that conforms to "certain criteria presumed to be evidence of mastery." If we knew these criteria, there would be no problem. These are the things that education theorists have been arguing about for two thousand years. I think it is irresponsible to engage vast resources of time and money in a movement that really amounts to no more than renaming what everybody is already doing.

I return to Professor Drummond's remark about not reading Stan Elam's article. I did read it, although I did not get it until after I had finished mine, but I edited mine after reading it. Stan Elam is an intelligent man, and he did what he was asked to do. He made a survey of all the things he had heard about PBTE. He found many things claiming that label. I did not reject his definitions, but I did stipulate a definition that would make PBTE a significantly different approach to teacher education. Reading reports of the various programs called PBTE, I come to no other conclusion than that either PBTE is innocuous or mischievous. If it is innocuous, let us forget it. If it is mischievous, let's see where it may be harmful. This I have tried to do. If it is to be the panacea, if this is going to take us to the Promised Land, then it should not have these gray areas and be all things to all men, although Professor Drummond dislikes sharp distinctions in ideas or birdseed.

I heard Dean Rosner say, "This is preparation for research into teaching." That is not the way PBTE has been advertised. That is not what the certification board in California thinks. That is not what the regents in New York think. That isn't what a host of legislators are thinking. They think we have an instrument with which to punish teachers and keep teachers colleges up to the mark. That is what PBTE has been advertising and promising. Where did the legislators get these notions, do you suppose?

DR. DRUMMOND: I notice that Dr. Broudy continues to establish beautiful dualisms, that PBTE is either up to mischief or that it is not. Everything in the world is either all one way or it is all the other—a proposition that most observations of the real world will not support.

The truth of the matter is that we do not know very much about teaching or about how one learns to teach if one views teaching as an applied science. I do agree with Dr. Broudy that one needs to look to see if there is any mischief in any kind of sponsored activity, but I do not see why he implies that competency based teacher education should be some sort of pure thought.

DR. BROUDY: There is very little pure thought in that.

DR. DRUMMOND: There is very little pure anything; PBTE has been conceived by a number of people who see schools operate the way they are, who have been trying to figure out ways for schools to be better. Now, such efforts do not always come out neat and tidy, and sometimes such efforts do not result in beautiful theory. Some theories, however, ought to come from practice and not necessarily vice versa.

DR. ROSNER: I am continually impressed by the fact that performance based teacher education is heralded as a panacea, that it is publicized as a way to revolutionize instruction. I do not know who authors this kind of publicity other than the elected or appointed officials of state and federal governments who somehow see in this movement an opportunity to emasculate the schools of education, to focus on the use of technicians, to save money.

The people with whom I have worked have not tried to sell it as a panacea. We have seen it as an approach to the clarification of much of the ambiguity that presently surrounds teacher education programs. We have seen it as an approach to the introduction of rigorous teacher behavior research. We have not seen it as an approach that will in one fell swoop solve all of the problems of teacher education or solve the problems of the public schools—but it is being sold that way. It seems to be that the sellers are the ones who perhaps may be irresponsible—but not the people whom I work with or the writers whom I have read. These people have tried to sell it as an approach to the introduction of clarity and rigor in teacher education.

MODERATOR HOWSAM: It seems to me there is little function in the issue of mischief as against good. The far more important way in which to look at this issue is to say that there are some anticipated consequences that can be predicted, foreseen, and sought for on the part of any movement. But there is always the hazard of unanticipated consequences arising out of our incapacity to see all the possibilities that might arise. I think it is much wiser to look at it in terms of good intent on both sides, but the possibility that blinders in one way may cause some anticipated or unanticipated consequences could become a problem. Within that context we arrive at much more defensible dialogue than we do out of the mischief notion.

DR. DRUMMOND: The real power of the PBTE movement lies in the response to the question, "What evidence do you accept that something is being done the way you intended it to be done?" That concern, the kind and amount of evidence the teacher is searching for in assessing his own teaching, continues to be a powerful idea. I concur with Professor Broudy that the most important effect of PBTE may be that teachers and teacher educators have had to struggle to make intentions clear. The PBTE movement calls for making public statements of intention, including some kind of statement regarding expected results. Pressing for clarity in the definition of goals is not new. To the best of my knowledge, none of the ideas normally associated with performance based teacher education is new.

PARTICIPANT FROM AUDIENCE: If Professor Broudy is right in his presentation, it might be reasonable to expect that some of the advocates of PBTE, as he presented them, might prefer having expert witnesses before the state departments of education, state boards of education, and state legislators, urging that they not mandate this thing with the power of the state behind it until there has been research experimentation.

DR. DRUMMOND: I have made such testimony myself.

DR. ROSNER: Professor Broudy alluded to the situation in the state of New York. I can assure you that those of us in the state of New York who have spent considerable time looking at performance based teacher education have presented many arguments to the New York State Regents and to the State Education Department, asking them to slow down, asking them to withhold their mandated change. If you like, I can send you a copy of a rather lengthy letter which I wrote to the Regents, telling them if they mandated performance based teacher education, they would have the result of prematurely aborting whatever power was inherent in the concept. I asked for the allocation of funds to support the necessary research and development that would lead to some degree of research before it was mandated.

The State Education Department—and I assume this is true across the country and not restricted to New York—is not concerned as much with teacher education as with teacher certification. They see in the performance based teacher education thrust an opportunity to introduce immediate changes in certification—to modify current certification and possibly tenure-related legislation and regulations in the guise of advocating performance based teacher education, whatever it means to them.

MODERATOR HOWSAM: It may interest you to know that we also have a mandatory implementation date in the state of Texas, and it may interest you to know that the PBTE people in Texas are greatly concerned over the precipitate nature of this and have also advised their agency to be very cautious about the use of the State Board of Education or of a legislative mandate. It is our perception, however, that the political process grinding on the agency from the one side is in many respects more powerful than the "take it easy, give us more time" kind of thing that comes from other sides.[6]

PARTICIPANT FROM AUDIENCE: Two mandates apparently are going on today: performance based teacher education and humanistic education. Are these philosophically opposite?

DR. BROUDY: I was accused of being too pure. In these days that is really a vice. But I think you raised a very interesting point in the politics of education today. I think there are two prongs to the attack on the public schools. One is coming from the efficiency people who demand accountability in terms of some kind of cost benefit analysis. I think they are the people who are advocating behavioral objectives, and I think Dean Rosner would agree that they have seized on these ideas as a way of coping with the rebellious taxpayer. The new humanistic attack, I think, comes from a different source but ends up aligning itself politically with the efficiency forces. The humanistic point of view, it seems to me, originated in the dissatisfaction of the minorities with the schooling their children got, on the ground that it was designed for the middle class establishment and was therefore antithetical to their needs.

Both sides say, "We do not want what we now have, so let's have something else." PBTE is one alternative, another is to concentrate on turning out teachers who "relate" to children. For that purpose, it has been argued, and I think with some cogency, teachers do not have to go to school at all—they can be taken out of the Job Corps, Peace Corps, and social work, that they should be people who can relate to people, and they can be put straight into the classroom. Whether they have studied anything formally does not make much difference.

There are two quite different attacks on the schools, differently motivated but having the same effect, namely, "Let's get rid of what we have and go on to something that bypasses the college of education." Sooner or later it comes down to the question, "How can we get around or reduce formal preparation of teachers?" Although I quite agree that my two panelists have not advocated this, some of their colleagues have allowed themselves to be co-opted into these efforts, and that is what I refer to as the death wish of many educationists.

DR. ROSNER: I wish I could say it as well as I would like. Because I am so involved with the political struggle to preserve teacher education, I just can't permit myself to leave without saying this.

All of us have a responsibility to look very carefully at where we are, to come to some decision about where we are going, and to make that decision clear and public. Otherwise, politicians concerned with economies will make those decisions for us.

NOTES FOR CHAPTER 6

1. Arguments presented in this section have been drawn from Harry S. Broudy, *A Critique of Performance Based Teacher Education* (Washington, D.C.: AACTE, 1972).

2. For an interesting explication of this view, see William T. Powers, "Feedback: Beyond Behaviorism," *Science* 179 (January 26, 1973): 351-356.

3. Broudy, *A Critique of Performance Based Teacher Education*, p. 3.

4. Stanley Elam, *Performance Based Teacher Education: What Is the State of the Art?* (Washington, D.C.: AACTE, 1971).

5. Ibid.

6. For a description of the Texas story with an analysis of the issues raised by proponents and opponents, see W. Robert Houston and Robert B. Howsam, "CBTE: The Ayes of Texas . . . ," *Phi Delta Kappan* 55, no. 5 (January 1974). In August 1973 the state commissioner of education requested an opinion of the attorney general as to the legality of the standards mandating PBTE. In January 1974 the attorney general ruled that, based on laws passed previously, PBTE as the *only* certification route was not legal; it could, however, be one of several preparation modes. His review was based entirely on legal rather than educational grounds.

7. Some Philosophical Issues

Elvira R. Tarr

From the time educators became self-conscious of our profession, we have looked to the "great teacher" as a model for our activities. Generations of students have not only read *The Dialogues, The Republic, Emile,* and *School and Society,* but have also been guided to a critical appraisal of the educational methods described in these classics. This was done very often with an imaginative reconstruction of the application of those ideas to the present. In addition, the implications of their adopting one or another or a combination of styles in their own teaching was part of the process of their preparation as teachers. In short, the presentation of models of educational systems and models of the great teacher offered students the opportunity to engage in conceptual analysis.

The addition of student teaching was an attempt to weld theory to practice. This is neither the time nor the place to review the vast literature devoted to questioning which courses should precede others, or at what stage of a teacher's preparation they should be taken.

What is important, I believe, is to set CBTE within the context of teacher preparation in order to understand and appraise this effort. Anything less than a constant critique running parallel to and informing about proposed educational practices would allow educational hucksters, who are always waiting in the wings, to take over center stage. Therefore, let us not be influenced by a bandwagon effect caused by such statements as, "It should be obvious that PBTE is a trend that is definitely catching on in education circles. Laymen as well as teachers are tuning in to this kind of thinking,"[1] or, there is "growing pressure to suggest a reform movement of great potential is in the making."[2]

Neither should we reject out of hand proposals for the improvement of teacher education. Without doubt the current push in educational circles is toward competency based teacher education. Before this "push" comes to "shove," perhaps it would be profitable to examine some of the philosophical assumptions that are implied in the idea and to suggest directions for exploration.

The AACTE invited Stanley Elam to write the pamphlet, *Performance Based Teacher Education: What Is the State of the Art?* His lucid explanation will serve as the primary basis for my analysis.

The description of PBE consists of five essential elements—see chap. 1, p. 9, for a full description. "These elements are generic, essential elements and only programs that include *all* fall within the definition of P.B.T.E."[3]

Several ideas are found in these five elements that are used uncritically and with systematic ambiguity. It is the purpose of this exposition to identify and clarify those concepts.

Among the implied characteristics is the allegedly "systematic" nature of the program. That is, the purpose determines the nature of the process, and the critical measure of the system is the accuracy with which the product reflects the purpose. But what is the purpose? What is a competent teacher? According to the definition of the word system, the critical measure of the system would be the improved learning of children.

Although there has been no thoroughly developed philosophical position to support CBTE, some attempts have been made to place this effort in one or another philosophical tradition. An examination of the claims made by a few of these writers should dispel the erroneous assumptions that attempt to justify educational practices. In this

way we will be able to objectively explore the strengths and limitations of CBTE without the mistaken importation of authorities to
support or vitiate the ideas.

Klingstedt claims the genesis of CBTE is experimentalism, and in a
naive and erroneous rendering of this philosophical position, he joins
it with the ideas of some experimental psychologists and then offers
the following justification for CBTE:

Performance based educational programs placed an emphasis on changing the
learner's behavior or performance. From an emphasis on performances identified
by "immediate suggestion," the movement became more focused and attempted
to zero in on performances arrived at, through reasons which were designed to
guarantee a given competency level. In the Experimentalist tradition, the method used to define competency was the same as Dewey's scientific method, e.g.,
in the area of teacher education the "felt difficulty" was that teachers were not
being adequately prepared; the "immediate suggestion" varied according to the
situation. Following the emotional reaction, reason was brought to bear and a
hypothesis or "contemplative theory" was formulated. Following this, procedures were established for testing the hypothesis; and, finally, constant reexamination of the program was built in. Experimentalists would support this approach because of their faith in the scientific method and its role in research.
The faith in research exhibited by people within the CBE movement indicates
their confidence in the compatibility of psychological data and educational practice (a fundamental idea of Experimentalism).[4]

This is an attempt to link Dewey's reading of the logic of inquiry
to the methods employed by CBE by their common "faith in research." I believe a correct reading of Dewey would indicate that the
problem, whether it originated in a "felt difficulty" of emotional or
cognitive origin, would lead to the development of testable hypotheses that took the possible consequences into account. These hypotheses were tentative and were to be altered as they were informed by
practice. The constant reexamination that Klingstedt alludes to was
not to be an intellectual exercise in the compatability of the program
with the proposed solution or an observation of the effect. It was, in
fact, an alteration of the program in the light of practice. This alteration was thus a possible reformulation of the original hypothesis.
Dewey's "faith" was not in research done in a laboratory, but in
ideas in action, in practice, and informed by a hypothesis that was
being tested. It is to be hoped that Klingstedt and others are aware of
Peirce's essay on the fixation of belief and the danger he ascribes in
affixing one's belief by the method of authority! Whether Dewey,
Skinner, or any other person is responsible for the genesis of an idea,

one is fighting a straw man if one denies the compatability of psychological research and educational practice.

The writings on CBTE at this time seem to suggest either that (1) a teaching theory is being explicated or (2) a "fruitful hypothesis" is being formulated.

If we take *theory* in its traditional sense, surely one can find little or nothing that has been written about the nature of society, the nature of human beings, or the good life. There is nothing that resembles *The Republic, Emile,* or even *Walden II.* The proposals developed so far do not present us with the large canvas that purports to describe or prescribe for American education.

If on the other hand we employ theory in a narrower sense, i.e., a series of "laws" or regularities covered by a fruitful theory or a hypothesis of predictive value, we come closer to what CBTE seems to be. Although Elam states that his elements are "theoretically based," what we are presented with is a "strategy" that seems to have its genesis in psychological research but is concerned with teaching.

Perhaps if we accept a rather simple distinction between teaching theories and learning theories, we can better understand Elam's statement that CBTE is "theoretically based." Teaching theories are primarily *prescriptive,* that is, they are concerned with what we "ought" to do to "facilitate certain kinds of learning."[5] These suggestions are bound up with our beliefs about what is worth teaching.

Learning theories are primarily *descriptive* in nature; they explain or describe how learning occurs. Of course, there is an implicit view of human behavior and the sources of knowledge. For example, Skinnerian behaviorism is "rooted in the belief that the only reliable source of human knowledge is that which can be directly observed."[6]

An examination of CBTE in the light of this distinction suggests that it is neither prescriptive nor descriptive, though perhaps a little of both. The proposal tells us how to facilitate learning but almost nothing about what is worth teaching. On the other hand, if we consider CBTE from the standpoint of a learning theory, it is defective in that it does not offer a consistent and coherent body of explanations.

The avowed goal of CBTE is the preparation of competent teachers. Note that it is not to prepare great, excellent, good, inspiring, or dynamic teachers, but competent ones. How is this to be achieved?

Of what does the preparation consist? Elam offers us the "essential elements," and says: "Some authorities consider it potentially superior to traditional strategies for developing the teacher knowledge, skills, and *attitudes* necessary to facilitate pupil learning."[7] (Emphasis added.) However, he says later, "There now appears to be general agreement that a teacher education program is performance based if . . . competencies (knowledge, skills, behaviors) [are] to be demonstrated by the student."[8] No reason is offered for excluding the word *attitudes* offered in the initial definition and the substitution of the word *behaviors*.

Although the current writing on CBTE makes innumerable references to the social and political ferment in society and in the schools, no recommendations are made for improving the situation to invalidate community criticisms of teachers. The work of Rosenthal and Jacobs (*Pgymalion in the Classroom*) and others concerned with the effect of middle class values or ethnic values, suggests that a teacher's attitudes are a highly significant factor in determining student learning. One must hope that it was not the lack of assessment measures that caused the deletion, for that would suggest that the imperfect state of measurement is decisive in determining what we will try to identify and develop in teachers!

Another essential element is that competencies are role derived from explicit conceptions. In fact, the competencies that have been identified have not been logically derived through analysis of a conception, but rather were empirically adduced. In any case, the lists of competencies being developed are formidable compendia.

A further requirement is that the competencies must be identified and be so stated that the student who is supposedly demonstrating the competency can thereby be assessed. In short, a stipulation is made that a competency can be stated in assessable terms, and any that cannot be are dropped from the list or perhaps placed on a waiting list.

The student's performance is used as the primary source of evidence, although what is meant by "performance" is not clear. One wonders if nonverbal performance is acceptable—and how would one assess it? If we cannot assess the raised eyebrow or a shrug of the shoulder, will these performances also be placed on a waiting list?

Much is made of the fact that the rate by which a student progresses through the program is determined by competence, not by time or course completion. We might see an additional six months or a year as attending to individual differences, but will the program planners allow five years or perhaps ten years? Is there any limit to the resources spent on an individual? While we may applaud the effort to remove narrow restrictions on entrance requirements, surely there will be *some* requirements. These may not be easily identified at this time, but the impression given is that anyone may enter and receive individualized attention. Perhaps only a few will enter. One can only speculate, although the end of the teacher shortage is mentioned several times.

Participation in the program is described as broad-based decision making. Thus such groups as college faculty, students, public school personnel, even community multi-institutional patterns of participation are possible. However, we are also told the actual designers of the instructional system are the students and the teachers. To suggest that students can design or help design a program of performances that will prepare them to develop into competent teachers for the real world of teaching is to ask for the finished product at the initiation of the program.

Finally, when the student has reached the point where he has an adequate conception of the goals of teaching, role integration takes place. The student moves from mastery of specific techniques toward "diagnosis and selective utilization of such techniques in combination." Anyone who has taught—not trained, but taught—preservice teachers will certainly recognize this as an aborted description of the teacher role.

As mentioned above, a major claim made for CBTE is that the program is systematic[9] and that the purpose determines the nature of the process. If the purpose is to improve or alter the education of young children, then the admission by everyone writing in the field that there is not enough knowledge about the relationship between teacher behavior and pupil learning strongly suggests that it would not be wise to mandate *one* process for teacher education. New York State has set a timetable for CBTE that is already moving many institutions in this direction. The ends or goals of education for children in the urban school setting in 1990 are surely not known now. The process suggested is just one of many strategies that might be employed. In addition, the description of the process barely takes into account the "world of informal learning, the streets, TV, friends, libraries and museums."[10]

The proponents of CBTE seem to share Plato's assumption that to know the good is to do the good, because nowhere are questions raised concerning the actual and continuing performance of those who have demonstrated their ability to perform. Research done by Horner indicates that most women who are capable in their work will not perform as well as they are able to when they are placed in a competitive situation with men.[11] Performance as an isolated factor is not as accurate a reflection of a person's ability as might appear. Variables such as the classroom itself, years of teaching, sex, etc. are factors that will influence actual performance on the job.

The area most neglected and probably of paramount importance is the problem of values. There are apparently no differences or priorities in values among the various competencies. What competence is of most worth? What guiding principles will the teacher use in setting up a field situation? The uncritical use of the word experience in much of the literature suggests that the writers believe that by placing a student in a field situation, the values will emerge from the situation itself.

Several questions not of apparent importance if only the substantive portions of the CBTE program are considered take on vital importance when the whole educational enterprise is considered. The first question is that of the lack of attention to the affective domain. It is not enough to say that all the performances are pervaded by the affective, nor that "objectives to develop the affective behaviors— those in the realm of attitudes, beliefs, and relationships—resist precise definition and thereby preclude the precise assessment which competency based approaches seek." We should not have to be reminded of the research done by Stanley Milgram not long ago, when "electric shocks" were given to subjects by students who unquestioningly followed the directions they received from their instructors. If we do not concern ourselves with the humanistic aspect of education, what kind of teachers will we be preparing?

For many years teacher education has included performance as part of its certification requirements. If CBTE is an attempt to rationalize what was previously sporadic and arbitrary, the attempt deserves attention. Perhaps a more fruitful approach would be to consider, as does Daniel, that the continuum should be perceived as performance based at one end with nonperformance factors (personality traits, intelligence test scores, knowledge of subject matter, etc.) at the other. However, "there is no agreement as to how far such a movement should go and how fast such a movement should proceed."[12]

The second question concerns the lack of attention to the cognitive domain. Although the question of goals seems not to be an important concern of CBTE program developers, when the area is discussed much is apparently assumed about the preparation of teachers. For example, *Developing Instructional Modules* states, "Designers of teacher education programs, by identifying the type of objectives they set and by emphasizing the more powerful ones, can improve the programs they design."[13]

The classification system includes four types of objectives: (1) cognitive based, (2) performance based, (3) consequence based, and (4) exploratory. Which of the four is most powerful? What is meant by "powerful"? No matter! The authors of *Developing Instructional Modules* state that in competency based teacher education "greater emphasis is placed on performance and consequence objectives than on cognitive objectives."[14] That is, more attention is paid to performing and causing change in others than in developing a sound knowledge base from which to operate. If there is justification for their choice, it is not made apparent to those who are learning how to develop a module. But then again, why should it be? The authors are demonstrating that they can have the reader perform and change behavior (write a module) while relegating to the less important domain the cognitive concerns.

If the reader's interest is piqued and he wonders what a consequence based objective is, perhaps this example will illustrate:

At the consequence level, the prospective teacher demonstrates that he can, for example, motivate pupils and change their attitudes. An example of a consequence objective of this area is: The prospective teacher plans and teaches a unit on dental health which results in 40 percent of his pupils demonstrating a positive attitude about care of the teeth by voluntarily brushing their teeth after lunch.[15]

This example in itself raises several questions about teacher performance. Would the teacher be judged competent if only 10 percent of his students brushed their teeth? Would he be considered competent if 80 percent brushed after lunch but not in the morning or the evening? If the children could go to the sink without asking permission to brush their teeth but were restricted during the remainder of the day, would that fact be a consideration in determining a "positive attitude"? To what extent were the children motivated by a supportive home that encouraged teeth-brushing behavior?

Professor Broudy has responded to the assumption that in teaching "the whole is merely the sum of its parts." His succinct refutation of that belief is equally applicable to another assumption implicit in the work of CBTE.[16] Although mention is made of the differentiated staff patterns in schools, we also know that many schools are using team teaching while others are developing variations of "open education." If CBTE is assuming that four competent teachers working together do *not* provide a sufficient qualitative difference in student performance than what is apparent in the addition of the four disparate performances, here is certainly an area of investigation that has been overlooked.

Throughout the writings on CBTE the claim is made that individualization of instruction is of paramount importance. However, the individualization is localized within the pattern set by the specificity of performances agreed to in advance. No provision is made for the student, who is perhaps better able to understand the nature of the problem if the problem as a whole is first set before him and is then broken down into an analysis of the components that make up the whole. What of the student who has an opportunity to observe or work with a few children and from that experience begins to identify and isolate the skills that he needs to develop into a competent teacher? This is the "felt need" that Dewey wrote about that is the impelling force for learning.

If we examine some of the competencies that have been enumerated, we will be in a position to make wiser recommendations. For example, the teacher should be able to

· Cause a student to feel free to seek knowledge, invent and try out ideas, and create;[17]

  · Cause a student to perceive the relevance of his learning;[18]

  · Organize and manage the classroom efficiently;[19]

  · Help children develop an inclusive patriotism.[20]

This brief sample should be sufficient to illustrate that any listing of supposed competencies without the activities that would provide the meaning through directly testable statements results in an empty concept of that competency. If these ideas are to acquire any meaning for the student, he must have the opportunity to develop a repertoire of possible behaviors that he could, in fact, use in a classroom. We must ask, What would constitute confirmation that a teacher was able to "*cause* a student to *feel* free to seek knowledge," etc.? What would the class have to do to demonstrate that the student was competent to do this? Or if, as is presently the case, the child is not considered, what would the trainer accept as the "required" level of performance? How does one justify the level—80 percent, 90 percent, 5 percent?

Pai points to the difficulty of developing a program when he states,

Putting a subject in sequence can be done according to the complexity of the materials, or the difficulty of the terminal behavior, or the logical structure of the subject, or a natural order inherent in the subject (e.g., history can be taught as a chronological sequence of events). Unfortunately none of these approaches to sequence has proven itself consistently useful.[21]

Skinner has also noted the difficulty of organizing the material, and says that "the most advantageous and effective programming is accomplished when sequence is based on the teacher's knowledge of the student's attainment and direction."

There is an admission by those who propose and those who oppose CBTE that there has not been sufficient research into the relation between teacher performance and pupil learning. Yet the raison d'etre of CBTE is to improve the education of teachers so that children will learn more. I will do no more here than note again this lacuna. However, it would be remiss not to point to other aspects of this problem.

We are aware that observation of objects, people, and events provides the opportunity for the child to obtain information. We do not know, however, just how the child processes this information or how this processing can be facilitated. Nor do children demonstrate every act they observe. "More basic is the question of the factors that control what the child observes in the first place, for the child cannot attend to all of the behaviors that are displayed in his environment."[22] For example, research by Horner indicates that the sex of the child plays a part not only in his receptivity to praise but in his performance itself; not only is there a distinction between ability and performance, but under some conditions one's sex can also play a role in impairing performance.

A final distinction to be drawn is that between learning and performing. Hilgard reminds us that "learning must always remain an inference from performance and only confusion will result if performance and learning are identified."[23] He points to the fact that learned behavior fails under the use of drugs or intoxicants. But we know that the person can exhibit that learned behavior at a later time without any intervening training.

The implications of the adoption of a competency based teacher education program are vast and too important for one to spend time considering the writings of men who say, "It is better to have a 'feel' of the concept than it is to explicate all of its nuances and subtleties," and then write, "because these plans (accountability) are comprehensive action systems, they avoid the narrow conception of teaching competencies. They avoid the 'myth' that if each teacher only had a 'basic set' of skills and used it, the children would inevitably learn."

While it is the case that the training of teachers needs serious and sustained attention, the importance of teaching children requires a critical appraisal of proposals in the field of teacher education. My purpose was not to play the role of Cassandra, prophesying doom, but to contribute to a better understanding of the meaning of the idea of a competency based teacher education program.

NOTES FOR CHAPTER 7

1. Joe Lars Klingstedt, "The Philosophical Basis for Competency Based Education," *Educational Technology* (November 1972): 14.

2. Stanley Elam, *Performance Based Teacher Education: What Is the State of the Art?* (Washington, D.C.: AACTE, 1971), p. 1.

3. Ibid., p. 7.

4. Klingstedt, "The Philosophical Basis for Competency Based Education," p. 11.

5. Young Pai, *Teaching, Learning, and the Mind* (New York: Houghton Mifflin, 1973), pp. 6-8.

6. Ibid.

7. Elam, *Performance Based Teacher Education*, p. 1.

8. Ibid., p. 6.

9. Ibid., p. 9.

10. Alvin Lierheimer, from *PBTE Quotations*.

11. Matina Horner, "Woman's Will to Fail," *Psychology Today* 3, no. 6 (November 1969): 36.

12. Fred K. Daniel, "Performance Based Teacher Education," *Multi-State Consortium on Performance Based Teacher Education* 1, no. 5 (December 1972): 5.

13. W. Robert Houston et al., *Developing Instructional Modules* (Houston, Tex.: University of Houston, College of Education, 1971), p. 79.

14. Ibid., p. 78.

15. Ibid.

16. Harry S. Broudy, *A Critique of Performance Based Teacher Education*, PBTE series no. 4 (Washington, D.C.: AACTE, 1972), p. 1.

17. Norman Dodl et al., *A Catalog of Teacher Competencies* (Tallahassee: Florida State University, November 1971), p. 32.

18. Ibid., p. 22.

19. Ibid., p. 32.

20. Ibid., p. 33.

21. Pai, *Teaching, Learning, and the Mind.*

22. Harold W. Stevenson, *Children's Learning* (New York: Appleton-Century-Crofts, 1972), p. 163.

23. Ernest R. Hilgard and Gordon Bower, *Theories of Learning* (New York: Appleton-Century-Crofts, 1966), p. 5.

8. Performance Based Certification: A Teacher Unionist's View

Sandra Feldman

The title of this chapter should make my bias very clear. My point of view is that of a teacher unionist, and my comments are based on a policy adopted by our union in New York City after considerable discussion and inquiry by a committee of about fifteen classroom teacher activists.

We were not "involved" in the performance based certification moves of the New York State Education Department; we ourselves decided to become involved. Our point of view is important because we have a strong organization and we intend to be heard.

Our committee did a lot of homework. We read all the material available and discussed it at length. We spent a day at the Educational Testing Service in Princeton, New Jersey, met with Fred McDonald and his staff, and looked at what they were doing. We met with a number of other experts in the field and attended conferences. We developed a position paper on the subject.

Since I am going to be critical and, I hope, controversial, I want to say at the outset that we do not oppose performance based teacher education. The concept is a welcome one. I will discuss first our positive feelings on the subject, and why we feel that way, and secondly our strong reservations, our opposition to performance based *certification*—and why. I will conclude with a summary of our recommendations.

We welcome the thrust of the performance based teacher education movement as an attempt to develop a coherent body of knowledge about teaching and the effects of specific instructional strategies on the learning process. We have felt keenly the inadequate preparation to which teachers have been subjected in the past—college preparation that is unrelated to the problems teachers face, even after student teaching, when they enter the classroom and take full responsibility.

For the most part, the organization of schools is such that principals are so harried with tending to administrative and community problems that little or no attention is given to the classroom training of new teachers. Visits from the supervisor are either meaningless exercises or threatening.

Schools face the problem of accountability by dropout, where in the absence of adequate supports thousands of new teachers simply leave teaching, demoralized and defeated. Then there is the problem of those who are demoralized and defeated and do not drop out.

There is also the basic, urgent problem of the failure of tens of thousands of children to achieve—a failure that has led to a loss of public confidence in the profession and has created a great deal of turmoil in many school systems. Such failure has also led to a proliferation of such phony structural changes as decentralization, filled with empty promises of educational improvement, and to such gimmickry as performance contracting and vouchers.

It is a crisis of confidence that we as educators have contributed to somewhat, for we are ever willing—as we should be—to talk about our own failures or about the need for educational improvement. But we are often too defensive to say outright that our nation's schools are full of really good teachers who were not "produced" by teacher training institutions, but became good teachers in a process of trial by fire in the classroom. Teachers are faced very often with the most difficult conditions and the least possible support.

We are now in a situation in which despite the fact that for the first time in many years we have enough teachers and potential teachers to provide individualized attention to children who need it—to reduce class size drastically—we are told there is a teacher "surplus." The public is less and less willing to spend on education. School budgets are being cut to the bone when additional resources are desperately needed. The government is using as justification and rationale the works of liberal critics of the schools, for example Moynihan and Jencks, who are busily pointing out that schools do not end inequality, that compensatory programs do not work, and that most money for education goes primarily to pay teachers' salaries.

More and more, teachers are looked on as the frontline agents for the failure of the schools. There are increasing attacks on teacher rights and a tendency toward scapegoating in the absence of real solutions. The public seems to feel that anyone can teach—that all one has to do is love children and be able to talk. This too is partly a result of our success, for thanks to the public school system we have a literate and educated public, many of whom feel they can do what teachers do. This attitude thrives partly because we have *not* developed a visible, clearly formulated "technology of teaching" that can be translated into concrete instructional skills and methodologies. We have *not* coherently assembled the expertise of experienced teachers to demonstrate a concrete, tangible body of knowledge identified as teaching.

Teacher education that is classroom centered, research oriented, and performance based provides a hope of doing that. It offers the possibility of providing teachers with real knowledge about successful classroom strategies and, beyond that, with the concrete skills they need to carry out those strategies.

For this reason, and because of the great need of the profession and of the schools for answers we don't now have, we look favorably on performance based teacher education. We oppose, however, a changeover to performance based certification at this time.

Before explaining why, we must consider the politics of schools, because our hesitancy on the issue of performance certification is very much rooted in the political situation. The thrust for this change cannot be separated from the political situation.

For the past decade and longer, schools have been the scene of conflict—a microcosmic reflection of the stresses and strains of the larger society. The great civil rights successes of the early sixties raised expectations but left unchanged the terrible conditions in northern urban ghettoes and in ghetto schools. One result has been racial conflict in the schools of the inner cities. In addition to this there is the increasing resentment among the lower middle class, overburdened by an unjust tax system and an inflationary economy. School budgets suffer as a result.

Throughout the country, different groups have understandably begun to organize themselves for power. Everyone—the poor, the taxpayers, the students, the teachers (who have even gone so far as to go on strike)—has been demanding a "voice" in decision-making, particularly in the schools.

It is not surprising that the schools—traditional vehicles for opportunity in American society, bastions of authority and respect for manners and learning—are immediately in the maelstrom of the storm of social protest. Nor is it hard to understand why people get emotional about schools: there are children in them. All the hopes and aspirations of adults are focused on the schools, not without reason. Yet thousands of poor children are not learning, while thousands more are ill-prepared either for the difficult competition of the higher education marketplace or for the increasingly complicated work skills required by an increasingly technological society, as well as by employer demands for higher job qualifications.

Furthermore, the schools are billion-dollar operations. Some groups, particularly in our larger cities, saw an opportunity for rebuilding broken patronage machines around the schools. There was the struggle over community control and decentralization, while in other areas consolidation and regionalization of school districts was the battleground. Integration, busing, and the like are important conflicts nourished by the failure of the schools to successfully educate large numbers of children and to solve *all* social and economic ills which, thanks to Christopher Jencks among others, people are just finding out schools cannot do. Educators have known this all along.

Blame-placing has always been a great sport in education. The public used to blame the board; the board blamed the superintendent; the superintendent blamed his deputy; the deputy blamed the principals; the principals blamed the teachers. Today it is different and much simpler. Everyone blames the teachers—or so the teachers feel—and with some justification.

Societal conditions are now providing the thrust for change within this atmosphere of blame placing and scapegoating. The schools in general and teachers in particular are bearing a great burden of blame for a great many problems *over which they have no control.* Teachers not only suffer the difficulties and strains of the classroom without adequate supports, but are also accused of "insensitivity," caught in conflicts and power fights, and constantly criticized. Recently they have been bombarded with new schemes for "accountability" in which they are told, for example, that their performance will be judged "objectively" on the basis of advancement in the standardized test scores of their pupils, or on the basis of pupil performance generally, as in the Stull Act.

Given this political situation and the fact that there is considerable confusion in the public mind and in state legislatures about just what the definition of "performance" is, we are opposed to performance based certification. It is a totally separate step beyond performance based teacher education, a step that is certainly premature at this time.

I hope we in education understand the difference between process and product, and the need to look at process and at teacher performance in an effort to determine what behavior, what instructional methodology, effects what learning and how. We know that many things besides specific teacher performance affect learning, and that teachers can be held accountable only for those things over which they have control. State legislatures and some state education departments do not understand this. They usually understand the assessment of performance as an evaluation of product. Translated, this means evaluating teacher performance on the basis of pupil achievement and nothing more. It is an easy and popular notion.

Furthermore, even if we are able to defeat (as we will) attempts to evaluate and certify teachers on a "piecework" basis—i.e., the number of reading score points made per child—and if performance based certification were to be introduced now, we would be making a significant change in teaching qualifications on the basis of vast ignorance.

No comprehensive and systematic scheme for observing and measuring teacher behavior has yet been developed. Educational Testing

Service is just beginning to develop instruments of measurement. The National Commission on Performance Based Education has been organized to support research and development, but it is still in the beginning stages.

There is no comprehensive and systematic evidence that any one methodology is superior to any other. We have no conclusive evidence that particular behavioral traits or "competencies" in teachers have a positive effect on learning in children. For example, we have some indications that "rewarding" behavior is better than "insulting" behavior. But we have no validated research conclusive enough to enable us to say that a teacher with X or Y particular skill or trait or competency is going to elicit X or Y learning response.

We *should* know; we should be working hard to learn these things. We should be working at it in our universities, in performance based teacher education programs, in the classrooms of our public schools, and with the aid and advice of experienced classroom teachers. We should be conducting research on the subject and making a massive commitment of funds for that purpose, for it is probably a key to improved education for children. We support performance based teacher education in hopes of getting the necessary research done.

What should be done until the research is completed? We can build a model based on the limited knowledge presently available and on what classroom teachers think is valid. We can go on with preservice preparation in that image and test it out when the new teachers are on the job. That is, research and development can be development and research.

To base certification on the existing uncertainties in an antieducation political atmosphere will simply open the door for some legislatures and state education departments to water down standards in the name of economy. There is some talk, for example, of doing away with the college degree as a requirement. After all, if a prospective teacher demonstrates the skills called for, why should he obtain a degree? If a teacher does not have a degree, why should he receive as much pay as one with a degree? Yet a degree *is* important. We want teachers to be educated people as much as we want them to be skilled technicians.

Some education departments may set up levels of competence, so that teachers at a "lower" level get paid less than those at a "higher" level—a form of differentiated staffing. Without research validated competencies, who will decide what competencies are required for what level? Who will decide how to assess each teacher's competencies? Are we, in fact, at some levels actually using teachers? How will we know and who will decide what "qualified" means?

The New York State Education Department is plunging into a performance based certification system. When we asked whether they were planning to do the research to validate competencies, they said no—they have no funds for that. The gentleman in charge said "we can't wait" for sophisticated instruments of measurement to be developed, even though he admitted candidly that what we do have is not very sophisticated.[1] Yet they are moving ahead to base certification on assessed performance or competency, and they are seeking to introduce "continuing" certification—not just "continuous career preparation," on this vague and undefined basis, so that every five years a teacher will be either recertified or decertified on the basis of demonstrating "required competency." Tenure will be destroyed, but no one yet knows:

(1) What the skills to be required are;

(2) How we will measure them when we figure out what they are; and

(3) Whether the skills we pick actually do affect learning.

As this same man said at a recent conference in New York City on performance based teacher education: "The direction is clear; the path to take us there is not so clear." We agree. That is why we oppose performance based certification.

As organized teachers who have struggled successfully for change, for a voice for teachers, for their right to be involved in educational decision making, we don't fear change. We welcome substantive institutional change; we foster it. But we have seen many proposals—full of sound and fury and signifying nothing—made, and sometimes adopted in the name of "change." While we see the thrust toward the development of real knowledge about performance as an important and necessary substantive change, we believe that the present efforts toward performance certification (aside from their being all form and no substance) will become engulfed in the turmoil of school politics. Like structural governance changes such as decentralization, lacking educational and intellectual substance and validity, it becomes all things to all people. If it dies on the battlefield of school conflict and if performance based teacher education dies with it, an opportunity to achieve an important change will have been lost.

CONCLUSION

Therefore, as organized teachers with a strong organization, we came to certain conclusions:

(1) We will cooperate with our universities in the effort to develop performance based teacher education programs with a research component. In the summer of 1972 we recruited over 300 classroom teachers to work with the City University of New York in the beginnings of a project to use the expertise of experienced teachers to work on the development of competency lists that can then be researched.

If we admit that no teaching strategies have been scientifically proven effective, we can begin to build a model based on the research now available and on what classroom teachers believe is valid. Using the classrooms of experienced teachers, we can teach student teachers in that image; its effectiveness can then be measured in the schools when the teachers so taught are on the job. If the research is built in and simultaneous with the development of a preservice training model, we think we'll go a long way toward improving teaching.

(2) We will insist that the much-needed, time-consuming, massive research be done to find out what we need to know about teacher behavior and its effects on learning. We will fight for the necessary funds for this research, and demand that teachers have a meaningful voice in its direction.

(3) We will continue to support the establishment of an on-the-job internship for teachers—whatever their preservice training was—so that during the first year new teachers carry only half a class load and work with experienced teachers the rest of the day. In the second year they would carry three-quarters of a load. They would have full classroom responsibility in the third year of probation.

(4) We will oppose any attempts (certainly here in New York) to institute performance certification before the research is completed.

We believe that in education we ought to stop reinventing the wheel, stop bringing in one tired "innovation" after another. For once, at least, we ought to base a fundamental change on substantive, proven knowledge instead of on public relations and guesswork.

We believe that experienced teachers have an important contribution to make, and if they are truly involved, in a nonthreatening way and with the time and conditions provided for, they will be telling us not just what to do for prospective teachers, but what kind of retraining and help they themselves need. Experienced teachers and the representatives of teachers must be involved in this if it is to succeed.

NOTE FOR CHAPTER 8

1. Vincent C. Gazzetta, director of the Division of Teacher Education and Certification, New York State Education Department, speaking to a conference on performance based teacher certification, Graduate Center of the City University of New York, February 19, 1972.

9. A Sociophilosophic Perspective on the Potential of Schooling

Frank H. Blackington III
Ann G. Omsted

Each fall cohorts of kindergartners, high schoolers, teacher education students, mathematics majors, and medical students gather in their respective classrooms and a new school year begins. While some individuals appear primarily because the law requires them to attend school, most appear because they and/or their parents believe they will be changed, improved, or even transformed by the school experience. (The very law requiring school attendance is predicated on society's belief that schooling is a transforming experience.)

During the course of the school year, the kindergartner is shown how to build with blocks and is taught the rules of a variety of circle games, but he is also expected to emerge from his learning experience a cooperative, self-disciplined child. The high schooler is provided with cello lessons and learns to perform the music literature played by his orchestra, but he is also expected to emerge from his experience as an adult who appreciates music and supports the arts. The

The authors are indebted to the Ford Foundation for support of this project.

teacher education student is taught to analyze critically children's literature, but he is expected to become a warm and accepting classroom guide, while the mathematics major is taught the rules and manipulations of Boolian algebra, but is expected to emerge from his experience a creative and loyal organization man. The medical student is taught to make incisions in the chest of a dog, but he is expected to become a wise and humane therapist and counselor. Thus, at all levels, the school tends to focus on the learning of sets of specific cognitive tasks that are age graded by difficulty (the kindergartner does not learn the rules of Boolian algebra, nor is the mathematics major permitted to build with blocks), while the societal support for schooling, though of course endorsing the learning of cognitive skills, is also importantly predicated on a belief in the transforming affective outcomes of the school experience, affective outcomes that are systematic and socially desirable.

When the kindergartner does not become cooperative and self-disciplined, the teacher not warm and accepting, the physician not wise and humane, the blame is typically assigned to the school. Though teachers not infrequently respond by pointing to student inadequacies, they are nonetheless likely to see themselves as somehow responsible for the undesired outcomes. Thus, while the public feels angry and frustrated and the teacher feels guilty and inadequate, the educational designers and planners too often define the problem as procedural and busy themselves devising new instructional methodologies, each of which tends to be viewed as a panacea. The disparity between expectation and reality, between input and outcome, between knowledge and behavior, is seen as the result of imperfect methodology rather than as a problem of conflict, competition, dissonance, and inconsistency in the demands put on the individual by the multiple social institutions to which he is tied, with resulting constraint on his possible range of behavior. If all institutions in the society placed value on the same facts, beliefs, and behaviors, any disparity between the society's expectation for the school and the reality of the school's outcomes could largely be explained in terms of imperfect methodology. However, this is not the case.

Though ability differences within any given group of students will be significant, the diversity of the life experiences, attitudes, and values of those who comprise the group are at least as great as the diversity in abilities. This diversity of abilities, backgrounds, and beliefs alone presents the school with a major problem. To make the problem more complex, the school experience occupies only a small part of the life of each student. It is only one among a number of socializing forces having an impact upon the student, each representing a set of experiences, attitudes, and values that compete or conflict with the school for the attention of the student. Even the five-year-old kindergartner is not an "empty vessel." He is a human being who, through interaction with others, brings to the school a life-style and a set of beliefs that, even if dysfunctional to school success, may be stubbornly resistant to change.

Moreover, the school experience does not typically involve a therapeutic relationship between practitioner and patient, but is instead characterized by sets of interactions that occur in the context of group life within a formally organized social institution. A number of implications flow from this. The teacher-student interaction, one of the more crucial interactions occurring in the classroom, is a forced relationship, in which neither teacher nor student chooses the other. This administratively mandated relationship is usually acted out before the student's peers, not behind the closed doors of the office or the conference room. Further, when conflicts arise between student and teacher, as they almost inevitably will, the relationship between student and teacher is essentially unequal. The teacher, as the socially and legally responsible member of the dyad, is able to enforce on the student her preferred beliefs, behaviors, priorities, and/or goals. At times the teacher may even be required by institutional rules or by social pressure from colleagues to impose on the student beliefs, behaviors, priorities, and/or goals that are alien to the student's life-style. The administratively mandated, publicly acted-out, power-based interaction between teacher and student occurs within a societally sanctioned, politically dependent institution, which must maintain itself by endorsing or at least acquiescing in the prevailing norms of the community that sanctions, oversees, and supports its activities. However, even the norms of the community may be in dispute, so that the values and behaviors espoused by the school and the priorities and goals that are set for the school may be more a matter of chance and caprice than they are of community consensus.

Thus, if it is not clear what facts, attitudes, values, and life-styles are societally preferred; if any given group of students is widely diverse in the psychological and social "baggage" it brings to the school experience; and if the critical interaction of teacher and student is, because of the structures of the classroom and of the school as an institution, inadequate to a therapeutic task, it is not surprising that students are seldom transformed by the school experience.

The rarity of personal transformation can be demonstrated at the empirical level through the findings of a longitudinal study of elementary teacher trainees.[1] Sixty-five students were followed through a special teacher training program that involved the standard first two years of college course work. This was followed by a year of full-time observation and student teaching in one or more elementary classrooms in the public schools of several Michigan communities, after which the trainees taught for two years as intern teachers, working in a regular classroom of their own, under the supervision of an intern consultant who was herself a master teacher. During the three years the students were in elementary classrooms learning to teach, special courses were brought out from the university so that pedagogical theory and practice were juxtaposed. The trainees also attended summer school on the campus to fulfill degree requirements. While the campus-based courses were no more personalized or individualized than any standard university program, the courses taken to the students in the community in which they were teaching were tailored to the needs of that student group.[2] Moreover, the relationship between supervising teacher and student teacher and between the intern teacher and her intern consultant was always intensive and sustained and usually intimate and open.[3]

Depth interviews were conducted with all students enrolled in the program when they entered the program and at the end of each of the three years they were enrolled. The data gathered at entrance to and exit from the program are the focus of our attention here.

Fifty-seven scales were developed reflecting the variables elicited from the data. A computerized profile analysis was applied to the data. Each person in the data pool was compared with every other person on all scales. Individuals were empirically assigned to stance types, so that every person in a group more closely resembled the group to which he was assigned than he resembled any other individual in the data pool. This profile analysis of entering data produced four stance types, to which the names *security seekers, authority seekers, achievement seekers,* and *self-actualization seekers*[4] were given. As the following brief description of the stances suggests, the stances are defined in terms of some mix of cognitive and affective variables.

The *security seekers* were those who were attracted to teaching because they saw teaching as offering good hours and working conditions at a job which they believed to be essentially indistinguishable from any other woman's job. The *authority seekers* saw teaching as an important job in which one was accorded respect and authority over the lives of others; in exchange for the grant of status and authority, one submitted to the authority of superordinates, principals, parents, etc. The *achievement seekers* saw teaching as offering mobility and an opportunity to succeed in a professional occupation; often, for them, classroom teaching was seen as a step in a career line that led to administrative or planning positions in public schools or to college teaching. The *self-actualization seekers* were attracted to elementary teaching because they saw the opportunity for personal growth and self-expression in working with children.

A similar analysis using the data gathered in the exit interviews was undertaken. Here seven stance types emerged, to which the following names were given: *time servers, contented conformists, task focusers, pragmatists, child focusers, ambivalents,* and *alienated.*

Time servers are characterized by a lack of concern for their own excellence or their own personal achievement. The belief that teaching neither demands special knowledge nor significantly serves society is a function of the lack of integrated beliefs about education. So, too, is the fact that the *time servers* are easily threatened by children and/or adults. Lacking an integrated belief system, they are reduced to keeping school, where all claims on them have potentially equal force.

Contented conformists do what is expected of them conscientiously, and often with skill. *Contented conformists* do not feel pressure because they think of teaching as doing what one is told rather than requiring one to make choices. When *contented conformists* follow the curriculum syllabus and the principal's directives, as they do, teaching provides them both security and self-fulfillment. They accept authority, just as they expect their pupils to accept their authority.

The *task focusers* define the teacher's purpose as guiding pupils in mastery of their assignments. School is a serious business for them.

Their focus is upon practical problems of motivation, concept development, etc. *Task focusers* are characterized by a certain perfectionism and a marked feeling of working under pressure. Time is the enemy of all teachers, but this is especially so for the *task focusers*. There is much to be done, and the choice is often between doing a thing well or dropping an activity from the curriculum. Both alternatives are intolerable for the *task focuser*.

The *pragmatists* are negotiators. They believe that experience teaches and are confident they have the skills to assess the lessons of their experience properly. Even when the *pragmatists* find themselves wrong, they are protected by their adroitness, for they are successful politicians. They prefer quiet horse trading to dramatic confrontations. They select allies who carry weight in the informal structure and they protect their lines of retreat. Moreover, they are, as good organization men should be, willing to accept responsibility. They are loyal, defending the school to outsiders even when they themselves are critical of it. Through moderating the conflicting needs and demands of the child and the school, they win autonomy for themselves.

The *child focusers*, as the label implies, are characterized by their single-minded devotion to the pupil as a child, as an unfinished personality whose special needs a teacher must understand and serve. While all teachers give lip service to this principle, *child focusers* act it out in their daily contacts with children. Cued in this way, the *child focusers* respond to children therapeutically rather than with disciplinary measures. For the *child focusers*, schools really do exist for children.

The *ambivalents* appear to be composed of individuals who are somehow in transition, for what they do is full of inconsistencies. If one were to hypothesize the plight of the *ambivalents*, it would be to guess that these are people for whom the disparity between what they believe about children and teaching and what they found to be the reality of the classroom is so great as to have fragmented their belief system. They cannot quite let go of their idealism and face the reality they perceive.

Finally, the *alienated* have an exit stance whose distinctive quality is the inability or unwillingness to identify with other teachers or to accept the worth of the tasks schools set for children. The *alienated* are the most heterogeneous of the exit stance types since the roots of their discontent are so various. Some reject the particular children with whom they work or the particular faculty of which they are a part. Others are dissatisfied with elementary teaching itself.

One striking observation is possible from even the most cursory perusal of these data. The students in this program entered with the several concepts of teaching described by the entrance stances. They exited from the program having more or less shaped their work as teachers to their original ideas about teaching, rather than having been transformed by the training process. The *security seekers* became, in order of likelihood, *time servers, dropouts, contented conformists,* or *alienated.* The *authority seekers* became, in order of frequency, *contented conformists, time servers, task focusers,* or *ambivalents.* The *achievement seekers* became, in order of frequency, *pragmatists, task focusers, ambivalents,* or *child focusers.* The *self-actualization seekers* became, in order of frequency, *child focusers, dropouts, alienated,* or *pragmatists.* In fact, if significant change—as contrasted to elaboration—occurred, it was in the direction of fragmentation, disillusionment, and destruction of the belief system with which the student came to the program, without that belief system being replaced by an integrated alternative system of beliefs.

The lack of movement from one concept of teaching to another is all the more striking when one takes into account the fact that this three-year program was individualistic, in that it was paced largely to the developmental level of the student; personalistic, in the sense of encouraging students to develop their own strengths and interests; and humanistic, in the sense of attempting to deal with beginning teachers as not just classroom teachers but as human beings with a whole round of concerns.

Of course, the program was neither infinitely individualistic, personalistic, or humanistic. It had to operate within a whole welter of constraints—not the least of which was the purpose of the program and, presumably, the purposes of the participants. The presence of constraints in human behavior is a constant. The content and context of constraints is variable. Those who pretend otherwise deceive themselves, as do the personalists who merely substitute the constraints that emerge in student-teacher interaction for more institutionalized forms.

This lack of fundamental change in stance type indicates that the students were relatively impervious to any transforming intent embodied in the program as a whole or to any particular teacher or set of teachers within the program. Yet transformation has long been the task assigned to and accepted by educational institutions at all levels—no less in professional schools where the young are to be inducted into the norms of that particular occupational group.

The acceptance of transformation as a possible and desirable goal has been reinforced by notions of urgent social necessity and by student reports of feeling transformed. Their personal identification with programs, institutions, and people have caused them to assert again and again that one or all (programs, institutions, person) made a startling contribution to their present condition in life: "... made all the difference."

Our data suggest that such is not typically the case. A large proportion of these students felt *transformed* when they had merely been *elaborated,* a crucial distinction. We are arguing that students entered with a stance; perceived the contexts in which they operated through the selective prism of that stance; developed skills, teaching styles, and attitudes selectively; and left the program as a much elaborated bearer of the initial stance.

It is this marked elaboration factor that gives rise to the appearance of and belief in the transforming capacity of schooling. We make this observation not to denigrate elaboration, but rather to distinguish what occurs in a school setting from what occurs in a therapeutic setting. In a school setting, "made all the difference" should be translated to read "enabled me to markedly elaborate my original stance."

Cast in this light and given the relatively low level of success even among psychotherapists in securing transformational change in their clients, the lack of significant directional change in our data is less than astonishing. In fact, a good case can be made that those who sensed the necessity for transformation (the security seekers and the self-actualization seekers) resisted the nonelaborative demands of the situation by becoming disenchanted or dropping out of the program.

This lack of transformation has been underscored here because it allows and indeed demands the raising of questions. With myth and ideology, death comes hard and reincarnation easily. Nevertheless, we shall proceed on the assumption that the validity of standard transformation expectations assigned to institutions and instructors has been sufficiently diminished by the facts, at least concerning this age group.

Assuming that formal schooling, including extended and intensive guided field experience, has a relatively low capacity for transformational and a relatively high capacity for elaborational impact on students, there are a host of policy questions that may be variously characterized as economic, moral, legal, and social. Current policies, however, reflect an assumption of transformability. For example, admissions policies primarily reflect some assessment of grade point average, lack of moral turpitude, and the presence of interest and/or commitment to teaching. It is assumed that satisfaction of these criteria will allow colleges, assuming adequate teaching, to produce the type of teacher they want to produce. While such criteria are not completely irrelevant, assuming our findings, institutional success in such ventures may be far more dependent on the stance types of the students who are attracted to the college.

It then becomes a significant question, in an economy of scarcity, whether society can afford to support the schooling of students without invoking the additional criterion of stance type in the initial selection process. Whether one measures cost in purely economic terms or in the more human terms such as disenchantment, frustration, and unfulfilled capacities that other avenues might better serve, the price of ignoring such an additional criterion is surely enormous. However, a selective admission policy requires a rather definitive picture of the desired product to which a college will commit itself.

Educators are not blind to the virtues of increased efficiency. Assuming a well-defined product, the selective device we have suggested has considerable promise. Efficiency has many faces, however. Facing decreasing enrollments, efficiency may well be interpreted as success in retaining a significant student population in order to maintain staff and justify current budgets. The fact that teacher success is locally defined helps to hide the inefficiency (in terms of definable product development) from all parties, while at the same time encouraging colleges of education to duck an explicit treatment of product definition. This avoidance also receives significant support from those who claim the inherent value of diversity. Consequently, a proposal for the addition of a criterion of stance type, having a surface plausibility of efficiency, can be seen as economic and moral shortsightedness.

The moral arguments are essentially relativistic. In brief, it is held that no person, school, or profession has a right to impose its values, world view, or knowledge claims on anyone else. Further, it is held that diversity and pluralism are inherently good, that they are instrumentally good in that the truth will out in the end as the educational forces guided by the hidden hand of open competition move us to ever-higher levels of practice. Part of the passion that inflames the literature and the committee meetings on these questions is a result of the continued belief in the transformational capacity of schooling; part also results from the desire to teach in the style and the content most comfortable to the professor. However, most of it is a result of a clear fear of "arbitrary behavior" on the part of others in the absence of generally accepted standards of judgment.

It would be easy to refute the relativistically oriented educators by pointing out that "It is wrong to impose one's values" is a tautology or that "Pluralism is inherently good" is an absolutist statement. Educators cannot avoid the problems of standard setting, valuation, and values by shifting emphasis from the institution to the individual, who can act out his will or perception without fear of justified conflict.

Whatever else might be gained from refutation of the relativistic position, it would be unlikely to reward one with a similar yield of changed beliefs. The case is similar when one is confronted with the radical claim that essentially nothing is known or can be known about the educative enterprise, so we might as well start from scratch. A demonstration that the surface plausibility of such claims is almost entirely dependent on equivocation on such notions as "know" is likely to have little impact on the true believer.

Any formalization of selectivity at the point of admission is likely to meet with violent reaction, and at the point of graduation is often defeated in intent by pro forma assessments. Aside from the acceptance of transformation as a goal, of relativism as a norm, or of more immediately self-serving conceptions of efficiency as a motivation, there is always the likelihood of a legal challenge of discriminatory behavior in an admissions process. The fact is that the courts are unlikely to uphold the challenge if the college can demonstrate that differential treatment was based on real and relevant differences. The ability to demonstrate that is entirely dependent on casting a clear statement about the type of product to be produced and the existing functional relationship of the relevant differences to the achievement of the product.

Indeed, a variety of institutions might choose quite different conceptions of the product assigned the label *teacher*. Each would be allowed, on demonstrating the functional relationships, to discriminate along the lines of demonstrated relationships. No monolithic notions are necessarily implied by this approach. Rather, there exists the probability of a variety of public and legitimately discriminating practices.

This is in stark contrast to the current scene where court action is far less likely but infinitely more justified. There is an immense amount of hidden discrimination, given failure of transformation. Judgments made along a "success" continuum are highly idiosyncratic and private. Of course, an assigned grade provides a kind of public notice, but there is very little, if any, public discussion of the basis for the assessment. This discrimination is particularly glaring in instances where there is demonstrated technical adequacy but low overall evaluation, or where there is technical inadequacy but high overall evaluation. During the training period, there are few overt challenges to this private, erratic, and ofttimes illegitimately discriminatory evaluation system. Even if the judgments are, in some sense, "correct," they are often arbitrary in that those involved cannot articulate a coherent basis for the judgment.

This may seem too harsh an indictment. If so, the reader might reflect a bit on any hearing before a tenure commission. These hearings are relatively rare. They are rare because public school evaluation practices are ordinarily a mirror image of college of education evaluation practices. School officials do not usually press their cases to a formal hearing because they know they are likely to lose in a court of law, not because they are necessarily "wrong," but because they have not raised their implicit and often incoherent assumptions about good teaching practice to an explicit level. This failure not only renders them unable to claim evenhandedness in applying principles, a notion fundamental to justice, but it leaves all in a state of confusion as to what would constitute evidence in the case.

To close with the assertion that confusion and indecision abounds is perhaps safer than an assertion of the existence of fundamental error. We would assert both. Our claim is that there is a fundamental error in believing that schools can typically transform people. This has been reinforced by the confusion of elaboration with transformation and has led, along with other forces, to indecision about the product to be developed. Our data clearly shows little transformational capacity, even under most favorable conditions. Further, our data were generated by empirically derived stance types. These stance types offer analytical power, as well as the opportunity to focus clearly on product definition and mechanisms for its realization. This would ensure that the definition and its functional relationships would be open to continuing public scrutiny, thus reducing the frequency of arbitrary evaluation in its many guises.

NOTES FOR CHAPTER 9

1. Ann G. Olmsted, Frank H. Blackington III, and W. Robert Houston, "Stances Teachers Take: A Basis for Selective Admission," *Phi Delta Kappan* 55, no. 5 (January 1974): 330-334.

2. For example, one campus-based faculty member, who taught a course in science methods to a group of intern teachers in the community in which they were teaching, reported that at the end of the term the interns asked what course they were enrolled in, because the issues discussed during the course had covered the range of concerns of the interns, rather than exclusively addressing the more circumscribed domain of science methods.

3. During the year of observation and student teaching, each supervising teacher worked with only one student teacher at a time and each student teacher remained with the supervising teacher for at least a ten-week term. In the first year of intern teaching, the intern consultants, whose full-time responsibility it was to work with the interns, were assigned five interns. This permitted each intern consultant to spend the equivalent of one day per week in the intern's classroom working with the intern and the pupils. During the second year of internship, each intern consultant worked with ten intern teachers, permitting the equivalent of a half-day per week to spend in the classroom of the intern teacher.

4. Self-actualization is used in Maslow's sense of the term.

Part 3
Models for
Competency Identification

10. Deriving Teaching Skills from Models of Teaching

Marsha Weil

INTRODUCTION

The purpose of this chapter is to illustrate how teaching skills may be identified by deriving them from teaching strategies, and to present some of the advantages this offers as a way of handling the skill unit of teaching.

The derivation of teaching skills from teaching strategies emerged naturally out of the Columbia University Teachers College teacher training program in that its conceptual framework and initial instructional core was built around a series of teaching strategies called the models of teaching.[1] However, the present predilection for this as a way of deriving skills has to do primarily with considerations of competency based program design. Two design concerns in particular have shaped this derivation of skills. First is the belief that a training program must have a high degree of conceptual or substantive unity among its various components. The frames of reference and examples a teacher candidate explores as philosophies of education or theories of learning must translate into sets of related concepts and behaviors that extend throughout all aspects of the training program, whether as interactive teaching skills, teaching strategies, curriculum planning, or instructional and institutional design. In other words, competencies have to mesh with each other conceptually, practically, and programmatically so that a student does not acquire the interactive skills for one role and the planning and design skills for another. Second is the belief that competencies come in different "sizes." For example, interactive competency in a particular teaching strategy is a much larger and more complex unit of behavior than the skill of asking questions at a certain cognitive level or pausing three seconds. Furthermore, large, complex behaviors are not the summation of smaller behaviors, but training in the latter can certainly contribute to greater effectiveness in more complex behaviors.

Many competency based program designs begin the delineation of competencies at the micro-level and continue to build a program of small behavioral outcomes. Columbia University Teachers College, for reasons of accident, ignorance, or intuition, began with the teaching strategy as the basic unit of program design. From there we have moved, in one direction, toward the philosophical and psychological program linkages and, in the other direction, toward the behavioral skill level.

We have explored competency in terms of performance in a teaching strategy. In the course of doing this, we have identified smaller micro-level behaviors or teaching skills that facilitate performance in a particular strategy. The search for teaching skills has taken place through deductive, theoretical extrapolation and inductive, empirical means. Every conceivable concept and technology of the field was used to pinpoint what goes on when a teacher implements a teaching strategy. As a result, a great many behaviors have been identified as facilitating a particular strategy.

This chapter attempts to look at the totality of these efforts in terms of their implications for the process of identifying teaching skills and for skill training. The skill derivation process presented here involves four stages which, not surprisingly, parallel the development of the models of teaching. Hence, the description of each step reflects the history and evolution of our work.

We will illustrate the process of extrapolating teaching skills from teaching strategies and present the findings of the research on teaching skills and strategies, as well as some issues that have arisen from this way of identifying teaching skills.

DEFINITION OF A TEACHING STRATEGY

Before going into the details of the particular strategies that will be used as examples, it seems essential to distinguish a strategy from a skill and to explain the concept of strategy embodied in the models of teaching, because it plays a large part in the theoretical derivation of teaching skills.

Teaching strategies are defined as complex behavioral events in which the teacher carries out a sequence of activities designed to implement particular educational objectives and goals. The specific activities and their sequencing are both important in implementing a teaching strategy. Teaching *strategies* may involve hundreds of communications (moves) between teacher and student. Teaching *skills,* in contrast, are smaller, more discrete units of teaching, often a single teacher move; they are essentially instructional techniques and procedures that may be used in different combinations in the flow of teaching. No particular educational outcome is theorized or associated with a single skill although skills in general are associated with effective teaching and greater learning.

The models of teaching represent an attempt to operationalize a particular theory of learning or philosophy of education into a teaching strategy (pattern of activities) that teachers can be trained to perform. We have invented a set of four concepts for extrapolating and describing any teaching strategy: syntax, principles of reaction, social system, and support system. Each concept can be a source for skill derivation.

(1) *Syntax* describes the model in action. If a teacher were to use the model, how would he begin? What would he do first, second, third? We call these sequences of events "phases"; they are descriptions of a broad class of activities, e.g., present material to the learner, develop confronting situation, etc. By comparing the structural phasing of models, the operational differences among them can be identified. An inductive strategy would not have the same type or sequence of phases as a deductive one.

(2) *Principles of reaction* guide the teacher's responses to the learner. In some models the teacher overtly tries to shape behavior by rewarding some student activities and maintaining a neutral stance toward others. In other models, such as those to develop creativity, the teacher tries to maintain a nonevaluative, carefully equal status so that the learners become self-directing. Principles of reaction provide the teacher with rules of thumb by which he can gauge the student and select his responses to what the student does.

(3) The *social system* includes a description of student and teacher roles, hierarchical or authority relationships, and the kinds of norms that are encouraged. The leadership roles of the teacher vary greatly. In some models he is a reflector or facilitator of group activity, in others a counselor of individuals, and in still others a taskmaster. The concept of hierarchical relationships is explained in terms of the sharing of initiating activity by teacher and learner, the location of authority, and the amount of control over activity that emerges from the process of interaction. In some models the teacher is the center of activity and the source of input; he is the organizer and pacer in the situation. Other models provide for relatively equal distribution of activity between teacher and student, while some place the student at the center. Finally, in different models different student behaviors are rewarded. In some the student is rewarded for getting a job done and sticking to a prescribed line of inquiry. In others he rewards himself by knowing that he has learned something. One way to describe a teaching model, then, is according to the degree of structure in the learning environment. That is, as roles, relationships, norms, and activities become less prescribed or externally imposed, more emergent, and within the students' control, we can say that the social system is less structured.

(4) The *support system* refers to the additional requirements beyond the usual human skills, capacities, and technical facilities that are necessary to carry out a model. For example, a human relations model may require a trained leader; the nondirective model may require a particular personality, i.e., an exceedingly patient, supportive one. For example, if a model postulates that students should teach themselves with the roles of teachers limited to consultation and facilitation, what support is necessary? A classroom filled only with textbooks would be limiting and prescriptive; support in the form of books, films, self-instructional systems, travel arrangements, and the

like is necessary. The support requirements are derived from two sources: the role specifications for the teacher and the substantive demands of the experience.

Teaching strategy in terms of the models of teaching includes behavioral specifications for several dimensions of the educational environment—instructional, social, psychological, and to some extent technological or physical. Each concept describes the characteristics of a part of the environment. The environment conception of strategy is crucial in the derivation of skills because the skills associated with a particular model are derived from descriptions of the principles of reaction (psychological environment) and the social system as well as from the syntax or basic instructional activities and procedures.

DERIVING TEACHING SKILLS FROM A MODEL OF TEACHING: FOUR STEPS

In the process of operationalizing a model of teaching and identifying small micro-behaviors or teaching skills we followed four steps: (1) initial extrapolation; (2) basic teaching skills; (3) instructional system development; and (4) clinical assessment and revision. Each stage yielded greater behavioral specificity. We tend to think of the behaviors we identify as a micro-behavior or teaching skill. However, not all the skills are demonstrative; some are cognitive skills having to do with the preactive or planning stages of implementing a strategy. Later we focus on two or three models so the reader can follow their behavioral delineation through the four steps.

INITIAL EXTRAPOLATION

The first step in operationalizing a model was to condense the original theoretical description and cast it in terms of the four basic concepts, syntax, social system, principles of reaction, and support system, using a textbook format as the mode of description.

Our initial efforts in writing *Models of Teaching* focused on behavioralization at a general level, particularly extrapolating the syntax. With some theories this required great inferential leaps in order to delineate and sequence phases of activity that were not immediately apparent. At this point we were not influenced by concepts from other language systems such as interaction analysis, nor were we thinking in terms of single behaviors.

The two strategies used as examples in this paper are interesting because the first—the *inductive thinking model*—is rather straightforward, requiring minimal extrapolation and concerned with the more familiar information processing or cognitive objectives. *Group investigation,* on the other hand, is more complex, emergent, and rests on implementation and behavioralization of long-argued concepts such as democratic process and inquiry. It focuses on the less familiar social outcomes of learning and requires considerable change from the usual teacher role.

The inductive thinking model was developed by the late Hilda Taba. Taba believed that one of the primary objectives of education is to teach concept formation: the process of interrelating and organizing discrete bits of information into categories through an inductive mode of thinking. Taba organized her means for achieving this objective explicitly in the form of a teaching strategy. That is, she expressed the procedures or method in terms of a sequence of activities:

Phase 1: Identifying and enumerating data;
Phase 2: Grouping items of data;
Phase 3: Conceptualizing and labeling groups of data.

The teacher's job is to move students through the phases by asking initiating questions, but because the process is inductive the teacher cannot initiate the latter stages until the preceding ones have been developed adequately. Taba discusses the relationship between the content focus of the teacher's questions and the data that becomes available for concept formation. For instance, the concepts of goods and services call for data-eliciting questions broad enough to generate examples of both. "What do you buy in the supermarket?" would tend to exclude services while "What do you see in the supermarket?" or "What do you need to open a supermarket?" is broader. Taba's materials provided examples of initiating questions and transcripts of classes engaged in the concept formation strategy.

The objective of group investigation, a strategy developed by Herbert Thelen, is to engage learners in academic inquiry through group processes. Teachers organize their children into problem-solving groups to learn simultaneously the social processes of democracy and the scientific process of academic inquiry. The essence of group investigation is that students develop objectives and procedures for their learning experience and take responsibility for the social processes. This model requires that teachers play a less dominative role than they are accustomed to. Thelen's writings included a narrative example of group investigation based on his own teaching experience at the college level. Joyce and Weil's extrapolation of the strategy appears in Table 10:1.

Compared to the inductive thinking model, group investigation is longer and more complex; the immediate behavioral meaning of each phase is much less apparent and the moves a teacher might make are not yet known.

The first attempts to train teachers in the models of teaching and to assess their performance occurred during 1970-71 at Teachers College, Columbia University. The chief means of assessment was to translate the initial specifications for the phases of a model and for the principles of reactions into interaction analysis terminology. We were then using a multidimensional interaction analysis system developed by Joyce and Hodges[2] to look at student-teacher interaction. The system reflects Joyce's environmental conception of teaching and included categories for procedures, sanctioning, handling information (based on Bloom's cognitive levels), and maintenance activities. The original efficiency scale for group investigation used by Wald[3] in her study appears in Table 10:2. The items are based on interaction analysis descriptions and points were given for each item. Wald did not train students in the inductive thinking model, but a similar efficiency scale for inductive thinking would have items referring to the presence of particular cognitive levels of interaction and the sequential ordering of these communications. Since Taba's is an inductive mode, communications of the lower factual levels would come before the higher cognitive levels. The reverse would indicate a deductive process.

Wald found that teachers could be trained to implement a variety of models of teaching calling for shifts in behavior from their natural teaching style and from model to model. Her initial effort at model assessment was based largely on interactional analysis concepts and methodology. The behavioral assessments indicated gross changes in teaching behavior and laid groundwork for formulation of the basic teaching skills.[4]

Table 10:1. Summary Chart: Group Investigation Model

Syntax

Phase 1	Phase 2	Phase 3	Phase 4	Phase 5
Encounter with a puzzling situation (planned or unplanned). Exploration of reactions to the situation.	Formulate study task. Organize for study (problem definition, role assignments, etc.).	Independent and group study.	Analysis of progress and process.	Recycling of activity.

Principles of reaction

Teacher plays a facilitative role directed at group process (helps learners formulate plans, act, manage group) and requirements of inquiry (consciousness of method). Functions as an academic counselor.

Social system

Democratic process, i.e., group decisions. Low external structure. Puzzlement must be genuine—it can't be imposed. Authentic exchanges are essential. Atmosphere of reason and negotiation.

Support system

Environment must be able to respond to a variety of learner demands. Teacher and students must be able to assemble what they need when they need it.

Source: Joyce and Weil, *Models of Teaching* (Englewood Cliffs, N.J., Prentice-Hall, 1972), p. 47.

Table 10:2. Efficiency Scale: Group Investigation Model

Points	Description
0	Did not do model. No P-3s or P-4s* present, indicating absence of verbal interaction over negotiated procedures.
1	P-3s and P-4s present.
2	Sequence, minimum of three student communications in a row, that is, P-3, P-4, P-4, P-4. Sequence must be present at least twice.
1	Presence of P-5, P-6, P-7, P-8. One or all of them present in any combination indicating interactive communications on the setting of standards, either directed or negotiated.
2	P-7, P-8 (P-5, P-6 cannot be present). Indicates negotiated discussion over objectives and standards.
2	More student talk than teacher talk.
1	Two or fewer negative sanctions by teacher following any procedural communication by student.

*P-3 and P-4 refer to the categories for student and teacher negotiation procedures.

THEORETICAL EXTRAPOLATION OF SKILLS: BASIC TEACHING SKILLS

Our first-year experience with the models convinced us of the need for greater training precision at a skill level. Most teachers seemed able to carry out the basic syntax, but the richness of the performance varied considerably among the teachers. In some cases the best performers achieved greater strength and precision in their moves; in other cases, once they had made the major initiating moves of each phase, they were able to draw on a wider range of moves in responding to the student's reactions than were the least successful implementers.

We began the attempt to identify the contributing micro-behaviors by defining skills that were basic to any instructional strategy. To do this, we returned to the environmental concept of teaching that is reflected in the four concepts for operationalizing any model and to the interaction analysis categories that had been used to represent the various intellectual and social dimensions of the environment. Three teaching skills were identified as basic teaching skills: (1) modulating cognitive level, (2) structuring, and (3) focusing.

Modulating is a skill that affects the intellectual quality of the learning environment. Skill in modulating cognitive level means the ability to shift the cognitive level of the discourse, e.g., to ask questions or design learning activities at three cognitive levels. Three cognitive levels have been identified: factual, conceptual, and theoretical. These are described in Table 10:3.

Table 10:3. Cognitive Levels and Activities

Cognitive levels	Cognitive activities
Factual	Recalling information. Recognizing or identifying information. Gathering or enumerating data. Translating information into one's own words.
Conceptual	Building categories and forming concepts. Generating examples of concepts. Comparing and contrasting. Making inferences about cause and effect.
Theoretical	Developing a principle or generalization, as in interpreting or explaining data. Testing a hypothesis. Making predictions. Making value judgments based on criteria or developing criteria.

From *Basic Teaching Skills* by Bruce R. Joyce, Marsha Weil, and Rhoada Wald, p. 51. © 1972, Science Research Associates, Inc. Reprinted by permission of the publisher.

Structuring influences the social dimension of the learning environment. It has to do with varying the distribution of control over behavior in such areas as the determination of learning goals, the content and form of the learning activity, the pacing, and who initiates and maintains the activity. Three conditions of structure are identified: teacher directed, negotiated, and student constructed. The actualization of each condition depends on the locus of control of the organizational elements, identified in Table 10:4.

Focusing affects the content of the learning environment and is used by the teacher to draw, maintain, or shift the student's attention to particular aspects of the topic or learning activity. The ability to establish, maintain, and shift focus constitutes mastery of this skill.

In the literature, teaching skill usually refers to discrete behavioral actions. Our definition differs in that it incorporates the notion of

Table 10:4. Structure as Determined by the Source of Control

Organiza-tional element	Type of structure		
	Teacher directed	Negotiated	Student constructed
Goal	Teacher selected.	Teacher selected.	Student selected.
Content	Teacher determined.	Teacher determined; student determined.	Student determined.
Activity	Teacher determined.	Student determined; teacher determined.	Student determined.
Procedures	Teacher responsible and paced.	Student responsible and paced	Student responsible and paced.

From *Basic Teaching Skills* by Bruce R. Joyce, Marsha Weil, and Rhoada Wald, p. 28. © 1972, Science Research Associates, Inc. Reprinted by permission of the publisher.

flexibility, the ability to perform a series of discrete behavioral actions that reflect a single behavioral continuum. We selected the dimension of the educational environment and found a means of expressing the possibilities along each dimension. The intellectual environment was expressed in terms of cognitive levels; the social environment was expressed in terms of degree of structure.

Each strategy can be described according to the basic teaching skills and translated into the skill moves required at each stage. Table 10:5 illustrates this process for the group investigation strategy.

It is also possible to characterize a strategy as having a dominant skill. The essence of group investigation, despite its intellectual dimensions, is in structuring: students develop objectives and procedures for the learning activity and take responsibility for the social process. This requires teachers to shift from their normal highly structured, instructional role to a more reflective, facilitating one. On the other hand, in the inductive thinking strategy, the structuring dimensions do not change much from traditional patterns, but it is absolutely essential that the teacher have the ability to question at different cognitive levels.

The theorized relationships between basic teaching skills and strategies were tested empirically. Several questions were explored: first, to what extent is competency in the skills related to effectiveness in a model of teaching; second, how much of performance in a teaching

Table 10:5. Teaching Skills in Group Investigation

Stage	Activity or task	Structuring	Skills Modulating	Focusing
1	Confront puzzling situation.	Teacher directed.		
	Identify differences in reaction.	Negotiated.	Varies.	Focus (differences in reaction).
	Formulate problem.	Student constructed.	Conceptual and theoretical levels.	
2	Further analyze task.			Refocus (planning and process).
	Break down task	Student constructed.	Conceptual and theoretical levels.	
	Analyze role requirements.			
3	Operations.	Student constructed.		
4	Reflection and evaluation.	Negotiated.	Conceptual and theoretical levels.	Refocus (previous ideas).
5	Conclusion or recycling.	Negotiated. Student constructed.		

From *Three Teaching Strategies for the Social Studies* by Bruce R. Joyce, Marsha Weil, and Rhoada Wald, p. 104. © 1972, Science Research Associates, Inc. Reprinted by permission of the publisher.

strategy is accounted for by the basic teaching skills; and third, how does performance on one skill relate to performance on another?

Table 10:6 presents the analysis of the relationship between competency in skills and strategies.

Table 10:6 indicates one significant relationship for each precision score: modulating cognitive level is correlated with the inductive thinking model (.515 significant at the .01 level); structuring is related to group investigation (.365 significant at the .01 level); focusing is related to inductive thinking (.472 significant at the .01 level); and overall precision is related to inductive thinking (.482 significant at the .01 level).

Table 10:6. Coefficients of Correlation among Precision Measures
and Effective Scores for Three Models of Teaching

Precision measures	*Effectiveness scores*		
	Inductive thinking model (N=30)	Group investigation model (N=30)	Role-playing model (N=30)
Modulating cognitive level	.515*	.039	-.087
Structuring	.264	.365**	.040
Focusing	.479*	.082	-.283
Overall skill average	.482*	.089	-.243

*Indicates significance at the .01 level.
  Critical r with 30df = ± .449.
**Indicates significance at the .05 level.
  Critical r with 30df = ± .349.

The predicted skill/strategy relationships among modulating cognitive level, inductive thinking model, structuring, and group investigation, were confirmed while the relationship between focusing and role playing was not. Focusing *was* found to be significantly related to the inductive thinking model. Since the latter is an information-oriented model and focusing is a content-based skill, a relationship between the two seems very reasonable. General skill or overall precision is related only to inductive thinking.

To gain a more complete picture of the nature of a teaching strategy as macro-behaviors made up of micro-behaviors, a step-wise multiple regression analysis was computed for the basic teaching skills and the three teaching strategies. The results appear in Table 10:7.

According to Table 10:7, the three teaching skills comprise .3054 of the performance in inductive teaching strategy, .1515 of performance in group investigation, and .1378 of performance in role playing. Most of the contribution in each strategy came from a single teaching skill: modulating in the case of inductive thinking (.2656), structuring in the case of group investigation (.1332), and focusing in the case of role playing (.0799).

These findings are interesting in two respects. First, a large part of the performance in a teaching strategy is accounted for by as yet unidentified elements. This implies a need to develop greater validity in present clinical assessment form for measuring model performance

Table 10:7. Regression Coefficients for Basic Teaching Skills
and Three Teaching Strategies

Model and skill	Beta weight	Multiple R	R^2	F
Inductive thinking				
Modulating	.5154	.5154	.2656	
Focusing	.3542	.5526	.3054	1.540
Structuring	-.0064	.5527	.3054	.001
Group investigation				
Structuring	.3650	.3650	.1332	
Focusing	-.1481	.3863	.1492	.508
Modulating	-.0618	.3892	.1515	.070
Role playing				
Focusing	-.2827	.2827	.0799	
Structuring	.2571	.2827	.1281	1.493
Modulating	.1270	.3712	.1378	.292

or, more likely, the design need to identify additional skills contributing to competency in a model. Secondly, multiple regression seems to be particularly appropriate analysis for competency based research in that it nicely highlights the macro-micro relationships. If micro-teaching competencies are derived from macro-units such as teaching strategies, multiple regression may be more useful in that search for program design and functioning than correlational analysis. From the multiple regression analysis, the program designer can determine which behaviors are made up of similar skills. This knowledge facilitates several kinds of programmatic decisions. For example, the style of a teacher candidate can be matched to those macro-competencies that are based on common micro-competencies with mastery expected in those areas or depending on the philosophy of the training program. Teacher candidates can be required to acquire competencies that increase the repertoire of micro-behaviors.

The third analysis focuses on the nature of the three skills. By definition, teaching skills are identifiable, discrete behaviors. Our assumption is that the notion of general competency is invalid and that competency in one skill is not related to competency in another. The results of a correlation analysis among the four precision scores appear in Table 10:8.

Contrary to expectations, Table 10:8 indicates that the teaching skills are highly interrelated. Modulating cognitive level correlates with structuring (.382 significant at the .05 level) and with focusing

Table 10:8. Intercorrelation among Precision Measures

Precision measures	Modulating cognitive level	Precision measures Structuring	Focusing	Overall average
Modulating cognitive level		.382*	.629**	.647**
Structuring			.520**	.719**
Focusing				.934**

*Indicates significance at the .05 level.
  Critical r with 30df = ± .349.
**Indicates significance at the .01 level.
  Critical r with 30df = ± .449.

(.628 significant at the .01 level). Structuring correlates with focusing (.520 significant at the .01 level). The three skills correlated with overall precision in the following way: modulating cognitive level (.647 significant at the .01 level), structuring (.719 significant at the .01 level), and focusing (.934 significant at the .01 level).

The high degree of relatedness among the three skills may be due in part to a common flexibility factor. Unlike most concepts of teaching skill, the basic teaching skills incorporate the notion of flexibility, each skill one of a series of discrete moves along a single behavioral continuum. Another possibility is that these teaching behaviors are made up of both process and substance, in which case focusing, a content-oriented skill, would be a part of modulating cognitive level and structuring. A third possibility is that mastery of any teaching skill reflects the ability to be precise. Like flexibility, there may also be a common precision factor indicating there may be some truth in the notion of general competence. However, that fact does not alter the competency based design necessity for behavioral specificity and determination of relationships. It does raise the question whether there may be a basic set of generic skills.

EMPIRICAL EXTRAPOLATION FROM
INTERACTION ANALYSIS

One of the goals was to generate a set of basic teaching skills with broad instructional applicability, both conceptual and behavioral.

Figure 10:1. Teacher Innovator Interaction Analysis System

I. Structuring

A. *Planning*

Goals and standards		Context		Procedures	
Directive	Negotiated	Directive	Negotiated	Directive	Negotiated
1	2	3	4	5	6

B. *Implementation*

Instructional	Noninstructional
7	8

Subscripts*

1. data	6. summarizing
2. cuing	7. reflecting
3. redirecting	8. integrating
4. clarifying	9. nonverbal
5. justifying	

II. Information

Level 1	Level 2	Level 3	Open	Opinion
9	10	11	12	13

III. Feedback

Positive	Neutral	Negative	Corrective	Repeat	Digression
14	15	16	17	18	19

*May be used with information processing (9-13) or structuring (1-8).

However, it seems possible through additional theoretical extrapolation to identify idiosyncratic skills that are unique to a particular strategy, especially utilizing existing skill formulations and teaching concepts. The categories of the previous interaction analysis system were revised to reflect the definitions of the basic teaching skills and other model-relevant dimensions. We also added a system of subscripts to the interaction analysis in order to broaden our description of model behavior. The subscripts moved us much closer to idiosyncratic skills, that is, skills applicable to a particular model. The revised system appears in Figure 10:1.

Some of the subscripts such as cuing are skills taught by other skill training systems. Other subscripts, such as reflecting and clarifying, are taken directly from the theoretical description of the teacher's role. All of these subscripts probably appear in at least one other category system. Together they represent a further effort to describe the behavior combining the theoretical specifications of the model with existing concepts of teacher behavior. Analysis of high performers and low performers in a model of teaching indicates that many of the teacher moves as described by subscripts distinguished high performers from low performers. For example, Table 10:9 shows the results of a one-way analysis of variance of these two groups on the inductive thinking strategy.

Table 10:9. Results of One-Way Analysis of Variance for Significant Indicators: Inductive Thinking Strategy

Behavioral indicator	F (ratio)	Greater mean
Management factor	3.041	Lo > Hi
Teacher reflects	7.322*	Hi > Lo
Teacher integrates	3.544*	Hi > Lo
Data	3.759*	Lo > Hi
Justifying	10.872**	Hi > Lo
Integrating	4.918*	Hi > Lo
Theoretical level information processing	4.671*	Hi > Lo
Factual level information processing	3.950*	Lo > Hi
Planning	4.266*	Lo > Hi

*Indicates significance at the .05 level with 22 df = 3.44.
**Indicates significance at the .01 level with 22 df = 5.72.

Several indices appear significant or near significant: theoretical level information processing, factual level information processing, planning, justifying. However, two additional factors show up as influencing model performance. The first factors show up in the behavioral indicators based on the subscripts of interaction analysis. This reflects the richness of the data exploration and the teacher's ability to focus on and probe a single idea. The communications of the low performers showed more behaviors characterized as data oriented, while high performers showed behaviors characterized as justifying, integrating, reflecting. These three indices proved to be significant discriminators of high performances on the inductive thinking model. Another way of saying this is that higher performers indicate a greater behavioral repertoire in handling ideas than low performers. Reflecting and integrating are elements of the skill of focusing, which proved to be significantly related to the inductive thinking model.

The second factor is the management factor. The low performers showed greater management problems than high performers. It seems reasonable that a low behavioral repertoire for handling information forces the narrow, factually oriented, teacher-directed classroom, with greater reliance on directive structuring as a means of social control.

INSTRUCTIONAL TRAINING SYSTEM

The task of developing an instructional training system to teach a model of teaching requires an analysis of complex behavior into smaller prerequisite and constituent behaviors and the design of a training sequence including provision for evaluation and feedback. The instructional training system is a third means for identifying micro-skills because the behaviors for which training sequences are developed and all the items of an evaluation measure can be thought of as micro-skills. For example, the training system for inductive thinking includes a sequence on the nature of a concept: what a concept is with practice in identifying concepts and attributes. The ability to do this is a cognitive or planning skill essential to carrying out the strategy interactively. Similarly, the assessment measure for evaluating classroom implementation of the inductive thinking strategy includes this item: "Did the teacher ask redirecting and justifying questions over the student's grouping statements?" In our experience with the models, we have found that these two types of questions characterized the better model performances.

There are four sources for breaking down complex teaching strategy behavior into its smaller, trainable parts: (1) the phases of activity; (2) key model elements like democratic process, confronting incident, or concept defined with precise behavioral meaning; (3) the teacher's role in each task; and (4) specific teacher moves or questions in each subtask.

First, each phase of activity can be treated as made up of separate subtasks, each with a separate training sequence. For example, Wald found that teacher candidates attempting to implement behavior modification had difficulty with the phase of the model that required them to carry out a contingency announcement with youngsters.[5] In the revised training system for this model, exercises were developed so that trainees could practice this behavior. Not all phases of a model need, or lend themselves to, a separate training sequence. The highly structured models are more amenable to phase training than less structured ones because the phases in the less structured models are emergent and depend more on student participation and control. In the less structured models, the teacher's role is better characterized as a series of moves or characteristic responses. In general the instructional training systems provide specific descriptions for the phase of activity setting forth the tasks to be accomplished in each and linking these to interactive moves or questions. Phase 2 of the inductive thinking strategy, discussed earlier as grouping items of data, is described in Table 10:10 with the following specificity in the instructional system.

The training for group investigation, which is a less structured strategy, benefited greatly from the prerequisites for designing an instructional system. The complex phases were broken down into their tasks, and the teacher's role in each task was described. See Table 10:11. Trainees were given specific training in carrying out some of the tasks. For example, our experience with this model before the instructional system was developed indicated that teachers had trouble formulating confronting incidents that might result in genuine academic inquiry; therefore, a portion of the training system is devoted to ways of planning confronting incidents and exercises in doing this.

The second source for task breakdown is the key elements of a

Table 10:10

Stage	Function of question	Question
2	To develop criteria for grouping.	What are some of the ways in which we can put these items together?
	To help students see relations between items.	What items belong together?
	To explore similarities.	What are some of the reasons why you put these items together?
	To explore differences.	Are there any relationships among the items that would justify organizing them into groups?
	To explore characteristics of various items.	Why does this item go here?

From *Three Teaching Strategies for the Social Studies* by Bruce R. Joyce, Marsha Weil, and Rhoada Wald, p. 30. © 1972, Science Research Associates, Inc. Reprinted by permission of the publisher.

model. For instance, some of the terms used by Thelen in describing group investigation were "democratic process," "inquiry," "group interaction," and a "problem for inquiry." We found these terms did not have adequate behavioral referents in teachers' conceptual or behavioral repertoire, so a training exercise was developed that discussed these key elements and had students analyze whether these elements were present in model protocols, or generate their own examples. One of these key elements is described in Table 10:12.

A third source for task breakdown is the teacher's role. Although we have not developed skill training sequences for roles, it is possible to imagine the sequences that might be developed for some of the roles described for group investigation in Table 10:13.

The fourth source has to do with specific types of teacher moves or questions used in a model. For example, in role playing the phases of the model were analyzed for the type of teacher moves. Some moves were repeated throughout the phases and could be found in many strategies; others were quite specific to a function in that particular strategy. Nine types of moves were identified in the training system. Examples of each type of move were provided and the phases were described in terms of the types of moves that are used.

Table 10:11

Stage	Activity	Task	Teacher role
1	Encounter and reaction	Confront puzzling situation.	To initiate confronting situation.
		React and discuss differences in reaction.	To reflect differences in reactions.
		Formulate problem focus and task.	To facilitate discussion.
			To clarify problem focus.
2	Organization of inquiry	Further analyze task or problem.	To reflect and clarify nature of problem, task breakdown, and role requirements.
		Break down task into sequence of activities. Analyze role requirements and distribution of roles.	
3	Operations.	Collect data.	To act as resource person.
		Analyze and interpret data.	To clarify and reflect analysis and interpretation.
4	Reflection and evaluation	Generalize about data and raise new questions. Synthesize. Reorganize ideas, modify plans, refine problem focus.	To clarify and reflect synthesis, ideas, plans.
5	Conclusion or recycling	Reach decision or solution. Recycle activities.	To clarify and reflect decision or solution.

From *Three Teaching Strategies for the Social Studies* by Bruce R. Joyce, Marsha Weil, and Rhoada Wald, p. 73. © 1972, Science Research Associates, Inc. Reprinted by permission of the publisher.

Table 10:12

Key element	Sample A				Sample B				Sample C			
	Yes	Somewhat	No	Can't tell	Yes	Somewhat	No	Can't tell	Yes	Somewhat	No	Can't tell

Democratic process
   (1) Did most of the students participate in planning the activities?
   (2) Were there diverse reactions?
   (3) Did students discuss each other's ideas and reconcile any differences?
   (4) Did decisions grow out of the group's discussions?
Inquiry
   (5) Was there a puzzlement?
   (6) Did the students identify or formulate the problem or activity?
   (7) Was there a consciousness of method (collecting data, associating ideas, formulating and testing hypotheses, studying the consequences, modifying plans, and so on)?
   (8) Did the students reflect on their experience by formulating conclusions or discussing the possibility of doing it again and the changes they might make?

From *Three Teaching Strategies for the Social Studies* by Bruce R. Joyce, Marsha Weil, and Rhoada Wald, p. 91. © 1972, Science Research Associates, Inc. Reprinted by permission of the publisher.

Table 10:13 shows the description of moves for each phase. The text explanation for three of the types of moves follows:[6]

Problem definition: to delineate the details and issues in the problem story. "Can you describe what happened in this story?" "And then what did he do?" "What is Tommy's problem here?"

Conceptualization of roles: to delineate and generalize about the character. "What kind of person is he?" "What is he like?" "What are some of the things he feels?" "Why does he behave that way?" "What are his parents like?"

Table 10:13

Step	Type	Function
(1) Warm up	Problem definition	Introduce problem and set climate.
	Participation	Focus attention and initiate discussion.
(2) Select participants	Conceptualization of roles	Get students to feel roles.
	Activity—specific	Select participants.
(3) Set the stage	Activity—specific	Set line of action.
	Conceptualization of roles	Restate roles, if necessary.
	Activity—specific	Get inside problem situation.
(4) Prepare the observers	Activity—specific	Assign observation tasks.
(5) Enact	Participation	Begin role play. Maintain role play.
	Reflection and summary	Break role play.
	Activity—specific	Monitor enactment.
(6) Discuss and evaluate	Participation	Open up discussion.
	Analysis of feelings	Analyze feelings.
	Analysis of behavioral reality	Probe reality.
	Consequences of action	Analyze events.
	Reflection and summary	Summarize ideas.
	Behavioral alternatives	Elicit proposals.
	Activity—specific	Monitor enactment.
(7) Reenact	Same as 5	
(8) Discuss and evaluate	Same as 6	
(9) Share experiences and generalize	Reflection and summary	Summarize ideas.

From *Three Teaching Strategies for the Social Studies* by Bruce R. Joyce, Marsha Weil, and Rhoada Wald, p. 155. © 1972, Science Research Associates, Inc. Reprinted by permission of the publisher.

Consequences of action: to establish the events and analyze the consequences of observed or proposed behavior. "What happened?" "What were the results of Nelson's behavior?" "When he did that, what happened?" "What will happen if Tommy doesn't give the money back?"

CLINICAL ASSESSMENT OF MODEL PERFORMANCE

The fourth means of deriving teaching skills are from the clinical assessment measures of model performance. Theoretically these measures make up the feedback tools of an instructional training system. In our case the clinical assessment measures required for research purposes have been developed somewhat independently of the original instructional system, though items from the latter were incorporated in the clinical assessment measure. The clinical assessment measure includes planning skills as well as interactive skill behaviors. An example of the clinical assessment measure for the inductive thinking model appears in Figure 10:2.

Figure 10:2. Clinical Assessment Inductive Thinking Model

Name_____   Task type_____
Date_____   Lesson no. _____

Planning
 *1. Was a concept determined by the teacher?   Yes_____   No_____
 *2. Were the attributes of the concept identified?   Yes_____   No_____
 *3. Did the material or source of the data adequately illustrate the attributes of the concept?   Yes_____   No_____
                              Planning subtotal (3)

Phase 1
 *1. Were the students asked to enumerate data?   Yes_____   No_____
 *2. Did the teacher's questions elicit the attributes of the concept?   Yes_____   No_____
  3. Did the teacher use redirecting and clarifying questions to facilitate the model?   Yes_____   No_____
 *4. Was the data identified without labeling the concept?   Yes_____   No_____
  5. Was the phase overextended, i.e., more data gathered than was needed?   Yes_____   No_____
  6. Were several students involved in enumerating the data?   Yes_____   No_____
                              Phase 1 subtotal (6)

Phase 2
 *1. Did the teacher ask students to develop their own groups?   Yes_____   No_____

---

*Essential items.

2. Did the teacher ask redirecting and justifying questions over the student's grouping statements?   Yes_____   No_____

*3. Did students develop criteria for grouping through justifying statements?   Yes_____   No_____

4. Did the teacher's questions and statements focus students so that their groupings reflected the concept in the lesson plans, guiding them to reshape their groups if necessary?   Yes_____   No_____

or

If alternate acceptable concepts were identified did the teacher develop or get the students to develop the attributes of these concepts?   Yes_____   No_____

Phase 2 subtotal (4)

Phase 3

*1. Did the teacher ask the students to identify the word that represents the groups?   Yes_____   No_____

2. Did the teacher and students discuss the label in terms of its attributes?   Yes_____   No_____

3. Were their reflective and integrative questions and statements over the labels?   Yes_____   No_____

Phase 3 subtotal (3)

Subtotal interactive score (16)

Total planning and interactive score (19)

The items in the clinical assessment measure are derived from three sources: (1) theoretical extrapolation; (2) clinical observation; and (3) empirical research. Those based on theoretical extrapolation come from the initial extrapolation, basic teaching skills, and the instructional systems. The empirical research of high and low performers mentioned earlier also contributed items. For example, as the correlates of behavior for high performers in inductive thinking were determined, these items were incorporated in the clinical assessment measures (Phase 1, item 3, Phase 2, items 2 and 3). Each of the items in the instrument is a potential skill behavior from which a training sequence can be developed. Zaikin[7] recently completed a training sequence in the inductive thinking model with a small group of preservice students. Her results included an item analysis of the clinical assessment measure which indicated the skill behaviors trainees found most difficult to implement.

CHARACTERISTICS OF MODEL DERIVED SKILLS

The skill behaviors that are derived from *Models of Teaching* are not necessarily different ones than those derived by other means, although some are very model specific in that they are not likely to have been formulated outside of a model. The chief feature of model-derived skills is that they have been conceptualized in a larger context, a fact that imbues them with several characteristics.

First, the models provide the teacher an implicit decision-making framework for calling on the skill behaviors. Some skills are exhibited because they are essential for carrying out a particular phase of activity, some because they involve principles of reaction to learner responses, and still others because they logically prompt the kinds of learner behavior described in the model. The decision-making characteristics of model-derived skills raises an important research question as to whether teaching skills are more successfully and permanently acquired when they are learned in the context of a teaching strategy.

A second characteristic of model-derived skills is relationships to other classes of skills. For instance, planning skills often bear a direct relationship to interactive skills. In inductive thinking the planning skill of selecting a concept and identifying its attributes is related to the teacher's ability to plan for and ask appropriate data eliciting questions and to help students develop criteria for their groups. Similarly, because the models outline the specifications for the intellectual, social, and psychological environment, interactive teaching skills such as modulating cognitive level (intellectual environment) can be perceived in their relationship to skills such as structuring, which regulate the social environment. In other words, the models describe skills.

ADVANTAGE OF STRATEGY LEVEL AS A STARTING POINT FOR SKILL IDENTIFICATION

There are several advantages in using the teaching strategy as the starting point for skill identification. First, although teaching strategies are functional units of behavior, they also possess substantive theoretical or philosophical properties. Because of these substantive properties, conceptual linkages can be built to the other components

Figure 10:3. Program Design Linkages

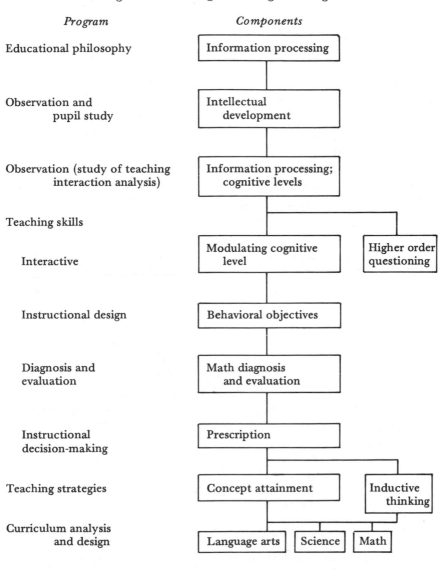

Program	Components
Educational philosophy	Information processing
Observation and pupil study	Intellectual development
Observation (study of teaching interaction analysis)	Information processing; cognitive levels
Teaching skills	
Interactive	Modulating cognitive level / Higher order questioning
Instructional design	Behavioral objectives
Diagnosis and evaluation	Math diagnosis and evaluation
Instructional decision-making	Prescription
Teaching strategies	Concept attainment / Inductive thinking
Curriculum analysis and design	Language arts / Science / Math
Classroom organization and management	
Institutional design and decision-making	

of a total program design. A teaching strategy which improves the analysis of social issues can easily be related to training components in child study, e.g., diagnosing and assessing the moral development of the learner or relevant social characteristics. Since a teaching strategy embodies or represents a philosophical view of education, it naturally relates to analytic training of alternative philosophical positions. Finally, a teaching strategy can be treated as a behavioral unit and broken into its constituent parts of skills. Since many levels of program design easily emanate from the teaching strategy, it is possible to build a "system" of competencies. Figure 10:3 illustrates sample program design linkages in the "intellectual" domain. The first advantage, then, is the facilitation of total program design.

The second advantage has to do with increased conceptual efficiency and meaning in teaching training. If the trainee perceives the conceptual unity of the total training program and if the concepts do function as educational linkages from one component to another, it would seem that the substantive and behavioral power of the entire program is increased. It would also seem, as mentioned above, that a behavior, such as a teaching skill, learned within a larger context with decision-making referents, such as a strategy, is easier to acquire and maintain.

Lastly, teaching strategies may be more directly linked to learner outcomes than is a single teaching skill. Some researchers maintain that learning is not the result of a single move but the cumulative impact of certain patterns. If this is true, we do not have to justify the skill selection and training directly in terms of consequential behaviors but can derive them from strategies that produce certain effects in youngsters. In other words, the learner output linkage of a strategy provides a rationale for the selection of teaching skills.

NOTES FOR CHAPTER 10

1. Bruce R. Joyce and Marsha Weil, *Models of Teaching* (Englewood Cliffs, N.J.: Prentice-Hall, 1972).

2. Bruce R. Joyce and Richard Hodges, "A Rationale for Teacher Education," *Elementary School Journal* (February 1966).

3. Rhoada Wald, "The Effects of Models of Teaching as a Program for the Training of Teachers" (Ph.D. diss., Teachers College, Columbia University, 1972).

4. Bruce R. Joyce, Marsha Weil, and Rhoada Wald, *Basic Teaching Skills* (Palo Alto, Calif.: Science Research Associates, 1972).

5. Wald, "The Effects of Models of Teaching as a Program for the Training of Teachers."

6. Bruce R. Joyce, Marsha Weil, and Rhoada Wald, *Three Teaching Strategies for the Social Studies* (Palo Alto, Calif.: Science Research Associates, 1972), p. 154.

7. Jane Zaikin, "An Assessment of the Effects of Practice on Execution of the Taba Model" (Ph.D. diss., Teachers College, Columbia University, 1972).

11. A Framework for CBTE

Herbert F. LaGrone
Sandy A. Wall

Changes are now occurring in the teaching profession that will reduce clerical and technical performances and enable teaching to approach true professional status.

The addition of paraprofessionals to the school staff in recent years has enabled teachers to delegate some of their nonprofessional duties to others. State governments are establishing standards for professional teaching practice. Training of teachers is no longer the sole prerogative of institutions of higher education, but is now cooperative, involving practicing members of the teaching profession as well as the college. Under such conditions there will be more opportunity for members of the profession to have control over those who enter the profession. Teacher organizations, although they have had

This chapter was prepared by Herbert F. LaGrone and Sandy A. Wall from a paper entitled, "The Meaning and Assessment of Professional Competence in Teaching," by John Lottes and Christabel Jorgenson of the Texas Christian University Teacher Center Staff.

general statements of ethics for years, are becoming more concerned with ethical standards that add the force of an element of accountability to teaching; societies are expecting teachers to do more than "keep school." With the change in societal expectations, a body of knowledge is developing that is essential to the teacher if he is to be professional and accountable.

A competency based teacher education program mandates a systematic organization of the body of knowledge and integration of the knowledge with practice. The study of teaching as a profession and the teacher as a professional provides a valuable approach to the organization and integration necessary.

A profession has three interrelated bases: a societal base, a knowledge base, and an ethical base.

A profession is supported by society because society expects and needs certain unique services that members of the profession can perform. Teachers help pupils achieve educational aims that society values. To provide this help, a teacher needs to know from society at least his pupil population, the educational goals to be attained, the expected teacher-pupil relationships, and the limits that are placed on this relationship.

The unique services to society can be performed because teachers have specialized knowledge that members of society do not usually possess in systematic form. Professional specialized knowledge consists of principles and techniques comprising the "know what" and the "know how" of the profession. The knowledge base is made up of interrelated definitions, rules, organizational patterns, lines of justification of professional action, and strategies.

Ethical bases provide a guide for the way the professional performs his services. This base guarantees the quality of service and protects the interests of the pupil, who is in effect the "client" of the teacher. One source of the ethical base is a formal statement of the obligations of the profession. But there are other standards and expectations that, in addition to basic human values, stem from the teacher's willingness to be held accountable for his professional actions and from a commitment to the profession of teaching.

Teaching requires goal-directed activity that includes advance planning and assessment of goal attainment. In order to perform these procedures under accountable conditions, in which one can explain or justify his actions, professional actions must be rational. Rational action denotes (1) the ability to make clear the goal of the action, (2) the ability to formulate a set of procedures that he infers will lead to the attainment of the objective, (3) the ability to make plain what will count as evidence that the objective has been attained, (4) the ability to put the procedures into effect, and (5) the ability to determine the effectiveness of the procedures.

In addition to rational action, teaching like other professions requires continued efforts to advance. Advancement is accomplished by individuals improving in their classrooms their own professional action, by individuals contributing additional knowledge to the bases of education, and by the corporate action of the profession as a whole seeking better ways to perform its services.

Within the context of the societal, knowledge, and ethical bases, and rational action and commitment to continued advancement, there are three dimensions of teaching action: formulation, validation, and improvement.

Formulation can be divided into the categories of foundational, planning, and implementation competencies. Foundational encompasses the development of the bases—societal, knowledge, and ethical—of the professional enterprise. Planning denotes framing goals, determining possible courses of action, and establishing standards of assessment. Implementation includes performing the previously planned courses of action in a teacher-pupil setting.

Validation includes evaluating the effectiveness of the plans, as well as explaining and justifying teacher action by determining such aspects as internal consistency, potential utility, compatability with a conceptual framework, and the correspondence between expectations and outcomes.

Improvement implies that the teacher adds to the common values, principles, aims, problem-solving methodologies, and assessment standards that comprise the bases of the profession. The teacher also utilizes new knowledge or previously unused information, and perceives and resolves problems that are unique to his circumstances, and thus improves the quality of his individual services.

The various dimensions of teacher action are not separate but are closely interrelated. Furthermore, the increase in knowledge, the alterations in society, and the shifts in value systems cause the professional bases to change. Therefore all aspects of professional teacher action need to be subjected to critical scrutiny and constant modification.

When teaching is consistent with the societal, knowledge, and ethical bases of the teaching profession and manifests the formulative, validation, and improvement classes of action, a teacher performing in this integral manner is competent. Teacher competency, then, is a unity embodied in professional action, and the dimensions are the significant areas of competency for professional teachers. The previously described dimensions form a classification for comprehensive teaching action:

Formulative action
 (1) Foundational competencies
 (2) Planning competencies
 (3) Implementation competencies
Validation action
 (1) Evaluation competencies
 (2) Explanation competencies
 (3) Justification competencies
Improvement action
 (1) Profession improvement competencies
 (2) Individual improvement competencies

FORMULATIVE ACTION

Foundational competencies underlie the structure of teaching, and include the societal, knowledge, and ethical bases of the profession. Competency in the societal base is demonstrated in such ways as identifying society's expectations of schools, recognizing the diverseness of pupils; making a critical study of statements of educational expectations at the state, local, and school level, and interpreting the nature of teacher-pupil relationships and the limitations society places on these relationships. Competency in the ethical base is demonstrated in such ways as determining the reasoning back of the professional value statements and making decisions about their validity, constructing a useful professional value system that is consistent with the formal statements of the obligations of the profession, analyzing the operational values within a classroom setting, assuming a willingness to be held accountable for one's professional actions, committing oneself to the responsibilities of the profession of teaching, and making decisions as to the professional services that the teacher ought, and is able, to provide.

Competency in the knowledge base is demonstrated in such ways as analyzing relevant information unique to teaching and assessing its worth, determining from the literature of relevant teaching areas the concepts that have applicability to teaching, acquiring knowledge of new concepts about teaching, and organizing significant information into structural ways of action.

Planning competencies are those used to organize for effective teaching. They include (1) constructing goals and curricular systems, (2) producing instructional plans, and (3) deriving standards for evaluating the curricular and instructional plans.

Competency in constructing goals and curricular organization is demonstrated in such ways as specifying curricular goals that are appropriate to the pupils and to the area being taught: articulating the cognitive, affective, and psychomotor characteristics of pupils; distinguishing those pupil characteristics that are necessary for attaining the goals; developing a curriculum pattern consistent with both the goals and pupil characteristics; and constructing curricular rules that prescribe content structure, indicate sequence, and organize the teacher-pupil relationship.

Competency in producing instructional plans is demonstrated in such ways as formulating sets of instructional objectives that are compatible with previously produced curricular goals and patterns, determining the prerequisite concepts that are necessary for the pupils to attain the instructional objectives, and formulating instructional strategies that are likely to enable the pupil to attain the objectives.

Competency in devising standards for evaluating curriculum and instructional plans is demonstrated in such ways as judging the coherence of the curriculum and instruction plans, judging the degree to which these plans can be tested empirically, judging the correspondence of these plans to the expected outcomes, and judging the relation between these plans and other systems.

Implementation competencies are those concerned with arranging the physical, social, and informational aspects of the learning environment and communicating with pupils.

The arrangement of the learning environment depends on such aspects as informational resources, spatial and social arrangements, and the schedules that will facilitate the designs that resulted from the planning actions. While the arrangements may include items such as grouping, individualizing instruction, team teaching, open class-room, independent study, educational media, or classroom management, the arrangement depends on making the previously established plans effective rather than on some specific activity which may be currently in fashion.

Communicating with pupils involves both receiving and sending aspects. Both verbal and nonverbal modes of communication are included.

Competency in implementing curricular and instructional plans is demonstrated by such items as comparing the arrangement of the aspects of the learning environment with the instructional plans; employing knowledge of pupil characteristics as a basis for arrangement; selecting implementation arrangements that are coherent with learning goals; transmitting teacher statements with meaning, coherence, and significance; analyzing and interpreting pupil statements and questions; translating and rephrasing specific aspects of the curriculum; administering effective tests; evaluating pupil performance; and diagnosing pupil difficulty.

VALIDATION ACTION

Validation competencies involve justifying and evaluating teacher action. If a teacher can provide sound reasons for his professional actions and is able to do so on demand of his pupils, his colleagues, or individuals in society supporting the teacher's services, then he has demonstrated competence in justifying his teaching action. Evaluating means to make a value judgment against specified criteria and to support it by evidence. A teacher's justification and evaluation are made in terms of all previous dimensions of his actions including the formulation aspects as well as the bases for the profession itself.

To explain a teaching action is to set forth a generalization from which specific action can be deduced. When the action meets the conditions of the generalization, it is justified.

Competency in validation actions is demonstrated by testing the coherence of specific professional actions to planning actions, assessing the relationship between specific professional actions and the societal, ethical, and knowledge bases; communicating with pupils and parents about objectives and operations; synthesizing plans and performances for colleagues and administrators; and judging whether pupils attain intended goals.

IMPROVEMENT ACTION

Improvement actions involve contributing to the collective knowledge of the teaching profession and bettering the individual planning, implementing, and validation competencies.

At least some members of the teaching profession must assume responsibility for improving the bases that govern professional action. Some may devote time to the development of foundational aspects of the professional bases. Others may improve the profession as a whole by conducting their planning and implementing competencies in such a way as to provide publicly useful empirical information. Teachers who work systemically and can articulate the grounds for their practical actions, as well as those who make adequate judgments about proposed changes in the services provided, in the codes of ethics, or in the ways of evaluating teachers, can make significant contributions toward improving the profession.

The individual professional teacher will have the values, concepts, and skills that will enable him to improve throughout his career. Such a teacher is able to effectively change any of the aforementioned competencies.

Competency in improvement is demonstrated by analyzing and developing generalizations about the professional bases; discovering new organizational schemes of the foundational competencies; designing and reordering planning and implementing competencies; communicating with other members of the profession about teaching; explicating teaching actions on the basis of logical judgments; changing ways of communicating with pupils; experimenting with various arrangements of the learning environment; developing better objectives, better strategies, and better pupil assessment instruments; and becoming more knowledgeable about the bases of the teaching profession.

This discussion makes it possible to define a competent teacher as one who is able to perform in a manner consistent with the ethical, societal, and knowledge bases of the teaching profession over all formulative, validation, and improvement classes of teaching action.

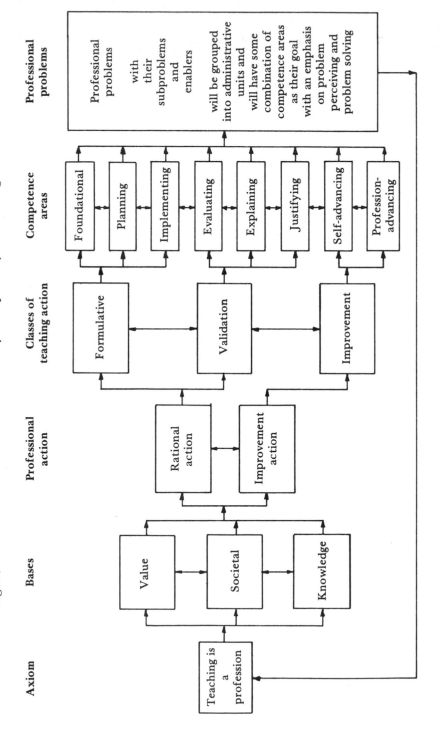

Figure 11:1 The Texas Christian University Competency Based Program Model

Derived from this definition of a competent teacher, a competency based teacher education program is one designed to provide education, training, and experience in an interrelated way over all classes of teaching action. To maintain the connectedness of competencies, the basic unit of instruction is the professional problem.

A professional problem is broad, including several competencies, and presents interrelated theory and practice of the competencies in the interrelated form in which the teacher is most likely to encounter them. A teacher does not distinguish those characteristics necessary for the learning at hand apart from communicating with students; he does not plan apart from evaluation of his planning.

Development of the problem includes the steps previously listed as characterizing rational action: a goal, a sequence of procedures, a statement of evidences that will indicate that the goal has been attained, a process for implementing the procedures, and a means of determining the effectiveness of the procedures. Discussion of the development of specific professional problems and the curriculum organization are not included in this chapter.

12. Determining Priorities among Competencies: Judgments of Classroom Teachers and Supervisors

Adele K. Thomas
Patricia M. Kay

One of the first steps in competency based program development has been the identification and comprehensive delineation of competencies.[1] A number of approaches have been developed for identifying those knowledges, skills, and behaviors that are to become the objectives of competency based teacher education programs.

In 1971 Dodl at Florida State University compiled a catalog of teacher behaviors, the *Catalog of Teacher Competencies*,[2] which represents an initial attempt to systematize intuitive statements of competence collected from a variety of educational sources. Statements of teaching skill were classified on the basis of relevant education level, content area, and teacher-pupil activity. Since there were no selective criteria in drawing up the statements, any and all competencies collected were included.

Another approach to generating teacher competencies has called for advisory committees to develop and evaluate teaching competencies for specific areas such as science education or psychological foundations.[3] Houston has identified a number of routes to competency identification that are variously based on reformulation of current course requirements, in task analysis of teaching roles and the needs of school learners, in theoretical stances on teaching style, or in the demands of clustered curriculum areas.[4]

Competencies arrived at through these varied approaches must be regarded as tentative until research has confirmed that they are indeed the most essential skills a teacher might possess. Ultimately, competencies may be apparent from the results of extensive research about the relationship between teaching characteristics or behaviors and pupil outcomes. The present state of that research demands that preliminary competency identification rest on the related research and theory of the social sciences, the demands of specific school curricula, and the culled experience of the teaching profession.

This study was concerned with methods of collecting data that culled experience of professional educators. A difficulty with the sets of competencies arrived at through all the approaches mentioned above is the problem of distinguishing crucial competencies from those considered nonessential, or as "icing on the cake." A consensus of opinion on what teaching behaviors and skills are more important than others is difficult to obtain, because such judgments reflect a broad range of values based on diverse philosophies of education and theories of learning.[5] In addition, judgments about necessary teacher competencies can be expected to vary according to different needs of particular communities.[6] Nevertheless, the need for determination of priorities among teaching skills is underscored by the practical constraints of developing programs which initially can focus on only a portion of all possible teaching skills.[7] Thus an important step in the development of performance based teacher education is the establishment of methods of ordering competencies, to reflect specified educational priorities.

Methods of ordering educationally relevant judgments have been reviewed by Stake in a survey that dealt with the data of program evaluation.[8] Stake urged that educational objectives and priorities be viewed as aspects of values and preferences, subject to empirical scaling analysis. In the area of curriculum development several attempts have been made to gauge preferences and priorities among educational objectives, using a variety of questionnaire formats. Differences in rankings of educational goals have been found among teachers, pupils, parents, and supervisors.[9] Similarly, the ratings of teachers, student teachers, and pupils have differed regarding desirable teacher characteristics.[10]

Educational rating forms that have been used in this work have included Likert scales,[11] Q sorts,[12] open-ended questionnaires,[13] and semantic differential.[14] Forced-choice questionnaires have had the advantage of eliminating coder reliability problems found in open-ended questionnaires.[15] However, the forced-choice format has been considered restrictive when the intent of scaling is the exploration of limits of complex attitudes or values.[16]

The present study was designed to explore the relative effectiveness of two traditional attitude measurement techniques and the use of open-ended group discussion for arriving at priorities among defined teacher competencies. Classroom teachers and supervisors were called on to rate statements of competencies on a five-point Likert scale and in a paired comparison format. In addition, to develop group-generated statements of teacher competence, group discussions were conducted that focused on the concept of performance based teacher education and those teaching skills deemed necessary for beginning teachers.

METHOD

Subjects

An open invitation to apply for eight two-day workshops on performance based teacher education was extended to teachers through the United Federation of Teachers, and to supervisory personnel through the Council of Supervisory Associations. Over 900 people responded. The 156 participants selected were chosen to represent a cross-section of educational levels (high, middle, and elementary), a range of teaching and supervisory experience, and various school districts throughout New York City. The eighty supervisors represented diverse administrative positions—e.g., director of psychological services, district coordinator of athletic activities, coordinator of drug abuse programs—in addition to positions from department head through principal. The seventy-six teachers as well as the supervisors who participated came from schools that varied in ethnic composition and socioeconomic level. Designation of socioeconomic status (SES) and ethnic makeup of schools was based on teacher reports. Subjects were paid honoraria for their participation.

Diversity of experience was an important aspect of participant selection to facilitate exploration of as wide a range of teaching competencies as possible; therefore no attempt was made to establish a sample that was representative of all New York City teachers and supervisors. Nevertheless, participants clustered on several characteristics. Teachers and supervisors were predominantly white, graduates of teacher education programs (69 percent), with six years or more teaching experience (70 percent). Participants came from schools that were racially mixed (82 percent) and low in socioeconomic status (63 percent).

Instruments

Three means of obtaining judgments about priorities among competencies were used: (1) a rating questionnaire, (2) a pair comparison instrument, and (3) a content analysis of directed group discussion.

The rating questionnaire consisted of 195 statements of teacher competency beginning, "A teacher should be able to. . . ." Each item was responded to on two five-point scales: one rating the degree of importance of that competency for a beginning teacher, the other for an experienced teacher.

One hundred fifty-two of the items were drawn at random from the *Florida Catalog of Competencies* and grouped into the seven categories of teacher behavior used in the catalog. The other forty-three items were selected from a set of competency statements drawn up by the Competency Based Teacher Education Project Committees at the City University of New York. These statements were also put in the *Florida Catalog* form and classified according to the seven teacher behavior categories. Table 12:1 contains definitions of the teacher behavior categories and the number of questionnaire items in each category.

The pair comparison instrument was constructed by randomly selecting three items from each of the seven categories of the rating questionnaire. Table 12:2 contains the selected statements. Each of the twenty-one statements was paired with all others in the set. The resulting 210 pairs were randomly divided into four subsets which became the four forms of the instrument. For each form, the order within pairs was reversed for half of the participants. Participants

Table 12:1. Teacher Behavior Category Definitions and Number of Rating Questionnaire Items in Each Category

Category	Number of items	
(1) Evaluation	43	Identification and assessment of pupil learning, achievement and emotional needs; familiarity with a variety of assessment techniques; self-assessment skills in affective realm as well as teaching skill.
(2) Planning instruction	43	Design of lessons; development of class goals and individual learning objectives; organization of material and plans for individual needs.
(3) Managing instruction	52	Conduct ongoing learning utilizing skills such as adequate feedback, resolution of class discipline problems, and use of effective questioning techniques.
(4) Communicating	16	Use of a variety of communication modes (written, nonverbal, etc.) related to diverse situations such as parent conferences, classrooms.
(5) Human relations	27	Emphasis on development of tolerance, self-esteem, cooperation, and openness in relating to students, parents, and other teachers.
(6) Instructional resources	9	Use of a broad range of community and school resources for enhancing learning and student development.
(7) Institutional administration	5	Implementation of school policy, classroom regulations, optimum use of school personnel.

responded to only one form and were instructed to select the one statement of each pair they judged to be more important for a beginning teacher to possess. The judgments were then pooled for analysis.

The group discussions that were content analyzed were either taped or summarized in writing by participants who volunteered to serve as group secretaries. Each group presented its own list of competency statements at the end of each workshop. Data from the taped group sessions, secretary notes, and written competencies were

Table 12:2. List of Competency Statements Comprising the Pair Comparison Instrument, Grouped by Teaching Skill Category

(1) **Evaluation**
Teacher should be able to analyze the effect of his/her own teaching behavior.
Teacher should be able to assess student learning problems.
Teacher should be able to identify a student's instructional needs on the basis of errors.

(2) **Planning**
Teacher should be able to involve students in teacher-pupil planning.
Teacher should be able to write behavioral objectives for several content areas.
Teacher should be able to design a lesson for the introduction of a concept.

(3) **Managing**
Teacher should be able to organize and manage the classroom efficiently.
Teacher should be able to provide relevant examples illustrating given content.
Teacher should be able to use positive and negative reinforcement and extinguishing in class.

(4) **Communication**
Teacher should be able to use techniques for formal and informal lecture.
Teacher should be able to utilize illustrations and examples in lecture.
Teacher should be able to use probing questions successfully.

(5) **Human relations**
Teacher should be able to accept feelings, whatever their nature, that others have toward him.
Teacher should be able to accept thinking strategy of a student as legitimate at that time.
Teacher should be able to respond to others in such a way that they are stimulated.

(6) **Instructional resources**
Teacher should be able to familiarize himself with community resources.
Teacher should be able to evaluate the quality of materials for instruction.
Teacher should be able to use a variety of media in the course of teaching a lesson or unit.

(7) **Institutional administration**
Teacher should be able to identify and utilize as resources a variety of personnel.
Teacher should be able to set up and utilize an individual record system.
Teacher should be able to maintain the amount and condition of physical resources for the classroom.

all analyzed by coding according to the seven teacher behavior categories and tabulating frequency of category mention.

In addition to analysis for teacher behavior category, the materials were also analyzed for attitudes about teacher training and recommendations for change in teacher education.

Independent ratings by two coders familiar with category definitions yielded 88.2 percent intercoder reliability. Since the seven categories in some respects represented overlapping teacher skills, coder disagreement arose because many competencies could fit into more than one category. After discussion about alternate choices, 100 percent agreement was achieved.

Procedure

The eight two-day workshops were conducted in summer 1972, with approximately twenty participants in each group. On the first day, each group was first introduced to the concept of performance based teacher education (PBTE) via a slide tape presentation.[17] A general discussion of the issues involved in a PBTE approach to teacher training followed. The workshop director led the discussion and supplied information about the current status of PBTE. After exploring issues concerned with the delineation and evaluation of teacher competency, participants completed the rating questionnaire and recessed for about an hour. The pair comparison instruments were distributed in the afternoon session, after which each large workshop group was divided into three subgroups according to grade level: elementary, middle (junior high), and high school. Each subgroup was instructed to react to the instruments to provide feedback on their format and content. At the end of the day, the entire group met to report on and compare the conclusions of each subgroup.

On the second day, subgroup discussion began in the morning session to specify the most critical teacher competencies. Each group was instructed to develop as detailed a listing of necessary teaching skills as it could produce. All subgroups came together in the afternoon to report their conclusions and discuss different viewpoints.

RESULTS

Rating Questionnaire

Since each teacher behavior statement was rated according to its degree of importance for beginning and experienced teachers, the relationship between these two ratings was measured by means of a Pearson product moment correlation. The ratings correlated .94, indicating teacher behavior statements were considered almost equally important for both inexperienced and experienced teachers. All further analysis was based on response data for the inexperienced teacher.

All competencies presented on the rating questionnaire were considered important (scale level four) or essential (scale level five) by approximately 75 percent of all 156 participants. Competencies judged unimportant (scale levels one and two) were so infrequent that the responses could not be meaningfully listed by percentage. Data analysis was based on the seven category subdivision discussed in the Method section. Within this scheme, analysis of mean ratings for teachers and supervisors was carried out according to several classifications, summarized in Tables 12:3 and 12:4.

Although ratings were clustered on the two highest scale levels, it was possible to rank the overall ratings of teachers and supervisors across the seven categories (see Table 12:5). Regardless of subgroup membership, teachers and supervisors consistently ranked human relations skills first and evaluation last. Between these extremes, rankings were more variable depending on educational and teaching background. Thus on the basis of overall means, teachers ranked communicating skills second highest, but new teachers who had one to three years experience gave this skill first priority. While elementary and middle grade teachers and teachers from low SES, predominantly black schools, ranked institutional administration skills second, secondary grade teachers rated institutional administration skills fourth, and teachers from schools of mixed race and class ranked them fifth. Communicating was given an overall ranking of third by supervisors, but elementary grade supervisors and those supervisors from predominantly white, middle-class schools rated communicating behaviors sixth. While teachers and supervisors on the whole gave planning instruction a rank of four, some discrepancies included teachers from predominantly black schools and high school supervisors, both of whom rated planning sixth.

To inspect differences within categories, a series of two-way analyses of variance was performed for each of the seven categories. The classifications of teacher education program, grade level, school SES, and ethnic composition were varied with teacher-supervisor classification. Since all supervisory teaching experience exceeded four years, a separate analysis of teacher experience was conducted by means of t tests.

Significant differences were found for only the teacher education classification. The main effect of graduation from a teacher education program was significant for the categories of planning, managing, and instructional resources ($F = 3.91$, $df = 1/152$, $p < .05$). Table 12:6 summarizes the results for these categories. Teachers and supervisors who had graduated from teacher education programs gave significantly higher ratings to the teacher skills involved in planning, managing, and instructional resources than those who were not graduates of formal programs.

It was found that new teachers (one to three years) gave significantly higher ratings than their more experienced colleagues (four years or more) to teacher behaviors related to planning ($t = 2.216$, $df = 74$, $p < .05$), managing ($t = 2.521$, $df = 74$, $p < .05$), communicating ($t = 2.419$, $df = 74$, $p < .05$), and human relations skills ($t = 2.035$, $df = 74$, $p < .05$). In fact, new teachers tended to give consistently higher ratings than any other group of participants.

Pair Comparison Instrument

Analysis of this rating was based on the twenty-one statements that appeared on the first rating questionnaire. Similarly, the twenty-one items were coded according to the seven teaching categories, with three statements assigned to each category. Investigation of the extent to which the statements might be ordered on a preference continuum was made on a category basis by collapsing the data into seven levels.

Scale scores for the seven categories were derived from how many times one competency statement of a pair was judged more important than all other statements. Rankings from pair comparison data (Table 12:5) may be contrasted with results of the rating questionnaire. There were several discrepancies in rankings for the two instruments. Pair comparison data reflected lowered values for teacher skills in planning and human relations and higher priority for instructional resources and communicating when contrasted to rating questionnaire rankings. In addition, while values on the rating questionnaire for all teacher skill categories clustered in a narrow range (mean responses of 3.7 to 4.5), the distance between the first (communi-

Table 12:3. Mean Teacher

Teacher skill category	All teachers	Teacher education program		Grade level		
		Yes	No	Elem	Mid	High
(1) Evaluation	3.932	3.973	3.869	3.950	3.906	3.941
(2) Planning	4.079	4.154	3.965	4.098	4.078	4.063
(3) Managing	4.051	4.118	3.949	4.058	4.060	4.036
(4) Communication	4.173	4.220	4.100	4.126	4.208	4.183
(5) Human relations	4.234	4.252	4.208	4.176	4.273	4.252
(6) Instructional resources	4.047	4.101	3.963	4.024	4.117	3.996
(7) Institutional administration	4.155	4.183	4.112	4.197	4.259	4.005
Number	76	46	30	25	26	25

Table 12:4. Mean Supervisor

Teacher skill category	All supervisors	Teacher education program		Grade level		
		Yes	No	Elem	Mid	High
(1) Evaluation	3.920	3.991	3.679	4.012	3.812	3.890
(2) Planning	4.081	4.114	3.864	4.194	3.997	4.061
(3) Managing	4.070	4.120	3.899	4.150	4.004	4.068
(4) Communication	4.099	4.154	3.912	4.143	4.034	4.137
(5) Human relations	4.254	4.287	4.131	4.271	4.281	4.191
(6) Instructional resources	4.055	4.140	3.764	4.173	3.920	4.065
(7) Institutional administration	4.160	4.176	4.105	4.270	4.146	4.131
Number	80	62	18	37	17	19

Responses to Rating Questionnaire

School socioeconomic status			School ethnic composition			Teaching experience	
Low	Mid	½-½	Black	White	Mix	1-3 Years	4 Years
3.982	3.981	3.791	3.940	4.094	3.881	4.195	3.856
4.112	4.226	3.976	4.087	4.199	4.039	4.371	3.995
4.092	4.174	3.930	4.106	4.135	3.939	4.358	3.963
4.223	4.074	4.046	4.222	4.216	4.080	4.499	4.079
4.296	4.107	4.080	4.288	4.275	4.134	4.450	4.172
4.106	4.019	3.888	4.099	4.102	3.945	4.186	4.006
4.268	3.705	3.895	4.241	4.172	4.005	4.311	4.110
54	2	20	44	6	26	17	59

Responses to Rating Questionnaire

School socioeconomic status			School ethnic composition			Teaching experience	
Low	Mid	½-½	Black	White	Mix	1-3 Years	4 Years
3.892	3.962	4.017	3.887	3.993	4.011	—	3.929
4.068	4.108	4.180	4.075	4.108	4.182	—	4.090
4.055	4.032	4.170	4.060	4.119	4.114	—	4.074
4.132	4.013	4.115	4.109	4.099	4.139	—	4.110
4.255	4.187	4.273	4.241	4.252	4.285	—	4.242
4.058	4.079	4.169	4.083	4.018	4.198	—	4.090
4.165	4.183	4.310	4.182	4.217	4.272	—	4.181
45	9	21	43	17	15	—	75

Table 12:5. Teacher Behavior Categories as Ranked by
Teacher and Supervisor Groups

	Teachers	Supervisors
High	Human relations	Human relations
	Communicating	Institutional administration
	Institutional administration	Communicating
	Planning	Planning
	Managing	Managing
	Instructional resources	Instructional resources
Low	Evaluation	Evaluation

cating) and last (evaluation) was considerable from pair comparison judgments.

Group Sessions

Sixty-five percent of workshop discussion focused on attitudes about teacher education and recommendations for change. It was apparently difficult for participants to judge teacher activity in an open-ended format without also discussing the school environment and traditional academic approaches to developing teacher expertise.

The eight workshop groups developed 758 teacher skill statements. The greatest proportion of competencies generated fell into three categories: human relations skills (24 percent), managing (24 percent), and planning (20 percent). Supervisors produced almost twice as many competencies as teachers, with middle and high school supervisors contributing the largest number (323 statements).

Although many participants considered the format of questionnaire statements to be general or vague, most group-generated statements were very similar in format. However, 10 percent of the skill statements developed were concerned with subject matter knowledge. Since middle and high school teachers and supervisors noted that competent performance must be grounded in mastery of specific subject areas, teacher behavior statements included activities directed toward the attainment and maintenance of subject knowledge. On the other hand, elementary grade teachers did not consider such specific skills crucial to competent performance; rather, they focused on generic teacher activities directed at maximizing pupil exploration and learning skills.

Table 12:6. Summary of Analysis of Variance of Ratings of
Teachers and Supervisors Who Were Classified According to
Graduation from Teacher Education Programs

Planning

Source	SS	DF	MS	F
A (title)	.0988	1	.0988	.30
B (teacher ed. program)	1.7306	1	1.7306	5.40*
AB	.0662	1	.0662	.20
Error	48.6846	152	.3202	

Managing

Source	SS	DF	MS	F
A (title)	.2019	1	.2019	.62
B (teacher ed. program)	2.0782	1	2.0782	6.38*
AB	.4472	1	.4472	1.37
Error	49.4927	152	.3256	

Instructional resources

Source	SS	DF	MS	F
A (title)	.2019	1	.2019	.62
B (teacher ed. program)	2.0782	1	2.0782	6.38*
AB	.4472	1	.4472	1.37
Error	49.4927	152	.3256	

Another unique classification stressed by groups was discipline. Approximately 10 percent of all competencies developed focused on activities that established teacher authority, class routine, and order. These activities were perceived as especially important for new teachers. Teacher and supervisory groups also found it necessary to designate separate teacher skill requirements to accommodate the special needs of minority, disadvantaged, and urban student populations. Generally categorized within the human relations area, these skills related to developing empathy for and awareness of minority lifestyles. However, teacher activities in reading and language arts were also developed for special use with disadvantaged students.

CONCLUSION

While both rating instruments were successful in identifying value hierarchies for teacher competencies, each offered somewhat distinct advantages. The positive aspects of the rating questionnaire included the relative ease with which a large number of statements could be judged. Although ratings tended to cluster across teacher categories, the rating questionnaire was effective in isolating variation in values based on differences in teaching background and the experience of participant judges. It was difficult to analyze the pair comparison data for information about value changes due to teacher background because different individuals responded across the total set of comparisons. However, the pair comparison instrument provided precise discrimination among the seven teacher competency categories. Where each participant rated all competencies against his own standard for the rating questionnaire, on the pair comparison task participants had to weigh the importance of each competency against every other statement. Thus, the scale level distance for pair comparisons between the first (communicating) and second (institutional administration) ranked teacher categories was considerable compared to similar rankings on the rating questionnaire. The more detailed discriminations required on the pair comparison task may also account for some of the discrepant rankings on the two instruments for human relations, planning, and instructional resources. It is possible that the seven teaching categories may not hold up as unitary classifications under the more rigorous pair comparison judgment task. While paired comparisons demonstrated finer distinctions among the seven teacher dimensions, the rating questionnaire provided useful information about differences among participants that can affect ratings. Depending on the type of needs to be met, either one of the rating scales may be effectively utilized in determining educational priorities. However, when objectives are loosely defined and exploratory in nature, the use of both instruments may be considered complementary.

The inclusion of group-generated products and subjective reactions to the concept of competency based teacher education was an essential part of the assessment process. Content analysis provided a method of analyzing participant reaction objectively. The data obtained via this method offered support for rating scale findings and added a dimension of emotionality that aided rating interpretation. Thus the low ranking for evaluation activities was reinforced in group sessions by a consensus of opinion that a large portion of evaluation responsibility might be better delegated to school personnel other than teachers. The high priority given to communicating and human relations was underscored in group sessions by discussions that focused on the difficulties new teachers have in fulfilling their teaching role while at the same time adjusting to the demands of inner-city school environments. Group discussion data also revealed differences in attitudes not apparent from questionnaire results alone. Grade differences were found for competencies relating to subject knowledge, while statements about discipline issues offered insight into why high priority was given to questionnaire competencies related to teacher administration activity. Group session results of varying teacher competency profiles for different student populations suggest that the task of assessing requisite teacher skills is a complex one which must take into account the specific nature of the social milieu in which teaching occurs.

It is noteworthy that workshop participants generally considered all the skills in the questionnaire statements important for teachers to possess. Both teachers and supervisors indicated considerable agreement in designating hierarchies of skills. School personnel themselves expected teachers to be competent not only in subject matter and instructional methodology, but also across several levels of interpersonal relations and community involvement. Participant concepts of the ideal teacher and the general obligation to be all things to all people made it difficult for groups to restrict areas of skill or to specify minimum rather than maximum levels of teacher competency.

In this respect it would appear that new teachers felt the burden of competence more than any other group of teachers or supervisors, as indicated by their uniformly high ratings. Similarly, the higher ratings for graduates of teacher education programs may be understood in terms of greater sensitization through training to instructional planning and management activities, as well as the use of instructional resources.

Finally, the workshop format used was extremely well received by both teachers and supervisors.

In retrospect, the present study produced two benefits. The feasibility of utilizing assessment techniques at an early stage of teacher competency development has been demonstrated. And, more fundamentally, the enlistment of school staff in initial planning for competency based teacher education was assured. Local teacher associations were keenly interested in the implications of competency based approaches in New York City and were eager to cooperate with the CUNY project.[18] Participating teachers and supervisory personnel became enthusiastic about concrete efforts to seek innovation in teacher education and were gratified to be able to influence implementation in equal partnership with traditionally distant teacher training institutions. The popularity of the workshop format, which stressed the importance of teacher input in new plans for teacher training, contributed considerably to the acceptance by teachers of the competency based approach. A bonus was the establishment of solid working relationships with teacher groups for future collaboration on teacher training development.

NOTES FOR CHAPTER 12

1. T. E. Andrews, *Manchester Interview: Competency Based Teacher Education/Certification*, PBTE series no. 3 (Washington, D.C.: AACTE, April 1972); F. K. Daniel, "Performance Based Teacher Certification: What Is It and Why Do We Need It?" paper prepared for a leadership training program conducted by the Florida Department of Education, Miami, May 1970; W. H. Drummond, "The Meaning and Application of Performance Criteria in Staff Development," *Phi Delta Kappan* (September 1970).

2. N. Dodl, J. Gant, P. Nelson, and H. A. Jung, *Catalog of Teacher Competencies* (Tallahassee: Florida State University, November 1971).

3. P. Kay, "The City University Competency Based Teacher Education Project," Instructional Materials Center Reports 4, no. 3 (New York: New York Network, 1972).

4. W. Robert Houston, *Strategies and Resources for Developing a Competency-Based Teacher Education Program* (Albany: New York State Education Department and the Multi-State Consortium on Performance-Based Teacher Education, 1972).

5. B. Rosenshine, *Teaching Behaviors and Student Achievement* (London: National Foundation for Education Research, 1971); H. D. Schalock, "Alternative Strategies and Foci for Teacher Education," paper prepared for 23d annual conference on teacher education, Austin, Texas, October 1970; R. E. Stake, "Objectives, Priorities and Other Judgment Data," *Review of Educational Research* 40, no. 2 (1970): 181-212.

6. B. O. Smith, S. B. Cohen, and A. Pearl, *Teachers for the Real World* (Washington, D.C.: AACTE, 1969).

7. B. Rosner, *The Power of Competency Based Teacher Education: Report of the Committee on National Program Priorities in Teacher Education* (Boston: Allyn & Bacon, 1972); B. O. Smith, ed., *Research in Teacher Education: A Symposium* (Englewood Cliffs, N.J.: Prentice-Hall, 1971).

8. Stake, "Objectives, Priorities and Other Judgment Data."

9. E. L. Baker, "Parents, Teachers, and Students as Data Sources for the Selection of Instructional Goals," *American Educational Research Journal* 9, no.

3 (1972): 401-411; P. A. Taylor and T. O. Maguire, "Perceptions of Some Objectives for a Science Curriculum," *Science Education* 51, no. 5 (1967): 181-212; S. Stemnock, "The Evaluatee Evaluates the Evaluator," *ERS Circular No. 5* (Washington, D.C.: Educational Research Service, 1970), p. 54.

10. R. W. Bybee, "The Ideal Elementary Science Teacher," paper presented at the annual meeting of the National Science Teachers Association, New York City, April 1972; T. L. Rosenthal, M. Coxon, M. Hurt, Jr., and B. J. Zimmerman, "Pedagogical Attitudes of Conventional and Specially Trained Teachers," ERIC no. ED 034 587 (Tucson: University of Arizona, Center for Early Childhood Education, 1969), p. 27.

11. Baker, "Parents, Teachers, and Students as Data Sources for the Selection of Instructional Goals"; Rosenthal et al., "Pedagogical Attitudes of Conventional and Specially Trained Teachers."

12. Bybee, "The Ideal Elementary Science Teacher."

13. F. F. Fuller and J. S. Parsons, "Current Research on the Concerns of Teachers," ERIC no. ED 063 257 (Austin: University of Texas, 1972).

14. Taylor and Maguire, "Perceptions of Some Objectives for a Science Curriculum."

15. Fuller and Parsons, "Current Research on the Concerns of Teachers."

16. Stake, "Objectives, Priorities and Other Judgment Data."

17. W. Weber, "Competency Based Teacher Education: An Overview," slide tape developed for the Center for the Study of Teaching (New York: Syracuse University, 1970).

18. S. Feldman, "Teacher Evaluation: A Teacher Unionist's View," see chapter 8.

13. The University of Florida's Childhood Education Program: An Alternative Approach to CBTE

Arthur W. Combs
Suzanne M. Kinzer

RATIONALE

Historically, teacher educators have sought to find *the* definition of good or effective teaching. Much research has been conducted in this search, but results have not yielded any set of criteria around which educators can rally. Much of this study has centered on the identification of traits, behaviors, or competencies possessed by "good" teachers. Another approach has been to view the teaching act as objectively as possible and try to see "what is." The work of Flanders, Smith, Soar, Medley and Mitzel, and others are notable examples. All of these efforts have added to the profession's conception of teaching; however, from our point of view, they seem to have provided little in the way of direction for teacher education program design. At the University of Florida, some began to feel that the search for answers may have been occurring in the wrong places. Thus, for our definition of good teaching, we began an exploration of a different order.

It is a notorious and maddening fact that despite three generations of careful research the teaching profession is still unable to define teaching in terms of any specific information or behavior that can be clearly shown to be always associated with either good or poor teaching. Arthur W. Combs and Daniel W. Soper sought some other approach to understanding the differences between good and poor practitioners in the helping professions. Looking at the various helping professions, including teaching, counseling, social work, pastoral care, and psychotherapy, it became apparent to these psychologist-educators that the common characteristic of all helping professions is "instantaneous response":

> All of the helping professions seem to be differentiated from more mechanical operations in the immediacy of response required of the helper. In teaching, for example, when the child says something to his teacher his teacher must respond instantaneously. The same thing is true in the interrelationships of the social worker and client, the pastor and parishioner, the nurse and her patient, or the counselor and his client. All of these professions are dependent upon immediate response. Professional helpers must be thinking, problem solving people; the primary tool with which they work is themselves.
>
> We came to describe this understanding of the nature of the helping professions as the "self as instrument" concept. . . . Effective operation in the helping professions is a question of the use of the helper's self, the peculiar way in which he is able to combine his knowledge and understanding with his own unique ways of putting it into operation in such a fashion as to be helpful to others. . . . This explains why the attempt to distinguish the helping professions on the basis of knowledge or methods falters. If effective operation in the helping professions is a personal matter of the effective use of self, then the search for a common knowledge or common method is doomed before it begins. Since the self of each individual is unique, the search for a common uniqueness is, by definition, a "built-in invalidation."[1]

The modern giant computer takes in mountains of information, fed to it by keypunch operators. This information is combined with the information already in the machine's memory bank to provide all kinds of answers to problems. With lightning speed, the computer provides us with the best possible answers from the data at its disposal. This is very much like what the professional helper is required to do. In the giant computer, instantaneous answers are determined by the nature of the program placed in the machine in the first place. In the computer this is usually a mathematical formula; in human beings it is the person's belief system. The perceptions people have about themselves and the world in which they live determine the goals they seek and the ways in which they behave in trying to reach them. Proceeding from this observation, Combs and Soper first tested the perceptual approach in a study of effective and ineffective counselors.[2]

The results of this study were so promising that a faculty-student seminar on the helping relationship was organized at the University of Florida in fall 1959-60. This seminar attempted to examine the problem of effective and ineffective helping relationships and produced a series of perceptual hypotheses about the possible differences between good and poor helpers in several professions.[3]

Over the next few years, these hypotheses were explored in a series of doctoral dissertations examining the perceptual organization of good and poor counselors, teachers, nurses, and Episcopal priests. Results were published in a social science monograph, "Florida Studies in the Helping Professions."[4] The results of these early studies have since been corroborated in a series of studies on good and poor teachers at the University of Florida under the direction of A. W. Combs, and at the University of Northern Colorado under the direction of Richard Usher.[5]

The perceptual approach to understanding the behavior of good and poor teachers seems amply supported. Good teachers are clearly different from poor ones in five major areas of perception:

(1) What the teacher believes is the proper data on which to base his operations. Good teachers seem always concerned with how things look to the persons they are working with, while poor ones believe the important data are how things look to themselves. That is, good teachers seem to be phenomenologically or perceptually, rather than behavioristically, oriented. A simpler description of this way of perceiving might be called "sensitivity" or "empathy."

(2) Good and poor teachers can be clearly distinguished on the basis of how they perceive themselves. Good ones tend to see themselves in positive ways, while poor ones see themselves negatively.

(3) Good and poor teachers can be distinguished on the basis of their beliefs about the persons they are working with. Good teachers tend to see other people in positive ways—as friendly, able, trustworthy, etc.—while poor teachers suffer grave doubts about the nature and capacity of the persons they are working with.

(4) Good and poor teachers can be clearly discriminated by the purposes they seek to carry out in their daily tasks. The purposes of effective teachers tend to be freeing, opening, expanding purposes,

while their ineffective counterparts pursue narrowing, controlling, directing goals.

(5) Good and poor teachers can be discriminated on the basis of the methods they use. This is not to say that there are "good" or "right" methods. Quite the contrary, the important thing about methods seems to be the authenticity or "fit" of the method to the teacher who is using it and the peculiar circumstances in which he is working. This is a personal matter that has to do with the teacher's discovery of the peculiar methods he needs to use to carry out his own and society's purposes.

The Florida and Colorado research on good teaching was so consistent that it became apparent perceptual approaches had much to offer our understanding of the nature of good teaching. Since it is the task of teacher education to produce good teachers, this research was also crucial for thinking about the goals and practices of professional education. Repeatedly, the research was saying, "This is the way good teachers typically perceive themselves and the world they operate in." How, then, shall a teacher of education program be constructed to produce that kind of teacher? To answer that question, Combs began the construction of a theory of teacher education combining the findings of perceptual research, on the one hand, with the understanding of the dynamics of perception provided by modern perceptual humanistic psychology on the other. The resulting theory was published in 1965 in *The Professional Education of Teachers: A Perceptual View of Teacher Preparation.*[6] From the basic outlines of that theoretical position, a series of assumptions for a teacher education program were developed.

ASSUMPTIONS FOR A TEACHER EDUCATION PROGRAM

Basic Principles[7]

(1) *The development of an effective teacher is a process of becoming.* It is not a matter of learning "how to teach," any more than becoming a lawyer is a matter of learning "how to law" or becoming a physician is a matter of learning "how to doctor." Just as one speaks of *becoming* a lawyer or physician, so we must speak of becoming a teacher. The professional education of a teacher is a process of personal discovery designed to assist a student to learn how to use himself effectively as an instrument for carrying out his own and society's purposes.

(2) *The process of becoming should begin with a feeling of security and acceptance.* It is a well-established psychological principle that the experience of feeling threatened interferes with the processes of perception, making the exploration of self and the world more difficult. Until a student knows he can survive in the classroom, there is little point in exposing him to ideas from curriculum theory and educational philosophy. Such high-flown concepts presented before a measure of security is gained are likely to be regarded as irrelevant and immaterial to more concrete and personal problems.

Counselors and psychotherapists know that, to help their clients grow, it is necessary to create an atmosphere in which the client feels accepted as he is and safe enough to risk examination of himself and his problems. This basic principle is just as applicable to the learning situations of a teacher education program. Since feelings of self-acceptance and security are essential conditions for personal exploration and discovery, teacher education programs should begin from an acceptance of students where they are, followed by a maximum diet of success and a minimum experience of failure.

(3) *Teacher education programs should concentrate on personal meanings rather than on behavior.*[8] From this point of view, behavior is only symptom; the *causes* of behavior lie in meanings—in one's perceptions and beliefs about himself and his world. Teaching teachers how to teach, how to behave, hasn't worked because it places too much emphasis on symptoms. If a student is taught the "right" way to teach, and this right way doesn't fit when he goes out to try his skills in the blackboard jungle, all he can do is fall back on what he has learned from previous experience. He then decides that what he was taught at teacher college is "for the birds," and other teachers who have been through the same experience are quick to corroborate his conclusion. This syndrome has defeated whole generations of teacher educators preoccupied with trying to teach "right" ways of behaving.

In light of this understanding of the symptomatic nature of behavior, teacher education programs preoccupied with behavioral approaches to teacher preparation may be creating their own roadblocks. The concept also raises interesting questions for the current national emphasis on behavioral objectives and for some applications of behavior modification techniques. It is conceivable that requiring a teacher education program to define precisely the behaviors it hopes to produce may be the surest way to destroy its effectiveness by concentrating everyone's attention on the wrong dynamics.

How a teacher perceives a child determines his behavior toward that child. It makes a great deal of difference, for example, whether a teacher approaches a difficult child with the perception that his behavior has to stop or that the child believes people don't like him. Either is a way of perceiving calls for quite different constellations of behaviors to deal with the problem. If we can be sure the teacher's ways of perceiving are accurate and constructive, it may not be necessary to know precisely how he will put his concern into effect. There are thousands of ways to express either of these perceptions in action. The crucial question for teacher education is not *which behavior,* but *how* to bring about appropriate shifts in perception.

(4) *To deal effectively with meaningful teacher education, programs should emphasize the subjective aspects of human experience.* The worship of objectivity, scientific method, and technological approaches to solving all problems is a way of life deeply rooted in the American culture. Nevertheless, if it is true that human behavior is a function of perception, the problems of behavior change must then be recognized as fundamentally subjective, having to do with the inner life of persons—their feelings, attitudes, beliefs, understandings. After all, even a fact is only what someone believes. It is interesting to note that in the Florida studies on the helping professions objectivity correlates negatively with effectiveness. In that research, one of the most important factors distinguishing good helpers from poor ones is the capacity to see nonobjectively; that is, subjectively, empathically, or sensitively. Good helpers are characteristically concerned about how things look to the people they are working with.[9]

To humanize teacher education and our public schools, an alternative humanistic psychology is needed—more specifically, a perceptual psychology capable of producing sensitivity, empathy, and capacity for effective interaction. No teacher college in these times can afford to base its functions on a single psychology. Humanistic approaches to psychological thought have been expressly designed to deal with the problems of perceiving and of becoming basic to current practice. It is time they were more widely adopted into the curriculum.

(5) *An individualized program aimed at personal discovery and meaning calls for an open system of thinking.* There are two major ways to approach the problem of changing human behavior. One is a

closed system of thinking. In such a system, ends or outcomes are clearly defined in advance. Thereafter, conditions are set in motion to achieve those ends, followed by some kind of assessment to determine whether the ends were truly achieved. It will be recognized that this is the pattern currently advocated in behavioral objectives, performance based criteria approaches to our educational problems. The system often works well when applied to comparatively simple outcomes capable of clear and unequivocal definition. Those conditions are not likely to be present in teacher education, especially not in the highly individualized, self-assessment instrument, personal discovery of meaning concept of effective teachers that has been outlined above.

A more appropriate system of thinking for the kind of teacher education we are advocating is an open system that does not call for specifically defined outcomes determined in advance. In an open system of thinking, teachers and students confront together problems whose precise answers may be unknown to either party. Donald Snygg once said, "The trouble with American education is that we are all trying to provide students with answers to problems they haven't got yet." A problems approach to learning avoids this error; teachers and students cooperate in finding effective solutions to problems of interest to both of them.

The advantages to an open system of thinking extend beyond the fact that it is likely to result in more personalized and effective learning. Professors do not *have* to be right and so can divest themselves of the burdens imposed by the necessity of being a "fountainhead of knowledge." The relationship between teachers and students is also likely to be much improved, for a problems approach makes teacher and student partners in a common project rather than separate or antagonistic participants. An open system built around real and relevant problems also solves the problem of motivation. People do not need to be rewarded, cajoled, or punished to deal with matters that affect them in important and immediate ways.

(6) *The dynamic importance of need in learning should be fully exploited.* Psychologists don't know much about learning, but they *do* know that people learn best when they have a need to know.

Applying the principle that learning proceeds best when there is first a need to know calls for rethinking the typical internship at the end of a teacher education program, which was put there with the idea that one learned how to teach and then went out and practiced it. Rather, field experience should be a time for discovering what the problems are, not a place to practice preconceived solutions. What the prospective teacher needs is an awareness of problems and help in finding answers. This calls for continuous practical experience throughout the training period. It probably also means the college will have to surrender to the public schools the job of supervision for a very practical reason: colleges can't afford it. College supervision is feasible if it is concentrated into a single experience. If field experience is to operate continuously throughout the program, few college budgets can stand the strain.

The principle that learning proceeds best when it follows need has even more striking connotations when applied to the substantive aspects of teacher training: it runs head-on into the traditional curriculum organization of courses. A course is a package, generally arranged in some orderly sequence determined by the nature of the subject and delivered at some predetermined point in the student's program. Student needs are maddeningly haphazard and unpredictable. If students are left free to pursue their needs, they do not learn in orderly sequence; they learn first and later discover an order in which to organize what they have learned. A program that honestly seeks to provide information in response to developing needs to know would have to abolish or drastically modify its customary course organization.

(7) *A program based on effective discovery of personal meaning should actively seek student involvement.* Since the person's self is his own private possession, it cannot be effectively changed without cooperation of the student. An effective teacher education program must therefore encourage maximum self-direction and student responsibility for most of the student's learning. Students need to be deeply involved in every aspect of their professional education, including the selection of experiences, making policy, and evaluation of progress. This may not be easy, for most students come to professional preparation after years of experience in a system that thoroughly indoctrinated them to an essentially passive role.

(8) *If the self-concept is as important a determinant of behavior as research suggests, teacher education should actively apply what is known about it.*

Research on effective helpers clearly demonstrates that such people see themselves in essentially positive ways—as being liked, accepted, able, dignified, and worthy—while poor helpers see themselves as unliked, unwanted, unable, and unworthy. If this is true, teacher education must produce teachers who see themselves in positive ways. This can only be done by giving prospective teachers positive experiences—a principle that is at variance with much current practice in selection, evaluation, and the maintenance of standards.

A person learns about himself from the feedback he receives from others. Good helpers see themselves as liked, wanted, able, and worthy because they are treated that way. To change education, then, one needs to ask: How can a person feel liked unless someone likes him? How can he feel wanted if no one wants him? How can he feel able unless somewhere he has had success? In answering these questions we shall find what we need to do to improve educational practices and produce teachers with positive views of self.

(9) *Since methods of teaching are personal ways of using self, they cannot be given; they need to be discovered.* Teachers colleges formerly often regarded their task as one of teaching students "good" or "right" methods, generally derived from observation of expert teachers in action. In the light of what now seems evident from research, such prescriptive tactics are likely to be only partially effective. Methods, we now understand, are highly personal and must be deeply related to the teacher's own beliefs, purposes, and conditions for action. This calls for a cafeteria approach to methods, in which students are given wide opportunities to confront all kinds of possible methods and are encouraged and assisted in trying out and modifying teaching techniques to fit the peculiar combination of characteristics of self, students, and the surroundings in which they may find themselves.

(10) *Since students come to teacher education programs from a wide variety of backgrounds and experience, professional education should allow for the widest possible flexibility for adjustment to such diverse needs.* Teacher education programs that require all students to move through the same sequence of experiences in the same time periods do violence to everything we know about the unique nature of persons. Some students are much more ready at the beginning of their program to take on full-time teaching than some stu-

dents will be at the end. Putting all students through the same program, at the same speed, is a grossly inefficient approach to teacher education. Teacher education programs should be so constructed that students can move through them at different speeds depending on their own readiness to begin and how quickly they can acquire the qualities that will make them effective practitioners.

(11) *Since people learn most effectively from their own experience, teacher education programs should demonstrate in their philosophy, practices, and human relationships a wide variety of models.* Historically, the role of the teacher as director has long held center stage. In this view the teacher is the determiner of objectives, manipulator of the machinery to accomplish them, and the tester and evaluator of outcomes. It is the role most familiar to students coming through our traditional educational system, commonly found on college campuses and heretofore most frequently encountered in teacher colleges as well. Modern education, however, increasingly demands of teachers two other roles less frequently seen in the past. One is the role of "teacher as facilitator"; it is required of teachers operating in an open system of thinking. It calls on teachers to focus primarily on the creation of effective processes for learning—they must know how to facilitate and assist students in a problems approach to education. The other role is that of "teacher as consultant." This role is demanded of teachers when students are actively engaged in their own development or in pursuit of their own special needs.

For a very long time teacher education has been preoccupied with the director role. In the complex modern world, however, teachers are increasingly required to operate in facilitating and consulting roles. If young teachers are to be effectively prepared, teacher education programs will need to model such roles.

IMPLEMENTATION

The Childhood Education Program (CEP) is based on a definition of effective teaching that is grounded in theory and research. Teaching is essentially a process of becoming—as Combs defines it:

The effective teacher is a unique human being who has learned to use himself effectively and efficiently to carry out his own and society's purposes in the education of others.[10]

Keeping this definition and our philosophical orientation in mind, program components have been designed to facilitate the student's development as an effective person-teacher. Other programs, based upon differing sets of assumptions, generally focus more on the development of specific teaching skills or behaviors—most recently labeled *competencies*. Both of these approaches to teacher preparation can be thought of as "competency based." The difference lies in definition. Our approach redefines the term competence in less specific (or more general) terms. Through participation in the various components of the program (field experience, seminar, and subject area work),[11] our students do develop competence; however, competencies may be very different for each individual. Our commitments, beliefs, and assumptions about the ways in which people learn and grow have led us to deal with the vital questions of competence and accountability in some rather unique ways.

What are some of the unique features of our program?

(1) Goals are derived from ideas about good teaching that are based on phenomenological theory. This theory supports the notion that programs should focus on the development of the person in the process rather than on a wide variety of performances. More explicitly, this focus relates to the development of a perceptual or belief system that includes:

- A positive view of self;
- Accurate perceptions of self and the world;
- Ability to confront the world with openness and acceptance;
- Deep feelings of identification with other people;
- An appropriate degree of knowledge and information.

(2) Program organization therefore facilitates:

- Close interpersonal relationships between faculty and students;
- Student involvement in programmatic and personal decision-making;
- Optional approaches to learning;
- Varied and continuous practical experiences that foster student identification of learning needs;
- Continuous evaluation and assessment of student (and faculty) growth as a person and teacher;

• Appropriate and individual knowledgeability about teaching, learning, child development, and curriculum.

(3) Instructional outgrowths or implications of this theoretical framework that are particularly relevant to our broad definition of competence are:

A. *Subject area work*

The substantive work is arranged in the traditional subjects approach fashion (reading, language arts, math, social studies, science, etc.). Each of these areas is under the direction of a subject area specialist. Rather than the typical course format, the substance of the area is organized into a series of learning activities or assignments that make up the requirements for each area. These activities are generally divided into three major categories to facilitate student choice and increase the student's opportunity to relate his substantive work to practical experiences in the schools. The categories are:

• Required—those activities that must be completed by all students or in which all must demonstrate competence;
• Selected—an array of activities from which students may select those that best meet their interests and needs;
• Negotiable—students contract the activity with faculty consultation and advance approval of a plan for study.

Interdisciplinary efforts are encouraged, particularly in the selected and negotiable activities. Students are, in fact, urged to negotiate so that the substantive work relates as much as possible to needs that have been identified as a result of experiences with children, and overlap and duplication are avoided.

Additionally, this kind of organization enables students to select learning modes that are appropriate for them. Workshops are sometimes required, sometimes optional. Students often request sessions based on a particular interest. Input can be obtained in a variety of ways, from large group sessions, if they are more appropriate, to small discussion groups and/or independent study. Students are encouraged to do some activities as group projects; it is not unusual to see students conducting workshops for other students. Thus, variety in approaches to learning is encouraged.

B. *Seminar leader-student contract*

Each quarter students make a contract with their seminar leaders in which the number of activities each student plans to complete is identified. At the end of the quarter, the student checks in with the seminar leader and reports on the degree to which he or she has met this commitment. A certain amount of procrastination and floundering is expected, particularly with new students; however, the contract provides a means of monitoring and aids students in the transition from a teacher-directed mode of operation to a personal acceptance of responsibility for learning.

C. *Student-directing teacher negotiation*

An additional kind of interaction occurs between students and the teachers with whom they work in the public schools. Students come to teachers with learning activities they want to complete, many of which involve work with children. Some of these have been identified by university faculty; others are initiated by the students; still others grow directly out of the students' work with children and conferences with directing teachers.

D. *Continuous seminar*

The ongoing seminar attempts to tie everything together, aiding students in the development of personal meaning and relating to each other all the experiences the program provides. The following areas are typically focused on in this program component:

· Communication skills;
· Values clarification;
· Analysis of group process;
· Development of problem-solving ability;
· Organizational skills;
· Personal and group decision making skills;
· General ability to analyze experience and identify "what it all means to me."

E. *Student involvement in decision-making*

Each seminar is represented by one or more students at regular program meetings, various curriculum committees, and any faculty retreats or general meetings held. Students are thus in a sense forced to become part of an open system of program planning and revision. They are actively involved in the solution of real problems that directly affect them.

ASSESSMENT

Each student's development is continuously evaluated in ways which are consistent with our underlying assumptions and redefinition of competence, and which at the same time keep us honest and accountable as teacher educators. Data is collected in the following ways:

(1) The various learning activities that are a part of the subject area work are evaluated regularly according to criteria established by faculty and, when appropriate, by students.

(2) Each quarter public school teachers identify students' teaching strengths, areas needing improvement, and kinds of experiences students have completed in their work with children.

(3) Seminar leaders and students, on a quarter basis, meet to assess students' progress and identify long- and short-term goals and the plans for achieving them. During this conference, data from the public school teacher, subject area faculty, and student self-evaluative perceptions are considered.

(4) Seminars are held weekly and students are required to attend. During these sessions, students help each other in identifying and exploring teaching problems, analyzing their experiences, evaluating and reevaluating alternatives, and generating ideas to be explored and assessed. Seminar leaders also gather data in these sessions. Much of it is subjective data based on impressions, perceptions, and feelings. Some is more formalized, as the leaders ask students to identify strengths and weaknesses in the development of human relations skills. The seminar leaders keep very complete records on all program activities and come to know the students very well. The leader plays a role analagous to that of the elementary teacher in an open setting. Anecdotal records are kept, individual conferences held, and the contract and its implications are explored.

(5) Self-evaluation has been mentioned; the students are encouraged—in fact required—to do a great deal of personal reflection. This takes varied forms, including informal and formal conversations be-

tween students and faculty; keeping diaries, journals, or logs; completing value sheets regularly; and examining behavior through a variety of group process analysis checklists, and sometimes through systematic observation systems.

(6) Students are formally evaluated in a midterm and a final review conference. The seminar leader, one other faculty member, and the student together assess progress. Even so, it is the student's responsibility to collect various pieces of information and, in essence, present his own case. The faculty play the roles of facilitator, clarifier, questioner, suggestor of consequences for one's behavior, and consultant.

SUMMARY

It is our intent to involve students in a teacher education program that is a model of the kind of education we feel most enhances continuous individual growth. At the same time, we are aware of our professional responsibility to be accountable. Our attempts to make assumptions and instructional implications explicit and to redefine competence and assessment procedures comprise, for us, a "happy medium."

Our students complete the program when all field work, seminar responsibilities, and subject area requirements have been completed. Judgments as to the appropriate exit time are based on data obtained from the sources mentioned above, analyzed primarily by the student, his seminar leader, and other faculty members with whom the student has worked. The seminar leader then writes a very thorough and specific final statement, evaluating the student's work in the program and his readiness to assume the responsibilities of a beginning teacher. This becomes a part of the student's permanent record; it is sufficiently explicit that it serves to replace letter grades in the student's professional sequence.

The University of Florida's Childhood Education Department and members of the other departments with whom we work have had frequent and heated dialogs about our professional responsibility to be accountable. We are now confronting the accompanying need to make more explicit our goals, competencies, and means of assessment. These important considerations have not been totally resolved. Our program is concerned with a "people-oriented" rather than a "thing-oriented" product, and therein lies our dilemma. The kinds of evidence we accept, the data we utilize, and the procedures we employ are all very human in orientation. Decisions are often based on data that are analyzed in a rather subjective fashion. We do not apologize for this, as we believe it is consistent with our assumptions and reason for being. Faculty and students together are involved in a continual search for ways to improve (1) our data collection procedures; (2) our program organization; (3) collaboration between public schools and universities; and (4) our identification of program goals, implementation, and evaluation.

In essence, we are constantly involved in an ongoing experiment in curriculum development and teacher education. We feel this is quite appropriate for people in education. One of the major concerns expressed by many among our faculty and students is the fear that increased specificity or explicitness will bring about rigidity, or at least reduced flexibility. The above statements are our response to that fear and the nationwide push for competency based teacher education. "We have only just begun!"

NOTES FOR CHAPTER 13

1. A. W. Combs et al., "Florida Studies in the Helping Professions," University of Florida Social Science Monograph no. 37 (Gainesville: University of Florida Press, 1969), pp. 10-11.

2. A. W. Combs and D. W. Soper, "Perceptual Organization of Effective Counselors," *Journal of Counseling and Psychology* 10, no. 3 (1963): 222-226.

3. A. W. Combs, "A Perceptual View of the Nature of 'Helpers,' " in *Personality Theory and Counseling Practice*, papers of First Annual Conference on Personality Theory and Counseling Practice (Gainesville: University of Florida Press, fall 1959-1960), pp. 53-58.

4. Combs et al., "Florida Studies in the Helping Professions."

5. Richard Usher and John Hanke, "Third Force in Psychology and Teacher Effectiveness Research at the University of Northern Colorado," *Colorado Journal of Educational Research* 10, no. 2 (winter 1971).

6. A. W. Combs, *The Professional Education of Teachers: A Perceptual View of Teacher Preparation* (Boston: Allyn & Bacon, 1965).

7. Idem, "Some Basic Concepts for Teacher Education," *The Journal of Teacher Education* 23, no. 3 (fall 1972): 286-290.

8. A. W. Combs et al., *The Professional Education of Teachers: A Humanistic Approach to Teacher Preparation*, 2d ed. (Boston: Allyn & Bacon, 1974).

9. Combs et al., "Florida Studies in the Helping Professions."

10. Combs et al., *The Professional Education of Teachers: A Humanistic Approach to Teacher Education*, p. 9.

11. Robert Blume, "Humanizing Teacher Behavior," *Phi Delta Kappan* (March 1971): 411-415.

Part 4
Competency Evaluation

14. Assessment in Teacher Education: Notes from the Competency Orientation

Bruce Joyce

Recently there have been a number of excellent papers written about assessment in teacher education. These reflect a resurgence of interest both in the technology of assessment[1] and in the major issues surrounding it since the current reform movement in teacher education (the competency based teacher education movement) has gathered momentum, creating several difficult problems. The assessment problems associated with competency based teacher education come in two categories. One has to do with assessing the competency orientation itself, that is, developing a data base that will help us judge the productivity of the competency orientation as compared with competing ones. The other category is the broad area of assessment *within* the competency orientation. It includes within-program assessments (assessment of components and units of components within programs) and between-program assessments (comparison of programs and program orientations, as well as the attempt to determine principles on which programs and elements of programs can be reliably built).

This chapter was to be concerned primarily with the problems of assessment *within* the competency orientation, dealing with the problem of assessing the competency orientation itself in only a general way. However, it has become evident that the comparative assessment of the CBTE approach is not only difficult, but is a controversial and value-laden area as well. Readers who are not afficionados of the competency orientation are probably more concerned with assessing it as a general approach than they are with the within-program technology. Furthermore, my stance on comparing the competency orientation with other orientations toward training has a preemptive character, and I would like it criticized as closely as possible. Hence this chapter is largely a look at the problem of comparing CBTE with other approaches. At the end I turn to some of the issues involved in within-CBTE assessment.

COMPETENCY BASED TEACHER EDUCATION AND ITS ALTERNATIVES

My position is that it is simply not possible to compare the competency orientation with any of the three most common competitor approaches to the education of teachers (the ones from which the bulk of comparator exemplars come). This is because it does not seem worthwhile to compare programs that have vastly different goals and means—each intending to produce a completely different kind of teacher and to use very different avenues for training. In other words, although we can with some precision describe several orientations to the preparation of teachers, their goals are so far apart and the means they recommend are basically so different that the products are not comparable. The suggestion most frequently offered is that we should compare the graduates of the differently oriented programs. My response is that we cannot do this because the basic assumption is that the teacher will work in completely different ways and under completely different conditions. We would not want a comparison to be made under conditions or criteria that disadvantage the graduates of any one of the competing approaches. The competency orientation differs philosophically from competing orientations to such an extent that its graduates should not be measured by the same criteria; its conceptions of education, teaching, and the nature of what constitutes acceptable knowledge about teaching effectiveness are fundamentally different from those of the competing orientations.

The three major approaches competing with the competency orientation at this time are (1) the classical or traditional orientation, (2) the academic orientation, and (3) the phenomenological approach. What are the goals and means of these competing orientations? Why are they so different from competency based teacher education as to resist empirical comparison?

The classical teacher education program is made up of sets of courses in the social foundations, the subject disciplines, and curriculum and methods, accompanied by observation and participation in classrooms and followed by student teaching or internship.[2]

The academically oriented approach is exemplified by the master of arts in teaching programs and includes programs for preparation of secondary teachers in many of the major universities.[3] These programs consist largely of preparation in the academic disciplines, a very brief exposure to methods and curriculum in the area of teaching specialty followed by a fairly short internship or student teaching.

The chief spokesman for the *phenomenological approach* has been Arthur Combs.[4] Combs and his associates begin with the stance that teaching is a process of self-actualization. The teacher and the student are equals in a learning situation in which they work out their educational lives together, with the teacher in a counseling relationship to the student. The counseling process is idiosyncratic to the counselor, for it is an expression of his unique personality. The counseling relationship itself is a product of the unique personalities of both the counselor and the student.

The competency orientation begins with a definition of the role of the teacher and expresses this role in terms of a set of interrelated competencies—a functioning model of the teacher. It is assumed by most advocates that the competency stance can embrace a wide variety of teacher roles (including the teacher as academician and the teacher as counselor). Where the approach differs from the classical, academic, and phenomenological is that the competencies are specified *beforehand* and that a *precise* working model of the teacher will be identified. Thus it is possible to evaluate the competency orientation by (1) providing a situation in which the teacher can practice that role and (2) constructing criterion measures both of the *process* of his performance and of the *product*—that is, the effect on children. In other words, competency based teacher education specifies the *conditions* of teaching, the *role* of the teacher, and the *competencies* that are components of that role. Assessment can be made by creating those conditions, presenting the teacher with professional role tasks in that setting, and observing his behavior. This kind of assessment is not possible under any of the three competing orientations, for in each of them the teacher is seen as a *unique* operator. This is why they cannot be compared with the competency orientation on an equal footing against the same criteria. For different reasons, each concept of teaching takes a stance that is antithetical to the definition of standard competencies or ways of assessing them. The *classical orientation* is most common, and we begin with it.

The Classical Orientation

Until very recently, teacher education in the United States has been guided by a very broad conception of the Teacher. The graduate of teacher training institutions has been conceived of as a liberally-educated general practitioner who should be able to use a large number of approaches to achieve a great number of school objectives and aims with a great variety of children. Given such a broad conception of the teacher, it is understandable that certification became the granting of a very general license for educational practice. The existing elementary license permits a teacher to teach almost any kind of child several subject matters in rural, urban, or suburban schools. The secondary licenses are somewhat more subject specific, but otherwise unrestricted.

Operating from this orientation, the tendency in teacher training programs has been to avoid sharply defined specifications of what a prospective teacher should learn and to favor instead the acquisition of general knowledge about education, subject matter and methods of teaching. This was expected to form a general reservoir which the teacher could draw on to solve the myriad problems of his broad role. In addition to seeking these broad (and often vague) goals, the form of teacher training employed by colleges has been indirect and not very well integrated. Courses in the philosophical, social and psychological foundations were designed to provide a general knowledge from which teachers could draw to solve particular educational problems. Surveys of methods oriented the student to general approaches to teaching various subjects. Courses in subject matter provided substance to be taught. And finally, a field apprenticeship to an experienced teacher was supposed to provide knowledge of the real world of teaching and an opportunity to apply what had been learned in all of the preceding areas. But the learning of subject matter, method, philosophy and psychology had been accomplished under conditions far removed from their use in teaching. Thus while student teaching provided a good place to become generally socialized to the classroom, it was overly distanced from the remainder of teacher education. Hence it did not really provide the opportunity to apply what had been learned previously but became an independent course in classroom teaching. Moreover, apprenticeship in classrooms also proved to be a difficult avenue for learning specific competencies not prominent in the style of the cooperating teacher. But, perhaps more important, capping off teacher training with apprenticeship exerted a very stifling and conservative influence on new entrants into the profession by socializing the new teachers into the ways of the older ones.[5]

Thus, the teacher is seen as a unique problem-solver adapting to his situation and making decisions appropriate to the situation. The apprenticeship in traditional schools is congruent with the assumption of traditional programs that the teacher should be able to work in the standard classroom situation. Within the classroom, his competence is to be manifested in the ways that he solves the problems of his relatively unique situation. Since teaching situations are different, the expression of competence is different for each teacher at each point in time.

The style of implementing classical programs has matched in action the individualistic problem-solving approach these programs expected their product to use.

The approaches taken within the components of the traditional programs have differed considerably. Instructors have been relatively free to create courses according to their likes and academic strengths. Cooperating teachers have tended to control the conditions of the student teaching experience, with the effect that these conditions also varied widely. Consistent with their general concept of the teacher as individualist, the traditional programs do not usually have standardized program components. Different instructors and differing student teaching conditions have resulted in many program variants. Quality control has been a matter of faculty initiative rather than of standardized monitoring procedures.

The use of indirect training to develop an idiosyncratic problem-solver combined with the nonstandardization of components and quality control results in a very hard-to-define entity, even though there *is* a distinctive, shared character to the programs. And (if we are to believe the recent empirical studies of teaching behavior), rather than becoming individualistic problem-solvers, these teachers show remarkable similarity in teaching styles and very little ability to set learning objectives, select instructional methods, diagnose learning difficulties, or assess progress![6]

The view of the teacher as a nonstandard operative combines with the contradictory tendency of the graduates of these programs to behave in quite similar ways to create a very difficult assessment problem. Thus far, research into the effectiveness of these teachers has been inconclusive.

The fruitlessness of the effort is exemplified by the long years of research attempting to identify the relationships between characteristics of teachers trained by that approach and growth by children. Essentially, the studies that Rosenshine[7] analyzed so thoroughly have been studies of the graduates of these programs. Rosenshine found that studies of teaching have not located any definitive characteristics of teachers or teaching styles that are associated with learning by students. His analysis supports that of Gage,[8] who holds that the attempt to study the general problem-solver teacher is fruitless, because that conception of the teacher is too broad and is made up of too many undefined and unstudied competencies to be meaningfully related to any pupil-growth criteria.

The situation is complicated by the close ties between classical teacher education programs and the traditional bureaucratic model of schooling, which has supported a teacher role best filled by a very direct, convergent teaching style. The vast number of studies of teaching made during the last decade indicate that graduates of teacher education programs have hewed to a directive recitation style for the most part, with perhaps 5 percent of the teachers manifesting styles different from a recitation pattern. That is, most of the teachers trained in the traditional methodologies have practiced the language game of the classroom much as Bellack described it.[9] This "game" is the quintessence of a bureaucratic administration of education to children. If education becomes a routine administration of materials, then individual differences among teachers probably would not have much effect on learning. The necessary competencies are rudimentary; almost everyone can master them to an adequate level. The trouble is that it is simply an inadequate model of education if one believes that a proper education requires a range of environments for children to respond to.[10]

The classical model of education depends for clinical training on its laboratory components (student teaching and internship). As the Brown[11] and Seperson[12] studies have shown, a prominent effect of student teaching is what Hunt[13] refers to as a "funneling" of teaching styles into the recitative pattern—a *reduction* of individual differences among teachers. As indicated earlier, this is contrary to the increase of variability that is the hoped-for result of the indirect training employed in the belief that teaching is best accomplished as an individual problem-solving activity rather than as an activity based on standard competencies.

Thus, the classical teacher education curriculum presents two obstacles to comparative assessment. One is the general nature of its model and the consequent idiosyncratic conception of teaching. The other is the apparent cooption of classical teacher education by the bureaucratic mold of the school and its corollary, the recitation method.

The Phenomenological Orientation

The phenomenological approach is even more difficult to assess than the classical one because Combs and others of his orientation take the stance that teaching is such a personal matter that there can be no such thing as a set of competencies defined in advance for any set of teachers. If teaching works itself out idiosyncratically and is a consequence of a personal interaction between a teacher who is actualizing *himself* and a pupil who is actualizing *himself,* then the problem of assessment actually defies solution by definition. There can be no standard measure of self-actualization because it is a very personal thing. There can be no standard measure of teaching competence because that is the ability to enter into a unique relationship with a student. There can be no standard measure of student performance because that is idiosyncratic both to the student and to the teacher. Thus the product of a phenomenological approach cannot be compared in any way to the product of the competency orientation, which assumes that the ends and means of education can be determined in advance and the roles and thus the competencies of the teacher can also be derived in advance (from an analysis of those roles). Combs and his associates oppose the competency based teacher education movement precisely because it depends on the selection of teaching competencies.[14]

The Academic Orientation

The academic (master of arts in teaching) approach also defies the notion that there is such a thing as clinical competency in teaching. Competency in the subject discipline, an intellectual orientation, and the desire to practice that orientation with like-minded students seem to be the qualities most sought for. The teacher, as a scholar, would not simply *administer* academic curriculums but also, acquainted as he is with the most rigorous orientations of the disciplines, would initiate academic inquiry with students. The result would be almost as idiosyncratic as the results of the phenomenological orientation. However, the master of arts in teaching orientation has a relatively clear conception of the teacher-scholar; its programs can probably be compared at least on general terms with like-minded CBTE programs. The arguments against the competency orientation by academic professors suggest that this would not please many of them. Broudy, for example, has argued that the CBTE programs are necessarily atheoretical—that is, they are not amenable to any role for academic theory in teaching. From his stance, any definition of competency in terms of mastery of theory is questionable. Apparently Broudy[15] (who is the spokesman of many from the academic and classical orientations) believes that the working out of theory into practice is a reflective-adaptive process that defies explication in before-the-fact competency terms. Broudy feels that the emphasis by CBTE proponents on observable, assessable competencies is "naive." He objects to the "reduction" of teaching to overt performances which a teacher can "execute on demand."

Shugrue's "Performance Based Teacher Education and the Subject Matter Fields" expresses this point in some ways even more strongly than Broudy. Shugrue feels that the "intelligent, humane use of human resources to foster individual student learning" is not expressible in competency terms.[16] He worries that the use of systems planning will result in a focus on the trivial competencies, for "the most important attitudes and values developed through a liberal education resist such codification and evaluation."[17]

By now it must be clear that I despair of meaningful comparative research. The academically oriented tend to believe that only what is trivial can be defined and assessed in competency terms. The phenomenologists see the world as a collection of unique selves, creating their own realities and, through teaching, creating unique relationships that facilitate individual development and fulfillment. Only competency based teacher education proponents operate in an assumptive world which embraces the creation of clear-cut standards against which comparisons can be made.

The commonly made suggestion that we limit ourselves to comparing graduates on pupil growth criteria is not philosophically tenable.

To do so fairly, the other orientations would have to assent to the competency based teacher education mode of assessment criteria.

Although there would be excessively great difficulties in comparing the four orientations in the area of pupil growth (the effects the graduates have on the learning of children), it definitely would be worthwhile to describe the behavior of graduates of the various programs in the classroom to discover whether they are significantly different from one another. If they did indeed behave differently, then it might be worthwhile to proceed to measures of student behaviors or to a series of studies to determine the possession of competencies. Schalock[18] has provided an excellent paradigm for engaging in comparative research, which I believe would be extremely effective if it began with descriptive comparisons of the teachers rather than with an effectiveness comparison. Traditionally, the first step in this type of research is to describe the hoped-for behavior of the graduates and then construct a reliable instrument for determining whether these behaviors occur in the graduates of some programs more than others. I believe that this methodology is more amenable to the competency orientation than to others and should probably be avoided. (One possibly acceptable variant would be to have program designers from each orientation decide how best to analyze the behavior of their graduates and then use the four instruments that would result to describe the behavior of a sample of graduates from each of the four program types.)

However, since the important question would be, "Do the graduates of the four program types behave differently?" the best methodology might be the broadest and most open-ended. I suggest that programs of the four types be selected and that several of their recent graduates be identified who were apparently responsive to and compatible with the program orientation. Five teams of microethnologists like Smith[19] would study the graduates. One team would make descriptive studies of graduates from each program. These would result in comparisons from the same base (Study One). The other four teams would each concentrate on one program type (Study Two). In Study One, hypotheses would be tested about differences between the behavior of graduates of the program types by direct comparison. In Study Two, we would test whether the ethnological descriptions would differ—whether the differences in graduates caused the ethnologists to describe their behavior in different terms.

Needless to say, if graduates of the various orientations behaved differently, we could proceed to try to locate the effects of those differences on student behavior and, ultimately, to explore questions of student learning.

TO WHAT EXTENT MUST THE COMPETENCY ORIENTATION PROVE ITSELF BEFORE IT IS IMPLEMENTED?

Determining the effectiveness of the competency orientation on its own terms is of a critical importance which is underlined by its differences from the other orientations. Its assumption that the role of the teacher can be expressed as an interlocking network of competencies—a model of the teacher—that can prove itself in its effects on children, requires that it be susceptible to empirical tests.

There is a particularly difficult issue in the suggestion that the competency orientation should not be implemented before we know that it will produce far more effectiveness than the other orientations. Shugrue, for example, relies heavily on quotes from James Hoetker, as, "There is, to put it bluntly, no more empirical, objective evidence that the application of systems technology to instruction will contribute significantly more to improving the effectiveness or efficiency of an educational program than would the installation of an official astrologer."[20] Whatever our stance on the overall effectiveness of competency based teacher education, there is no escaping the necessity for a rigorous effort to determine the effects of components of programs and to investigate the consequences of variations within the competency orientation.

WHAT IS THE ASSUMPTIVE WORLD OF THE COMPETENCY ORIENTATION AND WHAT EVIDENCE IS THERE THAT THESE ASSUMPTIONS ARE VALID?

We have taken the position that the competency based system of teacher education consists of identifying sets of models of teachers who are capable of fulfilling various educational roles. The model has to be expressed in terms of sets of competencies for fulfilling the roles, and these are linked also to sets of instructional systems designed to enable teacher candidates to acquire those competencies and to integrate them in terms of the overall functions of the teacher. These competencies and the instructional systems need to be related to a system that assesses when teachers have acquired particular competencies as well as the integrated competence necessary to fulfill the teacher role.

Assumptions about Goals

The first assumption is that it is possible to create models of teachers in terms of sets of competencies. Some of these models might be descriptions of the competency necessary to carry out the generalist role in the self-contained classroom. Other competency definitions might add up to the role the teacher plays when he is a subject or technological specialist such as an English teacher or a teacher of media. Other models of the teacher might be parts of plans for a differentiated staffing arrangement such as those in the Parkway School at Philadelphia or any integrated educational complex embodying the newer instructional and counseling roles. A corollary assumption is that the competency orientation is philosophically pluralistic—it can embrace a vast variety of teacher models. The model of a teacher for Summerhill, for Montessori nursery schools, for academic secondary schools, etc., can all be held comfortably within the competency orientation.

The response to the suspicion that the competency orientation will produce mechanical teachers or atheoretical teachers is that this orientation is not limited to any one type of teacher. Theoretical or personalistic teachers can be expressed in competency models as comfortably as can operators of machines. The Original Bureau of Research Models[21] need only be read to establish that, at least in terms of program design, the systems approach is pluralistic.

Assumptions about Training

Competency orientation also rests on the assumption that we are able to build instructional systems that will enable teacher candidates and inservice teachers to acquire the competencies necessary to play those defined roles. Many of these competencies are complex, so it is worthwhile to consider whether we have evidence that we can train teachers to a complex competency.

Our belief is that abundant evidence exists to indicate this can be done. Part of the evidence is in the teacher training field. Popham, Baker, and their associates have demonstrated that they can teach teachers to define behavioral objectives, select learning alternatives, and assess learning outcomes, and that those three types of competencies indeed result in increased pupil learning.[22]

Over the past ten years McDonald, Allen, and their associates have demonstrated that they are able to teach teachers to acquire teaching skills and complex teaching strategies.[23] Their work has been followed by that of Borg and Goll,[24] who have also demonstrated that it is possible, through self-contained, self-administering instructional systems, to train teachers to acquire both simple teaching skills and complex teaching strategies. Flanders has demonstrated that interaction analysis systems can be used to teach teachers to study their own behavior and improve their competency as teachers.[25] Joyce, Weil, Wald, and their colleagues[26] have demonstrated that it is possible to create instructional systems that can be used to permit teachers at the preservice and inservice levels to acquire complex models of teaching representing a variety of frames of reference for teaching and learning. Teachers representing many "natural styles" can use these instructional systems to acquire the new models of teaching, and they can do this even in classrooms where cooperating teachers do not either model or employ the kinds of behavior that the teachers are trying to acquire.[27] Joyce, Weil, and Wald have successfully built instructional systems representing personalistic views of teaching, as have Ivey and others.

Thus there is positive evidence that it is possible to build instructional systems that can be used to enable teachers to acquire teaching skills and strategies that they otherwise (i.e., without training) rarely display in the classroom.

Industrial and military applications of training psychology have resulted in similar findings. Simulators have been built in which astronauts are trained to the competencies necessary to permit them to go to the moon and return. Similar training systems enable pilots to learn the techniques necessary to fly very complex aircraft from place to place. Instructional systems have been developed which train military personnel whose jobs are highly complex, such as submarine commanders and tank commanders, as well as industrial personnel who engage in a wide variety of difficult roles.[28]

The Payoff for Children

Will the competency orientation result in increased learning to children? The answer is that we will not know for sure whether children can learn better from teachers who are trained to be competent than from those not so trained until we have studied the results for a long period of time. Teacher education is in the same position that medicine was before the Flexner report came out. Before the Flexner report was implemented, physicians were not universally trained to any particular set of competencies. Following the report, medical schools tried to teach physicians the knowledge and skills that would be most likely to improve the health of their clients. Over a long period of time it has turned out that the health of the American people improved following implementation of the Flexner report. Not all aspects of health have improved—cigarette smoking, stress, and other factors have actually increased deaths by heart disease despite increased competence by physicians. However, death from wounds received in battle has decreased enormously because physicians know how to handle conditions of shock, how to prevent infection, and how to make other applications of the physiological sciences to reduce human mortality. Before the training of physicians, many persons died of infection following operations; now death from infection following surgical procedure is almost unheard of. Thus it turned out that the competency orientation in the training of physicians has paid off. The assumption that competency trained teachers will benefit children is basic to the orientation, but the payoff will be gradual.

As was stated earlier, the issues over whether the competency orientation has to be proved generally effective before it can be implemented and the difficulties of comparing competency based teacher education to other types of orientations do not relieve the designers of CBTE programs from the responsibility of assessment within the orientation.

ASSESSMENT WITHIN THE COMPETENCY ORIENTATION

All the existing designs of teacher education programs that have been made from the competency orientation are exceedingly complex. Many have had a dozen major components, containing altogether as many as three thousand program elements or modules.[29] The competencies developed by the units of the programs eventually have to find expression in terms of ability to fill a given teaching role—a role in which the competencies have to operate in an integrated manner. Ultimately, assessment has to speak to the effectiveness of individual program elements (does the module achieve the objective?), to the integration of competencies (the ability to fill a teaching role), and to overall program effectiveness (power to train).

Whereas nearly all efforts at assessment have in the past been oriented toward the study of the teacher—searching out the most and least effective teachers—the focus in competency based teacher education assessment is the *program* itself. The program has to be assessed—in terms of particular elements, components, and the totality —in order to build a reliable CBTE system whose output of competencies can be assessed in its turn. If there is to be really meaningful within-program assessment, an assessment system has to be built that will yield data about components, units, or modules within components and the program as a whole, all on an ongoing basis which is linked to program renewal and redefinition.

There are a number of dimensions to this task. The first is to identify the types of competencies that make up the model of the teacher under the competency orientation. The ultimate competence is to carry out the role of the teacher as specified; and the performance of the role may not vary below certain minimum levels of performance. That is, we would expect a teacher who has completed the program to be in the same professional shape, comparatively speaking, as a pilot who had finished a course to prepare him to take modern commercial airliners across the ocean. We would not expect to license a pilot who could not get us from Kennedy to Heathrow. Nor would we permit any latitude; that is, we would not want *any* pilots who could not meet the minimum criterion, given reasonable conditions of the airplane and the weather. We would expect that above that level there would be a variation in competence, but we would not want to license anyone who was even close to the minimum level— that is, anyone who could just barely get us from Kennedy to Heathrow would be disqualified! We want people to be so far above the minimum criterion for getting the job done that there is 100 percent probability that they will get the job done *all* of the time. Marginal performers get the job done most of the time but not all of the time; just as we do not want to land in the Irish Sea within the tolerance of our licensing procedure for pilots, neither do we want children to end up academically maimed or emotionally damaged within the limits of our teaching license. Therefore, performance means performance well above minimum criterion levels. If our program were effective, we would expect all of the graduates to be able to carry out the role so well that research into their individual differences would tell us relatively little about which was the most effective. Given any reasonable educational objective within the scope of their training, we would expect them all to achieve it, just as, given a reasonable destination, we expect every pilot to achieve that.

Under previous orientations to teacher training, general training was first conducted and then programs of research were developed to try to learn who were the more effective teachers. Under the competency orientation program, designers decide on the roles they wish teachers to fulfill and then attempt to construct programs to train teachers to carry out those roles. Assessment is focused on the program elements rather than on the teacher.

Beyond the testing of the units themselves, it is unlikely that much useful data will come from isolated studies of the effectiveness of program elements or components. Very few modules and only a few major components are likely to account for a significant proportion of teacher behavior. However, the competency based teacher education format requires and makes relatively easy the testing of units (and their revision or replacement).[30] The most important area to assess, however, is whether the program prepares teachers for specifically defined roles.

MODULAR TESTING OR THE
DEVELOPMENT OF PRINCIPLES

There is a fork in the road in the near future for the assessment community as it approaches the problem of the competency orientation. It is possible to build an assessment system around the questions asked that are specific to program elements and to the integration of the competencies learned in the elements. Such an assessment system would have immediate use for tracking the progress of students and testing the strength of component elements.

However, as both McDonald and Schalock point out, it is far more important to search for trustworthy principles that can be used to guide future programs. Assessment systems can be designed to search for principles just as easily as they can be designed to test only specific elements of a program. For example, variations in feedback, modeling, task complexity, staff size, group size, type of feedback, etc., can be researched if the assessment system is designed to permit them to be studied conveniently. It is important to establish principles for several reasons. In addition to the obvious ones that are needed to learn what will work in teacher education, there is the need to establish the reliability of elements so that we do not have to test every student's acquisition of every behavior that is specified in the program. If we have reliable principles on which to build program components, then we can predict that trainees will achieve certain levels of performance if components are built around those principles. We do not necessarily have to assess its outcome every time it is used or for every trainee within a program. This is an extremely important issue when one considers the amount of testing that was projected for the original Bureau of Research models. In a complex program in which 2,500 or 3,000 competencies are specified and are linked to instructional devices of some sort, a student could be exposed to eight or nine assessments a day, a level far beyond what is necessary or could be tolerated. A sampling is far more reasonable and becomes increasingly feasible as principles are established on which components can be developed and implemented.

NOTES FOR CHAPTER 14

1. N. L. Gage, "An Analytic Approach to Research on Instructional Methods," *Phi Delta Kappan* 49, no. 10 (June 1968): 601-606; F. J. McDonald, *Problems in Assessing Teacher Effectiveness* (Washington, D.C.: AACTE, forthcoming); W. James Popham, "Identification and Assessment of Minimal Competencies for Objectives-Oriented Teacher Education Programs," paper presented at the AERA conference, New Orleans, 1973; H. Del Schalock, Bert Y. Kersh, and Jesse H. Garrison, "From Commitment to Practice in Assessing the Outcomes of Teaching," in *Competency Based Teacher Education*, ed. Theodore Andrews (Albany, N.Y.: Multi-State Consortium on Performance-Based Education, 1974); Richard L. Turner, "Levels of Criteria," Appendix A, in *The Power of Competency Based Teacher Education*, ed. Benjamin Rosner (Boston: Allyn & Bacon, 1972).

2. Margaret Lindsey, ed., *New Horizons for the Teaching Profession* (Washington, D.C.: NCTEPS, NEA, 1961).

3. Michael F. Shugrue, *Performance Based Teacher Education and the Subject Matter Fields* (Washington, D.C.: AACTE, 1973).

4. Arthur Combs, *The Professional Education of Teachers: A Perceptual View of Teacher Education* (Allyn & Bacon, 1965). In chapter 13 Combs and Kinzer describe his basic assumptions and the resulting preparation program.

5. Bruce Joyce, Jonas Soltis, and Marsha Weil, *Design Alternatives for Teacher Education*, PBTE series (Washington, D.C.: AACTE, forthcoming).

6. James Hoetker and William P. Ahlbrand, Jr., "The Persistence of the Recitation Method," *American Educational Research Journal* 6, no. 2 (March 1969): 145-168.

7. Barak Rosenshine and Norma Furst, "Research on Teacher Performance Criteria," in *Teacher Education: A Symposium*, ed. B. O. Smith (Englewood Cliffs, N.J.: Prentice-Hall, 1971).

8. N. L. Gage, *Teacher Effectiveness and Teacher Education* (Palo Alto, Calif.: Pacific Books, 1972).

9. Arno Bellack, *The Language of the Classroom* (New York: Teachers College Press, 1969).

10. Bruce Joyce and Marsha Weil, *Models of Teaching* (Englewood Cliffs, N.J.: Prentice-Hall, 1972).

11. Clark Brown, "The Initial Teaching Style" (Ph.D. diss., Teachers College, Columbia University, 1967).

12. Marvin Seperson, "The Influence of the Teaching Styles of Cooperating Teachers on Student Teachers" (Ph.D. diss., Teachers College, Columbia University, 1969).

13. David E. Hunt, *Matching Models in Education* (Toronto: Ontario Institute for Studies in Education, 1971).

14. Combs, *The Professional Education of Teachers: A Perceptual View of Teacher Education*.

15. Harry Broudy, *A Critique of Performance Based Teacher Education* (Washington: AACTE, 1972).

16. Shugrue, *Performance Based Teacher Education and the Subject Matter Fields*.

17. Ibid.

18. Schalock, Kersh, and Garrison, "From Commitment to Practice in Assessing the Outcomes of Teaching."

19. Louis Smith and William Geoffrey, *The Complexities of the Urban Classroom* (New York: Holt, Rinehart & Winston, 1968).

20. James Hoetker, *Systems, Systems Approaches and the Teacher* (Urbana, Ill.: National Council of Teachers of English, 1972), pp. 27 and 28 as quoted by Shugrue in *Performance Based Teacher Education and the Subject Matter Fields*.

21. Bruce Joyce, "Variations on a System Theme," in *Perspectives on Reform in Teacher Education*, ed. Bruce Joyce and Marsha Weil (Englewood Cliffs, N.J.: Prentice-Hall, 1972).

22. W. James Popham and Eva I. Baker, *Systematic Instruction* (Englewood Cliffs, N.J.: Prentice-Hall, 1970); W. James Popham, "Performance Tests of Teaching Proficiency: Rationale, Development and Validation," *American Educational Research Journal* 8, no. 1 (January 1971): 105-117.

23. F. J. McDonald and D. W. Allen, *Training Effects of Feedback and Modeling Procedures on Teacher Performance*, final report, USOE project OE-6-10-0178 (Stanford, Calif.: Stanford University, 1967).

24. W. B. Borg, M. Kelley, P. Langer, and M. Goll, *The Mini-Course: A Microteaching Approach to Teacher Education* (New York: Macmillan, 1970).

25. N. Flanders, *Analyzing Teaching Behavior* (Palo Alto, Calif.: Addison-Wesley, 1971).

26. Bruce Joyce, Marsha Weil, and Rhoada Wald, "Models of Teaching as a Framework for Teacher Education: An Evaluation of Instructional Systems," *Interchange* (summer 1973).

27. Ibid.
28. R. Glasser, *Training Research and Education* (Pittsburgh, Pa.: The University of Pittsburgh Press, 1962); Karl Smith and Mary F. Smith, *Cybernetic Principles of Learning and Educational Design* (New York: Holt, Rinehart & Winston, 1966).
29. Joyce, "Variations on a Systems Theme"; W. Robert Houston and Robert B. Howsam, *Competency Based Teacher Education* (Palo Alto, Calif.: Science Research Associates, 1972).
30. M. Vere DeVault, Norman Dodl, Bruce Joyce, and H. Del Schalock, "Closing the Knowledge Gap: A Proposal for a Long-range Program on the Efficacy and Design of Competency Based Teacher Education" (Tallahassee: Florida State University, National Consortium of CBE Centers, 1973).

15. Notes on a Model of Assessment That Meets the Requirements of CBTE

H. Del Schalock

In the first of a series of publications by AACTE on the nature of competency based teacher education and its contribution to the education profession, Stanley Elam has set in clear perspective the dependence of the movement on the evolution of a science and technology of assessment. While his definition of assessment is more limited than the one proposed in this chapter, he states the case well:

The overriding problem before which the others pale to insignificance is that of the adequacy of measurement instruments and procedures. PBTE can only be successful if there are adequate means to assess the competency of the student. The bulk of the effort in establishing PBTE is most likely to go into the development of new instructional materials, into working out arrangements with the bursar and registrar, into devising ways for practicing teachers and administrators to share decision making, into moving the program into the field, and—most important of all—into developing ways to use faculty and librarians most effectively in the operation of unconventional modules in a conventional system. But, when all this is done an institution will still not have moved beyond current conventional grading procedures unless new methods are found for assessing the complex cognitive and affective objectives which are such an essential part of the training of teachers . . . this is the foundation stone on which the program rests.[1]

A similar point of view has been taken by the Committee on National Program Priorities in Teacher Education,[2] the Florida Department of Education (the Florida Program for Improving the Training, Evaluation and Licensure of Educational Personnel, 1971), and others intimately associated with the CBTE movement.[3]

As of fall 1973, however, the idea of assessment as the foundation stone of the CBTE movement was not widely understood, or if it was it was not translated well into program operation. Few "competency based" programs employ any but the most rudimentary assessment procedures, and fewer still have anything that could be called an assessment system at all. As yet there simply is no sign of an emerging technology of assessment that meets the demands of the competency based teacher education movement.

While the general neglect of the assessment function within CBTE is beginning to prove embarrassing, a greater threat to the ultimate success of the movement is the relatively limited concept that most persons in the field have of that function. By and large the literature of CBTE tends to treat the problem of assessment as if it were equivalent to the problem of measuring teaching performance or "teaching competency." Given the emphasis that has been placed on the concepts of demonstrated performance, performance criteria, and the like within the CBTE literature, this is understandable, but it does not serve well the long-term needs of the movement.

To be sure, measurement problems within CBTE are great. This is particularly so when performance criteria are defined in terms of the demonstration of complex teaching skills under ongoing classroom conditions (Turner's criterion level 3), or the demonstrated ability to bring about short- or long-term learning outcomes in children (Turner's criterion levels 2 and 1). (On Turner's criterion levels, see chapters 6 and 17 in this volume.) But no matter how complex the performance, measurement is not enough. In addition to the process of measurement *judgments* have to be made about what has been measured, and *decisions* have to be made on the basis of those judgments. Obviously, a central question is whether a particular performance meets criterion. But a host of other questions must be attended to as well, e.g., if performance does meet criterion what should be done next? And if not, what should be done next? In either case what should be done with the information about performance that has been collected? Who should see it? What form must it be in to be usable? How should it be stored?

In this writer's judgment, the issue of what to do with information once it is collected is as critical to performance based teacher education programs as the issue of what information is to be collected in the first place.

The purpose of this chapter is to call attention to the full range of assessment problems that exist in competency based teacher education, to review the progress that has been made toward resolution of these problems, and to provide in outline form a model of assessment designed to overcome them. The substance of what is proposed is based on work being done in CBTE at Oregon College of Education; the concepts, examples, and language used reflect a teacher education context. It is anticipated, however, that the model being proposed will be as applicable to competency based elementary and secondary education as it is to teacher education.

Our premise is that for an assessment system to serve well the needs of CBE and CBTE, it must be viewed as a targeted, decision-serving information system, rather than a set of procedures that measure competence. This chapter attempts to present a convincing case for this premise, and to provide a language and set of constructs for thinking about it as well as suggestions on what such an information system might look like and how it might function. Until all education personnel adopt a more critical view of the role of assessment within CBE and CBTE programs, the power of the ideas underlying those programs have little chance of being realized.

PROPOSALS TOWARD A LANGUAGE OF ASSESSMENT

The language of competency based teacher education is fraught with confusion, to the initiated as well as the uninitiated. Some writers interchange freely the terms performance and competence; others interchange the terms objectives, behavioral objectives, performance objectives, performance standards, and performance criteria; and still others interchange teacher behavior, teaching skills, and teaching competence, or define teaching competence in terms of knowledge while others define it in terms of skills or products. The overall impression gained through the literature of the field, either on first reading or after extended study, is one of massive conceptual confusion.

The language that has emerged on assessment in CBTE programs is no exception. The terms measurement, evaluation, and assessment seem to be used interchangeably, and efforts are rarely made to tie a term used to the operations that give it its meaning. A case in point is the language used by Elam in his discussion of assessment as "the foundation stone" of the CBTE movement; on page 21 of the document he refers to assessment as "the development of appropriate *measurement* instruments and procedures," and on page 22 as "the creation of adequate *evaluation* devices" (emphasis added). McDonald's discussion of the role of evaluation in CBTE programs reflects a similar undifferentiated use of terms.[4]

The model of assessment that is outlined here is based on the proposition that measurement, evaluation, and assessment are terms that stand for different sets of operations, and whose meanings and uses should reflect those differences. Technically, measurement refers to the assignment of numerals to objects or events according to rules,[5] and evaluation refers to the assignment of worth or value to objects and events according to standards.[6] These are two different matters. The collection of information about performance (measurement) involves a different set of operations than does judging whether an observed performance meets the standards set for it (evaluation). We propose that these descriptions of operations be adopted as the formal definitions for these terms as they are used in the context of CBTE.

Unlike measurement and evaluation, assessment has not received formal technical definition in the education literature. Moreover, the standard dictionary definition in no way suggests its use as a synonym for either measurement or evaluation. In Webster's 1969 College Edition of the New World Dictionary, the first definition is "to set an estimated value on (property, etc.) for taxation"; the second is "to set the amount of damages (for example, a fine)." Because of this relatively narrow dictionary definition, and because the term is commonly used in conjunction with measurement and evaluation in educational contexts, we propose that assessment assume a technical meaning that complements the existing terms of measurement and evaluation. Specifically, we propose that the term assessment be used to refer to the identification, collection, reduction, analysis, and use of information in service of targeted, adaptive decision-making.[7]

Given the definitional framework proposed assessment becomes a more inclusive term than either measurement or evaluation. In fact, it incorporates these concepts. It also reflects the basic premise of the chapter, that is, that for an assessment system to meet effectively the demands of CBTE it must function as a targeted, decision-serving information system. The proposed relationships among measurement, evaluation, and assessment are shown in Table 15:1.

Table 15:1. Operations Included in the Proposed Definitions of Measurement, Evaluation, and Assessment

Operation	Measurement	Evaluation	Assessment
Identification of data needed	x	x	x
Collection of data	x	x	x
Reduction and synthesis of data		x	x
Analysis of data in relation to standards		x	x
Analysis of factors affecting data			x
Utilization of data in making decisions			x

Some may view the distinctions among these terms as arbitrary and unnecessary, others simply as further confusing the issue. They are indeed arbitrary, and it may be that operations have been assigned incorrectly to labels, or that a better set of labels may someday be found for the operations described. But what *is* important is that, whatever these functions are called, they must be recognized and attended to by the designers of CBTE programs.[8]

THE DEMANDS ON ASSESSMENT IN CBTE PROGRAMS

Two requirements of CBTE programs encourage the view of assessment as a targeted, decision-serving information system: (1) the requirement that designated teaching competencies be demonstrated as a basis for graduation from a teacher education program, and (2) the requirement that a program be continuously adapted, updated, or "renewed" on the basis of information on cost and effectiveness.

Both requirements depend on data to be collected (measurement), judgments to be made in relation to standards held (evaluation), and utilization of the information generated through measurement and evaluation in adaptive decision-making (assessment). Both, of course, relate directly to the higher order concepts of accountability and systemic design, concepts that have been central in the competency based movement in teacher education from its beginning.[9]

For a CBTE program to meet these two requirements, three general classes of data must be available on which to make decisions: data on student competencies; data on program cost; and data on program operations. Two other conditions must be met as well. First, information must be available on the extent to which demonstrated competencies, program expenditures, and program operations comply with performance standards. Secondly, the structures and procedures established must permit an analysis of conditions that affect performance in these three areas and short- and long-term adaptive decisions made in relation to them. An outline of an assessment system that can meet such requirements is presented schematically in Figure 15:1.[10]

The implications of this view of assessment are of major consequence, and when program staff or administration consider what it will take to establish and operate such an assessment system an immediate reaction is likely to be, "It's not feasible. Even if technology were available to establish and operate this system, the resources required would be beyond the reach of most if not all teacher education programs in the nation. Find a simpler model of assessment!"

This response is understandable. Developing measures of program cost and effectiveness, in addition to measures of teaching competency, is a lot to ask. Developing performance standards and formalized decision structures and procedures as well approaches the unreasonable. However, a lesser view of what CBTE requires by way of assessment denies the integrity of the whole idea of competency based education and teacher education. In our judgment, a compromise of that magnitude and consequence cannot be tolerated.

AVAILABILITY OF ASSESSMENT SYSTEMS THAT MEET THE DEMANDS OF CBTE

As of now probably no competency based teacher education program in the United States has an assessment system in operation that

Figure 15:1. An Assessment System That Can Meet the Information and Decision Requirements of CBTE Programs

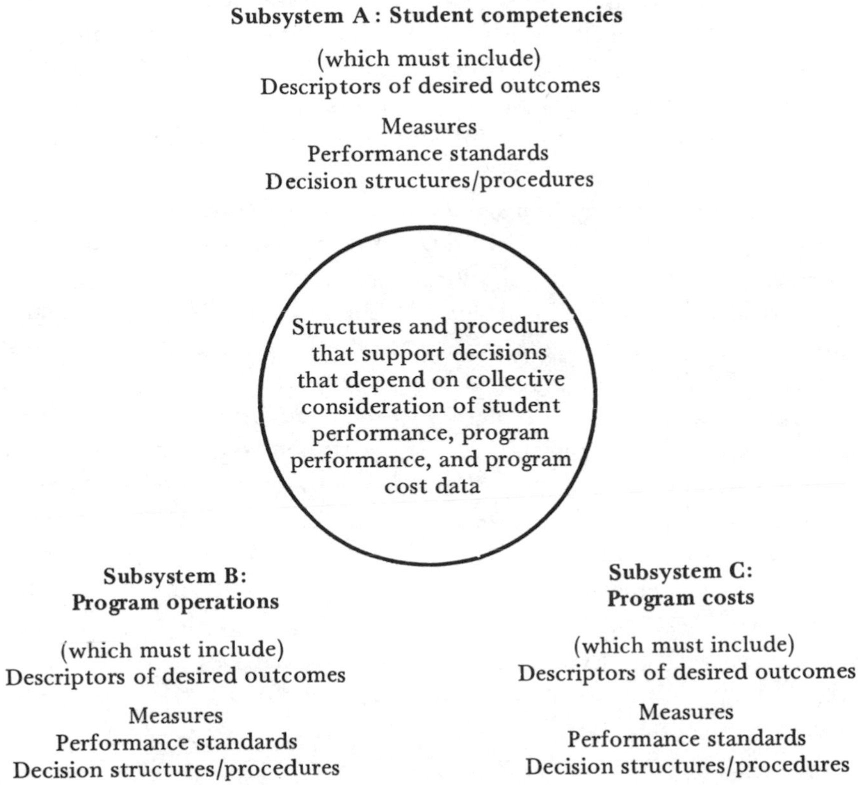

Subsystem A: Student competencies

(which must include)
Descriptors of desired outcomes

Measures
Performance standards
Decision structures/procedures

Structures and procedures
that support decisions
that depend on collective
consideration of student
performance, program
performance, and program
cost data

Subsystem B:
Program operations

(which must include)
Descriptors of desired outcomes

Measures
Performance standards
Decision structures/procedures

Subsystem C:
Program costs

(which must include)
Descriptors of desired outcomes

Measures
Performance standards
Decision structures/procedures

could anywhere near meet the specifications we have outlined. In fact, it is probably fair to say that no more than half-a-dozen CBTE programs have in operation, in other than rudimentary form, even one of the assessment subsystems suggested in Figure 15:1. This is even the case in assessing teaching competency, the recognized "cornerstone" of the competency based movement from its beginning.

Some would hold this to be too harsh a judgment, pointing to programs that have elaborate lists of behavioral objectives and identifying those that faithfully collect performance data in relation to these objectives. They would argue that such programs do in fact have the assessment of student competence well in hand.

In one sense this is true, *but only if competence is defined in terms of knowledge or simple teaching skills.* When competency is defined in terms of complex teaching skills (Turner's criterion levels 4 and 3), or the outcomes of teaching (Turner's criterion levels 2 or 1), it is apparent that fully functioning assessment systems are not as yet available. In fact, as soon as the definition of teaching competency extends beyond the knowledge of simple skill level, the matter of assessment becomes sufficiently complex that it demands more of the technology of measurement and evaluation than the technology is at present able to give.[11]

While assessment systems that focus on teaching competency are still in their infancy, even less development has been carried out on assessing program operation and program cost. This is puzzling, for a great deal of work has been done in the so-called "formative evaluation" methodologies that should be directly applicable to the assessment of CBTE program operations. The work that has been done in recent years on program planning and budgeting systems (PPBS) should be equally applicable to the assessment of program costs and to the calculation of cost-benefit relationships. In spite of the availability of such closely related methodologies, however, the writer knows of no competency based teacher education program today that systematically collects data on program effectiveness and cost; the conclusion follows that at present there probably *is* no CBTE program that systematically adapts program structure, content, or operation on the basis of data on program effectiveness and cost.*

---

*The importance of distinguishing among these three foci of assessment lies in the fact that the nature of measurement, evaluation, and information utilization varies as the substance of content (focus) of an assessment system varies. A system for assessing student performance, for example, must contain measures of teaching competency, standards for judging the acceptability of competency demonstrations, and decision rules for program placement or instructional planning depending on level of demonstrated competence. A system for assessing program performance, on the other hand, must possess the means of obtaining data on the problems and satisfactions encountered in program operation, the weaknesses and strengths of program operation, and suggestions as to how a program might be improved. A system for assessing program costs, of course, contains still different features. Because of this kind of variability the designers of assessment systems need to differentiate clearly as to the focus or target of a system, to be able to build into that system the content and sensitivities required to make it work for its users in the ways it is intended to work.

CHARACTERISTICS OF AN ASSSESSMENT SYSTEM THAT MEETS THE DEMANDS OF CBTE PROGRAMS*

Given the distinctions that have been made and the general point of view they carry about assessment, it is possible to sketch in outline form a model of assessment that meets the demands of CBTE. The model is based on the assessment system that has been developed and tested at Oregon College of Education. The model is theoretically grounded in the work of Williamson on systems theory and institutional change,[12] and has received additional testing within the contexts of Oregon elementary and secondary schools (John Adams High School in Portland; Crescent Valley High School and Hoover Elementary School in Corvallis). Although the proposed model extends somewhat beyond what has been implemented or tested thus far, the extension is minimal.

Three broad features of the model are described: its general characteristics, its major components, and the functions that need to be performed in operating an assessment system based on the model. Following the description of the model, attention is directed briefly to a strategy for integrating assessment and instruction within an on-going CBTE program. The chapter closes with a description of the assessment systems that have been developed at OCE as both an extension and test of the proposed model.

An Assessment System as a Decision-Serving Information System

One essential characteristic of the proposed model of assessment is its likeness to a total information system. Operationally, an assessment system that serves decision-making must contain specifications on what is to be assessed, standards by which to judge what is assessed, who is to be involved in making judgments about performance as it relates to standards, and rules that spell out what is to occur if performance standards are or are not met. In addition the system must have the data generation, reduction, storage, retrieval, and distribution capability implied by such specifications, including

*The work that is reported in this section was supported in part by the Teacher Corps and the National Center for the Improvement of Educational Systems, U.S. Office of Education. Intellectual debt is owed my colleagues at Teaching Research and OCE, Drs. John Williamson, Bert Kersh, and Jesse Garrison.

the decision-making structures needed to match data, time, people, decisions, and decision schedules. Finally, an assessment system that serves decision-making must contain a well-worked-out design that permits it to interact functionally with the program it supports and with the elements of the program that in turn support it. Without this close articulation, either the program will function in splendid isolation, or the assessment system will fail to function because of its isolation.

An Assessment System as a Targeted Information System

It is necessary to be clear about, and continuously reaffirm, the focus or target of an information system that is being developed. As mentioned earlier, this is because the nature of measurement, evaluation, and information utilization varies as the focus or target of an assessment system varies. Also, it is remarkably easy to seek information that will never be used in decision-making. For an assessment system to be functional and minimally efficient it must be designed with a clear view as to the kind of decisions that are to be made, the kind of information that is needed to make them, and who will need what information in what form and on what timelines for decisions to get made.

We have found in our work at OCE that targeting a subsystem of the overall assessment system on student performance, another on program performance, and still another on program cost provides a structure that permits the ordering of decisions, data, etc., into reasonably cohesive and coherent units. This is not to say that all decisions within each subsystem are the same, nor are all data collected in support of the various decisions within a subsystem comparable. However, *families* of decisions and related data sets can be identified within a subsystem that have considerably more in common than the decisions and data sets that appear in one of the other subsystems. Such commonality within subsystems makes the task of their development and operation considerably more manageable than might otherwise be the case.

An Assessment System as an "Open" Information System

Just as CBTE programs are to be continuously adaptive, so must the assessment system that supports such programs also be adaptive. In the language of systems theory, an assessment system must be an "open" system.

As used at OCE all three assessment subsystems are open on two counts: (1) to the influence of immediate context and (2) to the influence of long-term design considerations. While all three subsystems are "closed" at the time of a particular application—that is, they are applied in terms of a particular context and a particular design consideration—all are open to variation in context across applications and open to variation in design across time. An example from the OCE student assessment system may help explain this distinction between open and closed systems.

Oregon College of Education defines a teaching competency as "the demonstrated ability to bring about the expected outcomes of a role or function included in a job definition." In demonstrating a teaching competency a student must not only identify the teaching position for which he is preparing, as well as the outcome he expects to achieve within the role or function that he will be performing in the demonstration context, but he must also designate the specific context in which the competency is to be demonstrated. If he is to be an elementary teacher, this requires the selection of a group of students between first and eighth grade in a school within a thirty-to-fifty mile radius of the college. Thus, two students who are preparing to become general elementary teachers, and who choose to demonstrate competence in bringing about desired learning outcomes in pupils, may choose different grade levels in which to teach, different subject matter areas, and even different kinds of children to teach, for example, a group of slow-learning children and a group of fast-learning children. The point is that the student assessment system must be adaptive to such variation in demonstration contexts, and yet *at the point of application* in these varying contexts be "closed" to the point where reliable, trustworthy information can be obtained on each student's performance.

Being open to variations in context is one essential feature of a CBTE assessment system. Being open to change in program design is another. Consider, for example, openness to change in desired program outcomes. To be functional, a CBTE assessment system must be sufficiently open to change that it can accommodate the adoption of differing program outcomes over time yet sufficiently closed *at a point of application* that reliable, trustworthy information may be obtained on whatever outcome is being assessed at a particular point in time. Ensuring that an assessment system is responsive to change generally means that it must be open to data from both inside and outside the system. Data from within the system indicate how well presently held or previously held program outcomes have been realized; external data indicate the desirability of dropping existing outcomes or adding new ones.

Given the point of view that an assessment system must be open to variations in context and design, yet closed at the time of a particular application of the system, it becomes obvious that such a system will be time-dependent and program-specific. Put in other terms, a CBTE assessment system is likely to be appropriate only for a given point in time and only for the program that it has been designed to support. Of course, many parts of an assessment system will probably remain stable across time within a particular program, but it is not so likely that an assessment system developed within the context of one program will have utility in another. To the extent that another program adopts similar outcomes for program functioning, or similar definitions and performance standards for teaching competencies, an assessment system could be transferable. The history of experience with CBTE thus far, however, suggests that comparability across programs is rare.

An Assessment System as a Research-Serving Information System

Historically there has been a great deal of confusion in the operational meaning to be assigned the terms assessment (or evaluation) and research. Many have viewed assessment or evaluation as synonymous with research.[13] Others[14] have classified both evaluation and research as "methods of disciplined inquiry," but have drawn substantive distinctions between them. As used here a sharp distinction is drawn between evaluation and research, and between assessment and research. Both assessment and evaluation are seen as consciously designed decision-serving activities. Research, on the other hand, is seen as a set of activities that leads to the extension of reproducible knowledge. Once produced, knowledge may also serve a decision-making function, but increasing the effectiveness of decision-making within a particular program setting is not the primary reason for undertaking research activities.[15]

From the point of view of CBTE program operation these are important and far-reaching distinctions to make, and the designers of assessment systems need to be clear that a perfectly adequate system for purposes of program-related decision-making need not be adequate for purposes of either program-related or basic research.

For an assessment system to serve both decision-making and knowledge-production functions, two conditions must be met: (1) the measures employed must be of a quality that permits their use in research, i.e., they must be valid, reliable, and sensitive; and (2) experimental designs must be introduced within the program with sufficient rigor that "causality" can be attributed to the experimental or treatment variables investigated. Both these conditions are above and beyond the requirements of the kind of assessment system that has been outlined in this chapter, but both can be achieved through relatively simple extensions of such a system. When this can be done effectively obviously much can be gained, for knowledge production can be added to program operation at little added cost.

While it is possible for an assessment system to serve a research function by meeting these two conditions, it should be pointed out that considerable risk is involved in attempting such a venture. The risk comes with the added burden that each condition brings to an ongoing educational program. High quality measures, for example, are often difficult and costly to obtain, and requiring that program operations meet the constraints of experimental design almost always creates an unwieldiness and rigidity that frustrates program operators. Efforts to design assessment systems in the image of research programs have led to the nearly universal consequence of designing research programs instead of assessment systems—at least as assessment systems have been defined here. When this has occurred there has been a nearly universal reaction on the part of persons responsible for program operation and adaptation: it has been unsatisfactory![16]

A number of strategies have been proposed to overcome the temptation to design assessment systems in the image of research programs, but few strategies have attempted to design research programs in the image of an assessment system. The concept of formative evaluation is one attempt to design an assessment system that breaks away from a research paradigm. The concept of "illuminative evaluation," which calls for a substitution of an anthropological research paradigm for the classic "agricultural-botany" paradigm,[17] is another. The proposal here, of course, is that research programs should be designed as *byproducts* of assessment systems, rather than the reverse, and that this can be done by carefully and selectively adding to an assessment system the properties of design and measurement that make the data that emerge from the system functional within both a research and a decision-making context.

COMPONENTS OF AN ASSESSMENT SYSTEM THAT
MEETS THE DEMANDS OF CBTE PROGRAMS

Passing reference has been made to the elements that make up an assessment system that meets the demands of CBTE. Some of the elements had to do with the *components* of an assessment system, e.g., decisions to be made, the structures and procedures within which decisions are to be made, etc. Others had to do with the *functions* to be performed within an assessment system, e.g., collection, reduction, storage, and distribution of data. At this juncture both sets of elements will be dealt with systematically and in some detail, for they constitute the pieces and parts that must be considered in developing and implementing a CBTE assessment system. The components of an assessment system are considered first.

Component 1: Families of Decisions

An assessment system of the kind called for has to support an extremely wide range of decisions. If each decision required totally different data, or totally different decision-making procedures, the variability that would have to be dealt with would be overwhelming.

Two strategies can be adopted that reduce variability in program-related decisions to manageable proportions: (1) the development of "targeted" subsystems within the overall assessment system, and (2) the identification of "families" of decisions within each targeted decision area. Since the first strategy has already been discussed (see pp. 213-214, 218), only the strategy of identifying families of decisions within targeted subsystems will be considered at this point.

A family of decisions is simply a collection of decisions that have a number of features in common. The rationale underlying the concept is one of economy and manageability, that is, by clustering or classifying decisions on the basis of data needs, structural requirements, procedural requirements, etc., sufficient order is introduced to the decision-making process that supporting it with data becomes both manageable and economically feasible.

In the OCE *student assessment system* three families of decisions have been identified: program entry decisions, program planning decisions, and program exit decisions. In the OCE *program assessment system* two families of decisions have been identified: executive or management decisions and policy or governance decisions. No decision families have as yet been identified in the *cost assessment system,* but that is thought to be due to the relatively small amount of attention given to this system thus far.*

While a great deal of attention at OCE has been directed to the identification of decision clusters, it should be pointed out that they have been established arbitrarily and though they have proved to be useful no particular brief is held for them. It is likely that other programs will arrive at other family clusters, at least in the early years of CBTE, and that is as it should be. What is important at this point in the development of CBTE is to search for such clusters, and to compare the cost and effectiveness of assessment systems that are designed to serve alternative cluster definitions. It is only through such a procedure that the quality and efficiency of assessment systems designed to serve CBTE can be improved.

Component 2: Structures for Decision-Making

A "structure" for decision-making refers to the organizational vehicle or mechanism within which decision-making occurs. It may be a committee, a board, a conference, or a jury, but in all cases it defines the physical context in which decisions are made.

It has been our experience at OCE that in the overall design of an assessment system decision structures must be attended to with as much care as the clustering of decisions or the designation of the procedures to be followed in decision-making. It has also been our experience that the nature of decision structures varies with the nature of decisions to be made, the procedures to be followed in making them, and the persons to be involved in the decision-making process. We have found, for example, that decision structures vary considerably for program entry decisions, program planning decisions, and program exit decisions. Similarly, we have found that structures vary for executive and policy decisions, and even for various levels of executive and policy decisions. On-line decision-making in program planning with students, for example (a lower level executive decision) requires relatively informal decision-making structures, whereas

---

*With application it has been found that decision families can often be subdivided into even more homogeneous groupings. Where this has occurred the subgroupings have tended to be ordered hierarchically along some dimension, and have thus been called "levels" of decision-making. All families and levels of decision-making thus far identified at OCE are described in some detail below.

adjustment in program planning procedures for students (a higher level executive decision) or the redesign of program planning procedures for students (a higher level policy decision) require relatively formal decision-making structures. Apparently the biological adage of "form following function" holds for the design of assessment systems: decision structures (form) need to be tailored to the class of decision (function) to be attended to. This adage should be kept clearly in mind by the designers of assessment systems, for without attending seriously to decision structures, and without tailoring structures to the class of decision being made, the likelihood is poor that a functional and efficient assessment system can be established.

Component 3: Procedures for Decision-Making

When a decision or set of similar decisions (a family of decisions) has been identified, and when a structure has been established within which to make the decisions, procedural statements have to be prepared that spell out who is to do what, when, where, and how in carrying out the decision-making process. If, for example, a decision is an "on-line" decision that has to do with whether a student teaching performance meets specified standards, and the structure within which that decision is to be reached is a three-way conference among student, classroom supervisor, and college supervisor, the procedures that are to be followed by each person in the three-way conference, the rules governing the decision-making process, and what is to be done after a decision has been reached must be spelled out. Without such clarity of procedure, chaos or authority will reign.

Generally speaking, acceptable decision-making procedures are reasonably easy to establish if there is clarity as to the model or the principles that govern program operation! Program operation models and decision-making procedures may appear at first glance to be strange bedfellows, but they are in fact closely related. If, for example, a governing principle of a program is that all participants should share equally in decision-making, in all likelihood the procedures to be followed in arriving at any particular decision will reflect this principle. If another governing principle is that all decisions should be made only after data that pertain to a particular decision have been reviewed, then the procedures to be followed in arriving at any particular decision should also reflect this principle. Program principles serve only as general guides to decision-making, however, and the specific procedures to be followed in attending to each class or family of decisions must be spelled out in detail.

As in the case of families of decisions within a particular program, or the structures employed to deal with them, the procedures followed in decision-making will always be program-specific. They will always reflect the combined influence of the principles governing operation of a specific program, the families of decisions identified within a program, and the decision structures that have been established to deal with them.

Component 4: Participants in Decision-Making

As in the case of all other components, the choice of participants in a particular decision reflects a combination of factors. Chief among these factors are: (1) the class or family of decisions that is to be attended to, (2) the principles governing decision-making within the program, and (3) the nature of the program itself, e.g., is it a consortium-centered program or one in a college environment? Of these three factors, the class of decision that is being considered is probably the most powerful source of influence. If a decision is a policy decision, for example, and it is at a level of generality that affects total program operation, then all major participants in the program will probably be represented in the decision-making process. If, on the other hand, a decision is an executive decision that has to do with judging the adequacy of a particular teaching competency that is being demonstrated by a particular student, the participants may be only a school supervisor and the student involved.

The class or family of decision that is being considered, however, is not all-powerful in determining participation in a particular decision. If, for example, a program consists of a consortium of institutions and agencies that includes a college, students in a teacher education program, several school districts, the teacher bargaining agencies from those districts, and an R & D agency (as is the case at OCE), then the number and kind of representatives in policy decisions would be different than if a program were operated solely through a college, or through a college and a single school district. Similarly, participation in decision-making would vary if a program was governed by a principle that held that all participants in the program were to be represented in policy decisions, as opposed to a principle that participating institutions were to be represented in policy decisions only "where appropriate."

Recognizing that participation in decision-making depends on such a variety of factors should be helpful to a designer of a CBTE assessment system, for he or she must be clear about the participants to be involved in each class or family of decisions before a program goes into operation. This is important from the point of view of both persons in the program and persons responsible for the operation of the assessment system that supports the program. Knowing who is to be involved in what decisions reduces anxiety on the part of program participants and also enhances the likelihood of critical decisions being made. Knowing who is to receive what information in relation to what decisions reduces anxiety on the part of assessment staff, and enhances the likelihood of decisions being made on the basis of the information that is needed for them to be made soundly.

Component 5: Data Specifications

Ely[18] has recently documented what evaluators and program administrators have long known on the use of information in decision-making, namely, that information available to a decision-maker is rarely used in its entirety, and if it *is* used it is only one of a vast number of considerations that enter into making a decision. Ely has also documented another fact known to evaluators and administrators: Decisions get made in the absence of information, at least information that is organized in data form. The reality of an ongoing program is that decisions must be made; the counter reality is that with or without data they will be made.

This should not be too surprising, for the demands of time and responsibility in program operation are harsh. It does suggest, however, that the designers of assessment systems should not be deceived into thinking that information collected will always be seen as helpful or even relevant to decision-making. It also suggests that the amount of information that can be used by decision-makers in arriving at a particular decision is likely to be limited, so if information is to be valued by decision-makers it must be of critical importance. Finally, this fact suggests that any information provided to decision-makers must be in a form that is easily understood and easily applied in the context of a particular decision, and it must be available in a timeframe that permits its utilization when a decision is in the process of being made.

In light of these sensitivities, our position is that data specifications should be worked out in advance of program and assessment system operation, so that when the program begins to operate decision-makers will have access to information in a form and on a time-line that makes it useful to adaptive decision-making from the beginning. The development of such specifications is dependent of course upon designating the classes or families of decisions that are to be attended to within the program, the structures to be employed and procedures to be followed in making these decisions, and the participants who are to take part in them.

Component 6: Performance Standards

The remaining feature that is essential to the operation of an assessment system is the component that deals with performance standards. Performance standards are criterial statements for program operation that serve as guides to adaptive decision-making in relation to the program. Performance standards may be set for the competencies to be demonstrated by students in the program, for staff in the program, for program costs, for the performance of the program as a whole, etc. Such standards permit those responsible for program operation to know whether or not a program is doing what it is supposed to do, or is achieving what it is supposed to achieve, and thereby to know whether program adaptations are or are not needed.

The explication of performance standards for educational programs is an essential step in making rational the process of program adaptation. It is not a sufficient step, however, for unless standards are referred to in reviewing program performance, and unless there are data to show how a program in fact performed in relation to the standards set for it, they are of little use. It is important that the designers of assessment systems be sure that data are collected and treated in a way that permits judgments to be made about performance in relation to standards, and that both performance data and standards are reviewed when decisions about program adaptation are considered.

Our efforts to develop and apply performance standards at OCE has led us to respect both the subtlety and complexity of the concept. Some sense of the struggle we have had in implementing the concept is conveyed in this description of our efforts to establish performance standards for competency demonstration:

> Another aspect of the meaning of competency that had to be unraveled before progress could be made in the development of the assessment system was the matter of performance standards. This was a particularly troublesome concept for it was imbedded in both the nature of the competency to be demonstrated and the context in which it was to be demonstrated. For example, defining the objectives of instruction was a competency to be demonstrated, but there is nothing inherent in that competency descriptor that speaks to the quality expected (standard) in its performance. It also makes no reference to the context in which performance is to take place. This is equally troublesome since the performance standards for defining the objectives of instruction in the context of lesson teaching may be considerably different than in the context of short-term full responsibility teaching. Because of this interdependency of competency descriptor, the context in which a competency is to be demonstrated, and the performance standard set for its demonstration, the task of becoming clear as to what the assessment system was to do and how it was to do it was more difficult than anticipated.
>
> Another level of subtlety and complexity emerged in relation to performance standards as the assessment system developed. This was the distinction that had to be drawn between performance ratings and performance standards. As the system was planned initially it was anticipated that performance standards would apply to each competency that was being assessed. As the system evolved it was discovered that applying the concept of performance standards at that level of detail was simply not functional. Ratings of performance had to be applied at that level, i.e., at the level of each competency descriptor, but it turned out that performance standards seemed to apply best to performance within a particular demonstration context. Thus, as the system evolved during the first year of program operation, performance standards came to apply to performance patterns across competencies within particular demonstration contexts, rather than to individual competency demonstrations.[19]

In spite of the subtlety and complexity of the task, and the many false starts and blind alleys encountered, we have been able to establish what appears to be a functional set of performance standards for student performance, program performance, and program cost. While there is no claim to their quality, nor to the likelihood of their enduring, they are offered as examples of what performance standards can look like. Because the full set of standards runs to several pages, only illustrative standards are given.

Standards for Student Performance in Lesson Teaching

• Evidence of favorable performance on each of the teaching functions assessed in at least one of the three lessons presented;

• Evidence of favorable performance on the preponderance of teaching functions assessed in the three lessons presented. Preponderance is defined here to mean at least 75 percent of the functions assessed in the course of the three lessons presented will reflect evidence of favorable performance, and no more than 25 percent of the functions assessed will reflect evidence of unfavorable performance.

Standards for Program Performance (to be Applied at the End of the First Year of Program Operation)

· All students enrolled in the program, and who remain in the program for the two terms allotted, will qualify to engage in formal lesson preparation and presentation;

· At least 75 percent of the students who engage in lesson preparation and presentation will perform to the standards set for those activities in the minimum of three lessons. At least 95 percent of the students enrolled in the program, and who remain in it, will perform to the standards set for lesson preparation and presentation before the two terms allotted to the program close;

· At least 75 percent of the students enrolled in the program will qualify to enter short-term (two to five days), full responsibility teaching, and at least 75 percent of those who engage in such teaching will perform to the standards set for it;

· Program staff and administrators (both college and school) will judge the program upon its completion to be sufficiently worthwhile and sufficiently free of problems that its continuation is recommended.

Standards for Program Cost

· The cost of operating the competency based elementary teacher education program will not exceed the moneys available to the college for its operation from regular sources of revenue.

FUNCTIONS TO BE PERFORMED IN THE OPERATION OF AN ASSESSMENT SYSTEM THAT MEETS THE DEMANDS OF CBTE

The components described above constitute the foundation stones of a CBTE assessment system, but they do not by themselves make up such a system. For an assessment system to be operational at least five functions must also be performed: (1) data collection, (2) data reduction, (3) data storage, (4) data retrieval and distribution, and (5) the management of the assessment system per se.

Data Collection

Central to the operation of any assessment system is the collection of data that are to serve the decision-making process. No constraints should be set on the kind or amount of data collected, nor on the methodology used in its collection. At least three principles, however, should guide the collection of data in the kind of assessment system that is being proposed:

(1) The kind and amount of data collected should be in keeping with the directives of the data specifications component of the assessment system;

(2) The methodologies employed in collecting data must yield measures that are reliable, valid, sensitive, etc.;

(3) The methodologies employed in collecting and reducing data must be cost-effective.

The implications for data collection when an assessment system is to support research as well as adaptive decision making are discussed on pp. 220-221.

Data Reduction

Once data has been collected it must be reduced, ordered, and summarized in a manner that makes it usable by decision-makers as they consider a particular decision. This process will vary according to the nature of the data collected, the methodology used in its collection, and the data specifications that govern its ordering and summarization. It is not unusual for the data reduction and summarization process to require as many resources as data collection, so careful estimates must be made as to the resource requirements for these two functions so that they do not exceed the resources available to them.

Data Storage

Most of the data collected through a CBTE assessment system does not need to be stored for long periods of time. This of course varies by class of data, or perhaps more correctly by class or family of decisions being served by a particular set of data, but in most cases the storage of data beyond a year is unnecessary. Data that support on-line decision-making in relation to student performance, for example, ordinarily need not be kept for more than a term. Data that support entry or exit decisions may need to be stored for a longer period, but when this is the case it is usually in highly summarized form so it does not require a great amount of space or manipulation.[20]

Similar variation in storage requirements is likely to be found in program assessment data. Data used for purposes of simple program adjustments rarely need to be kept for longer than three months. Data used in support of major program adaptations or major policy decisions may be kept for longer periods of time, but these also are usually in highly summarized form.

In addition to the question of length of data storage is the question of how it is to be stored. A computer obviously affords an attractive storage vehicle, especially since it facilitates the data retrieval process, but computers are surprisingly limited in the amount of information they can store and they become more and more expensive as storage requirements increase. For these reasons only a very small proportion of the data used in the CBTE program at OCE ever finds its way to a computer. With the exception of summary measures of student competency demonstrations, all information having to do with student assessment, program assessment, and program cost is hand-stored.[21]

Data Retrieval and Distribution

Given the point of view that data has utility only to the extent that it gets in the hands of decision-makers in a form and on a timeline that makes it useful to a particular decision, the data retrieval and distribution function is extremely critical to the overall effectiveness of an assessment system. The best of data can be collected, the best of data summaries can be prepared, and the best storage system possible can be devised, but without timely retrieval and distribution of the stored data this is all of little use. Like any complex system, the overall performance of an assessment system is only as good as its weakest link. All too often the weakest link is to be found in the data retrieval and distribution function.

One major source of difficulty typically encountered in data retrieval and distribution is lack of understanding about what is to be distributed to whom, in what form, and on what timeline. With the preparation of the data specifications called for in the proposed assessment model, this problem can be essentially eliminated. Using these specifications, data can be collected, reduced, and summarized, and stored if need be, in a form designed expressly for use by a particular decision-maker or set of decision-makers in considering a particular decision or set of decisions. Moreover, the timeframe for the distribution of such data need not be ambiguous. With this kind of clarity the data retrieval and distribution problems typically encountered in program operation should be largely bypassed.

A note of caution is worth entering at this juncture: Even when it is possible to achieve the kind of clarity and efficiency that has been called for, it is still desirable that someone who is completely familiar with the data be on hand to introduce, present, and interpret it to those who are to use it, and to be generally available for questions while the data are being reviewed. For data to be understood and used, there seems to be need for a great deal of "human interface," at least when working within the context of education and teacher education. This is true no matter how finely or simply or elegantly the data are reduced and presented. At OCE we have established the practice of accompanying all data summaries with a cover sheet that both interprets the implications of the data set for a particular decision, and identifies questions raised by the data that bear on the decision. We have also established the practice of having data summaries presented orally at the beginning of a decision-making session by a person who is intimately acquainted with the data.

System Management and Governance

As proposed in this chapter, an assessment system that effectively supports CBTE programs constitutes a relatively large and complex operation. Because of its size and complexity, and because of the careful coordination of its various pieces and parts that is required, it demands a great deal of attention. It also requires manpower, consumable resources, and space, just as each of the functions within the system requires manpower, consumable resources, and space. All this simply speaks to the reality that all the factors that need to be considered in developing and operating a CBTE program also have to be considered in developing and operating an assessment system to support a CBTE program, even to the point of the assessment system being turned on itself and functioning in relation to itself! The kind of specifications needed to manage and govern a CBTE assessment system can be found in the feasibility study of the ComField Model for Elementary Teacher Education at OCE.[22]

Because of the complexity of this assessment model it is not difficult to conceive of assessment within the context of CBTE programs consuming as many resources as instruction. Given the nature and history of teacher education, however, this is not likely to happen. Our estimate at OCE is that in the foreseeable future assessment will have to operate with 10 to 25 percent of the resources allocated to instruction; however, this represents an entirely adequate funding base if care is taken in the design and operation of the assessment system.[23]

The general features or *characteristics* of the model of assessment we are proposing for CBTE programs have been spelled out, the critical elements or *components* that comprise the model have been detailed, and the activities or *functions* called for by the model have been elaborated. Obviously, the level of description provided on each of these items is more general than some would like, particularly if they wished to implement or test the model. Considering the limited experience we have had with the model, however, the level of detail provided is probably appropriate. Hopefully, it will afford at least a general sense of what is being proposed, and a general sense of how to proceed to implement it. If so this chapter will have achieved its purpose.

The next step is to refine the model and test it in a variety of contexts. As it stands the model represents only a first step on a long road that has yet to be traveled, but it should represent a step in the right direction.

Three sections remain in the paper. The first deals with the complex and delicate task of integrating an assessment system with an instructional program. The second summarizes progress that has been made at OCE in implementing an assessment system that reflects the characteristics of the model that has been proposed. The third returns to the issue of the relationship between assessment and research, an issue that was touched on briefly earlier.

A STRATEGY FOR INTEGRATING INSTRUCTION AND ASSESSMENT

Designing and developing an assessment system that meets the demands of CBTE programs is one thing. Integrating such a system with instruction is another. How, for example, is the traditional mistrust of assessment on the part of both college faculty and the staff of participating schools to be overcome? How are the realities of the college-based and school-based instructional programs to be translated into the assessment model? In short, how is assessment to become conceptually and operationally an integral part of CBTE instructional programs?

The premise underlying the efforts at OCE is that an assessment system can become an integral part of an ongoing CBTE program only when three conditions are met: (1) when an institution recognizes the impossibility of separating assessment from the operation of a CBTE program; (2) when assessment is conceived as broadly as it has been in this chapter; and (3) when intellectual and financial resources can be made available to support the development and implementation of such a system.

In addition, however, a strategy must be pursued to actually get the integration to take place. At OCE the strategy followed has been one of "assigned" responsibilities but "shared" operations. In terms of who actually does what, OCE instructional staff and the clinical supervision staff from cooperating schools have primary responsibility for the instructional side of the program, while the office of the Dean of Faculty and staff of the Teaching Research Division of the State System of Higher Education have primary responsibility for the assessment side of the program. However, while *responsibilities* are divided in this way, *actual work performance* is not.

At OCE and the Teaching Research Division we are of the opinion that within the context of CBTE, instruction and assessment problems cannot be separated and staff members must work jointly on both sets of problems. The assessment staff, for example, share in the task of spelling out the competencies to be demonstrated by students in the program and participate in adaptive decision-making about the program. Instructional and administrative staff are involved in devising and administering measurement procedures, and processing and distributing the data that derive from them. Perhaps most important, however, any staff member who carries out a set of measurement operations within the program must be involved in the decision-making activities that utilize the data that derive from those operations. So far, the strategy has worked well. Whether it will continue to do so remains to be seen.

APPLICATION OF THE PROPOSED MODEL OF ASSESSMENT AT OREGON COLLEGE OF EDUCATION

As with any developmental effort, the assessment system that has evolved at OCE reflects the design that was initially held for the system, but at the same time is much different than what the original design called for. Similarly, the model that now guides the assessment system reflects the experience of a year of operation, and is quite different than it was a year ago. The model now outstrips the existing reality. Even so, just as it seems appropriate to present the model, recognizing its limitations, it seems appropriate to present where development in terms of the model now stands at OCE, and to project where development is expected to be a year from now.

Background

The context within which the OCE assessment system was developed was an experimental elementary teacher education program initiated on a pilot basis at the college in fall 1972. The program grew out of an early test of the feasibility of adopting at OCE—and in Oregon generally—the ComField Model for Elementary Teacher Education program, one of the eight elementary models designed under a grant from the U.S. Office of Education.[24] During the course of the feasibility study OCE refined the initial specifications for the ComField Model, applied those specifications to program development and operation at the college, tested the model-based program for its cost and feasibility, and worked out a plan whereby program efforts at OCE could be diffused throughout Oregon and adapted to fit the particular needs of other teacher education institutions in the state.

As implemented, the experimental program at OCE was to serve both as a test of the soundness of the principles of the ComField Model as those were elaborated in the feasibility study, and of the feasibility of a set of standards recently adopted by the state of Oregon for the accreditation of education personnel development programs.[25] The program was also to serve as a center for research and development in teacher education in Oregon, taking as its primary objective for the first year of operation the development of an assessment system consistent with the model of assessment outlined in this chapter.

A number of features of the experimental program at OCE had major implications for the design and operation of the assessment system that was to accompany the program, including the following:

• The program was to be operated within the context of a consortium for teacher education, the consortium consisting of a number of school districts, college faculty from education and related subject matter areas, a research and development agency, and students who were taking part in the program;

• Program management and governance decisions, where appropriate and possible, were to include representatives of all participating institutions, agencies, and groups;

• Teaching competency was to be defined in terms of the ability to bring about the outcomes expected of a teacher in a certificated teaching position, including the ability to bring about desired learning outcomes in pupils;

• Standards for the performance of teaching competencies were to be made explicit and public at the level of program operation, but idiosyncratic and personalized at the level of a particular demonstration context;

• Program operations were to be "data dependent," that is, to the extent possible decisions within the program were to be made only after data were considered that related to the decision; and

• The data used for purposes of decision-making were to be of a quality that permitted them to be used with confidence in a wide range of research activities that related to the program.

It is important that the reader have some awareness of these program characteristics for, as we indicated above, the nature of the program being implemented determines to a large extent the nature of the assessment system that needs to be developed.

Forty-three students entered the experimental program. The program was staffed by two full-time education faculty, six quarter- to full-time faculty from related subject matter areas, forty-three school supervisors, and the equivalent of one full-time specialist in measurement and evaluation. The program was limited to the pre-student-teaching aspects of professional preparation, and extended over a period of two terms (fall and winter). Students received thirty-six hours of college credit when they met the requirements of the program.

Progress on the Student Assessment System

During the first year of program operation relatively limited goals were set for development in the student assessment system. The major goal was the development of those aspects of the system that would permit the assessment of teaching competencies in ongoing school settings at the precertification level. If time and resources permitted, attention was also to be directed to the development of competency assessment procedures at the level of initial certification, but that was of secondary importance. In the language of "decision families," attention during the first year was to be directed to program planning decisions, with program entry and exit decisions receiving developmental attention only if time and resources permitted.[26]

As the year progressed the goal for development turned out to be an assessment system that functioned at two levels of competency demonstration: (1) lesson teaching and (2) short-term (two- to five-day), full responsibility teaching. Lesson teaching became the first and simplest context within which teaching competency was to be formally demonstrated in the program. Short-term, full responsibility teaching was the second context, and as such was to serve as the staging ground for student teaching. Short-term teaching was to be engaged in only after competency had been demonstrated in lesson teaching, and student teaching was to be engaged in only after competency had been demonstrated in short-term teaching.

A third demonstration context received some attention during the year, but not as much as the first two contexts. This was a *student teaching equivalency demonstration context*. It required full responsibility teaching for a five- to ten-day period, and could be entered only under conditions of exceptional performance in short-term, full responsibility teaching. Successful performance in the student teaching equivalency context was accepted as evidence of the level of teaching competency required to receive initial certification.

The student assessment system now represents little more than a beginning of the system that ultimately must evolve. Two major components of the system have been developed, and a third started, but all of these have undergone major revision in preparation for the second year of program operation. Undoubtedly, they will undergo at least one more major revision before they stabilize. In addition to revision of what has already been developed, however, the system must be extended to cover assessment of competency for purposes of initial, basic, and standard certification (program exit as well as program planning decisions). This represents a major developmental undertaking, for as the Oregon Process Standards now read, initial certification requires competency demonstration in a two- to five-week full responsibility teaching situation (student teaching), basic certification requires competency demonstration in a one- to three-term full responsibility teaching situation (intern or protected first year teaching), and standard certification requires competency demonstration in a two- to three-year full responsibility teaching situation after the basic certificate has been received.

Finally, the system must be extended to cover program entry decisions as well as the knowledges, skills, attitudes, and personal characteristics needed for a student to perform effectively as a teacher. These two sets of decisions could become intricately linked but as yet little substantive attention has been directed to them.

It can be seen from this brief outline that the work that remains on the student assessment system far exceeds the work that has been done. Reasonable clarity has been achieved as to the "family" of decisions that need to be made in assessing student performance, but all other components called for in the proposed model of assessment have been developed only for the precertification levels of competency demonstration. This is viewed as important progress, however, in that the foundation has been laid for the development of the system as a whole, and there has been a reasonably good test of the adequacies of the assessment model that has been outlined. Schalock, Kersh and Garrison describe the student assessment system that is now in operation at OCE in some detail.[27]

Progress on the Program Assessment System

In recent years persons concerned with program assessment or evaluation have come to think of assessment as either "formative" or "summative" in nature. As used by most persons, formative assessment refers to the monitoring of program content, operations, and procedures as they are being developed and implemented, with an eye to correcting or adapting them as needed. Summative assessment is generally seen as an evaluation of how well a program has done what it has set out to do; it typically occurs at a terminal point in the program, and typically involves an overall judgment or set of judgments as to the success or worth of a program.

The concept of program assessment that has been employed at OCE has taken a slightly different form. Program assessment is seen as the provision of information that permits various levels of adaptive decisions to be made relative to program operation. A course or program structure at OCE is always viewed as an approximation. It represents the best that can be done at a given point in time, but it is always seen as one step in the evolution of an ever more powerful, useful way of organizing learning experiences for the preparation of prospective teachers. Because of this dynamic quality courses and programs are subject to day-by-day, term-by-term, and year-by-year adaptation. The purpose of program assessment is to obtain data that will facilitate and make more sophisticated this continuing process of program change.

As initially conceived, the program assessment system was to serve four levels of adaptive decision-making, each decision level representing a "family" of decisions. The simplest level was associated with the change of program structure, procedures, and context to meet the expected or unexpected demands of day-to-day operation. Such demands arise from student differences, breakdowns in communication, unexpected complications in scheduling or field conditions, illnesses, etc. Adaptation at this level can appropriately be called *maintenance* adaptation; its essential feature is its limited scope as far as fundamental alterations of program structure, objectives, and content are concerned.

A second level of adaptive decision-making involves change in program structure, content, procedures, and objectives so that the nature or scope of the program is fundamentally altered. These adaptations, made while a course or program is in progress, generally arise in response to emergencies or pressures that force basic program change. Because such adaptations occur in the context of an ongoing course or program, however, they are generally restricted in scope and are seen as more temporary or tentative than more reflective program changes. This level of adaptive decision-making has been labeled *adjustment* adaptation; its defining features are its scope and its occurrence within the context of an ongoing course or program. Adjustment adaptations are generally characterized by more upheaval than maintenance adaptations, and are generally made with greater reflection and with a broader base of decision-making than maintenance adaptations.

A third level of adaptive decision-making that occurs within the context of CBTE programs—or any other teacher education program for that matter—occurs after a course or program has been given and there has been opportunity to reflect on what has occurred as a consequence of its being given. This is the kind of adaptation that typically occurs between the first and second terms of a course, before a course is given, or after a course has been given and before it is to be given a second or third time. It has been labeled *design* adaptation, and is characterized by its holistic considerations, its reflectiveness, and the presence of a relatively broad data base on which to make design decisions. This level of adaptation is typically associated with course or program development by an individual faculty member, or by a small group of faculty. It is less inclusive than the level of adaptation that is typically associated with curriculum development and change.

The fourth level of adaptive decision-making considered at OCE, and by far the most complex and far-reaching level of adaptation, centers on the reshaping of a curriculum or set of course offerings as a whole. Adaptations at this level are generally made in response to major shifts in the knowledge or technological base of a discipline, major shifts in the value structures or needs of a society, or major shifts in the basic orientations of an institution. These are generally adaptations that involve extensive reflection over a long period of time, and command a wide data base and wide involvement in decision-making. Adaptations of this kind have been labeled *reformulation* adaptations.[28]

In its first year of operation the program assessment system developed at OCE served only the first three of these four levels of adaptive decision-making. In serving these three levels, however, the system reflected to one degree or another all of the components and functions called for in the proposed model of assessment. Decision families were identified; decision structures, procedures, and participants were matched to decision families; data specifications were established; and well-defined procedures were carried out for the management and governance of the assessment system. All the assessment functions called for in the model were also implemented. It was this experience that formed the basis for the present description of the assessment model as a whole.

After using the four-level scheme for a year, we have come to the view that a two-dimensional scheme that incorporates increasingly complex "levels" of decision-making along each dimension is a better way of conceptualizing the adaptive decision-making process than a single-dimension scheme. We have labeled the two dimensions, respectively, executive or *management* decision-making and policy or *governance* decision-making. Using this scheme, the four levels of decision-making used in the first year of program operation divide evenly along the two dimensions, with maintenance and adjustment decisions falling on the management dimension and design and reformulation decisions falling on the governance dimension. This placement is in keeping with the generally accepted notion that policy decisions are more far-reaching than management decisions, and accordingly tend to be carried out more reflectively and with wider participation in the decision-making process.

For 1973-74 we are adding a third level of decision-making to each dimension. What were labeled as on-line decisions are to be added to the management dimension, and what were labeled as administrative decisions are to be added to the governance dimension. These become the lowest order or least complex decisions in the two-dimensional scheme, corresponding to the day-in day-out, routinized decision-making that is the stuff of program operation. The relationships between these various levels and dimensions of decision making can be shown schematically in Figure 15:2.[29]

By and large the program assessment system functioned during the first year of program operation as planned. It supported the three levels of adaptive decision-making remarkably well, and it proved to be cost effective (once developed, the program assessment system was operated—including the collection, reduction, distribution, and interpretation of all data—by one work-study student working fifteen hours per week!). The decision structures, procedures, participants, and data collection tools used in support of program-related decision-making during the first year of program operation are summarized in Table 15:2.

It can be seen from Table 15:2 that work on the program assessment system has progressed farther than work on the student assessment system. This is deceptive, however, for while the program assessment system is relatively far along in its development it is much less complex than the student assessment system. Also, even though much progress has been made much remains to be done. Families of decisions need to be refined; decision structures, procedures, partici-

Figure 15:2. Program Decision Structure Employed at OCE

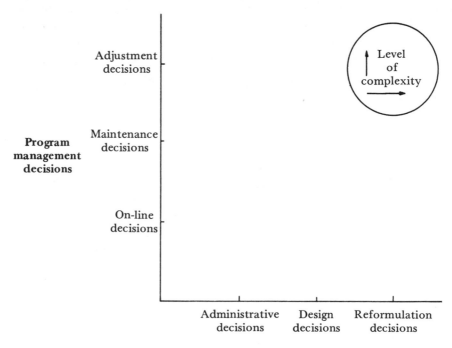

Program governance decisions

pants, and data specifications need to undergo major revision during the coming year to accommodate the expansion and formalization of the consortium within which the program operates; and program standards must be expanded and tested. (Standards were stated for the first year of program operation but they were not used formally as guides to decision-making. A set of program goals were used instead. While these proved to be reasonably satisfactory substitutes for a start-up year, formal performance standards will have to be used in the years ahead.) All in all, however, the work that has been done on program assessment is encouraging. The major conceptional and methodological problems that relate to it have apparently been solved, and the model that is outlined here apparently holds up. A description of the program assessment system that is in operation at OCE will be available in monograph form in fall 1974.[30]

Table 15:2. Structures, Procedures, Participants, and Data Sources
Used in Support of Program Adaptation Decisions

Model components	Maintenance decisions	Adjustment decisions	Design decisions
Structure	An hour-long meeting each week	A two-hour meeting each month	Six three-hour seminars and a full-day program planning exercise over the course of a term
Participants	College faculty; students; assessment staff	College faculty; school supervisors; students; assessment staff	College faculty; school supervisors; college and school administrators; students; assessment staff
Procedure	Maintenance level data reviewed; meeting then opened to discussion and related problem-solving	Adjustment level data reviewed; meeting then opened to discussion and related problem-solving	Adjustment and design level data reviewed by selected topics; seminar then opened to discussion and related problem solving. Program planning exercise focuses upon simulated program related decision making
Formal data sources	Program maintenance survey (administered to a 10% sample of students and school supervisors, and a 50% sample of college faculty)	Program adjustment survey (administered to all students and college faculty, and a 25% sample of school supervisors); selected interviews	Program design survey (administered to all students, college faculty and school supervisors, and selected college and school administrators); program cost reports; selected interviews; student performance data*

*It can be argued that data on student performance is the one valid measure of program effectiveness, and so should be the only measure used. The view taken at OCE is that while it is a necessary measure of program effectiveness, it is not by itself sufficient. Nor is it a particularly good measure from the point of view of being informative as to how a program should be modified to function more smoothly, efficiently, or effectively within the resource constraints that exist. As a consequence the other data sources that are listed are attended to with as much care, and given as much authority, as measures of student performance.

Progress on the Cost Assessment System

As yet the cost assessment system being developed at OCE is not fully operational. A procedure for determining program costs has been field tested and some cost data collected, but actual program costs have not been calculated except those associated with the development and operation of the assessment system. These data are presented in Table 15:3.

The basic cost assessment procedures developed and tested so far involve recording the time spent in particular activities within the program, the materials used in various aspects of the program—including paper and printing, and unusual expenses associated with the program generally, e.g., consultants, travel, retreats, equipment, etc. Where we have not made a great deal of progress is in the presentation of cost data. It is unclear, for example, whether we should present cost data by program activities, program objectives, program components, or all of these. We are also unclear as to how cost data are to be combined with program effectiveness data and student performance data in arriving at overall program management and policy decisions. These decisions will be made in at least preliminary form before the beginning of the 1973-74 academic year, however, for costs associated with program operation are to be monitored closely during the coming year. Reasonably complete data on cost of program operation, as well as the methodology, decision rules, etc., that need to accompany its collection, will be available by summer 1974.

**Contribution of an Assessment System of the Kind
Proposed to Research on Teacher Education**

Our emphasis thus far has been on the role of the proposed assessment system in program operation and adaptation. Some attention has been given the requirements that an assessment system would have to meet if data produced by the system were to be of a quality that supported either program related or basic research (see pp. 220-221, but nothing of a substantive nature was said about such research.

Historically, research in education and teacher education has been disappointing.[31] A host of reasons have been offered for the small yield from educational research, including the argument that the world of education is simply too complex to yield to the strategies of

Table 15:3. Resources Utilized in the First Year of the Experimental
Teacher Education Program at OCE*

Cost items	Regular "junior-block" program			Experimental "junior-block" program		
	Fall	Winter	Spring	Fall	Winter	Spring
Program operation						
Education faculty	1.5 FTE	1.5 FTE		1.5 FTE	1.5 FTE	
Subject matter	1.5 FTE	1.25 FTE		1.75 FTE	1.50 FTE	
School supervisors	2 hrs. p/wk	2 hrs. p/wk		3 hrs. p/wk	5.25 hrs. p/wk	
Secretary/clerical	Normal	Normal		+50%	+50%	
Supplies/services	"	"		Normal	Normal	
Administration	"	"		+10%	+10%	
Program development						
Education faculty				.5 FTE	.5 FTE	
Assessment faculty				1.0 FTE	1.0 FTE	
Secretary/clerical				.75 FTE	.75 FTE	
Supplies/services				$750	$750	
Administration				+10%	+10%	
Program adaptation						
Education faculty						.50 FTE
Subject matter faculty						
School supervisors						6@ 5 hrs. p/wk
Students						12@ 5 hrs. p/wk
Assessment faculty						1.0 FTE
Secretary/clerical						1.0 FTE
Supplies/services						$500
Program-related research				$500	$750	$500

*Of the 44 students enrolled in the program, 37 completed it.

science, but it is the writer's opinion that the major reason for this poor showing is the lack of adequate dependent or outcome measures. No matter how powerful a research design, nor how powerful a treatment condition, research results of significance will not be forthcoming unless the measure of effect is strong.

One of the most hopeful features of competency based education and teacher education is that they are designed by their very nature to overcome the perennial problem of outcome measurement. Competency based education should yield new and powerful measures of learning outcomes in pupils, and competency based teacher education should yield new and powerful measures of teaching performance. If these measures are of the kind and quality anticipated, and the research community recognizes them as such and takes advantage of their availability, research in education and teacher education could enter a new phase.

It is within this context that the development and operation of the kind of assessment system that has been outlined here is being called for. If constructed and operated carefully, such a system could serve both the data-dependent decision-making and research functions that are so desperately needed at this juncture in American education.

In spite of good reason for optimism, a note of caution should be injected. Obtaining cost-effective measures of educational outcomes that have meaning to the public at large and utility in program operation, as well as a level of quality that permits them to be used for purposes of research, is a complex and demanding process. It requires a great deal of careful conceptual and technical effort, and a continuous monitoring of the quality of the measures that are being taken. This may be more than can be asked of educators at this time, even though the competency based movement carries such demands. It is the opinion of the writer, however, that unless competency based education and teacher education are served by measures of high quality, the movement will become a mockery. Unless research in education and teacher education can be served by measures of high quality it would be better left undone.

NOTES FOR CHAPTER 15

1. Stanley Elam, *Performance Based Teacher Education: What Is the State of the Art?* (Washington, D.C.: AACTE, 1971), pp. 21-22.

2. Benjamin Rosner, ed., *The Power of Competency Based Teacher Education* (Boston: Allyn & Bacon, 1972).

3. Frederick J. McDonald, "Evaluation of Teaching Behavior," in *Competency Based Teacher Education: Progress, Problems, and Prospects*, ed. W. Robert Houston and Robert B. Howsam (Chicago: Science Research Associates, 1972); H. L. Jones, "Implementation of Programs," in *Competency Based Teacher Education: Progress, Problems, and Prospects*, ed. Houston and Howsam; and H. Del Schalock, B. Y. Kersh, and Jesse H. Garrison, "From Commitment to Practice in Assessing the Outcomes of Teaching: A Case Study," in *Assessment in Performance-Based Teacher Education*, ed. Theodore E. Andrews (Albany, N.Y.: Multi-State Consortium on Performance-Based Teacher Education, in press).

4. Frederick J. McDonald, "Evaluation of Teaching Behavior," in *Competency Based Teacher Education: Progress, Problems, and Prospects*, ed. Houston and Howsam, pp. 56-58.

5. S. S. Stevens, "Mathematics, Measurement and Psychophysics," in *Handbook of Experimental Psychology*, ed. S. S. Stevens (New York: John Wiley & Sons, 1951), pp. 1-49.

6. G. V Glass, *The Growth of Evaluation Methodology*, AERA Curriculum Evaluation Monograph series (Chicago: Rand McNally, 1971).

7. After completing this chapter the author came upon a report by Dr. Frank Womer, "Developing a Large-Scale Assessment Program" (Denver: Cooperative Accountability Project, 1973), which supports the proposed use of the term assessment. Womer defines assessment as "a program to improve educational decision making by securing information about the outcomes of education" (page 1). He also points out that assessment as a term did not enjoy widespread use until the advent of the national assessment project (started in the mid-1960s), but that in recent years the term has begun to be used in place of testing.

8. Kaplan has expressed well the necessity of carefully delineating concepts and terms in an enterprise as complex as competency based teacher education. He has also expressed the provisional nature of any such delineation: "The process of specifying meaning is a part of the process of inquiry itself. In every context of inquiry we begin with terms that are undefined—not undefineables, but terms for which *that* context does not provide a specification. As we proceed, empirical findings are taken up into our conceptual structure by way of new specifications of meaning, and former indications and references in turn become matters of empirical fact." A. Kaplan, *The Conduct of Inquiry* (San Francisco: Chandler Publishing Co., 1964), p. 77.

9. Walt LeBaron, "Systems Analysis and Teacher Education," in *Competency Based Teacher Education*, vol. 1, ed. James M. Cooper and M. Vere DeVault (Berkeley: McCutchan Publishing Corp., 1973), pp. 15-31.

10. By and large, structures and procedures that support short-term decisions will vary from those that support long-term decisions. They tend to be less complex, less time consuming, less demanding of data, and require fewer people to take part in them. Short-term decisions, for example, rarely take into account data from more than one or two aspects of program operation at a time or involve more than two or three people, whereas long-term decisions almost always involve a larger number of people and collective consideration of student performance, program performance, and program cost data.

11. Schalock, Kersh, and Garrison, "From Commitment to Practice in Assessing the Outcomes of Teaching: A Case Study," in *Assessment in Performance-Based Teacher Education*, ed. Andrews, p. 3.

12. John Williamson, "The Inquiring School: A Model of Knowledge Utilization in a Self-Renewing Learning Environment," paper presented at AERA, Chicago, 1972.

13. M. Guttentag, "Models and Methods in Evaluation Research," *Journal of the Theory of Social Behavior* 1 (1971): 75-95.

14. G. V Glass and B. R. Worthen, "Educational Inquiry and Educational Practice," in *Conceptual Frameworks for Viewing Educational RDD&E*, vol. 3, ed. H. Del Schalock and G. R. Sell (Monmouth, Ore.: Oregon State System of Higher Education, Teaching Research Division, 1972), pp. 68-120.

15. H. Del Schalock and G. R. Sell, "A Framework for the Analysis and Empirical Investigation of Educational RDD&E," in *Conceptual Frameworks for Viewing Educational RDD&E*, vol. 3, ed. Schalock and Sell, pp. 197-265.

16. M. Parlett and D. Hamilton, "Evaluation as Illumination: A New Approach to the Study of Innovatory Programs," Occasional Paper, Centre for Research in the Educational Sciences, University of Edinburgh, Scotland, October 1972.

17. Ibid.

18. D. E. Ely, "The Myths of Information Needs," *Educational Research* 2 (April 1973): 15-17.

19. Schalock, Kersh, and Garrison, "From Commitment to Practice in Assessing the Outcomes of Teaching: A Case Study," in *Assessment in Performance-Based Teacher Education*, ed. Andrews, pp. 18-19.

20. Only summary measures of competency demonstration are maintained in the OCE permanent files. These are stored in two forms: (1) a computer-prepared competency demonstration profile, which is treated as a second transcript for each student graduating from the program, and (2) a competency demonstration study that is maintained for purposes of research. The nature and content of both storage vehicles are described in some detail in ibid.

21. All student performance, program performance, and program cost data collected at OCE are maintained in open files. This includes the data that are computer stored. Considerable effort is directed toward making these files available to and usable by students, college faculty and administrators, and participating school personnel.

22. H. Del Schalock, B. Y. Kersh, and L. L. Horyna, *A Plan for Managing the Development, Implementation, and Operation of a Model Elementary Teacher Education Program*, vol. 1 (Washington, D.C.: Government Printing Office, 1970), pt. 4.

23. This should be regarded as a tentative projection, however, for two reasons: (1) There are as yet only the most preliminary data on costs associated with assessment within CBTE programs, at least as those costs are distinct from instructional and administrative costs; and (2) costs allocated to assessment will depend on what one chooses to define as an assessment cost. It is perfectly possible, for example, as well as perfectly reasonable, to treat most assessment costs that pertain to student performance as instructional costs, for the instructional program is dependent on such data to operate effectively. It is also possible and reasonable to consider program asssessment costs as part of program management or governance costs, or program administration costs, for program design and adaptation decisions are dependent on such data. The estimate of assessment costs amounting to 10 to 25 percent of instructional costs is based on the assumption that all formalized measurement and evaluation operations would be identified as assessment costs, while the utilization of the data that derive from

these operations in decision-making would be considered as either instructional or administrative costs.

24. Schalock, Kersh, and Horyna, *A Plan for Managing the Development, Implementation, and Operation of a Model Elementary Teacher Education Program,* vols. 1 and 2.

25. "Process Standards for Educational Personnel Development Programs," Oregon Teachers Standards and Practices Commission, August 1973.

26. The recently adopted "Process Standards" (see note 25) for educational personnel development in Oregon call for three levels of certification: initial, basic, and standard. Competency demonstration is required at all three levels. As the level of certification increases the competencies to be demonstrated increase in number and kind, and performance standards increase in difficulty.

27. Schalock, Kersh, and Garrison, "From Commitment to Practice in Assessing the Outcomes of Teaching: A Case Study," in *Assessment in Performance-Based Teacher Education,* ed. Andrews.

28. These four levels of adaptive decisions were designed to parallel the "levels of inquiry" that John Williamson has proposed as essential to the operation of schools or other organizations for self-renewal.

29. Dr. John Parker, director of the School Component of the Rural Schools Program of the Northwest Regional Educational Laboratory, has pointed out that this schema is much like Bale's two-dimensional model of decision-making in social groups. Bale's model labels the vertical axis a task orientation and the horizontal axis a power orientation to the decision-making process.

30. H. Del Schalock, "The Oregon College of Education System for Program Assessment," monograph (1974).

31. N. L. Gage, ed., *Handbook of Research on Teaching* (Chicago: Rand McNally, 1973); B. Othanel Smith, ed., *Research in Teacher Education: A Symposium* (Englewood Cliffs, N.J.: Prentice-Hall, 1971); and R. M. W. Travers, ed., *Second Handbook of Research in Teaching* (Chicago: Rand McNally, 1973).

16. Some Measurement Issues

Thomas J. Quirk

In recent years the main focus of concern in teacher education, in terms both of discussion and of potential impact in the training of teachers, has been related to the problems connected with designing, implementing, and subsequently defending so-called "competency based" programs of teacher education (CBTE).

The movement toward CBTE has so far focused primarily on the administrative, organizational, and operational procedures necessary to establish and maintain a competency based program in teacher education. The general requirements for such a program have been presented by Elam.[1] A number of descriptions of competency based programs are available.[2] A working description of the principles of operation and structure of these programs is also available.[3]

The major emphasis of the Teacher Corps and in the Model Elementary Programs has also added to the general movement toward

This chapter was adapted from a paper presented at the annual meeting of AERA, New Orleans, February 1973.

deciding on a teacher's competence on the basis of what the teacher *can* do rather than simply on what he knows or says he will do when faced with a certain teaching situation. The fervor with which this movement has been presented within teacher education has been expressed by Houston and Howsam:

Rarely, if ever, has any movement swept through teacher education so rapidly or captured the attention of so many in so short a time as has the competency based movement. Already well underway, the approach holds promise of renovating and regenerating teacher education. Equally significantly, it appears probable that it will do so in record-setting time . . . ; by early 1972 some seventeen states either had announced certification changes to be based on competencies or had declared their interest or intentions.[4]

A committee that was formed to study national program priorities in teacher education has recently produced a substantive report, *The Power of Competency-Based Teacher Education*, which included formal recommendations for program planning, training laboratories, individual laboratory development and operations, instructional materials, instrument development, and career development. One of the recommendations of this committee in its five-year plan was: "To develop approximately 250 school-based criterion measures leading to competency based certification at the paraprofessional, provisional, and permanent certification levels."[5] The following recommendation on the development of instruments as part of the competency based movement in teacher education was also made:

The preparation of instruments to define performance criteria is the *sine qua non* of competency based certification. The Committee cannot emphasis too strongly the needed development of measures of teacher performance in the classroom. If BEPD had to support a single effort to establish competency based teacher education, it should invest in the development of instruments to assess teacher competencies.[6]

Such a strong statement from such a distinguished committee is likely to provoke even stronger support for the competency based programs within the teacher education movement. Before this happens, it might be helpful to consider a different focus, to think about some of the measurement problems connected with any program of teacher education—whether or not it is qualified for the label of "competency based." Instead of parading such catchy terms as "personalized," "self-paced," "individualized," "precise behavioral objectives," "criterion referenced tests," it might be fruitful to consider some of the implications of such terms from a measurement point of view.

THE DEVELOPMENT OF LISTS OF
PERFORMANCE OBJECTIVES

One prominent characteristic of CBTE programs is their haste to create long lists of performance objectives as proof that their programs are truly competency based. Occasionally these programs will state that they intend to include on the candidate's university transcript those performance objectives which the candidate has successfully achieved. Presumably, this list would be helpful to administrators in school districts who are considering hiring that person. The general idea is that the placement office of the training institution could provide a service to the school districts by sending portfolios describing special teaching skills or abilities of teacher candidates.

Many examples could be provided of this approach: Burke states that there are at least 300 behavioral objectives in the Weber State College model[7]; Jones identifies 2,700 modules in the elementary education program in the Michigan State University model.[8]

The main measurement problem with these long lists of performance objectives has to do with the reliability of the individual measures. Within the more popular standardized tests an analogous example is found by comparing the reliability of different subtests within a battery of tests to the reliability of the total test score. Table 16:1 presents the appropriate measurement principle related to this approach, i.e., the reliability of the test is a function of the number of items.

Breaking down the performance of a prospective teacher into finer elements could produce a result in which the reliability of individual judgments about the teacher's competence is inadequate. To illustrate using the Spearman-Brown formula,[9] suppose that a fifty-item test were reduced to five separate subtests of ten items each so that each block of ten items was related to a specific performance objective (a not too unreasonable assumption, given the fine level of specificity in the objectives of some CBTE programs). If we assume that these subtests have equal standard deviations and equal intercorrelations, and that the reliability of the fifty-item test was .80, the reliability of each of the ten-item tests would be only .44. This result could hardly inspire confidence in the accuracy of the statements about each of these five performance objectives.

Another way to illustrate this point is to consider that a test with a reliability of .44 has a standard error of measurement that is almost

Table 16:1. A Contrast of Principles of CBTE Programs
with Related Principles of Measurement

Principles of CBTE programs	Related principles of measurement
Competence should be defined in relation to lists of well-defined behavioral objectives.	In general, the fewer the number of items in a test, the lower the reliability of the test.
Superior ability in one critical area or skill should not be allowed to compensate for less-than-adequate competency in another critical area or skill.	The reliability of individual difference scores (either between different objectives or within retesting the same objective) is a function of the reliabilities and intercorrelation between the two sets of scores. Restricting the range of scores on a test decreases the predictive validity of the test.
The competencies of individual candidates, rather than the process characteristics of the teacher training programs, should be the most important measurement emphasis.	The reliability of the score of an individual candidate is lower than the reliability of the scores of a group of candidates. The standard error of measurement is a function of the reliability of the test. Restricting the range of scores on a test lowers the reliability of the test.
The effectiveness of a teacher should be determined in relation to pupil development.	Interactive teaching between a teacher and a group of pupils produces a situation in which neither the stimulus nor the response is well controlled; more importantly, this situation is subject to a wealth of interactive influences—some of which are positive and some negative in their contribution to the outcome.

three-fourths of a standard deviation of the test itself—a considerable error of measurement. While it is possible to make accurate statements from tests that contain only a few test items, one should consider the accuracy of these individual statements carefully.

THE RELIABILITY OF PERFORMANCE MEASURES

The emphasis on performance tests is a logical development, away from the concern with only the process objectives of teacher training toward the more direct concerns of what the teacher can do in an actual or simulated teaching situation. While a knowledge of the teacher's understanding of the subject matter he intends to teach is obviously helpful in determining his competency for teaching, it is hardly sufficient in itself. For example, there is little reason to think that a test of verbal ability or general education would serve as a good predictor of management skills, tutoring skills, planning skills, or the like.

A performance test requires the respondent to *do* a particular task, rather than merely to say what he will do in a particular situation or to select the single best answer from a list of alternatives. The use of performance tests to determine teaching skills is especially attractive when one considers that the act of teaching is a very different phenomenon from that represented by a paper-and-pencil test. Teaching is basically a sociopsychological situation in which neither the stimulus nor the response is well controlled. The teacher and the students *react* to each other, and it is this reactive content that is so difficult to capture in a written test. In this respect, microteaching and other simulated teaching situations present an opportunity for the prospective teacher to demonstrate what he can do in an interactive situation with students. The history of the research on the stability of teacher behavior is not encouraging, however.[10]

There are also a host of critically important research questions about microteaching tests or other simulated tests that need to be answered before such devices become a standardized part of a reporting system for teacher competence. How consistent over time is the teacher's behavior? What is the effect of familiar as opposed to unfamiliar pupils on the behavior of the teacher? What is the effect of pupil practice within the microteaching setting on teacher behavior? How is teacher behavior related to pupil learning? What are the correlations between simulated teaching tests and paper-and-pencil tests? So far, the important questions far outnumber the adequate answers.

THE USE OF THE PERCENT CORRECT PASSING SCORE

The practice in some CBTE programs of setting a fixed cutoff percentage of correctly answered items as the passing score for each performance objective makes little sense from a measurement point of view. "The candidate will answer correctly at least 80 percent of the items related to this objective to be considered as having achieved mastery" sounds semiscientific, but it does not possess much substantive value. The percentage of objective-related items that a candidate answers correctly is a function not only of the content of the items, but also of their difficulty. An estimate of the difficulty of the items can be obtained either from a logical judgment based on a study of the specific items or from empirical item analysis data. Obviously, the best way to make a program appear effective is to ask the candidates a lot of items of low difficulty levels.

Applying the fixed cutoff score to a different form of the test if the candidate does not achieve mastery on the first testing, as has been suggested by a number of CBTE programs, presents additional problems. Not only is it difficult to match two forms of the test in terms of both content and item difficulty, but, for the scores to have similar meaning, the two test forms should be equated statistically.[11] Unless they have been equated, the results could have quite different meanings even though the tests attempt to measure the identical content.

Retesting the candidate, either with the same test or with a different form of the test, presents further measurement problems connected with the reliability of the difference score between these two testings. Perhaps an analogy dealing with students would be helpful to illustrate the problem. Some junior high schools require that their students achieve at least a certain grade equivalent score on a reading test in order to be promoted into high school. This can easily produce the ludicrous situation in which the student is retested on the same or an alternate form of the test until some coincidence of regression toward the mean, practice effect, the standard error of measurement, and random error combine to produce the magical cutoff score on a single occasion. The confidence that could be placed in such a score can best be evaluated by asking, "How often would that test be given to that student again after he had once achieved the passing score?" The answer would undoubtedly be, "Never," and there is a good measurement reason for this inaction that is related to the reliability of the difference scores, about which we will have more to say later.

THE MULTIPLE CUTOFF MODEL

Correlation coefficients in validity studies are usually related to one of two types of statistical models: (1) *the linear multiple regres-*

sion model and (2) *the multiple cutoff model.* The linear multiple regression model assumes that a higher degree of ability or skill in one area can compensate for a lower ability or skill in another area by a special kind of statistical averaging or weighting. The multiple cutoff model assumes that a minimum passing score is set for each predictor, so that the candidate is not considered to pass unless he achieves at least the minimum score on each of the predictors; in this model, a lack of talent in one area cannot be compensated for by superior talent in another area. This latter model seems to apply more generally to the purposes and intentions of CBTE programs; its main difficulty has been nicely summarized by Hills:

> The most unfortunate thing about the procedure is that its administrative simplicity makes it readily available for uninformed and thoughtless use. Cutoff scores can be set arbitrarily without adequate evidence on the validity of the variable that is being used for selection or on the yield of admitted candidates that can be expected for any given set of minimum scores. . . . It also happens that an available measure may erroneously be assumed to be valid. The combination of invalid measure and arbitrary cutoff is, perhaps, the nadir of sophistication in selection.[12]

The use of profile reporting on performance objectives has also been advocated. This procedure has the attractive product of a graph of the candidate's performance across a series of performance objectives, like the one presented in Figure 16:1. This type of profile reporting has been called the *parallel stalk model.*[13] An unsophisticated user of a profile like that presented in Figure 16:1 might be tempted to say that the candidate performed better on Objective 4 than he did on Objective 3. But if these two objectives are highly

Figure 16:1. A Hypothetical Profile of a Candidate's
Achievement on Performance Objectives

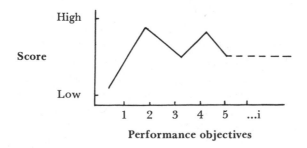

correlated, the reliability of the difference scores between these objectives would be low, even if we assume that the reliability of the measures of Objective 3 and Objective 4 are high.

In fact, if the average reliability of the measures of the two objectives is less than the intercorrelation between the two measures of the objectives, the reliability of the difference score between the two objectives would be negative.[14] To say that a candidate performed better on Objective 4 than he did on Objective 3 makes no sense unless the reliability of the difference score between these two objectives is adequate. This same concern would apply whether we were studying the performance of the same candidate on two different objectives or on a retesting of the same objective.[15]

To the extent that the range of scores for a test is restricted, the predictive validity of the test will also be affected. For example, if the original predictive validity of the test were .70, and the standard deviation of the test were reduced from 50 to 30, the predictive validity of the test would be lowered to .50 even if nothing else changed.

THE INADEQUACY OF THE PUBLIC SCHOOL TEACHER EVALUATION MODEL

In the typical teacher evaluation program in the public schools the principal, assistant principal, or department chairman rates the competency of the teacher according to some checklist or rating scale. The usefulness of this procedure in weeding out teachers of dubious competence can probably best be estimated by remembering that few teachers are denied the opportunity to continue teaching because of this evaluation model. If almost every teacher is judged satisfactory under this model, either the teachers who are being trained are of outstanding quality, or the model is dysfunctional.

To some extent, the course grade assigned to practice teaching follows a similar model. Such grades are typically based on a wide variety of factors, combined by some unknown weighting process; even within the same training institution their meaning is of doubtful value because the range of individual differences is so small. If practically every candidate receives a grade of A or B in student teaching, the ability of this experience to predict future teaching performance would be seriously curtailed—a point we have tried to illustrate throughout this chapter.

To the extent that such checklists or rating scales are used in CBTE programs, the same concerns apply.

CONCLUSION

We have attempted to call attention to certain measurement problems that should be the concern of any system that attempts to assess teacher competence, whether or not that system would like to include itself under the general rubric of "competency based." The measurement of teacher behavior is an extremely complex problem and care should be exercised in it, so that the zeal with which a label or set of principles is adopted does not cloud the larger measurement issues.

This does not mean that all programs called "competency based" should wait patiently until the measurement experts catch up with the promoters. That way lies paralysis of progress. The problem of trying to link teacher behavior to student outcomes is an extremely challenging one, and it will be met only if the preservice measures of teacher competence are of adequate reliability and validity.

NOTES FOR CHAPTER 16

1. Stanley Elam, *Performance Based Teacher Education: What Is the State of the Art?* (Washington, D.C.: AACTE, 1971).

2. Theodore E. Andrews, *Manchester Interview: Competency-Based Teacher Education/Certification* (Washington, D.C.: AACTE, 1972); Caseel Burke, *The Individualized, Competency-Based System of Teacher Education at Weber State College* (Washington, D.C.: AACTE, 1972); Iris Elfenbein, *Performance-Based Teacher Education Programs: A Comparative Description* (Washington, D.C.: AACTE, 1972); Frederick T. Giles and Clifford Foster, *Changing Teacher Education in a Large Urban University* (Washington, D.C.: AACTE, 1972); Benjamin Rosner, ed., *The Power of Competency-Based Teacher Education* (Boston: Allyn & Bacon, 1972), p. 26; James M. Cooper and Wilford Weber, *Competency-Based Teacher Education: A Scenario* (Washington, D.C.: AACTE, 1972).

3. Theodore E. Andrews, *New Directions in Certification,* ERIC ED 043 796 (Denver, Colo.: Improving State Leadership in Education Project, 1970); Harry S. Broudy, *A Critique of PBTE* (Washington, D.C.: AACTE, 1972).

4. W. Robert Houston and Robert B. Howsam, eds., *Competency Based Teacher Education: Progress, Problems, and Prospects* (Chicago: Science Research Associates, 1972), pp. viii-ix.

5. Rosner, *The Power of Competency-Based Teacher Education,* p. 26.

6. Ibid., p. 30.

7. Burke, *The Individualized, Competency-Based System of Teacher Education at Weber State College.*

8. H. L. Jones, "Implementation of Programs" in *Competency Based Teacher*

Education: Progress, Problems, and Prospects, ed. Houston and Howsam, pp. 102-142.

9. E. E. Ghiselli, *Theory of Psychological Measurement* (New York: McGraw-Hill, 1964).

10. Barak Rosenshine, "The Stability of Teacher Effects upon Student Achievement," *Review of Educational Research* 40 (January 1970): 647-662.

11. William H. Angoff, "Scales, Norms, and Equivalent Scores," in *Educational Measurement,* 2d ed., ed. R. L. Thorndike (Washington, D.C.: American Council on Education, 1971), pp. 508-600.

12. J. R. Hills, "Use of Measurement in Selection and Placement," in *Educational Measurement,* 2d ed., ed. Thorndike, p. 694.

13. W. W. Cooley, "Techniques for Considering Multiple Measurements," in *Educational Measurement,* 2d ed., ed. Thorndike, pp. 601-622.

14. H. Gulliksen, *Theory of Mental Tests* (New York: John Wiley & Sons, 1950).

15. There is considerable debate as to whether the intercorrelation between the two tests should be assumed to be zero, since the two scores are earned by the same person. Using this assumption, the intercorrelation between the two tests would have no bearing on the standard error of the difference. The writer is indebted to Dr. Donald Medley of the University of Virginia for calling this point to his attention.

17. Evaluating the Validity of Assessed Performances: Methodological Problems

Richard L. Turner

This chapter is written from the viewpoint of development and evaluation, rather than research. It avoids reliance on research findings or theory generated from research to support the value of a particular kind of teacher or preparatory teacher performance. The problem attacked is thus a practical one. Having developed a set of teaching competencies to which priorities have been assigned, as well as methods for assessing teacher performances that are taken to stand for these competencies, how can the value of the assessed performances be estimated? To put the question a bit differently, how can one increase his confidence that a spectrum of teacher performances, as assessed, is worthwhile?

The problem can best be dealt with by separating it into two parts.

One part deals with the degree to which assessed performances among preparatory teachers group or cluster in such a way as to yield

Adapted from a paper presented at the annual AERA meeting, New Orleans, February 1973.

interpretable classes of performance that can be isolated from the context in which they are assessed.

Assuming that stable classes of performances can be identified, the second part of the problem is to show that these classes, formed during the preparatory phase of the teacher's career, are useful for predicting where the teacher subsequently stands in an array of criterion variables, to each of which value has been attributed. The worth or value of the performance assessments is thus inferred from the relationships they hold to the valued criteria.

This way of dividing the problem is closely related to the six levels of criteria for teacher performance suggested in an earlier paper.[1] The lower criterion levels (6 through 3) employ as criteria teacher knowledges and teaching skills, tested for and observed in different types of contexts. These criteria are implicit in the first part of the problem, and are described below in relation to the contexts in which they would typically be assessed. The upper criterion levels (2 and 1), which primarily involve assessment of the *consequences* of the actions of the teacher, relate to the second part of the problem. They are substantially expanded later in the chapter to include criteria other than pupil learning.

CONTEXTS, PERFORMANCE ASSESSMENTS, AND COMPETENCIES

Teacher preparatory programs usually provide three types of contexts for training, and collaterally for the assessment of performance:

(1) *Symbolic context.* Much instruction and subsequent performance assessment occur in a college or university context, characterized by reading, writing, and talking. Hence the stimuli consist of words, as do the responses. Typically, only verbal performance—or what the teacher "knows" as opposed to what he actually does—is assessed.

(2) *Simulated context.* Some instruction and performance assessment occurs in a laboratory context in which audio materials, films, video tapes, and other kinds of aids and materials are employed. Teaching of a restricted kind, usually microteaching, also occurs. This context is concrete or quasi-concrete on the stimulus side, but it usually remains verbal or symbolic on the response (performance) side, although sometimes materials construction and arrangement are included.

(3) *"Work" context.* Student teaching and various types of class-room observation and participation occur in most preparatory programs. This context is described as "real" or concrete on the stimulus side, and involves an integration of teacher words and actions on the response side. In this context performance assessment may be made by systematic observation or by expert ratings of teacher skills.

These contexts are shown at the left in Figure 17:1 as segments of a column, ordered according to the degree of reality of the stimuli that typically appear in each context, with "symbolic" lowest and "real" highest. Within each segment is a matrix. The horizontal rows of the matrices represent conceptually derived classes of competencies, such as writing/sequencing objectives, questioning/probing, supporting/reinforcing, or whatever one thinks should form a class of competencies. The rows are replicated in each segment, from symbolic to real, so that every class of competency may recur in every type of context. The vertical columns in each segment represent occasions for assessment, a form of assessment, a substantive content (e.g., math or social studies), or all three. Different substantive contents are unlikely to occur within the same occasion.

For example, suppose we are interested in a competency such as sequencing objectives, which we shall label a. This competency can be assessed in all three types of contexts, symbolic (a_{sy}), simulated (a_{si}), and real (a_r). Moreover, within each context one could assess it on more than one occasion: $0_1, 0_2, \ldots 0_n$. Thus, for competency a there are several contexts for assessment, and, within each context, several possible occasions for assessment. A context-by-competency-by-occasion matrix (or three competency-by-occasion matrices) is thereby formed.

The methodological problem posed by these matrices and context segments bears directly on how competency is operationally defined. A competency is usually taken to mean an ability to perform. Presumably this ability is superordinate to the context in which it is assessed, to the occasion on which it is assessed, and to the specific form of required performance by which it is assessed. Moreover, one competency is at least hypothetically separable from another. Questioning/probing is presumably an ability separable from supporting/reinforcing.

Assuming that this concept of a competency is accurate, it follows that one should be able to develop a scale—specifically, a factor scale—that defines the competency. If the scale is a true or valid one, it

Figure 17:1. A Sequence of Moves for Evaluating the Validity of Assessed Performances

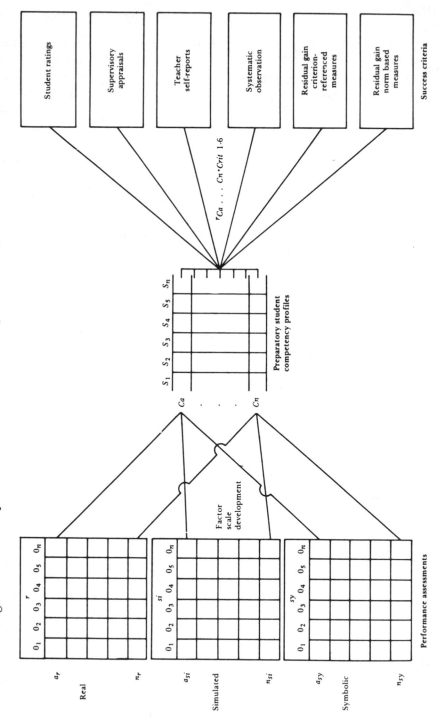

will represent the class of competencies conceptually defined in each parallel row, e.g., the *a* row of the matrix for each segment real, simulated, and symbolic, and will not represent a particular context or particular occasions or particular forms of assessment.

To grasp the situation, the central or "competency profile" portion of Figure 17:1 may be examined. To derive the rows of the competency profile, e.g., of competency C_a, all the occasions (0) in matrices *r*, *si*, and *sy* on which *a* was assessed (a_r, a_{si}, a_{sy}) must show loadings on factor *Ca* and not on some other factor *Cn*, and in addition no factors representing 0 should be extracted. If this condition can be met, a clear-cut set of competencies can be established.

The columns in the competency profile represent students, S_1, $S_2, \ldots S_n$, while any particular student, S_1, will vary across *Ca* ... *Cn*.

The methodological subproblems that attend the development of such competency scales include: (1) finding the minimum number of performances to establish reliable competency scales, (2) the storage and retrieval of accurate records of performance assessments for each preparatory teacher, and (3) developing a method for deriving scales if every person assessed is required to attain "mastery," which presumably means that no variation among persons will appear. Hence, statistical methods depending on variation among observations cannot be employed.

There are two important reasons for deriving competency scales. First, if performances assessed in symbolic and simulated contexts can be shown to correlate consistently with performances in "real" contexts, increased confidence in the value of the symbolic and simulated performances is provided since they predict performances in "real" contexts. Secondly, if one is going to decide on the worth of a set of performances—i.e., a competency—by correlating it with subsequent criteria, he needs to be as certain as possible that he has derived a true scale of competence and that this scale is highly reliable, i.e., that it contains maximum true score variance.

If one pursues these methods, at the end of two or three years he should emerge with a set of factor scales, each representing a competency. The variables loading on each of these scales will be the assessed performances of teachers that, taken together, define the competency. Presumably some performances will not load on these competency scales; they will represent either small unique competencies or error attributable to assessments contexts, assessment occasions, or the form of assessment itself. These performances would in all likelihood be discarded, and scale scores for each student would be derived from those performances that best represent each competency. The end product would be a profile of scaled competencies for each student. Basically, the scales in these profiles are potential predictors using multiple criteria of the teacher's future success.

THE DEVELOPMENT OF CRITERION VARIABLES

The premise underlying a performance or competency based approach to teacher training is that the preparatory teachers who show the highest levels of performance on various competency scales will be more successful teachers, while those showing less performance, or very little competence, as assessed, will be less successful. The question, of course, is what criteria will be taken to represent success. I suggest that six criteria be used:

(1) *Student ratings.* This criterion cannot easily be used with younger children, but is employable with older pupils. It tells the degree of satisfaction pupils have with teachers and is probably an index of what pupils report about teachers to their parents. It is thus a kind of representation of the image a teacher has among his or her clientele.

(2) *Supervisory appraisals.* Supervisory appraisals of teachers represent what principals or supervisors believe to be true of a teacher; they create the image of the teacher these authorities convey to other authorities in the bureaucratic hierarchy. Undoubtedly this image is important to the employment success of the teacher and to the type of informal feedback a preparatory institution receives about its graduates.

(3) *Teacher self-reports.* Since preparatory teachers are the consumers of competency based programs, they represent credible sources of reports about the utility of such programs to many persons. The reports of teachers about the utility of their preparatory program in their particular teaching situation are a criterion worth noting.

(4) *Observation of teacher-pupil classroom behavior.* Certain observation schedules involve scales that may be regarded as important with respect to the kind of life, intellectual and interpersonal, that

students lead in classrooms. For example, some schedules report on relationships among students, the teacher-pupil relationship, classroom climate, teacher dominance, and the like. Since pupils experience the classroom day in and day out, such scales deserve attention as indices of the *quality* of classroom life.

(5) *Residual pupil gain on criterion-referenced tests.* Pupil increases in knowledge as assessed by criterion-referenced tests may be considered important, if agreement can be reached on the value of the criteria against which the test is constructed.

(6) *Residual pupil gain on norm-based tests of achievement and of divergent thinking, or "creativity."* As in the past, these sets of criteria remain important ones since general achievement and creativity continue to be valued.

In the literature on teacher effectiveness, criteria 1, 2, 3, 4, and 6 have usually been shown to have little relation to each other; therefore, the criterion variables may be regarded as heterogeneous. This fact does not negate the relevance of any of the criteria; it simply makes satisfying all of them simultaneously with any one competency very difficult. If, however, one has developed multiple competency scales that are orthogonal to each other—i.e., that provide a heterogeneous array—then having a heterogeneous set of criteria provides the possibility that different competencies will relate well to different types of criteria.

The desired situation may be represented visually in a form like that shown at the right in Figure 17:1. An array of factor scales representing competencies $C_a \ldots C_n$ at the end of student teaching or an internship year are to be correlated with each of the criteria (1 through 6) of teacher success.

The methodological problems involved in relating the competency scales of individual preparatory teachers to success criteria are centrally procedural difficulties that arise from logistical and financial constraints. Graduates of a preparatory program should be appraised for success during each of the first two years on the job. If there are many graduates or if they are widely dispersed, obtaining the necessary criterion data will be extremely expensive and very difficult to manage.

One strategy for minimizing expense and management difficulties is to divide graduating students at random into three groups; then assign assessment on only two of the success criteria to each group.

Since all of the competency scales are represented in each group, all get tested against each criterion but not in every group. This methodology does not allow examination of the relationships among the full array of criteria, but it nonetheless provides the basic data necessary to determine the extent to which observations on each competency scale correlate with the criterion variables.

The product of this approach to the validation of assessed performances will be a set of zero order correlations between the competency scales (predictors) and the criterion variables or relevant components thereof. The pattern of the significant correlations among predictors and the criteria will indicate which of the competencies are more powerful in predicting success, and what kind of success they predict. It will also indicate which competencies seem to be of little worth, that is, correlate with few or no criteria. What this approach will *not* reveal is much information about the relationships between teacher classroom behaviors and pupil achievement or other outcome criteria. The latter, however, are the domain of research and need not, in the writer's opinion, be regarded as a significant omission in the development and evaluation of the assessed performances of preparatory teachers.

NOTE FOR CHAPTER 17

1. R. L. Turner, "Programmatic Themes and Mechanisms," in *The Power of Competency-Based Teacher Education,* ed. Benjamin Rosner (Boston: Allyn & Bacon, 1972), pp. 196-201.

18. Measurement Techniques: What We Have and What We Need

Patricia M. Kay

One of the most serious issues that confronts any teacher education faculty wishing to implement a competency based program is the lack of appropriate reliable procedures to assess complex teaching performance. This chapter presents arguments for the construction of a set or sets of instruments that might fulfill this need in a way that presently available measurement systems do not, and attempts to place the use of such instruments in the broader context of a total assessment strategy.

The distinction between assessment strategies and measurement systems is particularly important as it applies to competency based teacher education and certification. A total assessment strategy consists of the full set of procedures for collecting evidence that prospective teachers have acquired specified levels of mastery of critical concepts and skills. The assessment strategy may make use of many measurement techniques, ranging from the familiar paper-and-pencil objective tests of knowledge outcomes to videotaped recordings of

269

complex teaching situations in which specified behaviors may be observed and rated or counted.

The need for a total assessment strategy arises from the very essence of competency based teacher education (CBTE), while the need for certain measurement procedures arises from a gap in the technology of teacher behavior research. While this chapter is addressed primarily to those measurement procedures which, for the most part, are yet to be developed, it is important to place these procedures in the total assessment picture.

To be certifiable under CBTE, a prospective teacher must be able to demonstrate under actual classroom conditions the possession of those behaviors, skills, and knowledges by which good teaching practice is defined. This is a necessary condition whatever the program characteristics of the preparing institution. Some programs may be modular in format; others may more nearly resemble traditional programs. Some programs may emphasize field experiences; others may be more dependent on laboratory simulation activities. In any case, assessment under actual classroom conditions, whether real or simulated, is still necessary if huge inferential leaps are not to be made.

To implement an assessment strategy, essential teaching skills and knowledges must be identified, described, and defined, and priorities set among them. The set of measurement techniques that will determine the level of mastery of the defined behaviors must be constructed or collected, and the conditions or context in which prospective teachers will be assessed must be designated.

We do not intend fully to discuss the numerous approaches to identifying specific competencies, but several points should be noted. Almost all of the current approaches to defining competencies are variously based on available research, social science theory, the demands of specific curricula, and the experience of the teaching profession. Previous research, while not clearly establishing the importance of many teaching behaviors, does support the testing of hypotheses concerning some of them. The experiences of teachers, supervisors, and teacher educators, as well as "educational theories," also contribute to hypotheses concerning which teaching behaviors seem to make a difference in pupil learning. Whatever the basis for identification of competencies, the results at this time are mostly hypothetical and should be regarded as strictly tentative, subject to validation studies centering on the question, Is this the set of behaviors that is the most powerful in bringing about desired pupil change?

Once a set of tentative competency descriptions has been agreed on, measurement procedures must be matched to them. This is a major problem.

While there is no dearth of instruments for measuring teacher *behavior* (for example, the *Handbook of Research on Teaching, Mirrors for Behavior,* and the research literature contain references to literally hundreds), these presently available instruments fall roughly into two categories, neither wholly appropriate for the overall reliable assessment of teaching *performance.*

The first category contains instruments like those currently used by school systems to evaluate teaching personnel. They are, typically, rating forms that in essence ask the rater to make global judgments of various general aspects of teaching and teaching-related performance. Such instruments are notoriously subjective, primarily because of the lack of definitional consensus of categories within forms. Validation studies are nonexistent—if such are possible or even make sense. At best they may be thought of as forms on which to record employer satisfaction; they are not appropriate for measuring teacher competency. The proliferation of such forms for use in teacher education and certification, lacking as they do a host of desirable measurement characteristics, would be a serious detriment to the future of competency based teacher education. Dependence on this kind of procedure for collecting evidence of prospective teachers' levels of performance would likely bring to a halt the necessary teacher behavior research for validating competencies.

The second category of available instruments contains those measures that have been constructed primarily for use in research on or training for teaching. These measures usually focus on highly defined and very specific teacher behaviors and may be grounded in some theoretical position about teaching, learning, or teaching-learning interactions. While the reliability and validity of some instruments in this category may be at a higher level, their use is better suited to formative evaluation of teacher training: to give prospective teachers and their trainers feedback as students acquire the specific, isolated pedagogic skills and behaviors that are components of a training program. Dependence on these kinds of measures as a sole means of acquiring evidence of prospective teachers' skills would be a disservice to the future of competency based teacher education. While a set of these measures might provide evidence that prospective teachers do possess the specified skills in isolation, they provide little if any assurance that in a complex, day-to-day classroom situation the teacher can and will use those skills.

Thus, we are left with "measures" of employer satisfaction and measures of specific skills that are suitable for formative evaluation of prospective teachers. What we lack for the overall assessment strategy is measures that lie in between global evaluations and isolated pedagogic skill measures. These measures might be termed procedures for summative evaluation of prospective teachers' performances; they would assess competencies under the conditions of having to "get it all together." Del Schalock has aptly referred to them as judgments about the students' abilities to "orchestrate" all the knowledges and skills for which training has occurred,[1] and Richard Turner has pointed to this type of procedure as providing the most logical criteria for the provisional certification of teachers.[2]

The development of instruments to measure teacher performance under real classroom conditions will, no doubt, be extremely expensive but is crucial to the establishment of competency based teacher education. The Committee on National Program Priorities in Teacher Education has suggested a five-year-plan to develop approximately 250 such criterion measures, and has recommended that if the U.S. Office of Education were to fund a single effort to establish competency based teacher education, it should invest in the development of these instruments.[3]

To proceed with instrument development, an overall coordinating structure is necessary to avoid duplication of effort and achieve some degree of agreement on specifications.

Since it is not possible to measure all teaching behaviors in all possible contexts for each student, assessment situations will have to be sampled from a domain of teaching situations, which might be defined by situations in which teachers find themselves and the kinds of tasks they are required to perform. One guiding structure that might be useful is the Master Coordinate System, developed by B. Othanel Smith to guide the development of protocol materials for teacher education. This system is role defined and as free as possible from conflicting doctrines about what teachers do or ought to do.

The system is illustrated in its most basic form in Figure 18:1. It can be expanded in all three dimensions, but for these purposes particularly in the sources of behaviors dimension. It should be noted that the system itself will not generate the assessment situations.

Figure 18:1. Master Coordinate Systems of Settings,
Behaviors, and Levels

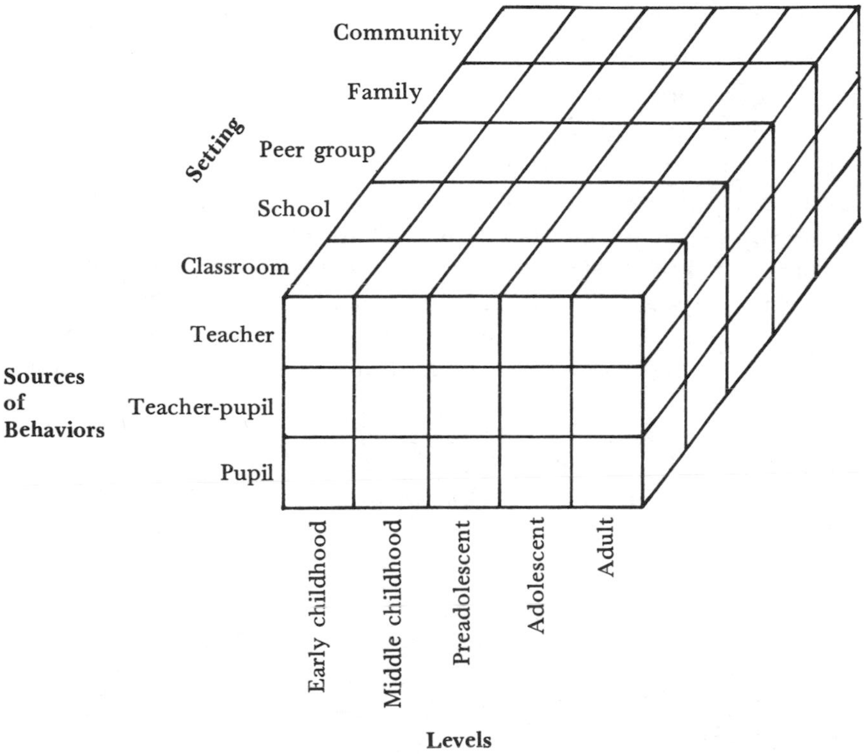

Source: B. Othanel Smith, *Catalog of Protocol Materials* (Tallahassee: Florida
State Department of Education, 1971).

Rather, it would be useful in much the same way that a "two-way
grid" is useful in test construction for defining the domain of possible test items. Items themselves are generated by the demands of
the subject matter. Here, assessment situations would be generated
by the demands of specific curricula, theory of the social sciences,
and practice of teaching. The appeal of this system lies in its ability
to provide for the development of instruments to assess competencies derived from a variety of theoretical positions.[4]

For the blocks of the expanded system, tasks would need to be developed to elicit the critical behaviors appropriate to the particular setting, source, and level. For example, for the classroom setting, middle childhood level, teacher-pupil sources, one task might be to ask prospective teachers to diagnose informally the arithmetic skill levels of a small group of elementary school children. The responses to this task and to several others might provide indicators of skill level for a number of competency areas (interaction, accurate diagnosis, planning, etc.) while allowing for the idiosyncracy or creativity of individual trainees. No one assessment situation would suffice to assure minimum competency but a sample of tasks appropriate to the certification and employment goals of the trainee could.

Table 18:1 illustrates how the evidence from a series of assessment tasks might be applicable to a number of competency areas. The competency areas used in the table are purely hypothetical but have some conceptual basis in teacher behavior research. The first *six* have

Table 18:1. Example of How Evidence of Competencies Might Be Gathered over a Series of Assessment Tasks

Hypothetical teacher competency areas	Assessment tasks		
	A programmed test of decision-making ability in reading instruction	A one-week teaching unit in science	A semi-microteaching math task
Teacher's ability to:			
Use informal assessment procedures	*	*	
Use formal assessment procedures	*	*	
Select content	*		
Set terminal performance goals	*		
Choose and construct materials	*	*	
Choose and devise procedures	*	*	
Explain		*	*
Interact		*	*
Give directions		*	*
Provide feedback		*	*

*Indicates that further defined behaviors pertaining to competency area might be assessed using task.

to do with teachers' planning and decision-making skills: formal and informal evaluating, goal setting, and strategy, materials, and methods selection. The last four areas encompass those skills that usually come to mind when performance measures are discussed, and have to do with teachers' abilities to implement plans in the classroom.

Similarly, the three assessment tasks used as examples are only possibilities. They have not been developed as described here, but the technological feasibility of each has been demonstrated in another context. A similar programmed test procedure has been successfully used for the evaluation of medical students by Christine H. McGuire at the University of Illinois.[5] A two-week teaching unit assessment situation is currently under development at Educational Testing Service by the Teacher Behavior Research Group under the direction of Frederick J. McDonald, and the utility of microteaching situations has been demonstrated in a number of contexts.

The programmed test of reading instruction skills in Table 18:1 is a simulation approach to assessing a prospective teacher's decision-making skills in planning for reading instruction. Under this approach, information would be presented and the teacher would be required to indicate the necessary next steps. The consequences of the teacher's decision would then be presented and another decision step taken and so on.

Materials that might be used in the simulation could include a group of children's cumulative folders containing data on family background, the child's interests, samples of written work, standardized test scores, anecdotal reports, and records of prior performance and materials used. They might also include films or audio recordings of samples of the children's oral reading as well as films or videotapes of a group reading lesson.

The second assessment task in Table 18:1 is an actual teaching situation where the prospective teacher must plan and conduct instruction to meet some prespecified pupil goals in science education over a period of one week. This task would, of course, be more standardized and also elaborated on more fully for the student. Responses that might be rated in addition to time-sampled video recordings for observation could be lesson plans, selected teaching materials, end-of-unit tests for pupils, etc.

The third example is a semi-microteaching kind of task in which the prospective teacher is asked to teach a specific math concept, using specified procedures, to a small group of children.

For each situation and task that would be developed into a measure (or set of measures), instrument specifications would need to be drawn up to include: the critical behaviors to be elicited; setting descriptions; stimulus and response modes; scoring procedures; administrative procedures; and cost estimates.

The critical behaviors to be assessed for each task follow from the identification and specific description and definition of competencies.

There is little doubt that the context in which assessment takes place strongly influences the outcomes. Therefore the setting in which assessment is to take place must be carefully described. The same task may be administered in several settings (open classroom/traditional classroom, urban youngsters/suburban youngsters, etc.), but for two important reasons each must be described. First, information on context variables will be needed for validating instruments and teacher training curricula and, more immediately, would be useful information for prospective employers. Furthermore, if normative information is required, assessment settings will have to be standardized or otherwise taken into consideration in some manner.

Stimulus and response modes could be specified from a number of available alternatives. Prospective teachers might respond to paper-and-pencil directions in a videotaped mode—or vice versa. Films, audiotapes, and actual demonstrations are other possibilities. Responses need not be limited to overt teacher behavior as the only teacher "product" but could include products such as lesson plans, teacher-made tests, reports to parents, and other record-keeping and planning outcomes. And of course one stimulus may produce a series of responses in various modes.

Scoring procedures will have to be determined for each of the critical behaviors of a task. The appropriate scoring procedure for each task will probably be arrived at only through both logical analysis and empirical comparisons.

There are two points on scoring procedures that seem to be critical. First, the desirability of obtaining a profile of competencies across tasks for each prospective teacher cannot be emphasized too strongly. Referring back to Table 18:1, competency areas like those listed might form the basis of a profile. Evidence gathered from each task could be combined in some manner to yield a score that indicates the level of mastery of that particular competency area.

This brings us to the second point, which involves a popular misconception about competency assessment. Along with the conceptual development of competency based teacher education, the idea has spread that competency assessment should proceed on, and be recorded and reported on, a criterion basis. This notion has probably grown out of a combination of factors: the systems approach, which has influenced so heavily the development of competency based teacher education; the growing concern that CBTE retain humanistic properties; perhaps even the notion that levels of skill needed would differ from context to context and must, to some extent, be negotiated from situation to situation.

It will be unfortunate, however, if assessment for teacher education and certification proceeds solely on a criterion-referenced basis. The major problem lies in agreement on criteria. If we are ever to agree on what levels of teaching skills (as well as what combinations of teaching skills) are needed to influence pupil behaviors, it will be necessary to know what each skill is and what constitutes varying levels of that skill. It will be necessary to reliably measure differences in skill levels and subject those results to validation studies. At that point, varying criterion levels for varying purposes (i.e., provisional versus permanent certification) may be set with some degree of confidence.

Finally, in planning for instrument development and in drawing up specifications for specific assessment tasks, two types of cost estimates should be generated: one for instrument development and one for ongoing use of the instrument. Cost estimates might include estimates of faculty and student time, space requirements, availability of public school pupils, and settings, as well as purely dollar costs. Unrealistic or unreasonable costs in any direction may dictate revision of specifications.

CONCLUSION

We have outlined, very briefly, one path that might be taken to arrive at some measures of teacher competency under the conditions of "getting it all together." Granted, it is an extremely ambitious plan and there is little likelihood of one institution or program developing it all. Such a plan might, however, form a basis on which cooperative efforts could be undertaken.

NOTES FOR CHAPTER 18

1. H. Del Schalock, "Performance Based Teacher Education," paper presented to City University of New York, Trainers of Teacher-Trainers (TTT) Conference on Performance Based Certification, New York City, 1971.

2. Richard L. Turner, "Relationships between *Teachers for the Real World* and the Elementary Models Programmatic Themes and Mechanisms: Payoffs, Mechanisms, and Costs," in *The Power of Competency-Based Teacher Education*, ed. Benjamin Rosner (Boston: Allyn & Bacon, 1972), pp. 188-221.

3. Benjamin Rosner, "Recommendations for Competency-Based Teacher Education and Certification," in *The Power of Competency-Based Teacher Education*, ed. Rosner, pp. 24-35.

4. B. Othanel Smith, *Catalog of Protocol Materials* (Tallahassee: Florida State Department of Education, 1971).

5. Christine H. McGuire, "An Evaluation Model for Professional Education—Medical Education," *Proceedings of the 1967 Invitational Conference on Testing Problems* (Princeton, N.J.: Educational Testing Service, 1968).

19. Using Pupil Data to Assess Teacher Competencies

Wilford A. Weber

INTRODUCTION

However else they may be defined and described, there appears to be general agreement that competency based teacher education programs are instructional systems that have been designed to prepare competent teachers.[1] As with other types of instructional systems, the purpose of assessment in a competency based program is to provide information on which to base operational decisions. Many of those who advocate competency based instructional systems for teacher education do so largely in the belief that such an approach provides better information on which to make program decisions. That is, competency based instructional systems call for assessment procedures that provide data which are less inferential and, consequently, more predictive than those data available in more traditional approaches.

The purpose of this chapter is to explore the extent to which data from pupils taught by teacher education students may be utilized to improve the quality of those decisions that are required in a CBTE program, beginning with a consideration of the purposes of assessment in competency based teacher education programs: that is, a discussion of the types of data-based decisions that are most crucial in a competency based instructional system.

PURPOSES OF ASSESSMENT

Banathy has suggested that assessment has two major purposes: (1) the evaluation of learner performance; and (2) monitoring the instructional system's effectiveness and economy.[2] Many who have described assessment in competency based instructional systems seem to have expanded this notion to include what they consider to be other equally important functions. For example, Houston suggests three functions to be served by assessment: (1) the monitoring of student performance; (2) the improvement of program effectiveness; and (3) the improvement of program operation and management.[3] DeVault also cites three purposes; he says: "Assessment data, continually collected, make possible the essential monitoring of student progress, provide feedback on the effectiveness of instructional activities, and suggest the appropriateness of a given teacher's associated personal goals, instructional program, and ultimate career expectations."[4] Dodl suggests four uses of assessment in competency based teacher education programs: (1) assessment of student-trainee performance; (2) evaluation of program effectiveness and efficiency; (3) collection of "beyond program" data useful to program decisions such as recruitment[5]; and (4) validation of specified competencies.[6] These authors and others, including Schalock and Smith,[7] have provided good descriptions of the role assessment plays in the competency based certification of educational personnel. Thus, it may be seen that in a competency based instructional system, assessment procedures are expected to provide information that enhances the quality of a large variety of data-based decisions.

The discussion which follows is most centrally concerned with the three decision areas that appear to be most crucial in the design and operation of competency based teacher education programs: (1) the monitoring of student progress and the determination of student achievement; (2) the evaluation of program effectiveness and efficiency; and (3) the validation of specified competencies. This discussion is followed by an examination of the ways in which pupil data—as opposed to or in conjunction with data from other sources—might be used to enhance the predictive validity of decisions relevant to the areas identified as most crucial in competency based instructional systems.

Monitoring Student Progress and Determining Student Achievement

Competency based instructional systems require: (1) the utilization of formative assessment procedures that provide data on student progress; and (2) the utilization of summative assessment procedures that provide data on the extent to which the student has demonstrated mastery in those competencies that are specified as program expectations. The monitoring of student progress and the determination of student achievement have been described by a variety of authors, but perhaps no one has done it better than Airasian in his discussion of the role of summative and formative evaluation with regard to mastery learning.[8] In a teacher education context, his assertions could be paraphrased in this form: On the one hand, the instructional system demands constant, ongoing formative evaluation to provide information useful for (1) student decisions in selecting objectives and learning experiences from among those alternatives and options which the program has provided, and (2) instructor decisions on which instructional processes might be best used to facilitate student growth toward competency. Assessment procedures are formative in that they are utilized to indicate how students are progressing with respect to explicitly stated instructional objectives related to specific competencies. On the other hand, the instructional system also requires summative data about student achievement; this is useful in making decisions such as awarding academic credit, degrees, and certification. This type of assessment provides data that indicate whether or not the student has met certain program requirements. In short, formative evaluation provides data about how students are becoming competent, and summative evaluation provides data about whether or not students have become competent.[9]

Evaluation of Program Effectiveness and Efficiency

The adequacy of a competency based instructional system is judged in terms of its intended purpose—the preparation of teachers who have acquired and demonstrated the competencies the program has deemed desirable. This means that the teacher education program must continuously assess the degree to which its students are demonstrating and have demonstrated those competencies. Such continuous evaluation and analysis provides program managers with information on both program effectiveness and—to a lesser extent, given our present level of sophistication in this regard—program efficiency. Decision-makers must have this information if they are to make intelligent judgments about program refinement and modification. Such decisions are best based on formative data that provide feedback on the appropriateness of program objectives, the adequacy of instructional processes, and the competence of program graduates. Only assessment procedures which provide such feedback can promote the development and operation of an open and regenerative system. Schalock notes that, "by and large, the kind of data being called for here are data that serve on-line decision making and are thereby best thought of as data that derive from either formative or summative-comparative evaluation activities rather than research activities."[10] Several advocates of competency based instructional systems for the preparation of educational personnel have provided descriptions of what have been called data-dependent program operation. Among the best of these are Schalock and DeVault.[11] For the purposes of this discussion, it is sufficient to say that the quality of information obtained and available largely determines the ability of program managers to make decisions intended to optimize both the effectiveness and the economy of the instructional system.

Validation of Specified Competencies

Both advocates and critics of competency based teacher education view the validation of the competencies specified by programs as absolutely essential to program effectiveness. It can be argued that teacher educators must be committed to empirically testing the validity of those competencies specified. "Each and every competency must be treated as an assumption which must be tested in terms of its purported relationship to pupil outcomes deemed desirable."[12] It should be noted that it is a most difficult—but not impossible—necessary task to establish relationships between specific teacher competencies and pupil outcomes.[13] A strategy that seems quite feasible is to be found in programs that perceive competency selections as untested assumptions to be treated as testable hypotheses. Such a program holds itself accountable for presenting evidence that supports or rejects those hypotheses. In addition, competency based programs have been described as environments within which such competency validation research might take place.[14] The point is simply this: If the purpose of the instructional system is the preparation of teachers who are competent, that program must be able to provide data which indicate that the competencies specified are indeed related to pupil change, however this is defined by the program.

ASSESSMENT CRITERIA

Having established that CBTE programs are instructional systems that have as their purpose the preparation of competent teachers, and having identified three of the more crucial types of decisions for which assessment is expected to provide information in competency based instructional systems, we now turn to an examination of those criteria that are viewed as appropriate for satisfying those data needs.

Many of the assessment procedures that have been advocated by proponents of competency based instruction can be traced to developments which have come from the teacher effectiveness research efforts of the past several decades; for example, improved assessment models, measurement tools, and statistical procedures. Indeed, in describing assessment criteria thought to be useful in assessing teacher competency in teacher education programs, most writers appear to build on the classic model of teacher effectiveness research proposed by Mitzel.[15] Using an input-process-output systems model, Mitzel provides a very useful description of three types of criteria that might be used in studying teacher effectiveness: (1) presage variables, which include teacher personality attributes and teacher knowledge; (2) process variables, which include teacher and student classroom interaction behaviors; and (3) product variables, which include the effects of teaching in terms of changes in student behavior. His model suggests that there are teacher (and student) personality attributes and knowledge—presage factors—which influence the nature of teacher-pupil classroom behaviors—process factors—and that these behaviors influence the pupil learning outcomes of that interaction—product factors. Numerous writers have built on this model although they have given the criteria different labels: knowledge, performance, and product criteria[16]; knowledge, skill, and competence criteria[17]; performance criteria which are knowledge referenced, skill referenced, and output referenced[18]; cognitive-based, performance-based, and consequence-based criteria[19]; personal attribute, process, and outcome criteria[20]; and knowledge, performance, and consequence criteria.[21]

Regardless of the labels used, a cursory examination of the writings of these authors seems to suggest that the selection of assessment criteria in a CBTE program should be fairly straightforward. Since the purpose of the program is to prepare teachers who are competent, and since the role of the teacher is to bring about desirable learner outcomes, it follows that teacher competency is best determined by measuring the growth of pupils taught by the teacher. The logic of this position has caused some to perceive it as being universal. For example, McDonald states: "There is almost universal agreement that the ultimate criterion for evaluation of a teacher is the effect of his teaching behavior on the performance of his students."[22] However, words of caution come from several sources, including Gage, McNeil, and Smith.

Gage claims that "the phrase 'the criterion of teacher effectiveness' betokens a degree of generality that has seldom been found in any branch of the behavioral sciences."[23] And McNeil says: "A criterion is a standard for judging and the criteria of teacher effectiveness should be derived from the goals of the educational system. Since in any system there are usually several goals, it is unlikely that there will be a single concrete and universal criterion for teacher ability."[24]

In addressing the issue of "optimum criteria" with regard to certification, Smith states: "The third criterion—ability to produce changes in pupil behavior—is perhaps the most rigorous [criterion]. It requires that the candidate's behavior produce an acceptable level of pupil learning under specified conditions, and over a specified time. The growth of pupils must be reflected not only in cognitive development, but also in affective development."[25] A bit later he adds: "But the matter is not so simple as it appears. In the first place, this criterion demands more evidence than can be readily provided. In the second place, it requires more evidence than is demanded of any other type of professional."[26] He goes on to make a very logical case for his position.

SOME CONSIDERATIONS

The "no single criterion" notion of Gage, McNeil, and Smith's comments suggests that there are, and perhaps appropriately should be, conflicting views among teacher educators on this issue. Because they have different concerns they hold differing opinions about the usefulness of knowledge, performance, and/or consequence criteria in assessing teacher competency. One is better able to understand these differences through an examination of reports from two conferences which reflect input from a relatively large number of teacher educators concerned with problems related to the assessment of teacher competency.[27]

A description of competency based teacher education assessment criteria was generated by participants who attended a conference in August 1971 on performance-based teacher education, sponsored by the American Association of Colleges for Teacher Education in August 1971: "Assessment of the students competence: (1) uses his performance as the primary source of evidence; (2) takes into account evidence of students' knowledge relevant to planning, analyzing, interpreting, or evaluating situations or behaviors; and (3) makes use of evidence on the consequences of student behavior where valid and feasible."[28]

In describing the problems of criteria selection as viewed by teacher educators who attended a U.S. Office of Education-sponsored conference in May 1971, McDonald notes that "participants described two kinds of criteria: (1) the criterion of classroom performance, and (2) the criterion of pupil performance. Both were recognized as significant criteria, but there was general agreement that the ultimate criterion is that of pupil performance. Much of the discussion centered on the interrelationship of these two criteria and on the problem of determining when each should be used."[29]

An examination of the views that were discussed above suggest that of the several factors that might be considered in the selection of assessment criteria and strategies, three considerations are foremost: (1) the purpose for which the data obtained will be used—data-need considerations; (2) the validity of the data—predictive validity considerations; and (3) the feasibility of applying those criteria in an instructional system context—feasibility considerations. A similar observation is found in the recently published monograph by

Merwin.[30] The discussion below briefly describes these considerations and attempts to make a case for their importance.

Data need considerations. The kinds of data-based decisions that must be made in competency based instructional systems differ in their perceived complexity and importunity. Thus, the assessment of student progress and achievement, the evaluation of program effectiveness, and the validation of specified competencies supply information for different types of programmatic decisions and are seen as meeting different types of data needs. That is, decisions which are seen as crucial are viewed as requiring information which allows great confidence—highly predictive, low inference data. For less important decisions, more inferential and less predictive data may be considered useful.

The point is that all teacher education programs require information on which to base certain kinds of decisions, and competency based teacher education programs are no different. However, where CBTE programs *do* differ is the extent to which they attempt to make decisions that are less inferential and more predictive. They do so by employing more rigorous assessment criteria and procedures in measuring teacher competencies. It is likely, then, that in making programmatic decisions in a competency based instructional system, teacher educators make significantly more demands of the data than is generally found in more traditional programs. However, the literature suggests that there is far from unanimity of agreement about the kinds of data that are required for specific kinds of programmatic decisions. A good case in point is the issues relating to the initial certification of teachers. In short, such judgments are program specific; few, if any, universal truths exist in this regard.

Predictive validity considerations. The quality of decisions that program managers are able to make is directly related to the validity of the data they use in making those decisions. Decisions made on the basis of data that have a high degree of predictive validity are likely to inspire confidence. Conversely, decisions that are made on the basis of highly inferential data are likely to be considered suspect. Those concerned with issues relating to predictive validity find themselves faced with numerous measurement problems, including: the inadequacy of measurement instruments and procedures[31]; the inadequacy of measures of teacher behavior and the lack of an adequate taxonomy of teaching behaviors[32]; the difficulties involved in isolating teacher influence from other influences on pupils, the lack of appropriate statistical methodologies, and the inadequacy measures and procedures for determining student growth of various kinds but particularly with regard to higher cognitive levels[33]; the many problems related to sampling and to obtaining objective, reliable information[34]; the tendency to specify and measure the easily measured competencies and to fail to measure those—often more important—that are difficult to measure[35]; the inadequacy and/or inappropriateness of measurement procedures, statistical analyses, and evaluation models[36]; and the use of norm-referenced measurement in systems calling for criterion-referenced procedures.[37] And in their excellent chapter on the assessment of teacher competence, McNeil and Popham note the great deal of support educational researchers have given the notion that the ultimate criterion of teacher competence is his impact on the learner. But they add that "reservations in accepting pupil change as the chief criterion of teacher effectiveness have arisen both from technical problems in assessing learner growth and from philosophical considerations."[38]

Our present level of psychometric sophistication does not permit the accurate measurement of human behavior of a complex nature in what are largely complex situations, except at extremely great expense. To claim otherwise is to contradict the present reality. The problems of measurement are many and largely unsolved. They seriously limit our ability to collect and utilize data that are of high predictive validity. On the other hand, recent years have shown great progress; there has been marked improvement in the ability to measure both objectively and reliably within the research context, and these gains are being reflected in the instructional context as well.

Several points are worthy of mention here. First, teacher education programs, competency based or not, are faced with very complex measurement problems. It is highly unlikely that solutions to all these many problems will be forthcoming in the near future. In the meantime, programs are daily faced with the making of operational decisions which—to the extent possible—should be based on information that is objective, reliable, and valid. Secondly, teacher competence measurement problems are not only the concern of competency based instructional systems. All teacher education programs face similar problems. The issue, then, is not whether or not to measure but how well to measure. Competency based instructional systems must be committed to the establishment of assessment procedures that will provide program managers access to the best available information, given "state of the art" and resource realities. And, thirdly, it is painfully obvious that those assessment procedures that are most likely to provide valid data are the most difficult and the most expensive.

Feasibility considerations. Competency based teacher education programs operate in the real world. In making decisions relevant to program design and operational procedures, program managers are faced with time and resource realities, and a program's assessment procedures will reflect that reality as program managers perceive it. Thus it is that concerns about feasibility impose themselves on decisions in assessment of teacher competency in a competency based instructional system. Merwin states the case nicely: "Regarding the measurement system itself, one should also apply a 'utility' criterion. Basically, this is asking of each data gathering effort whether the cost of time, money, and effort can be justified by the extent to which they reduce risks for decision makers."[39]

That such decisions will be dependent on those priorities that have been established by a program's decision-makers is clear. Again, decisions must be program specific. No attempt is made here to prescribe what those priorities ought to be, but it is easily recognized that highly predictive data are often most difficult to obtain. Consequently, assessment procedures that involve the collection and analysis of pupil growth data are likely to require far more resources than those that focus exclusively on the behavior of the teacher. Similarly, assessment procedures that utilize systematic observation of teaching behavior are likely to cost more than procedures that measure only the students' intellectual abilities and cognitive understandings. Program decision-makers should examine their need for assessment data in cost-effectiveness terms; they should view the resources used to obtain these data as invested, not spent.

Our recommendation here is that those who are faced with problems related to the assessment of teacher competencies within a competency based instructional system context will find better solutions if they give due consideration to: (1) the purposes of the system and their perceptions of the importance of the data-based decisions to be made; (2) the kinds of assessment criteria and procedures that will yield data at a level of predictive validity with which they would be satisfied; and (3) the "cost" of the data to be collected through the application of those criteria and procedures selected. The task is one of obtaining the "best" information possible at a "cost" the program can afford, given the purpose of the program and perceptions about the importance of the decisions to be made on the basis of that information. This task is a program-specific process in which decision-makers must determine what is most useful and practical in their context. Because different programs will be based on differences of opinion as to which types of assessment data are most useful and practical in assessing teacher competencies within the context of that program, seemingly conflicting views will result.

Before moving to an examination of several of those somewhat conflicting views that result from these differences of opinion, it seems appropriate to attend to a closely related issue which has interesting implications for those who consider questions on the use of pupil data in assessing teacher competencies. On the assumption that the purpose of a CBTE program is to prepare competent teachers, such programs have been viewed here as instructional systems. Many advocates of the competency based approach call attention to the need for teacher education instructional systems which incorporate what can be viewed as research subsystems[40] and accountability subsystems.[41]

Schalock has provided a most eloquent case supporting the need for what he calls "a shift from an essentially training function to a research, development, and training function" in teacher education programs.[42] The essence of his argument is that the effective, efficient operation of teacher education programs is dependent on research and development activities. He argues that a "performance-based, output-referenced, and data-dependent" instructional system provides the best possible context within which to mount research and development activities which are intended to provide the program with empirically validated solutions to programmatic problems. This has particular appeal within a professional school context, which includes an emphasis on research and development activities which will expand the "validated knowledge base of the teaching profession."

Two words of caution are offered here:

(1) Research and development efforts must support the instructional function; that is, research and development efforts should be

shaped by the data needs of the program; research and development costs should be viewed from a viewpoint of "what can the instructional program afford"; and research and development activities should be seen as requiring very vigorous data—data that are extremely expensive to collect and analyze, and which may in their vigor far exceed the realistic data needs of the instructional system.

(2) The degree to which a teacher education program should emphasize the research and development function depends on several factors; these factors include the extent to which the program has been built on the validated knowledge base, the extent to which the program can obtain useful research and data from sources external to itself (research and development centers and regional laboratories, for example), and the extent to which the program has been and is able to allocate resources necessary and appropriate to such efforts.

Within the context of this discussion, our point is this: The purpose of a research and development component (research and development subsystem) within a CBTE program (instructional system) is to provide certain kinds of data that meet the data needs of the program. The purpose of a research and development program (research and development system) is to provide data that meet the data needs of the profession (the suprasystem). The data needs of a program and those of the profession are similar but not identical. Each program requires only data that are useful in the program context; the profession, however, must have data that can be generalized to all programs. The assessment criteria and procedures necessary to generate generalizable data useful to the profession make resource demands far in excess of what might be reasonably expected of most teacher education programs. Great care must be taken not to expect CBTE programs to do that which is unreasonable. In this context, one must ask to what degree residual pupil gain data—*the* ultimate criterion of the researcher—can and should be *the* criterion of the teacher educator.

Concerns about the function of assessment in accountability efforts in competency based instructional systems are similar to those that have been described above about the function of research. As long as accountability efforts—whether student and/or program accountability—are both formative and summative processes that are intended to assure that program graduates are competent, all—pupils, students, the program, the profession, and society—are well served.

Unfortunately, most "systems of accountability" are not intended to facilitate the acquisition and demonstration of competence but are rather intended to prove cases of incompetence. This is somewhat less true in preservice teacher education than it is in the inservice setting, but its effects are often contradictory to the purposes of an instructional system. This view receives support from McNeil in his thoughtfully written book on the issues of accountability and assessment and improvement of teacher competency.[43] His notions about the utility of contract plans and clinical supervision techniques are well worth noting. As long as efforts to hold students accountable for meeting the expectations of the program—and as long as efforts to hold the program accountable for the quality of its graduates—are viewed in terms of the purposes of the instructional system—the preparation of competent teachers—such efforts are necessary and appropriate functions in which assessment plays a key role.

There is a great temptation to utilize pupil data in assessing teacher competency. Because the teacher's role is to facilitate pupil growth, it follows that the teacher education student should be held accountable for demonstrating the ability to change pupil behavior in desirable ways; and because the purpose of the teacher education instructional system is to produce competent teachers, it is equally appropriate to hold programs accountable in terms of the ability of program graduates to bring about appropriate pupil outcomes. However, if data are to be considered adequate for "due process" purposes, they must be of a very vigorous nature and beyond suspicion, for these data are expected to generate a degree of confidence that most likely can only come from an application of pupil gain criteria. Again, it should be noted that such data may be more vigorous than what can reasonably be expected of a teacher education program. Thus *the* criterion most appropriately applied in accountability situations may not be *the* criterion most useful to teacher educators. It is more likely that it will be but one of a number of criteria the teacher educator may appropriately use in making program decisions.

The point here is to reemphasize the notion that decisions regarding assessment criteria and assessment procedures are best made when decision-makers maintain a program-purpose perspective. It is important that teacher educators distinguish between those demands for research and accountability that are presently reasonable within an instructional program context, and those that are not. It is also helpful to be able to separate what is a reasonable expectation for the future from flag-waving rhetoric.

Concerning those considerations that might be taken into account when selecting assessment criteria procedures, three have been given priority here: (1) data-need considerations; (2) predictive-validity considerations; and (3) feasibility considerations. It has been suggested that these data considerations must be balanced by those who would choose to use knowledge, performance, and/or consequence criteria in competency based teacher education programs. The central task of the teacher educator is to establish a set of assessment criteria and assessment procedures that result in the availability of data that are sufficiently valid and at the same time reasonable in cost. The criteria selection process is a matter of opinion and judgment, not of fact, for differences of opinion result in conflicting views.

DIFFERENCES OF OPINION AND CONFLICTING VIEWS

An examination of the literature on assessment confirms the view that various teacher educators offer somewhat conflicting views, based on their perceptions of what is reality in light of their concerns about purpose, validity, and feasibility.

Turner provides a most useful discussion of the assessment criteria problem in his expansion of the knowledge, performance, and consequence criteria into six levels.[44] He attempts to make clear the points at which certain kinds of feedback data could be generated and the points at which certification could occur. He suggests that his levels of criteria are applicable to all teacher education programs that are oriented toward pupil outcomes, and summarizes them:

Criterion level six is concerned with the effects of a training program on improvements in teacher knowledges and understandings. Criterion levels five and four are concerned with the effects of teacher training on improvement in pedagogic skills under laboratory or simplified training conditions. Criterion level three addresses itself to the effects of training on the teacher's behavior under actual classroom conditions. The concept of pupil change as a criterion of teacher effectiveness is introduced at criterion levels two and one. Criterion level two is concerned with changes in pupil behavior that can be effected in a relatively short time period (one or two weeks) and under actual classroom conditions. Criterion level one is concerned with the long-range effects of teacher behavior on changes in pupil achievement and well-being.[45]

While Turner's conclusions concerning the utility of various criteria levels appear to be both logical and practical, their bases lie in opinion. Thus, it is not surprising to find others with seemingly conflicting views that appear equally sound. Reshaping Turner's six levels of criteria into the knowledge, performance, and consequence distinctions made earlier in this chapter makes it possible to compare Turner's conclusions with those drawn by others who have examined criterion problems associated with the assessment of teacher competency. It seems reasonable to suggest that the following results from a reshaping of Turner's six levels of criteria: (1) knowledge criteria (criterion level six); (2) performance criteria (criterion levels five, four, and three); and (3) consequence criteria (criterion levels two and one).

An examination of the positions taken by those who have been most centrally concerned with the selection of criteria and procedures for assessing teacher competency within a teacher education program context suggests that they share certain common perceptions: (1) residual pupil gain is the ultimate criterion of teacher competency; (2) measurement and analysis procedures on the application of pupil-gain criteria are costly and severely limited; (3) the utilization of knowledge criteria is not worthwhile for summative purposes (indeed, several questioned its value for formative purposes); and (4) each viewed the position he had taken as something of a compromise between the ideal and the realistically practical. Two major positions emerge about using pupil criteria in assessing teacher competency: (1) assessment procedures which emphasize the use of performance criteria[46] and (2) assessment procedures which emphasize the use of consequence criteria.[47]

Performance Criteria

Some have concluded that the utilization of performance criteria yields data that are sufficiently valid as predictors of teacher competency. Their position is that, in light of present realities, performance data are sufficiently powerful to meet the data needs of a teacher education program. This position is best summarized by Soar:

It may be feasible, perhaps even desirable to assess the competence of the teacher to promote lower level learning objectives by measuring change in pupils, but that for the attainment of higher level objectives or more slowly developing objectives, the more appropriate procedure would seem to be to measure the behavior of the teacher and compare it to behavior which is thought or known to be related to the development of higher level objectives in pupils. And such a procedure appears feasible of implementation. . . . the attempt to measure the attainment of all objectives by measuring growth of pupils is likely to be a disaster and to foreclose the possibility of implementing a procedure which, in the long run, would represent a real advance in teacher education, certification, and evaluation.[48]

Because they are logical, practical, and optimistic, it is impossible not to respect the opinions expressed in these conclusions. However, it is possible to take—as some have—an equally appropriate conflicting stance.

Consequence Criteria

Others who have examined the issues on the assessment of teacher competency have concluded that performance criteria alone do not generate data that are adequate predictors of competence. They take the position that it is necessary—and feasible—to utilize pupil data in the assessment of teacher competency within a teacher education context. While they recognize that great problems exist in measuring and analyzing pupil growth, they argue that these problems can be dealt with in ways that are cost-effective. The additional predictive power consequence-based assessment provides as compared to performance-based assessment justifies the additional resources required.

Our view is that several strategies using pupil data, often in combination with systematic observation, in assessing teacher competency have demonstrated their worth. Foremost among these are the contract plan and the performance test advocated by McNeil and Popham, who have provided the following description of contract plans that use pupil gain:

The essence of this technique involves the development of a carefully selected set of objectives for the pupil. Supervisors and teachers agree in advance what they will accept as evidence that the teacher has been successful in changing the skills, competencies or attitudes of his students. An agreement is drawn up before the teacher instructs and is designed to counter the prevailing practice of trying to make an ex post facto judgment about the desirability of ends. Subsequently, evidence is collected to see how well the learners achieved the stated objectives as well as whether unintended outcomes have emerged. . . . teacher competency is judged in terms of the results the teacher gets with learners, not by the procedures he is following in the classroom.[49]

McNeil notes that the contract plan is more than an assessment strategy.[50] It also affords students with opportunities to analyze their teaching in terms of what they were able to accomplish. This process provides feedback that serves as a basis for decisions regarding improvement. The contract plan has allowed each student to establish both the learner outcomes and the strategies he or she will use in attempting to promote the achievement of those outcomes.

Performance tests are similar to contract plans, but they require the student to demonstrate his competence by promoting the achievement of prespecified pupil outcomes under more controlled conditions. A most adequate description is provided by McNeil and Popham:

A number of teachers are given one or more identical objectives and a sample of the measures based on the objective(s) to be administered to pupils following instruction. The objectives may be cognitive, affective or psychomotor in nature. The teachers may also be given resource materials from which to plan a lesson designed to accomplish the objectives. The instructional tactics to be employed are left entirely to the teacher. . . . The teachers are allowed a specific period of time for planning the lesson and for teaching it. Groups of learners, perhaps only a few students per group, are assigned to the teacher as pupils. . . . Following the teacher's instruction a test is administered to measure pupil attainment of the objectives. Although the nature of the test may be inferred by the teacher from the objective, the actual test is not available to the teacher and, indeed, is usually administered by someone other than the teacher. The mean posttest score becomes the criterion of effectiveness. In some instances test scores may be adjusted for the initial abilities of the pupils.[51]

The use of contract plans and performance tests is based on the assumption that they provide a feasible process for applying pupil data criteria in assessing teacher competencies. Because they are a fairly recent development and relatively untested, there is need for caution in making claims for their predictive validity. But at the very least they must be described as a promising step forward, although they are not likely to fully satisfy the rigorous requirements set by some researchers. A comment by Gagné is relevant here: "Perhaps the whole business of 'testing,' in whatever form, has become too formal and too complicated a procedure."[52]

SUMMARY

Although residual pupil gain is *the* ultimate criterion of teacher competency, such a position—rigidly taken—does not give adequate consideration to the problems created by a real world. At the least, this includes concerns about program purposes, predictive validity, and feasibility. The answer is not to be found in the use of pupil data as *the* criterion, but in the use of pupil data when, in the judgment of program decision-makers, it is valid and feasible to do so. It is clear that decisions about validity and feasibility are matters of judgment, and that conflicting views may result is also clear. In deciding whether or not to use consequence criteria, teacher educators should be encouraged, and indeed should be expected, to exercise good judgment. However, they should not be expected to arrive at the same conclusions.

NOTES FOR CHAPTER 19

1. Wilford A. Weber, James M. Cooper, and W. Robert Houston, *A Guide to Competency Based Teacher Education* (Westfield, Tex.: Competency Based Instructional Systems, 1973).

2. Bela H. Banathy, *Instructional Systems* (Palo Alto, Calif.: Fearon Publishers, 1968).

3. W. Robert Houston, *Strategies and Resources for Developing a Competency Based Teacher Education Program* (Albany: New York State Education Department, Division of Teacher Education and Certification, and Multi-State Consortium on Performance-Based Teacher Education, 1972), p. 89.

4. M. Vere DeVault, "An Operational Plan for Program Development in Teacher Education," in *The Power of Competency-Based Teacher Education*, ed. Benjamin Rosner (Boston: Allyn & Bacon, 1972), p. 57.

5. Norman R. Dodl, "Program Evaluation and Student Assessment," in *Competency Based Teacher Education: A Systems Approach to Program Design*, ed. James M. Cooper, Wilford A. Weber, and Charles E. Johnson (Berkeley: McCutchan Publishing Corp., 1973), p. 119.

6. Norman R. Dodl, "Selecting Competency Outcomes for Teacher Education," *The Journal of Teacher Education* 24, no. 3 (fall 1973): 197.

7. H. Del Schalock, "The Focus: Knowledge, Teaching Behavior, or the Products?" in *Performance-Based Certification of School Personnel*, ed. Joel L. Burdin and Margaret T. Reagan (Washington, D.C.: ERIC Clearinghouse on Teacher Education and the Association of Teacher Educators, 1971); B. Othanel Smith, "Certification of Educational Personnel" (Tampa: University of South Florida, 1971).

8. Peter W. Airasian, "The Role of Evaluation in Mastery Learning," in *Mastery Learning: Theory and Practice*, ed. James H. Block (New York: Holt, Rinehart & Winston, 1971), chapter 6.

9. Ibid., p. 78.

10. H. Del Schalock, "BEPD, NCERD, and Teacher Education That Makes a Demonstrable Difference," in *The Power of Competency-Based Teacher Education*, ed. Rosner, p. 123.

11. Ibid.; M. Vere DeVault, "Systems Approach Applications in Designing Teacher Education Programs" in *Competency Based Teacher Education: A Systems Approach to Program Design*, ed. James M. Cooper, Wilford A. Weber, and Charles E. Johnson (Berkeley: McCutchan Publishing Corp., 1973), pp. 19-32.

12. James M. Cooper, Howard L. Jones, and Wilford A. Weber, "Specifying Teacher Competencies," *The Journal of Teacher Education* 24, no. 1 (spring 1973): 19.

13. Barak Rosenshine, *Teaching Behaviours and Student Achievement* (London: National Foundation for Educational Research in England and Wales, 1971); Barak Rosenshine and Norma Furst, "Research in Teacher Performance Criteria," in *Research in Teacher Education*, ed. B. Othanel Smith (Englewood Cliffs, N.J.: Prentice-Hall, 1971).

14. Rosenshine and Furst, "Research in Teacher Performance Criteria": Richard L. Turner, "Levels of Criteria" and "Relationships between *Teachers for the Real World* and the Elementary Models Programmatic Themes and Mechanisms: Payoffs, Mechanisms, and Costs," and Schalock, "BEPD, NCERD, and Teacher Education That Makes a Demonstrable Difference," in *The Power of Competency-Based Teacher Education*, ed. Rosner; James M. Cooper and Wilford A. Weber, "Who Has the Potential to Become an Effective Teacher?" in *New Directions in Education: Preparing and Qualifying for Admission to Teaching*, ed. Keith Goldhammer (San Francisco: Jossey-Bass, 1973), pp. 103-125; Margaret Lindsey, "Performance-Based Teacher Education: Examination of a Slogan," *The Journal of Teacher Education* 24, no. 3 (fall 1973); Ned. A. Flanders and Anita Simon, "Teacher Effectiveness," in *Encyclopedia of Educational Research*, 4th ed., ed. Robert L. Ebel (New York: Macmillan, 1969), pp. 1423-1434.

15. Harold E. Mitzel, "Teacher Effectiveness," in *Encyclopedia of Educational Research*, 3d ed., ed. Chester W. Harris (New York: Macmillan, 1960), pp. 1481-1486.

16. Wilford A. Weber, "Competency-Based Teacher Education: An Overview," slide/tape materials (Westport, Conn.: Videorecord Corp. of America, 1970).

17. Schalock, "The Focus: Knowledge, Teaching Behavior, or the Products?"

18. Schalock, "BEPD, NCERD, and Teacher Education That Makes a Demonstrable Difference."

19. Houston, *Strategies and Resources for Developing a Competency-Based Teacher Education Program.*

20. John D. McNeil and W. James Popham, "The Assessment of Teacher Competence," in *Second Handbook of Research in Teaching*, ed. Robert M. W. Travers (Chicago: Rand McNally, 1973).

21. James M. Cooper and Wilford A. Weber, "A Competency Based Systems Approach to Teacher Education," in *Competency Based Teacher Education: A Systems Approach to Program Design*, ed. Cooper, Weber, and Johnson, pp. 109-123.

22. Frederick J. McDonald, "Evaluation of Teaching Behavior," in *Competency-Based Teacher Education: Progress, Problems, and Prospects*, ed. W. Robert Houston and Robert B. Howsam (Palo Alto, Calif.: Science Research Associates, 1972), p. 70.

23. N. L. Gage, *Teacher Effectiveness and Teacher Education* (Palo Alto, Calif.: Pacific Books, 1972).

24. John D. McNeil, *Toward Accountable Teachers: Their Appraisal and Improvement* (New York: Holt, Rinehart & Winston, 1971), p. 25.

25. Smith, "Certification of Educational Personnel," p. 4.

26. Ibid., p. 5.

27. Weber, Cooper, and Houston, *A Guide to Competency Based Teacher Education*, p. 2.

28. Ibid. Within the context of the present discussion it is interesting to note that in Elam's elaboration of that description (p. 7), he does not mention the use of consequence criteria.

29. McDonald, "Evaluation of Teaching Behavior," pp. 69-70.

30. Jack C. Merwin, *Performance-Based Teacher Education: Some Measurement and Decision-Making Considerations*, PBTE series no. 12 (Washington, D.C.: AACTE, 1973).

31. Elam, *Performance-Based Teacher Education: What Is the State of the Art?*, p. 21.

32. McDonald, "Evaluation of Teaching Behavior."

33. Robert S. Soar, "Accountability: Assessment Problems and Possibilities," *The Journal of Teacher Education* 24, no. 3 (fall 1973).

34. Merwin, *Performance-Based Teacher Education: Some Measurement and Decision-Making Considerations*.

35. Wilford A. Weber, "Assessment in Competency Based Teacher Education: Let's See What the Kids Think," paper presented at the annual meeting of AERA, New Orleans, February 1973.

36. Thomas J. Quirk, "Some Measurement Issues"—see chapter 16 in this volume.

37. Richard C. Cox, "Confusion between Norm-Referenced and Criterion-Referenced Measurement," *Phi Delta Kappan* 55, no. 5 (January 1974).

38. McNeil and Popham, "The Assessment of Teacher Competence," p. 218.

39. Merwin, *Performance-Based Teacher Education: Some Measurement and Decision-Making Considerations*, p. 21.

40. Elam, *Performance-Based Teacher Education: What Is the State of the Art?*; Rosenshine and Furst, "Research in Teacher Performance Criteria"; Robert S. Soar, "Assessment Strategies" (Gainesville: University of Florida, 1972); and Schalock, "BEPD, NCERD, and Teacher Education That Makes a Demonstrable Difference."

41. W. Robert Houston and Robert B. Howsam, "Change and Challenge," in *Competency-Based Teacher Education: Progress, Problems, and Prospects*, ed. Houston and Howsam; DeVault, "An Operational Plan for Program Development in Teacher Education"; and Soar, "Accountability: Assessment Problems and Possibilities."

42. Schalock, "BEPD, NCERD, and Teacher Education That Makes a Demonstrable Difference," p. 124.

43. McNeil, *Toward Accountable Teachers: Their Appraisal and Improvement*.

44. Turner, "Levels of Criteria" and "Relationships between *Teachers for the Real World* and the Elementary Models Programmatic Themes and Mechanisms: Payoffs, Mechanisms, and Costs." See also chapters 6 and 17 in this volume.

45. Ibid., p. 7.

46. Smith, "Certification of Educational Personnel"; Soar, "Assessment Strategies" (Gainesville, University of Florida, 1972); Soar, "Accountability: Assessment Problems and Possibilities."

47. McNeil, *Toward Accountable Teachers: Their Appraisal and Improvement*; Howard L. Jones, "Implementation of Programs," in *Competency-Based Teacher Education: Progress, Problems, and Prospects*, ed. Houston and How-

sam; Houston, *Strategies and Resources for Developing a Competency-Based Teacher Education Program*; Schalock, "BEPD, NCERD, and Teacher Education That Makes a Demonstrable Difference"; Eva L. Baker, "Teaching Performance Tests and Dependent Measures in Instructional Research," paper presented at the annual meeting of AERA, New Orleans, February 1973; Cooper and Weber, "Who Has the Potential to Become an Effective Teacher?"; McNeil and Popham, "The Assessment of Teacher Competence"; W. James Popham, "Applications of Teaching Performance Tests to Inservice and Preservice Teacher Education," paper presented at the annual meeting of AERA, New Orleans, February 1973; Gilbert F. Shearron and Charles E. Johnson, "A CBTE Program in Action: University of Georgia," *The Journal of Teacher Education* 24, no. 3 (fall 1973); Ned A. Flanders, "The Changing Base of Performance-Based Teaching," *Phi Delta Kappan* 55, no. 5 (January 1974).

48. Soar, "Assessment Strategies," p. 15.

49. McNeil and Popham, "The Assessment of Teacher Competence," p. 234.

50. McNeil, *Toward Accountable Teachers: Their Appraisal and Improvement.*

51. McNeil and Popham, "The Assessment of Teacher Competence," p. 236.

52. Robert M. Gagné, "Observations of School Learning," *Educational Psychologist* 10, no. 3 (fall 1973): 116.

20. A Research Strategy

David A. Potter

The movement toward performance based teacher education has at its foundation the idea that teachers should be trained to do those things that cause or facilitate educational growth in their students. No one, however, really knows as yet what these teacher behaviors (or performances or competencies) are. This lack of a firm knowledge base is recognized and lamented by virtually everyone involved in or affected by the PBTE movement, for it represents a dilemma that must be resolved if performance based teacher education is ever to become anything more than another educational fad.

There is a real need for a systematic, large-scale research effort aimed at discovering the linkage between patterns of teacher behavior and student change. Without such research, PBTE cannot hope to answer those critics who claim it is a mechanistic, simplistic approach that cannot hope to comprehend the essence of real teaching.

The other side of the dilemma is the real and immediate need of teacher educators for ways to improve the teacher education process today. Many teacher educators, recognizing the problems inherent in traditional approaches to teacher education, have already begun to move their programs and courses toward a performance base. These educators, while they need data-based knowledge about the linkage between teacher behavior and student behavior, have a more real and immediate need for techniques to permit them to assess the skills their trainees possess and provide training in those skill areas where the trainees' performance is inadequate.

The resolution of this dilemma lies in a comprehensive research and development effort aimed at the production of performance based training and assessment modules. With such an approach, the development of assessment strategies and procedures so urgently needed by teacher educators becomes an integral part of a basic research program for specifying and validating teaching skills. This union of the two aspects of teaching performance—the development of procedures for measuring the level of teaching skill along with the behavioral definition of the skill and the demonstration of its utility in terms of student achievement—is not being proposed on purely pragmatic grounds. In fact, the opposite is true; the two aspects are so intimately related as to be practically inseparable. The process of defining and describing in behavioral terms the precise nature of teaching performance is part and parcel of the process of developing assessment procedures. An assessment procedure cannot be developed without a clear description of a skill, testing the relationship of the skill to student outcomes cannot be done unless one has first developed procedures for assessing teacher performance and student achievement. Furthermore, the relationship between teacher behavior and student outcomes cannot ultimately be tested without simultaneous development of training modules for each teaching skill to be studied.

A short digression may help to clarify this point. Performance based teacher education rests on the assumption that a causal relationship exists between certain patterns of teacher behavior and specifiable student outcomes. This relationship cannot be examined at all without first defining and describing in behavioral terms the nature of the teaching performance to be studied, so that we can at least tell when the behavior has occurred—in other words, we must at least be able to measure teacher behavior at a nominal or categorical level. In addition, we must be able to measure student outcomes in a reliable, objective manner. It is to be hoped that these measures will include not only lower level cognitive objectives but also measures of higher level cognitive functioning, as well as affective and attitudinal measures.

These two steps—the development of reliable and objective measures of student behavior and of student outcomes—will allow us to examine the relationship between what the teacher does and what happens to the students. However, we will not know whether this relationship is a causal one until we have conducted experimental studies in which teacher behavior is itself manipulated and consequent changes in student outcomes are measured. But what the experimental psychologist calls an experimental manipulation is closely related to what the educator calls training. In both cases, the goal of the process is the same: shaping teacher behavior in a specific way. Thus, procedures which the educational researcher uses to test his hypotheses about the relationship between teacher behavior and student outcomes are tools that can readily be adopted by the teacher educator to help teachers acquire specific teaching skills. Teacher educators can, without disrupting their role as educators, make substantial contributions to educational research.

What we are suggesting is that the needs of the PBTE movement will best be met by a programmatic research and development effort aimed at the production of performance based training and assessment techniques. Such a research and development program will provide a solid empirical base on which to rest the growth of the performance based movement. On the one hand, it will provide empirical evidence on the linkage between patterns of teacher behavior and student outcomes; and on the other, it will provide teacher educators with the training and assessment techniques they so urgently need. Nor are these aspects independent, for the training and assessment techniques developed will meet with an unprecedented level of acceptance. They will be accepted not because of a publisher's promotional efforts or because of the developer's reputation; rather, they will be accepted because they work—because they have proven their usefulness for training teachers in skills whose validity has been established in well-designed research. The techniques will be accepted as the means through which performance based education can fulfill its promise of improving education by improving the quality of the training received by prospective teachers, and by providing mechanisms for carrying out the evaluation of inservice teachers.

So far we have described the direction that the research and development program for performance based teacher education should take. To be maximally effective, this program must have certain definite characteristics. For one thing, it should be field centered rather than laboratory centered. Although laboratory research would have a distinct place in the program, the major emphasis should be in the field, with as much work as possible being done in the context of ongoing teacher education programs. This emphasis would not involve any relaxation of the rigorous design or methodology often associated with laboratory research; in fact, it might well be argued that standards could be raised, since the rigorous design would be supplemented by the constraints imposed by reality.

This field-centered approach has several distinct advantages. First, and perhaps most important, is the constant contact and interaction among researchers, educators, and students—a process that could do a great deal to ensure that the products of the program are attuned to the realities of teaching and of teacher education. This same process would greatly facilitate the transition from experimental training and assessment procedures to those that can be and are used effectively in the teacher training process. Finally, of course, there are political advantages: Procedures developed through the participation of all interested members of the educational community would probably meet with more ready acceptance than procedures perceived as having been developed by "ivory tower researchers."

A second characteristic of this research and development program is that the ultimate criterion for program success must be the outcomes achieved by the students of teachers trained by the program. There is of course tremendous difficulty involved in making this criterion operational, and it is not suggested that student learning measures be used as the sole criteria for evaluating individual teachers or teacher education programs. But, in the final analysis, the only valid reason for training teachers at all is to help them facilitate the educational growth of students in their classrooms. Moreover, the dissatisfaction that prompted the present move toward performance based teacher education arose from serious doubts about the efficacy of the procedures currently available to classroom teachers. In a very real way, then, the research and development program proposed here can justify itself only by proving its ability to improve student outcomes by changing teacher behavior.

Turner has formulated six levels of criteria for the assessment of the effectiveness of teacher education programs. While individual elements or modules of a program may be evaluated in terms of lower criterion levels, the program described here must be focused as a whole on criterion level 1, which has two parts: (1) the observation of the acts or behaviors in which the teacher engages in the classroom, and (2) systematic analysis of the outcomes achieved by this teacher's students. Turner specifies that this analysis of outcomes must take place over a relatively long period of time, "probably at least two years (on a time sampling basis)," in order to avoid errors resulting from random fluctuations in both teacher and pupil behavior. In other words, a program's success in training teacher candidates to perform a specified set of basic skills represents only partial success; ultimately, success can only mean that program graduates use these skills in their own classrooms and that their students learn more as a result.[1]

A third characteristic of the proposed research and development program is that competencies should be selected on a conceptual rather than an eclectic basis. The literature already notes a sufficient number of competencies, skills, and performances that are independent of any conceptual model of the teaching process. The interrelationships among the listed competencies, moreover, are relatively haphazard. Instead of developing procedures based on similarly unrelated lists of competencies, it would seem preferable to base our research and development efforts on some clear statement of philosophy or model of teaching. Our own experience with teacher behavior research and our contact with the profession have led us to believe that certain competencies are probably more ideally suited for some models of teaching than others; consequently, it would seem most efficient to select for further development those competencies that fit together, forming a coherent whole rather than a set of unrelated, isolated elements. One way of doing this might involve selecting a number—perhaps five or so—models of teaching from those proposed by Bruce Joyce and Marsha Weil in *Models of Teaching,* and to develop lists of the competencies required by each model.[2]

The fourth and final characteristic of this research and development plan is that it should involve an orientation to the teaching process that is molar rather than atomistic. Performance based teacher education is behavioristic, that is, it regards the teaching process as essentially a behavioral process. We believe that teachers have an effect on their students through their own behavior, and our goal is to discover the ways in which teachers can behave in order to optimize their effect on their students. This does not mean that we must regard teaching as merely the ability to assemble a set of relatively simplistic basic skills. We may start with basic skill assessment—that is, we may begin by assessing the prospective teacher's ability to perform such basic skills as questioning, planning, or explaining—but we would not stop at this point. Instead, we should expand our procedures to include teaching strategies—in other words, we must develop procedures for training and assessment of teaching as a whole. We often hear that teaching is not a set of discrete acts but requires the ability to "put it all together." The teaching process may in fact be analyzed in terms of some set of behavioral acts or basic skills, but we must also recognize the importance of being able to put it all together.

What we are recommending as the basic research strategy for performance based teacher education is a comprehensive, field-centered, conceptually oriented, research and development program aimed at the production of performance based training and assessment procedures. Such a program might begin quite simply. For example, many teacher educators are currently engaged in the production of instructional modules, some of which are more or less performance based. In the normal course of events, these modules are designed, tried out on colleagues, and then distributed to teacher education students for whom the modules serve much the same purpose as do traditional courses. The similarity with traditional course structures extends to module evaluation, which when it exists at all is generally quite informal.

None of this involves any criticism of the teacher educator who designs and uses modules. Working in this manner, he adequately fulfills his role as a trainer of teachers. But think for a moment how easy it would be to move beyond module design and utilization and into teacher behavior research. A module, after all, is designed to shape some particular facet of the teaching act. This shaping is analogous to what the educational researcher would call a manipulation of teacher behavior. If this shaping, or manipulation, is done within the context of a teacher education program, we call it teacher education; if it is done under relatively controlled conditions and if the consequences (in terms of student outcomes) are adequately measured, we have moved on into educational research, into the linkages between teacher behavior and student outcomes.

The technology for such research already exists in many teacher education programs. Microteaching, for example, provides a vehicle that can readily be used not only for training but also for research. Well-designed microteaching programs are similar to experiments in that they involve the performance of specified teaching tasks under highly controlled conditions; they differ from experiments primarily in the absence of any control or comparison group, a difference that can easily be eliminated. Nor does the inclusion of a control group in an educational process have any inevitable ethical implications (e.g., "How can we withhold this invaluable training from the control group?"). The control group can receive alternate, equally invaluable instruction, it can receive the experimental instructional package at a later date, or it can receive both.

Such a program might proceed as follows:

(1) The teacher candidate population is randomly divided into experimental and control groups;

(2) The experimental group receives and works through the experimental module, while the control group works through an alternate, unrelated module;

(3) Both groups take a performance test—that is, they teach in a standard microteaching format;

(4) (Micro) student achievement in the microteaching session is measured;

(5) Teacher performance on criterion behaviors in the microteaching session is coded, and teacher performance is then compared across experimental and control groups;

(6) Observed differences in teacher behavior are correlated with measured differences in student achievement.

This paradigm allows causal inferences to be made about the effectiveness of the training procedures, e.g., was teacher behavior actually shaped as the trainer-experimenter intended? In addition, and even more important, it also permits causal inferences to be drawn regarding the relationship between teacher behavior and student achievement, e.g., teacher behavior A actually caused student outcome A. It is precisely this sort of causal inference that is so urgently needed by teacher education today, and it is this sort of research paradigm that will allow such causal conclusions to be drawn.

An entire teacher education program could readily be built on developmental units like that described above. In point of fact, programs converting to a performance base often proceed much as we have described but without the research component. In such programs, performance based modules are designed and utilized, but no systematic effort is made either to evaluate their effectiveness as training procedures or to determine the relationship between the criterion teacher performances and student outcomes. As already indicated, however, the additional investment required to explore these relationships would be small relative to the probable outcomes of such an effort.

A teacher education program built on this premise would have a two-fold premise: it would attempt to validate competencies and training and assessment procedures, while at the same time it would capitalize on current knowledge in order to train teachers as effectively as possible. Such a program cannot be built quickly. Attempts to change existing teacher education programs—indeed, attempts to change any existing organization—are opposed not only by those who have vested interests in present ways of doing things, but also by diverse forces that collectively add up to what might best be termed organizational inertia. So powerful are these factors that it is almost impossible to impose change on an organization from without. Only when those affected by the change are involved in and committed to changing the organization is there any real hope of success. Moreover, even under the best of circumstances, attempts at total change are an invitation to disaster, for the failures that inevitably accompany any experimentation will multiply rapidly and be seized on by those opposing the change as reasons for maintaining the status quo. Change proceeds best by a series of small, successful steps; a program like the one outlined above is designed to move in just this way.

NOTES FOR CHAPTER 20

1. Richard L. Turner, "Levels of Criteria," in *The Power of Competency-Based Teacher Education,* ed. Benjamin Rosner (Boston: Allyn & Bacon, 1972), p. 4.

2. Bruce Joyce and Marsha Weil, *Models of Teaching* (Englewood Cliffs, N.J.: Prentice-Hall, 1972).

Part 5
Changing
American Education

\

21. Exploring Alternative Strategies for Institutional Change

W. Robert Houston
Robert B. Howsam
James M. Cooper
Wilford A. Weber

Man is an inventor; he strives to change the human condition. Though his inventions in the technological and material realms are more readily apparent, he also invents within the social dimensions of his reality; he invents, changes, renews, and dissolves institutions and organizations.

The consequences of inventive behavior—of change—are further change. Changes in the technological or material world inevitably affect the social world. Thus, in a world of change, man is constantly required to behave adaptively. He changes his behavior, and he modifies his institutions.

Thus, it is problematic, indeed paradoxical, that man should tend readily to encompass technological and material change but resist institutional and individual behavior change. Because of this, he experiences severe discontinuities and dissonances in times when the pace of change is rapid.

This chapter was originally prepared for a Deans and Directors Conference, Teacher Corps, 1973.

It seems evident to all that we live in a period when change occurs at an accelerating rate. One-fourth of all people who have ever inhabited this planet, and 90 percent of all the scientists, are alive today. The population shifts toward urban living as fewer persons are required to produce foodstuffs. Such urban concentrations breed new problems as well as new promises. In this cauldron of evolving social and technological flux, institutions—and particularly the primary institutions of home, school, church, and community—are forced to examine and reexamine their missions, their strategies, and their effectiveness.

Similarly, perhaps in part because of the weakening of the social fabric, the individual increasingly finds his levels of tolerance tested. While we might wish for the "nice safe cage" of Ogden Nash, we are not likely to find it. Our lot is a world that refuses to stand still. In a world of change, the law of survival is *adaptation*. The law applies no less to institutions than to societies or to species. Translated, it means that there needs to be institutional change as adaptive response to changing conditions.

Yet this concept, institutional change, appears itself to be a paradox. The concept of *institution* connotes conflict with the concept of change. Institutions view themselves and are viewed by others as stabilizing and regularizing systems, as powerful embodiments of the status quo. By definition, change challenges the status quo. Those who elect to foster change in organizations or institutions do so with the knowledge that they challenge those whom the status quo favors.

THE NEED FOR PLANNED CHANGE

It is commonly observed that schools have been remarkably slow to adapt in response to changes in society. Even less responsive have been teacher education programs.

Public education in particular—including the education of teachers—has long been on the horns of a dilemma. Should it promote change or resist it? Should it actively and adaptively seek to keep abreast of current development, or preserve the past? In the true nature of a dilemma, the alternatives often are seen as equally unacceptable. To change is to upset the culture, to trade the known and loved for the unknown, to substitute uncertainty for apparent relative certainty. Not to change invites a gap between the culture and emerging reality with which it is impossible to cope. The choice properly belongs to the people, but it is the responsibility of the educator to assist in the decision-making process. Educators have long neglected this role.

It took the upheavals in the large cities of the 1960s to awaken society and educators to the crises in education. Schools were found to be serving only some segments of the society. Teachers were being prepared for service in middle class neighborhood schools. Additionally, the schools had fallen behind markedly in their capacity to meet the educational needs of the time.

During the past decade, extensive efforts have been made by the federal and state governments, foundations, and teacher educational institutions to improve professional education. At the local level often the efforts were spasmodic, uncoordinated, and even conflicting; they were customarily supported by too few resources. Most of these efforts at change were additive in nature. That is, they attempted to induce change by adding new programs onto existing institutions, hoping that the institutions would change in the process. Usually they did not. Additive and linear approaches generally lack the power to bring about the needed level of change. What is needed is a systemic approach which recognizes the complex and interactive nature of change.

INSTITUTIONS INVOLVED IN PLANNED CHANGE

Change in one part of a system impacts all other parts of the system. Change in complex social systems is not likely to occur unless all the elements are collaboratively involved. Planned change involves identifying these elements and developing strategies of intervention that concentrate and focus the inputs. Teacher education is such a complex effort. Change strategies should involve:

- Colleges and universities
  Professional units
  Academic units
- School districts and other employing units who collaborate in the field aspects of teacher training and conduct inservice programs
  Administrators
  Teachers
  Public

- Professional associations of teachers and other educators
- State governmental units and their subsystems (county; intermediate units)
- Teacher education students

Teacher education—preservice and continuing—as a modern functioning system, demands the active participation of all these institutions or components.

TARGETS FOR PLANNED CHANGE

Collaborative efforts require a high-level capacity to plan and coordinate. Management must deal with the major targets of the change process. These targets are:

(1) The attitudes, values, and behavior systems of people who are concerned with teacher education;

(2) The organizational and communication structures within which such programs operate; and

(3) The curricula studied by trainees.

Target One: Change in People

Changing people for more effective responses in an evolving institutional frame is not simple. Human systems have a considerable capacity to resist change, to achieve a new equilibrium that closely approximates the old. Difficult as it is to change people, this remains the critical task. Schools will not improve until teachers are more effective; programs for preparing teachers will be no better than the teacher educators who train the teachers.

Target Two: Organizational Change

In the past teacher education has been responsive only to a limited institutional input. The college or university has dominated the process and the program. Institutional change in teacher education implies changing the power base and sharing decision-making with other institutions that have interrelated missions. Each of these institutions has its own set of mandates and primary missions in society, its own organizational structure, its own resources, and its own responsibilities which it is reluctant to share. Moving from independent operation and token cooperation to a genuine consortium can promote commitments to action, but such growth and development requires careful nurturing. Institutional change is not easy; interinstitutional change is yet more difficult.

Target Three: Curriculum Change

Teacher education curricula are changing more rapidly to meet evolving needs and to incorporate new concepts of teaching, learning, and content. Competency based teacher education, for example, with its emphasis on clear and concise objectives and its program and evaluation processes, provides a powerful vehicle for facilitating and assessing the effectiveness of the new programs.

These targets of the institutional change process cited above are interactive and interdependent. Changing one target area affects them all. However, change does not exist in a vacuum; it has a context and takes place over a period of time. Accordingly, strategies for change must take into account the specific context, the individuals involved, resources available, and many other variables.

PROPOSITIONS FOR INSTITUTIONAL CHANGE

While strategies for change must be implemented in specific contexts, it is possible to state some basic propositions that are believed to be valid and indigenous to successful change in educational institutions. These propositions have been grouped under the following categories: goals and objectives; organization and administration; reward system; communication; staff development; interinstitutional relationships; and evaluation: accountability.

Goals and Objectives

Clearly explicated goals and objectives tend to facilitate change. Although almost all educational institutions have some vague statements to which they owe allegiance, many do not have clear goals and objectives. Goals, so often wrapped in the cultural mantle, are generally accepted but provide little direction. Because their goals are long-range, global, and difficult to achieve, institutions often excuse themselves from accountability for their delivery.

Objectives formulated by projects that seek change are more likely to be achieved if they are compatible with the explicit values and goals of the institution. The objectives of externally funded projects often are derived exclusively from the funder (e.g., to train special personnel, research a topic, write a paper, consult on a topic); just as often, the institution does not perceive these activities as contributing to its goals. The project is considered a drain rather than a contribution to the resources and mission of the primary institution. In such cases the project is less likely to positively affect the institution, its programs, or its personnel.

Change is facilitated when objectives are short-range, specific, and relatively restricted in scope. This does not imply that broad, long-range goals are not important. It does suggest that macroproblems be divided into microproblems and realistic strategies. Short-term objectives that are made public are more likely to be achieved than vague, comprehensive statements which require extended time periods to achieve.

Organization and Administration

Agents and projects created to introduce change into an educational system must be perceived by affected personnel as being integral parts of the system. Impact is minimized when projects are perceived to be working outside the regular system.

A temporary system or project is likely to make enduring contributions only if the commitment to change exists within the regular system. Far too many institutions have adapted to the provisions of federal or foundation funding with grantsmanship. They have become entrepreneurial of posture and big business in orientation. For them, a measure of success is the size of the cumulative outside funding for the year. Under such circumstances institutional change is unlikely to occur. Staffing of projects, including even the director, is by soft money appointments; those who prove effective soon depart for the haven of hard money and the prospects of tenure. This approach results in projects being separate efforts that have little or no contact with or impact on the regular program.

Major changes in institutional purpose or processes often are accomplished with as much success as are relatively minor changes. Resources and focused change efforts are more likely to be well planned and coordinated when the change effort is major. As one educational innovator has phrased it, "A little change hurts; a big change hurts only a little more."

Changes should be planned and executed in such a way as to demonstrate maximum concern for human values. Emphasizing achievement of organizational goals must not negate an equal concern for the needs of the individuals in the institution. Particularly in primary institutions such as education, a high priority must be placed on human values.

Managers who are perceived as having little status or influence with their superiors are able to exercise little influence with their subordinates. Projects involving institutional change will have a great chance of success and of making a difference if the person placed in charge is perceived as having (1) competence and status within the organization, and (2) influence within the decisional and management processes of the institution.

Reward System

What is valued should be rewarded; failure to do so invites discontinuance of the valued behavior. People who try new approaches and find themselves unsupported by the organization and unrewarded for their efforts tend to give up their innovative efforts.

The institution that wishes to encourage change should express its commitment through a set of expectations which encourage adaptive behavior, and a rewards system which assures that those who innovate will be recognized and rewarded. This principle customarily is not applied in institutions. Indeed, the opposite is true when institutional flirtation with change begins and projects and experiments are undertaken. Essentially these usually are low risk since at this stage no attempt is made to redevelop the institutional thrust or its norms and rewards. Those who commit themselves to the innovative programs are often unaware of the extent to which the institution has "hedged its bets" and end up frustrated over the reluctance of others to "go all the way." Additionally, they often end up finding that their forays into innovation are not rewardable under the traditional rewards structure.

Communication

Institutional change is enhanced when people are aware of decisions and events that affect them. People are more threatened by not knowing what to expect than by decisions with which they disagree.

It is much more difficult to cope with uncertainty than with decisions that are viewed as adverse.

People will accept responsibility and accountability only for that which they have planned or shaped in some meaningful way. Individuals who perceive themselves as having a vested interest in the outcomes of change will work harder to achieve these outcomes. Further, the threat from change is eased by involvement of the affected parties in the processes of decision-making about directions and procedures.

Institutional change is enhanced when organizational managers receive systematic data flow regarding operations and quality of the product, enabling them to make enlightened decisions. Needed communication about how change efforts are working will flow up the line to management—if the climate of the institution is positive. Punitive or threatening responses to negative feedback causes adaptive behavior that dries up the source of data needed in decision-making.

Staff Development

Changing people in an institution is critical in changing the institution. The most important changes are the ones that occur in people. Only through people-changes can structural and organizational changes work. Conversely, to make organizational changes without also providing for the necessary staff development will prejudice the organizational changes.

Individuals are affectively involved in all change processes, regardless of how cool and rational they may appear. Time to adjust and assistance with the process are needed.

Extreme freedom and autonomy among staff members are likely to inhibit change. When individuals are insulated by the institution from the consequences of their actions, they are less accountable for maintaining relevancy. Professors in some colleges can choose to isolate themselves, whereas a tough-minded peer interaction facilitates creativity, inventiveness, and change.

Interinstitutional Relationships

Interinstitutional change is more readily accomplished when the institutions share common goals and mutual self-interest. When attempting to create interinstitutional change, the change agents generally operate from a less powerful base than they would in trying to create intrainstitutional change. They do not control the reward system as effectively; there are different constituencies and, frequently, different agenda. With all these complexities, the best chance for creating interinstitutional change occurs when the institutions share some common purposes.

In collaborative relationships, each member gives up some measure of his specific power in the interests of greater ability to get things done (more collective power). If collaboration is to be real, each party must have the capacity to influence decisions. Token collaboration is soon discovered and rejected.

Evaluation: Accountability

Without clearly defined goals and objectives, it is not possible to evaluate change or to hold anyone accountable for success. Further, the degree to which objectives are made explicit determines the depth of evaluation possible.

The processes of change are enhanced by ample use of formative evaluation. Change is continuous; it is neither discrete nor terminal. Thus evaluation must necessarily be a continuous process, providing data for revision and refinement of procedures. Premature use of summative evaluation tends to hinder the processes of change.

Personnel can be held accountable for either products or processes, but not both. If personnel are to be held accountable for achieving certain results, they cannot simultaneously be told what to do to achieve those results. If they follow the prescribed process perfectly and do not achieve the desired results, accountability remains with the initiator. Decisions must be made as to whether products or processes are the accountable item.

THE SYSTEMS PERSPECTIVE

One of the most useful ways of perceiving reality and for incorporating the above propositions into a meaningful strategy is through the concepts of general systems theory. Systems theory considers all phenomena—whether natural, technical, or social—as complexes of elements in constant interaction with each other. Accordingly, change is not a simple process; it involves multiple elements. Any attempt to intervene in changing the system will of necessity invoke predictable principles; a knowledge of these principles may serve to improve the intervention strategies and avoid serious errors or omissions. The following statements can be made about social systems:

(1) Systems are complexes of elements in mutual interaction.

(2) All phenomena, whether natural, social, or technical, may be perceived as being organized in systems.

(3) All systems have common properties.

(4) Though in theory and actuality everything interacts with everything else, for practical purposes groups of elements may be identified.

(5) Such systems are said to be bounded (inside the system). Everything not inside the boundary, then, exists in its environment (e.g., if Teacher Corps is defined as the system, the boundary separates those in from those not in).

(6) Systems exist for purposes.

(7) Systems are normative and sanction bearing. That is, they have expectations for their members (elements), and they have means of rewarding conformity to the norms and for punishing nonconformity.

(8) Systems are composed of smaller elements which are themselves systems; these are termed subsystems; e.g., a center within the Teacher Corps.

(9) Similarly, they are parts of larger systems called suprasystems, e.g., Teacher Corps within USOE.

(10) Systems (open) exchange energy and information with their environment (inputs and outputs).

(11) Systems are accountable to their suprasystems (which have created them for specific purposes).

(12) Effective systems are responsive to the other systems with which they share life space; they therefore relate.

(13) Changes in one part of a system inevitably produce changes in the other parts of the system.

(14) Change in a system may occur in consequence of developments within the system or of inputs from the environment.

(15) Systems tend toward stability, equilibrium, steady state, predictability (homeostasis).

(16) Systems also tend toward progressive segregation (splitting into smaller and smaller more specialized parts and functions).

(17) The tendencies of equilibrium and segregation both lead towards entropy, e.g., an incapacity to act effectively.

(18) To counter the tendency to entropy, to survive and be effective, systems need to seek a dynamic equilibrium. Such systems are adaptive, responding to changes in the environment by changes in themselves.

(19) The use of feedback (knowledge of results in terms of purposes fed back into the system as input) is a central feature of adaptive and dynamic systems.

(20) Systems are capable of responding to relatively minor change inputs by returning to their previous steady state.

(21) Change is more likely to occur when either massive or multiple change inputs are experienced.

(22) Change inputs to systems cannot properly be viewed as linear (one after the other) or additive. Rather they are viewed as interactive and cumulative. In times of rapid environmental change systems change tends to be exponential in nature (the pace quickens and the plotted change swings upward rapidly).

(23) Initial change in complex social systems usually appears to be painfully slow. If inputs are maintained, however, the pace is likely to quicken. There are few if any "instant" results in social systems. Changes involving cultural systems tend to be extremely slow; whole generations may be required before the change output is clearly observable.

(24) In modern times, the ability to develop technical systems has advanced rapidly through the application of science. A change in the technology of a social system impacts all of its parts (institutions, organizations, groups, individuals). The rapid pace of technical change places great stress on the social and human systems which (so far) have shown an incapacity to adapt rapidly enough. Schools are considered by many to suffer from this incapacity.

(25) Outside intervention in an attempt to change institutional systems should take into account as many as possible of the consequences. Unanticipated consequences will accompany any effort; some may be undesirable and serious.

THE CUTTING EDGE

The dynamic nature of institutional change implies direction and goal setting, value orientation, data-based decision-making, and willingness to take risks. Initial results of such efforts may appear to elicit only modest results. In complex social systems, change is at first slow, but with continued efforts the rate and extensiveness accelerates. *Institutional change occurs exponentially, not linearly.* Far too many innovations have been initiated as bright new ventures; before they could test their basic assumptions in examined practice, they were discarded as unfeasible or unworkable.

The role of educational change agent is not a comfortable one. Pressures are exerted from those with differing philosophies or strategies as well as from those desiring no change at all. With such pressures for maintaining the status quo, the temptation must be resisted to continue the current programs and practices unexamined. Only continuous, data-based, thoughtful, institutional change will contribute to improved educational programs.

Of such is the cutting edge. . . .

22. The Process of Curriculum Change in a Dental School

Horace C. Hartsell

External pressures and internal demands are forcing change in education. The tenor of the time is expressed in demands for more efficient and effective programs that will increase flexibility, reduce costs and learner time, and provide students with a curriculum based on problem solving. Educational planners and developers must translate learning situations into goals and objectives that are performance based; they must plan for the development and management of the learner environment; they must establish a measuring and evaluation system based on performance behavior.

Planning for teaching and learning includes two different processes: a developmental system and an instructional system. The selection of content and the learner environment provisions are a part of the development system. The instructional system consists of the teachers' management role and the students' learning and development role. A working definition of each follows:

The *developmental system* is that complex of instructor(s) and specialist(s) created to make decisions related to specific actions within the instruction system.

The *instructional system* is that complex consisting of learner(s), material(s), and technician(s), given inputs and designed to carry out a prescribed set of operations.

Bodies of knowledge have structure, and in the planning process a review of the research in technology must be made. Teachers cannot easily select the resources and arrange the appropriate environment without asking some penetrating questions: "What must we teach?" "Will it make a lot of difference how we organize our facilities (space, hardware, software)?" "How will we know the students are performing at the expected levels?" The arrangement and selection of instrumentation are based on the curriculum objectives, not on the building space and print and nonprint media. Unfortunately, many of our learning programs are dependent on the building space that we have. Available space frequently dictates the nature and type of methods, and the limitations on content resources and expected performance.

The planners must carefully identify the performance and effectively select the resources that are basic to student development. Success depends on knowing what is expected student behavior; on this basis judgments can be made about curriculum core content, sequence, and modes of instruction. The plan for teaching and learning must include information on the kind of learner space, simulation, hardware, and software, for it is when instructional decision-making is linked to explicit learner objectives that we begin to sense the implications of environment instructional technology for education. Many schools have added instructional developers to their faculties to organize a team to assist the faculty in implementing the teaching and learning systems needed to achieve a particular set of learner objectives.

Professional schools have similar concerns for instructional decision-making. This chapter describes The University of Texas Dental Branch at Houston education program, its conceptualization, rationale, and developmental processes. The contributions made have been in terms of new curriculum design; that is, (1) interdisciplinary integrated topic teaching (a scheduled *time* curriculum) and (2) a self-directed program (a *rate* curriculum). The latter concept is strongly student oriented as far as time management and study organization are concerned, because there are no scheduled classes and laboratories. These approaches were not created just to be different or to have something new, but because they more nearly provide those teaching and learning processes and procedures that support the desired student and teacher performances. The processes have become accepted procedures for instructional decision-making systems, resulting in continual pursuit of answers to the questions to be asked, answers that improve the learner environment.

Some of the concerns dealt with are (1) identification of essential course content, (2) systematizing the content, (3) sequential arrangement or relocation of content, (4) early clinic participation, (5) audiovisual communication (machine teaching), and (6) self-directed methodology. A few dental schools have already recognized these concerns and over a period of years have acted to seek solutions. Some have turned for answers to instructional technology systems.

SOME INSTRUCTIONAL DEVELOPMENT ASSUMPTIONS

Before describing the conceptualization, rationale, and developmental processes of the UTDB dental school program, several assumptions that guided our efforts should be listed:

(1) "Performance based" is the word of the day.

(2) The instructional designer is not a line and staff position, but rather a role one or more people can play. The instructional designer may be a teacher, a media professional, an audiovisual or library person, an instructional developer, a principal, a superintendent, a dean, and/or a college president.

(3) The curriculum design may be teacher centered (*scheduled*) or student centered (*rate based*).

(4) Students must be guided by clearly stated performance based objectives.

(5) Students must be tested and evaluated by these same stated objectives.

(6) Students must be participants, not spectators.

(7) The facts of the situation are that

    (a) If a teacher tells the students what they are to learn and at what level they are to perform, they will most likely succeed.

    (b) Students can teach each other, as well as the teacher teach-
ing the students.

    (c) Students can learn with or without a teacher present, but if
no learning takes place can a teacher be said to have
taught?

(8) Teachers can go through procedures that will enable them to
benefit from the instructional technology.

(9) Educational specialists are to serve teachers in their instructional planning.

(10) The hang-ups resource specialists may have with the teachers
that prevent them from helping must be removed.

TO MAKE A START

Among other factors, improvement of dental education requires a
high level of faculty involvement in systematic reexamination of instructional goals; reorganization of course content and modes of instruction; optimum use of educational technology; and careful evaluation to determine the efficiency and effectiveness of ongoing procedures. The dental schools' functions of *teaching, service,* and *research*
are dependent for their successful achievement on the excellence of
their faculties and on the resources available to the faculties to do
their work. Dental schools in this country show signs of high institutional "acceptability" for creating services in instructional development and technology, including adequate administrative provisions
(organization, funds, and personnel) for providing learning resources
and services to efficiently put the instructional plans into effect.

To get started at The University of Texas Dental Branch, a developmental procedure for identifying and involving the early innovator
was used. The first effort was to establish a space area for faculty
planning; faculty carrels, consultant help, and supplies were provided. The second act was to encourage the faculty committees to
put their thoughts and plans on paper. This was not a media support
effort, but an instructional development effort. The faculty began to
consolidate an integrated dental curriculum plan, which consisted of
eight topics. Biomedical communication support was expanded. A
developmental procedure for establishing a student-oriented, performance based learner environment was the natural result of these
efforts.

To achieve the stated objectives, the faculty developed a model for instructional decision-making. This model contained instructional decision-making roles of professors, departments, topic chairmen, the teaching committee, the curriculum coordinating committee, and the office of the dean. The dean insisted that publications of these various groups be reviewed and revised each year; a new cover with the current date was important, for as he stated, "I do not want our faculty to feel that we have arrived and that the job is over. If we knew how to do our job of instruction better for greater student achievement, we would begin to change today."

Instructional technology procedures at The University of Texas Dental Branch at Houston begin with a written order of instructional decisions, in the form of a handbook. Guidelines and answers as to how the dental school's *objectives* and educational philosophy will be achieved, by whom and by what methods, make up the content of the instructional decision-making model. This helps the faculty overcome the constantly developing problems associated with change and/or modifying a curriculum. Areas of responsibility have been delineated, rationale and guidelines developed, and definitions and statements of purpose provided.

A focus on dental education rather than on media systems places the emphasis on teaching and the accent on learning. Most important, it suggests caution in promotion of "easy-to-adopt" packaged programs just because they are the trend of the times. Figure 22:1, derived from the 1972-73 UTDB *Handbook for Topic Teaching,* shows the interaction and progression of coordinating decisions in curriculum development. Each instructional medium is carefully selected for its contribution to student performance objectives. The system is an orderly plan for making man-machine instructional strat-

Figure 22:1. Instructional Decision Model

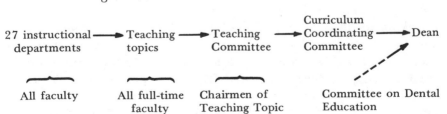

egy decisions. Multimedia technology, used as a result of systematic planning, supports the learning process and the mode(s) of instruction. To act in this manner is to accept that the learning system includes all the people, hardware, buildings, software, and procedures needed to achieve a particular learning objective.

Curriculum planning and development is a faculty role. All full-time faculty are assigned by department chairmen to represent their departments on one or more of the eight teaching topic committees. The function of the topic committees is to structure the content for their particular area of interest. In addition to organizing the course material, the faculty work closely with the Teaching Committee, the Curriculum Coordinating Committee, and the Instructional Development Services in generating performance based objectives for the instructional modes and modules and developing self-instructional material and evaluation instruments.

Instructional Development is a service force composed of professional and technical personnel. There are four graphic artists, four photographers, five television specialists, one motion picture photographer, and one technical writer who are assigned to a production division referred to as Medical Illustration. This team designs and produces the media resources identified in the instructional plan. Prior to production, qualified instructional developers consult with the faculty and committees on matters pertaining to learning, media, and evaluation. The library staff also plays a significant part in such planning. These persons are the professional and technical personnel who help plan and develop the instructional modes by locating and/ or producing the appropriate media resources.

THE FACULTY AND THE CURRICULUM

An annual faculty workshop has served as a prime force for curriculum study and change. Being away from one's family for two and a half days and some distance from Houston provides an excellent opportunity for the faculty to review the activities of the academic year and to take a good look at plans for the new year. Workshop proceedings are edited and published in a bound faculty resource book.

In the *Sixth Annual Faculty Workshop* publication, Professor James Rout reviewed curriculum changes. Prior to his presentation he asked one of the senior faculty members, "What year did Dean

Olson charge the faculty with developing an integrated program? Was it 1959 or 1960?" The professor answered, "Well, it doesn't make much difference because the work began on this program when you were my student and that was a long time ago."

The point is that curriculum must *not* be constructed; it must be developed and this takes planning and time. Dean Olson charged the faculty with developing an "integrated curriculum." He encouraged each faculty member to try to improve the curriculum for more meaningful learning and better teaching. Some accepted the challenge, while others hoped the charge would go away. The early work was carried on by a very small group of dedicated people.

In 1955, The University of Texas Dental Branch moved into a new building which provided new teaching facilities. The emphasis was on students taking more responsibility for their study and learning, and on learning from each other. In 1960, the School of Dentistry faculty accelerated the intensive study of its subject matter and methods of instruction. The new building design of unit laboratories predicated unified instruction. In fall 1966 the first class was enrolled in what was called Plan IV of the curriculum. Content from the various disciplines was arranged into unified topics. To prevent topics from becoming as numerous as former courses, the faculty selected eight broad areas of instruction as umbrellas to cover the integrated subject matter identified by twenty-seven teaching departments.

Management teams, each representing most of the departments, were structured as teaching topic committees which had the job of organizing subject matter from departments into unified patterns and presentations. By starting first-year students in Clinic Practice, presentation of a considerable amount of theoretical material was delayed until the upper levels of instruction. The faculty identified a core curriculum that was to be finished by the end of the third year; thus, to a major extent the fourth year didactics were either elective or supplemental.

A planned effort toward identifying students of superior ability and competency paralleled the integrated topic teaching curriculum development. This allowed them to advance into individually designed programs of experience. The nature and results of faculty participation were described by Dean Olson, in his message to the faculty at the Fifth Workshop, 1970:

As Dean, I feel that we do have an obligation to produce an outstanding program for other dental schools to examine, and even to copy, either totally or in part. I would like to see our faculty included in dental history as one that has made some of the most outstanding contributions to curricular development, to the identification of educational goals and objectives, and to the development of teaching media.

. . . .

In retrospect, I am glad that we decided to enter into a total program, and not to have part of the class as a "control" and another part labeled an "experiment." While it sometimes seems wise to have "controls" and "experiments," this also has many disadvantages to the students or classes who become labeled. Also, when this is done, I doubt that it is particularly useful, for I imagine that it would be difficult to teach a control group without some of the advantages of the new experimental teaching program rubbing off. Were that to happen, then the benefits of having a "control" group would be completely lost.

At the moment, I am even grateful that a few faculty members were not too enthusiastic about entering into this new program. These were men who apparently were convinced we had a good program originally, and we really ought not to "knock" success. However, most of us felt that nothing is so good that it cannot be improved. Also, those who preferred the former methods paid us two favors: First of all, they were constantly reminding us of standards that we had set for the students previously, wanting to be sure that we upheld these standards of quality and excellence. Secondly, these men constituted "doubters" in a way, but they gave a challenge to the rest of the faculty to explain the new program more convincingly and more thoroughly than we might otherwise have felt the need to do.

I guess what I am saying is that there is really nothing wrong with a "two-party system" even in dental education. But, as in politics, we hope that everyone would be open-minded and willing to listen to sound arguments from the proponents of each party—even willing to cross over party lines and become a member of the other group, when convinced it had a better program, in this case, a better curriculum.

In 1971, Plan V was activated by selecting eight students over the one hundred normally enrolled to become the developmental self-directed pilot group. This modular self-directed integrated curriculum has the flexibility for a dental student to learn and experience at his own rate and ability and to plan when he will graduate. It may shorten the time but not the curriculum experiences; it encourages faculty and students to develop criteria for quality assurance. There was no intent in this modular teaching structure to do less than was being accomplished in the excellent four-year ongoing topic teaching program. We hope it will make it possible for the students to better synthesize and integrate basic health knowledge and to apply this knowledge in developing those skills essential to accuracy in clinical performance and patient care.

While emphasizing quality standards, the self-directed curriculum makes it possible for a student to reduce the time to complete a D.D.S. program. The rapid learner can progress at a faster rate and still develop the same degree of competency as is expected in the four-year program. The self-study delivery strategy provides a learning environment for those who are capable and motivated to finish in less than four years, and the time could become as short as two and one-half years. Thus, health manpower needs could be more adequately met by this potential increase in dentist output. A four-year dental curriculum reduced to three calendar years can provide an increased dentist output only once—that being the first graduating class from the three-calendar-year program. Compared to this, a modular self-directed program could make it possible to admit new students when some of the first-year dental students have completed the first sequence, thereby opening up space and freeing material, equipment, and faculty. This accordion effect would keep the educational facilities at a maximum capacity without forcing the student into a four-quarter year.

THE TEACHING TOPICS

The use of teaching topics was the structure by which the integration of teaching of courses at UTDB took place. The teaching topics became umbrellas for a curriculum that contained a "core" program for fulfilling the basic requirements of dental education from the clinical and biological viewpoints. Around the "core," the student can build his own special course of studies with an elective program.

The eight specific teaching topics are (1) Cell and Tissue Biology, (2) Human Biology, (3) Developmental Biology, (4) Restorative Therapy, (5) Prevention, (6) Applied Biology and Diagnosis, (7) Medical and Surgical Therapy, and (8) Clinical Practice.

The stated purposes for each of the topics include definitions and statements of concern. For example, the definition and statements of concern for the topic "Cell and Tissue" are stated in the *Handbook for Topic Teaching* thus:

Definition
Studies of morphology, biochemistry, biophysics, and physiology of cells and tissue during health and disease.

Statements of Concern
1. A knowledge of fundamental structure and physiology of the basic building units of living organisms is essential in order to work with the macroscopic problems.
2. A broader knowledge of the predictability of tissue response is essential to diagnosis, treatment, prognosis, and leads to an understanding of some aspects of the organism's response.
3. The development of concepts and vocabulary to improve professional communication is essential.

Certainly, the fact that flexibility was built into the new curriculum was very important. Wise selection of the "core" teaching topics also helped guarantee a good measure of success. It is also well to remember that the topics chosen are truly *teaching* topics. They were selected as vehicles for helping the student learn in classrooms of faculty members from many different departments, as well as from modules for self-directed study.

The use of teaching topics is really not a "method" of teaching or learning, but a structure in which the entire faculty can help the student achieve that competence which the faculty and the profession agree he must possess before he is presented to a licensure board for evaluation. In addition, The University of Texas Dental Branch must be proud to have him as a practicing alumnus in any community.

For each of the seven first-year classes that have started in the new integrated curriculum, the program and the scheduling have been different. This doesn't mean a state of confusion, but rather that the faculty is constantly reviewing its objectives and course content and that revisions are made when it is apparent that they are needed. This is a healthful sign for a sound educational program.

A considerable amount of repetition and overlap has been eliminated. Faculty members have sat down together, talked about each area's problems, and realized their own as well as their colleagues' instructional difficulties. Each member has become more cognizant of what is needed to graduate a well-rounded professional man in dentistry. Cooperation has been excellent. The graduates have not suffered in shifting from the traditional curriculum to the modified (horizontally integrated) approach. In fact, the results of the National Board Examinations have shown superior achievement compared to previous classes. We have produced a graduate more knowledgeable of the role he is to assume in the professional world of dentistry and of the responsibilities he has in the community where he practices. The work that the faculty has done on the curriculum is such that it has been requested by several foreign countries, as well other dental schools in the United States.

Today's problem is to supply, distribute, and make accessible the necessary personnel to provide the forecasted need for dental services. How to cope with such pressures is foremost in thoughts of dental educators. The faculty has advanced in its thinking, and is involved in finding solutions to these problems.

Through experience in the integrated curriculum, some faculty could see the next steps to take, which included flexibility in curriculum to accommodate the advanced student. They began to talk about behavioral objectives for the student and how to evaluate him at certain points in his educational progress. This is the self-directed curriculum with an instructional module structure. The working definition for a module of self-directed instruction is a *set of stated performance objectives with sufficient appropriate instructional material, print and nonprint media, and human resources to permit a student to master the objectives at his own rate and ability in a self-directed learning environment.*

Why the great interest in self-directed instruction? What can it do for the dental student? It offers the following advantages:

(1) Learning can take place more rapidly, perhaps because of the removal of "clutter" and because the material is better organized.

(2) Learning can be more enjoyable, especially when the process is fast and easy and extraneous material has been eliminated.

(3) Self-directed instruction is based on performance objectives; the student does not have to guess what he is supposed to learn from the material presented.

(4) Self-directed instruction can be adapted to individual differences. Materials can be studied at a time and often at a place selected by the student. His rate of progress will depend on his abilities and not on the pacing provided by the lecturer.

(5) Techniques of self-directed instruction utilize research that emphasizes retaining the material learned. Learning is better retained perhaps because the method of presentation is more conducive to learning than that provided by a conventional text or lecturer.

These advantages may make it appear that the instructor and the lecturer are passé and should be phased out of the schools. In regard to lectures, that is largely true. However, teachers in the self-directed program have a more important function. The self-directed program enables the teacher to interact with the student at a synthesizing and creative level of behavior.

A student in the self-directed curriculum must assume the responsibility for scheduling his time and executing the study plan. A faculty member preparing the self-directed modules accepts the responsibility for providing a clear, concise package containing specific content, objectives, list of resources, and stated evaluation procedures. A study plan is provided to direct the student and show relationships to other modules in the integrated sequence. The study plan should contain what the student should be looking for, when to search for it, and where to find it.

Standardization is essential to instructional module preparation. The student must be able to find a module's essential ingredients (identity and classification, content, study plan, objectives, resources, and evaluation) in the same order and format regardless of topic or phase.

A guide has been provided for the faculty to use in preparation of the module and its format. This instrument serves the need for basic criteria to evaluate the module. Each element making up an instructional module is identified with explanations as headings on work sheets. These planning forms have been significant in standardizing the format and upgrading the modules. The headings on the work sheets are as follows:

The statement of content should
Present an overview of the subject matter to be studied which will
 • Guide and assist students in organizing and scheduling his own time for study and evaluation;
 • Show relationship and relevant aspects of the knowledge and skills to dentistry.

The study plan should
(1) Guide the student in his study and use of learning resources provided;
(2) Advise the student as to procedure and location of clinic and laboratory supply and didactic learning resources;
(3) Show relationship and relevant aspect of knowledge and skills to dentistry.

The objectives should
(1) Clearly state behaviorally what the student is to know and perform;

(2) Specify performance levels expected;

(3) Contain information as to the what, the why, and the how of the learning (stated in a clear, concise manner using action words) and as to what the student must be able to do in a specific situation.

The instructional resources should include

(1) Media material:

- Instructional media should be listed by type, title, location, and availability for each submodule.
- Media should be relevant to the instructional module objectives and to dental education.

(2) Human resources:

- How, when, where, and for what purpose should be stated for individual student/teacher contact.
- Seminars and group discussion should be built into the instructional module.
- Scheduled times for small group interaction should be repeated two or more times to permit the student to progress at his own rate.

Self-evaluation and teacher's evaluation should

(1) Reflect the stated objectives;

(2) Be phrased in such a way as to guide the student in his test preparation;

(3) Include a self-evaluation test sufficient for letting the student know when he is ready to take the examination for topic and phase credit;

(4) Assure the students that the objectives are stated in action terms and that the evaluation instrument will be measuring only those areas, actions, and conditions stated in the objectives.

SUMMARY OF UTDB METHODOLOGY AND CHANGE

Traditionally, curriculum has been vested in the department that is teaching the subject. Most faculty members can recall their undergraduate years when before answering a particular question on an examination, or starting a clinical project, they had to make the decision either, "Who wrote the question?" or "Who will evaluate the project?" Because of an instructional decision flow of department to student and student to department, conflicting views could exist for certain situations. These conflicts were not readily apparent to teachers, as there was no mechanism for interdepartmental decision-making.

As a result of the faculty topic teaching experiences, the Administration and Curriculum Coordinating Committee prepared a *Handbook for Topic Teaching* to serve as an instructional decision-making model for the UTDB School of Dentistry. The first handbook was prepared in 1968. Of necessity, it has been modified each year as experience grows in the topic curriculum. An instructional decision-making model has helped to answer how the aims and philosophy of UTBD will be achieved, by whom, and by what methods. The handbook is "to help the faculty overcome the constantly developing problems associated with change and/or modifying a curriculum. Areas of responsibility have been delineated; rationale and guidelines have been developed; and definitions and statements of purpose have been provided."

The methodology includes all of the dental faculty working in one or more of the teaching topic committees. Part-time and full-time faculty interact within the department. All full-time faculty are assigned by department chairmen to represent that department on a topic committee, which group structures the curriculum content for their particular area of interest. Each of the topic committee chairmen sits as a member of the Teaching Committee, which reports to the Curriculum Coordinating Committee. For matters of major curriculum interests, the dean has available the Committee on Dental Education as his advisory group. The office of the dean is the final step in the progression of coordinating decisions and approving curriculum change. This sequence occurs in both the scheduled *time curriculum* and in the self-directed *rate curriculum*.

PERT (program evaluation and review technique) for a five-year period to end by 1977 is being followed. The commitments include enrolling twenty-four students each year in the self-directed program, in addition to the one hundred in the scheduled program. May of each year has been indicated as the decision period for the faculty and the administration to decide whether or not the entering class of 124 will continue to be divided by curriculum format or enter the self-directed program. The plan forces a decision that will bring all entering students into the same integrated curriculum design. The result may be a combination of the best of the scheduled and the self-directed programs, or the integrated self-directed program in its entirety. The processes to follow should be worth observing and the rationale for the final decision worth examining. The University of Texas Dental Branch at Houston welcomes you to learn with us.

23. Planned Change in a Developing Institution

Richard Wollin

Colleges will not change in the 70's for the sake of change, but for the sake of themselves and humanity. In higher education as elsewhere change does not necessarily assure progress but progress implacably requires change.

—Henry Steele Commager

Southwest Minnesota State College is one of the Midwest's newest institutions of higher education. Six years ago cornfields bordered the eastern edges of Marshall, Minnesota. Today over $30 million in modern facilities have replaced those farmlands. The present enrollment of 2,500 students is drawn mainly from nineteen counties in southwest Minnesota—a predominately rural area. The largest community in the area is approximately 14,000; metropolitan St. Paul-Minneapolis lies 160 miles to the northeast. Half of the ninety-eight school districts in the area the College serves have a total school enrollment of fewer than 500 students in grades K-12.

The College has had the unique opportunity to incorporate concepts, innovations, and experiments into its total program that would be difficult to implement in more established institutions. At the same time, the College has recognized its responsibility to develop academic programs that reflect the highest quality of instruction and performance. In a sense, the opportunity has been afforded to combine the best of traditional approaches to education with those reputable innovations marking the frontiers of academic life in higher education today.

The development of our teacher education program has attracted the attention of professional personnel from colleges and universities, state departments, public schools, professional organizations, and the public because of efforts to develop a "competency based professional program." What does one do? How does one proceed to develop a new program in a new college with a new staff and new facilities? The task has been exciting, but demanding.

FACTORS INFLUENCING PROGRAM DEVELOPMENT

The educational programs at the College were developed within a number of institutional and value systems that have had important influences on the nature of those programs, including teacher education.

Mission of the College

As approved by the state legislature and the Minnesota State College Board before the opening of the College in 1967, the stated Mission of Southwest Minnesota State College identified three major references for program development:

First, the College is to be supported by public funds and therefore should endeavor to meet the needs of the public it is to serve.

Secondly, the College is to be a liberal arts and technical college, with certain professional and preprofessional programs. Major emphasis should be placed on developing plans to meet regional needs for elementary and secondary teachers and to provide programs for preservice teachers.

Thirdly, the College is to serve the nation, the state, and particularly rural southwest Minnesota. The curricula should recognize and be related to the needs of the region.

Academic Guidelines

While the unifying force in the academic programs of the College has stemmed from these statements, the curricula that comprise the educational program were to reflect a number of assumptions about learning programs for students. A sample of these assumptions that were found in the early literature describing the college reflect the "climate for learning":

(1) Education is primarily a process that goes on within the student; it is more than a procedure by which information is delivered by a professor, digested by the student, and recalled at expedient times.

(2) Educational programs should be open ended, exposing the student to various points of view. Instructors will assume responsibility wherever possible for relating assignments and materials to issues and problems that are and will be of concern to students.

(3) The climate for learning at this College is more important than the product it will turn out. The College will place primary responsibility upon the student for his or her education.

(4) Technology should be increasingly used to achieve desired learning for the student. If learning is viewed primarily as an internal process, the traditional pattern of an expert lecturing to novices can be extended to a larger range of possibilities through helping the student assume greater responsibilities for his own education. Ideally, in any program most factual information should come to the student via print, audio or video tape, film loops, slides, records, etc. Instructor and class time may be concerned with levels of learning beyond the merely factual.

More specifically, the Committee on the Liberal Arts and Teacher Education that functioned before the opening of the College suggested the following recommendations for initiating the teacher education programs:

• In the first two years, programs for potential teachers should have a broad liberal arts content, with possibly one introductory course in "orientation" to the field of education.

• All courses in professional education should be restricted to the junior and senior years.

• Some of the liberal arts faculty should be selected specifically on the basis of interest in building a strong program in teacher education.

· Time should be made available to selected faculty members to work with the elementary and secondary schools when these schools request consultation and inservice training.

· Outstanding high school teachers who meet the necessary standards should be brought in on a temporary basis as teaching assistants in those courses normally taught in high school, e.g., higher algebra, beginning languages, etc.

· Specialists should be provided to cooperate with high schools in coordinating programs such as student teaching, curriculum study, and counseling.

Consultants, Consortia, Cooperation

The chairman of the Division of Education was employed as a member of the charter faculty, half-time with the College and half-time with the Southwest and West Central Minnesota Educational Research and Development Council (ERDC), a consortium of ninety-five school districts cooperating to provide shared services not available to single school districts. This dual appointment (which has continued during the past five years) offered an excellent opportunity to develop preliminary plans for the teacher education programs at the same time that other programs at the College were being developed and initiated. It also provided an opportunity to work directly with public school personnel locally and in the state in examining the needs of schools for preservice and inservice programs.

The ERDC grew out of expressed needs on the part of public school officials for inservice programs dealing with curriculum and instruction. Educational service centers were developed in five communities, to provide diagnostic, prescriptive, and remediation programs for children with special learning problems. Studies with teachers and administrators during this period consistently indicated their need to define and to develop the knowledge and skills necessary for individualizing instruction. Over two hundred workshops and seminars on curriculum and instruction were conducted during this initial planning period. These activities culminated in the development and funding of a Title III ESEA project that involves twenty-three elementary schools that are implementing Individually Guided Education (IGE) programs. It was apparent that the development of new models for teacher education should be based on changing conditions in schools.

In fall 1968, the College participated in a consortium with two other agencies, the Kansas State Teachers College (Emporia, Kansas) and the Menninger Clinic (Topeka, Kansas), in drafting a proposal for Phase I of the Model Elementary Teacher Education Project to be funded by the Bureau of Research, U.S. Office of Education. Although the project was not funded, it did require involvement of a large segment of the College staff. One important component of the future program was identified: the importance of interaction skills in the defined role of the teacher.

The College also responded to the Bureau of Research request for Phase II proposals for "feasibility studies for the development, implementation, and operation of a teacher preparation program designed by one or more of the groups engaged in Phase I of the project." In cooperation with the Upper Midwest Regional Education Laboratory, St. Paul, Minnesota, a project proposal was submitted to USOE in spring 1969. Although the proposal was not accepted for funding, the components of the program, described below, began to emerge.

Extensive use of personal contacts and consultants was, and continues to be, used. Visits to other programs and visits by others to the SMSC campus have helped staff to incorporate new ideas into the program.

Public school personnel were and are used extensively. During the initial planning period an advisory council of administrators and teachers was appointed to develop recommendations on the general nature of teacher education and on the specific role that the public school could, and should, play in the preservice component of the program. This council has since been replaced by the teacher center council and coordinating committees. Contacts were maintained with personnel from the state department of education. Their openness to competency based education greatly facilitated the program development at the College. It should be noted that Task Forces appointed by the state department of education in recent years have consistently recommended changes in certification standards based on competencies rather than on courses per se.

In all these efforts it was found that consortia, consultants, and cooperative planning helped to create the desired "climate for change."

Staff Development

Certainly one of the advantages of developing programs in a new institution is the fact that staff can be recruited to fill specific roles. Using the information and materials described above, it was possible to assemble a unique staff within the College Division of Education. All have had extensive experience in innovative programs in public schools and colleges, and had proven themselves as change agents. Few had previous college teaching experience. They were hired to positions in four "learning centers" within the division: the Center for Educational Studies, the Center for Management of Educational Systems, the Center for Applied Instruction, and the Media and Learning Laboratories. The use of centers was a deliberate effort to avoid traditional department designations and to force redefinition of traditional teaching roles.

The first group of faculty in the division assembled two weeks before classes began in fall 1969. Several types of activities were initiated that have helped the group develop team spirit and mutual respect:

(1) Three members of the group had training and experience in human relations activities. Time has been set aside periodically for problem-solving activities, values clarification, peak experiences, etc.

(2) Extensive use has been made of materials collected from other sources. Of particular assistance in the early planning were the preliminary reports of the model elementary education projects. Staff members have been assigned to review selected materials and share their findings with others.

(3) Early in the initial planning sessions, three days were spent going through "we agree" sessions, which essentially developed the initial rationale for the programs. The words "we agree" are written on the chalkboard. Members are free to suggest a statement that is then accepted, rejected, or changed by others. It is a difficult and time-consuming process, but the agreement on rationale is probably the *most important component* in the design of any teacher education program. This "we agree" process has been used again at the beginning of each year to help new staff feel a part of the program and to develop an understanding of others. It has also been used extensively by the staff with public school faculty in helping them prepare for changes in their school program.

(4) Staff members were assigned to teams to work with elementary and secondary students. These teams now meet weekly and have been a constant source of inservice training. Each staff member is responsible for assigned curriculum areas, but each must function on one or more teams. Each works in both the elementary and secondary programs. In addition to team meetings, regular divisional meetings are scheduled. Student schedules are arranged to free Fridays for the division team meetings and for conferences with students. There has been no hesitation to cancel class schedules at the beginning of a quarter or during the year to work on problems or program components. Time in class becomes less important in a competency based program!

(5) The College has gone through two self-studies in the past three years for approval by the state department of education for certification of teachers and for accreditation by the North Central Association of Colleges and Secondary Schools. These processes have helped to clarify goals, to identify strengths and weaknesses, and to focus on finding solutions to problems.

Thus, the development of the competency based program that is individualized, personalized, and field centered has been the result of many factors, including many hours of hard work and dedication by the staff.

PROGRAM COMPONENTS

Identification of Competencies

Competency based teacher education has been defined as a program designed specifically and explicitly to provide the prospective teachers with learning experiences that help prepare them to assume agreed-on teaching roles. The program is successfully completed when candidates can demonstrate that they are competent to assume the role for which they have been prepared, i.e., they must provide satisfactory evidence, not only that they possess specified knowledge, but also that they can carry out in practice teaching tasks and functions and, in some cases, achieve learning outcomes with children.

While the identification of competencies cannot be traced to a single source or process, the ComField model, developed by the Northwest Regional Laboratory in Portland, Oregon, has helped to develop the role definition needed for competency identification. In this model four elements must be identified: (1) the pupil outcomes that are desired (i.e., the needs of society, needs of children, goals of education); (2) the conditions that bring about the desired pupil outcomes (the instructional programs within schools); (3) the competencies needed by teachers to bring about the instructional program and pupil outcomes in schools (the goals of teacher education); and (4) the conditions that bring about those competencies (the teacher education program).

Analysis of the process suggested that alternative models to the self-contained, graded, discipline-centered classroom must be considered. In cooperation with students and cooperating school personnel, the staff at SMSC identified several model school organizations as appropriate: (1) the nongraded continuous progress model; (2) the British primary school; (3) the multiunit, Individually Guided Education (IGE) model, and (4) the "humanized" secondary school. Since instructional materials are available and operational schools are located close to the college, Southwest Minnesota State College students have a unique opportunity to be prepared in IGE types of schools. (It is assumed that teachers who are prepared to accept roles in these schools can also assume roles in "traditional" classrooms.)

The staff also adopted a model for the systematic approach to instruction that provides a plan for organizing the curriculum for the teacher education program, for teaching identified competencies, and for the teacher to use once he is employed in the public school. This model is outlined in Figure 23:1.

The model in Figure 23:1 suggests that teachers need:

(1) Competencies in specifying educational objectives that reflect issues relevant to education and to living in our modern day society;

(2) Competencies in determining conditions of learners in relation to agreed-on objectives;

(3) Competencies in selecting, preparing, and using appropriate content, materials, and activities for the learner;

(4) Competencies in organizing and managing a variety of learning environments that promote learning for individuals and groups of students; and

(5) Competencies in evaluation procedures to determine if mastery of learning objectives has been achieved.

Figure 23:1. Instructional Management Model

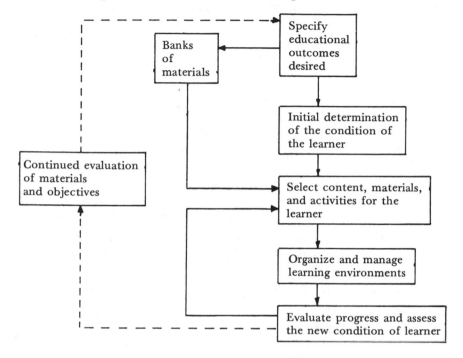

Incorporated in each of these clusters are competencies in establishing learning environments that promote positive self-esteem in all students.

The Learning Program

The program components and learning programs for students can probably best be described briefly by following a preservice elementary teacher through the program.

Approximately 450 junior and senior students are enrolled in the elementary and secondary education programs. They do not enter the teacher education program until the junior year. By this time, they have successfully completed two years of a liberal arts education, the same general studies program required of all other students at Southwest Minnesota State College. The students have the option of developing a major in an academic area, two or more academic concentrations, or an interdisciplinary program in addition to developing a major of 48 quarter-hours in elementary education.

Once the preservice teacher is accepted into the program, he or she enrolls for Elementary Block I, which is the first of five blocks (each block is six quarter-hours) required in the program. The flexible concept of the block rather than a course allows the development of individualized programs of study for each student. Research has implied that preservice teachers must focus on themselves before they can reach out and care about others; hence activities in Block I allow the students to clarify their own goals, values, and self-concepts and to see themselves in a school setting so they can determine what knowledge, skills, and competencies are needed to be a teacher.

Each student is assigned to an advisory group of fifteen to twenty students; the faculty member assigned to the group becomes the student's adviser. The student will stay in this group until graduation, unless he requests change of advisers. The advisory group is one of the most effective aspects of the program, and it serves several important roles. The group serves as a stable home base where students share learning problems, clarify goals in interaction with fellow students, get reactions to their progress, team up to work on individual study units, and, most important, are provided a humanizing dimension in the program. Contracts are written in one-to-one conferences between the adviser and advisee.

Each week a comprehensive seminar schedule is developed. Students have the option to attend seminars to achieve specific competencies. Seminars are conducted by faculty, public school personnel, and students.

Much of the student's time is spent working on the individual study units, called competency packages or ComPacs, which are units with clear goals and procedures. They proceed as much as possible from knowledge to application of that knowledge. There are over two hundred of these units currently filed in the Individualized Learning Center.

The ComPac is organized into seven basic components: (1) The objective states clearly the competency the student is to achieve. (2) In some cases there are prerequisites. (3) A pretest may allow the student to test out of the unit if he or she can do so. (4) The treatment section tells the student what he or she is to do. (5) A materials section indicates what resources are available. (6) Evaluation is based on the objective. (7) A quest section suggests additional in-depth study for the student. Films, filmstrips, video tapes, etc. provide intensive support to various kinds of print materials. The traditional textbook has been replaced by many books, many articles, and many materials from many sources.

Students work in public schools one half-day per week before they go into student teaching. They directly assist teachers as well as work on ComPacs that require the public school program for application level objectives.

After completion of three elementary blocks, the student may apply for student teaching. All field experiences are accomplished in one of the teacher education centers. The concept of the teacher education center was developed and tested by the University of Maryland. It is a unified approach to the study of teaching and supervision, a coordinated program of preservice and inservice experiences planned and administered cooperatively by the college and the public school systems. The program is designed to serve the needs and interests of the experienced professional as well as those of the inexperienced undergraduate student. An individualized approach makes it possible for each to become a student of teaching in accordance with his own particular stage of professional development. Coordinating the continuing career development program in each center is a teacher education coordinator, who was jointly selected and employed by the college and the public school. His role is to plan an effective program of laboratory experiences for the college student assigned to the center schools and to coordinate an inservice program for the center staff (the regular teachers of the school district who work with the students).

The teacher education center approach comes from the mutual desire of the college and the public schools to work together to improve the instructional program in the school and to develop a more effective teacher education program. Continually renewed commitment from both is required for the center to succeed. The public school must assume an increased and continuing responsibility for preservice training. The college must assume an increased and continuing responsibility for inservice training.

Several school districts in southwestern Minnesota were interested in becoming teacher education centers. Five school districts were selected. The criteria for selection were: (1) commitment to the teacher education center by the board, administration, and faculty; (2) interest of the school district in individualized instruction; (3) size of the school district; and (4) location of the school district in relation to the College. The Teacher Center Policy Committee, made up of one member from each center and one from the College, sets policies for the overall program; the Center Coordinating Committee, made up of teachers and administrators in each center, determines specific policies for each center.

Students are assigned to centers for field experiences for the junior year and for student teaching. Student teachers are assigned in their senior year to the teaching center as part of an instructional team, not to an individual teacher. This gives them the opportunity to associate and work with many faculty members. The student teacher assumes instructional responsibility for specific aspects of the curriculum. The center coordinator individualizes each student's teaching experience, using a wide variety of intensive and extensive experiences geared to meet the needs of the particular student. Each center is equipped with video equipment for microteaching and for recording classroom performance. Competency packages and the required support materials are also available for both preservice and inservice work. Weekly seminars are led by the teaching center coordinator to personalize and to evaluate the student teaching experience for each student teacher assigned to the center.

After students complete the student teaching component, they return to the college for a final evaluation. A student's graduation and certification both depend on demonstrated teaching competencies. These competencies include knowing what to teach, preassessment skills, selecting appropriate materials, choosing effective instructional strategies, and evaluation.

COMMENTS

The specific elements of the Southwest Minnesota State College program are still in the process of change and modification. What is important are the ideas on which the program is based and the effects they have on learners. The staff has focused on one basic question: "What does a teacher need to know and be able to do to teach in the modern public school?" Emphasis has been given to activities that seem to foster learning in schools that must serve a rapidly changing society. In developing the rationale and assumptions for the program, the staff has focused on the pupil outcomes that are desired in schools and on the conditions needed in school programs to foster these learnings. The other elements of the program design have developed from the rationale—competencies, specific objectives, levels of expected mastery, clusters of competencies and objectives, a management system, testing of material and processes, and ongoing evaluation systems.

In this type of program, staff members must trust each other and their students and believe that each learner has the desire to change, to learn. Students want to feel competent, to feel important, to feel successful. Students can set specific goals and long-range objectives that are meaningful to him or her. Students can become self-directed, but like most skill development, time and practice are required. As one student put it, "I really feel good about my experiences. I had an opportunity to see what it is actually like to be a teacher. I had a chance to prepare and to work with students. I discovered some of my strengths and weaknesses. Now I know what to work on."

The program is an extremely demanding one for staff and students. The staff spends their time developing curriculum and learning experiences for students, monitoring and evaluating student progress, attending planning meetings, and working with public school personnel. They constantly seek ways to improve learning programs for students. Students find that they must make decisions, expose their ideas and demonstrate skills, and make a commitment to their professional program.

Competency based programs can be, but need not be, impersonalized and dehumanized. Individualized instruction means learning in ways, places, and times appropriate to the learner. Working alone is one learning mode; working and interacting with others is greatly enhanced by the processes used.

CBTE is essentially an evaluation system. Very little is known yet about the essential competencies needed by students or about the criteria necessary to demonstrate competence with children. The emphasis in the SMSC program has been on teaching behavior rather than on consequence outcomes. Preservice teachers can learn the process of evaluating pupil outcomes and can demonstrate that process in field experiences, but because they have minimal control over factors affecting pupil learning, there is doubt that exiting the program can be based solely on demonstrated pupil outcomes.

It is increasingly apparent that personnel from public schools and professional organizations will provide the key to the success of these programs. The practicing professional should have a voice in determining competencies and standards necessary to enter the teaching profession. With this opportunity should also go the shared responsibility of evaluating teacher behavior of preservice teachers.

CBTE provides no panacea for all issues and problems in education. But it does provide the means by which decision-making processes can be shared by teacher educators, state department personnel, public school personnel, professional organizations, students, and lay citizens.

Programs and projects are means to ends; they should be used to meet needs of individuals. Too often individuals are used to develop programs. Social organizations, including teacher education, derive their significance from their promise to serve human beings, to fulfill their potential, and to enhance their dignity. Solutions have been found to many of the difficult and complex scientific and technical problems of our times. It is obvious, however, that we have not found solutions to the more critical problems of helping people relate to other people, people to society, and society to people. Education, including competency based education, cannot solve all society's problems, but teacher educators cannot afford to put their heads in the sands of time in hopes that the problems—the human problems—of the modern decade will disappear. The self-examination required by the design of CBTE programs is difficult, but it can be rewarding for those who have the "courage to change those things that need change, the humility to accept those that they cannot, and the wisdom to know the difference."

24. The Student in a Competency Based Program: Does He Have an Active Role?

Donna Dolinsky

One of the main ways in which a competency based teacher training program differs from a traditional teacher training program is in the amount of necessary planning before the program can be implemented. Before instruction, decisions must be made as to what competencies will be mastered by students, how mastery will be defined and measured, what instructional procedures will occur, how the program itself will be evaluated in terms of its success in bringing about these competencies, and also how the program will be managed. These decisions are usually made by university faculty and administrators with input from teachers and school administrators. This chapter investigates the question of student involvement in making decisions about the variables listed above. Students in three different competency based programs will be looked at in terms of the amount of input they have, whether changes occur as a function of this input, and whether students should have this input and why or why not.

Three groups of students will be referred to: (1) undergraduate students presently enrolled in the University of Toledo's competency based teacher training program; (2) Teacher Corps interns from the University of Toledo who are teaching a half-day at Washington Elementary School and who have all their education classes at the elementary school; and (3) doctoral candidates in educational psychology at the University of Toledo. The undergraduate teacher training program has been functioning as a competency based program since September 1972. The Teacher Corps program is evolving toward a competency based program, and the doctoral program is in part competency based, that is, certain courses are competency based, others are not. The third group of students is included because the Educational Psychology Department is considering a competency based doctoral program and doctoral students have been involved in deciding which competencies are needed by someone who will call himself or herself an educational psychologist. Differences in student involvement will be seen to be a function both of the kind of student involved and also the state of development of the program.

DEFINING SKILLS AND STATING OBJECTIVES

Do Students Have Input?

Generally, students in the undergraduate program have not been able to help decide which skills should make up their program. Most of the skills and their related behavioral objectives were decided on by the faculty before the program was implemented. Changes have occurred in the program; certain skills have been refined or dropped for various reasons and new skills added, but so far student input has not been responsible for these changes.

In the Teacher Corps program, individual students have stated the need to acquire certain skills, such as dealing with certain reading problems or acquiring classroom management skills. These students are teaching a half-day in an elementary school and see both the instructional aspects of teaching and the administrative side. A few of the interns have questioned if some of the skills they have learned can feasibly be implemented in a public school. These students felt that part of a CBTE program should include skills in changing administrative structures so that they could implement some of the instructional skills they had developed in the program.

In deciding what skills should compose the graduate program in educational psychology, the department met with graduate students for three grueling hours a week for one quarter to try to make some decisions about terminal goals of the doctoral program. Most of the doctoral students felt that they should acquire skills in college level teaching before graduating from the program and that they should have research skills long before beginning the dissertation. One student suggested that each student be able to set some of his own objectives. The feeling was that a doctoral student in educational psychology should be able to seek out and define problems that were interesting to him and set up a procedure for investigating problems, for generating, testing, and evaluating solutions to problems. However, most of the objectives were set by the faculty, but they were discussed and evaluated by the students.

In terms of the three developmental stages of these programs and these three types of students (a three-by-three factorial with 66 percent of the cells missing and an N of one in each remaining cell), one hypothesis would be that student input, when given equal opportunity, is probably more a function of the student than of the developmental stage of the program. The more experience the student has had in approximating the professional activities for which he is training, the more likely he is to have input into a competency based program—not a startling statement.

An interesting thing has happened to undergraduate students, however, as a function of being in a fully functioning competency based program. When a student has missed a class, he doesn't ask what was covered that day, but rather what objectives he had to master. This behavior is quite different from some graduate students who have not experienced competency based instruction; when they miss a class, they want to know what was covered or discussed. These students, even though they may have had extensive teaching experience and other related progressional experiences, need to learn the "form" of a competency based program before they can give meaningful input. The undergraduates understand the form of the program (having lived through it) and can easily differentiate between types of objectives and procedures and can apply the concept of an instructional system, but they have difficulty making meaningful decisions about the content of the program. By providing experiences in classrooms, we are hoping that they will "perceive a need" for some of the skills that they will acquire in the program.

Do Changes Occur as a Function of Student Input?

When Teacher Corps interns specify skills they feel they need to master, provisions are made (as often as possible) for a faculty member from the university to set up a program for the intern to help himself to learn that skill. We feel it is imperative that the intern receive feedback on the degree of his mastery of that skill, so the faculty member spends time in the classroom with the intern and gives feedback. This individualized program is in the beginning stages and obviously takes a lot of faculty time for observations. One of the mistakes made at the beginning was to make observations of interns before any specific need or skill was specified. The faculty observer didn't know what to observe so he chose something that was in his area (behavior modification, group process, etc.); the intern didn't quite know how to behave and there was little communication. Now when faculty members observe interns, they observe performance related to specific competencies—very often competencies that were decided on by the intern himself. Interns' ideas were incorporated primarily in the areas of value clarification and ethnic awareness in writing a proposal for the Teacher Corps.

Some of the doctoral students' ideas have been incorporated into present courses. For example, in a course in applied instructional systems, one doctoral student is designing, implementing, and evaluating an instructional module for the undergraduate program.

In the few cases where students have given input into these three competency based programs, changes have occurred and are still occurring.

Should Students Have Input into Defining Skills and Stating Objectives, and Why or Why Not?

Probably the best criteria for evaluating whether or not students should have input into designing objectives for competency based programs are if it is good for the program and if it is good for the student—not necessarily in that order. Skill input from students will be good for the program if future teachers who learn those skills are more successful in having their students learn than are teachers who did not acquire those skills. Unfortunately, we can't wait to externally validate skills in the program but must internally validate them on some criteria, for example, (1) present effectiveness of teachers demonstrating those skills or (2) hypotheses about future use of skills based on predictions of what classrooms will be like in the future and what children will have to be able to do in order to be successful human beings.

Input from classroom teachers could be very useful for the program because university professors with minimal classroom contact are sometimes not aware of the day-to-day problems that teachers encounter. However, this input is definitely not enough, since future teachers should be concerned not only with acquiring the competencies that many present teachers can demonstrate, but also in acquiring new competencies so they can be successful in the classrooms of the future. For example, many new packaged materials are based on using a systems approach to instruction and involve management systems. For maximum student learning, teachers and future teachers should be familiar with concepts like criterion-reference evaluation, skill groups as opposed to ability groups, recycling, formative evaluation, etc., and be able to use these concepts in implementing new materials.

The organizational structure of classrooms is also changing, as evidenced by the concept of Multiunit Schools with Individually Guided Instruction, Individually Prescribed Instruction, using the community as a source of both objectives and instructional procedures, problems-oriented teaching, an emphasis on inquiry, etc. Lecturing and traditional classroom management skills may not be especially useful in the future. However, to make reasonable predictions about the kinds of skills that might be useful to future teachers, an understanding of what teaching is about now as well as an understanding of CBTE may be necessary, but they are not sufficient. One must also have an understanding of the complex interaction of social, political, economic, and psychological influences in order to make reasonable predictions about which skills to teach.

A second criterion for making decisions about student input into designing objectives for a CBTE program is whether this is good for the student. It is probably an extremely good idea, because it forces students to look at our teaching in terms of their own learning, as defined by objectives, and this frame of reference may transfer to their own teaching. Also, probably the best way to learn about CBTE is to do it.

One of the most important reasons for student involvement in all facets of CBTE design and implementation is because, if something is being done to someone, he is usually happier if he understands what is being done, why it is being done, and has some control over it. We have found that students having problems with the program become very useful to the program (and thus to themselves) if we patiently and nondefensively listen to their complaints and *try to involve them in generating solutions.* Students who are happy in a program, who have a "good attitude" toward it, will probably tend to exert more effort and thus learn more. The sometimes unpleasant confrontations with troubled students were worth the long-range gains. The more we were open to confrontation with students at the beginning of the program when we were having some problems, the fewer problems we had later. Students who say that their input had made some change continue to give input, and to feel more a part of the program.

DESIGNING ASSESSMENT

Do Students Have Input?

Until students understand the relationship between objectives and assessment, they are likely to make decisions about assessment that reflect their own particular test-taking skills rather than the objective being assessed. Most of the terminal performance objectives in the undergraduate CBTE program are performance objectives, so the decision about assessment had been made at the same time the objective was designed. Since students are being given TPOs in advance, there is usually little input, unless criteria for assessment are not too clearly stated.

In the doctoral program, students have a great deal to say about their final assessment. They feel that this exam should measure what they have learned in graduate school and not what the faculty members learned when *they* were in graduate school. Educational psychology faculty and doctoral students are now working on this problem.

The input from Teacher Corps interns on assessment was essentially that the intern is training to be a teacher by actually teaching; therefore, any assessment of skills should be carried on in the classroom. This is being done as much as possible.

Do Changes Occur as a Function of This Input?

The students' reactions to unclear assessment criteria have made changes. Criteria were better thought out and made public in those cases.

The problems of assessment in the doctoral program appear to be much greater. One change that has occurred is that final exam questions are chosen much more carefully than in the past and are chosen with the individual student's program (with related objectives) in mind. More important is that the Educational Psychology Department is now working to set up measurable competencies that will be presented to students *before* they start choosing courses. Assessment will not necessarily be paper and pencil (except maybe for some content comprehension objectives and objectives dealing with planning), but will be observation and analysis of competencies such as teaching of educational psychology, research and development, product organization, and administration and interpersonal interaction. These areas are being task analyzed into skills and enabling objectives; the final assessment will be based on these objectives.

Should Students Have Input into Designing Assessment, and Why or Why Not?

One of the main reasons that students should have input into designing or evaluating assessment is that it keeps the professor "honest" by making it imperative that objectives of instruction are stated before instruction begins and that the student understands the objectives. The experience is also valuable because, by doing CBTE, a student is learning about it.

DESIGNING PROCEDURES

Do Students Have Input?

Students in the undergraduate program probably have not had as much input into designing instructional procedures as could be desired. One of the reasons for this is that when the objectives were designed, the instructional procedures were planned for many of the objectives at the same time. Another reason is that we have tried to incorporate as many different types of instructional procedures as possible (and meaningful), so that when it came time to study instructional procedures as an objective, the students would have common experiences to analyze. As a matter of fact, at times instructional procedures were chosen for this longer-range objective rather than for the immediate objective (which of course is questionable). For example, we realized that in a sequence of about eight modules, the students were never involved in a simulation game; we decided to use one for that objective (writing behavioral objectives) even though alternative methods would have probably been no more or less successful.

Teacher Corps interns have had input into design of instructional procedures. Rather than being told what to do and how to do it, e.g., teach elementary math operations with Cuisinere Rods, they often ask that they be shown in their classrooms, with their pupils, how this can be done. They then do it, are observed, and are given feedback. The doctoral students have varying amounts of input into designing instructional procedures. Those who have been successful designing and carrying out individual study are often very good at designing their own instructional procedures and are given opportunities to do it.

Do Changes Occur as a Function of Student Input in Designing Procedures?

In the case of the Teacher Corps interns, the faculty involved tries to model behavior as much as possible. However, in many cases this procedure is not sufficient for the intern to acquire competencies. If a professor goes into an intern's classroom to teach a skill, is successful, and then suggests that the intern on his own look into more about that skill—e.g., read a little—the intern is more likely to do so than if the professor first asks the intern to read or lectures to him. Fortunately or unfortunately, university education professors have lost some of their creditability with idealistic students who are actually teaching. Sometimes, students have to see that things work before they will believe that they are possible.

Doctoral students probably have the greatest *say* in designing their own instructional procedures. Many choose to work on their own in a tutorial fashion.

Should Students Have Input into Designing Instructional Procedures, and Why or Why Not?

Students would probably have input into designing their own instructional procedures if: (1) this helps them to reach the objective,

(2) they learn something about different instructional procedures, (3) they learn something about criteria for selecting alternate instructional procedures, and (4) they learn to become a little more independent and to take responsibility for their own learning.

We have found that some students avoid reading as an instructional procedure because they are not very good readers. While they may have a better chance of reaching an immediate instructional objective through another method, do we have any responsibility to help them become better readers? If so, might requiring a student to reach the objective through reading be one way of helping him to become a better reader? Suppose students always choose solitary methods of instruction, such as reading, viewing film strips, etc., and never choose anything that involves other humans? Is that appropriate behavior for a future teacher? Maybe if we give students a choice in selecting instructional procedures, we should set up constraints such that they choose from different types. This might help them to meet the general objectives above. Objective (4) probably could not be reached by students other than by designing their own instructional procedures. That might be an interesting skill to have in a CBTE program, e.g., given series of behavioral outcomes that the teacher trainees must meet for evaluation, the teacher trainee will design an instructional procedure such that he reaches mastery on each objective. Each instructional procedure must be of a different type. If mastery is not reached with the first choice of instructional procedure, the student will design instructional procedures until he is effective in reaching mastery.

An objective like this followed by an analysis of the relationship between different instructional procedures and different objectives might help the student make better decisions about choosing instructional procedures for his own teaching.

PROGRAM EVALUATION

So far, none of the students who have participated in the entire program has completed student teaching so we have no external validity data on the program.

The internal structure and management of the programs, however, are constantly being evaluated and changed. Student input has been necessary here, and it has been very easy to get, especially when something is not going well.

In the undergraduate program, students are generally pleased with the mastery of competencies notion and adapt to the new system easily. The idea of failing on pretests was at first confusing and disturbing to many, until they better understood the reason for a pretest. In some cases they have their choice of taking the pretest or not and have learned to study the terminal performance objectives before deciding to take a pretest. Since the students are on many different levels because of their different entry points into the program, it is possible (and does happen) that students pretest out of modules.

Most of the student input, probably the most valuable, has dealt with the management of the program. Self-pacing was a problem for many students; they asked for a lot of structured feedback on where they were in the program and what modules they still had to complete. Many students complained about all the papers they were getting at different times, and that they had difficulty coordinating everything. The second quarter of the CBTE program, students received a list of objectives for modules and due dates. The following quarter, along with the module outline, students received all the modules for the quarter bound together; and this relieved much of the confusion. One of the media students suggested that faculty members from different areas such as curriculum and educational psychology were talking about many of the same concepts but calling them by different names. To avoid the semantics problem, he suggested that a glossary be made up. The faculty responded with a concerted effort to speak only standard English. There are certain words that everyone uses that are not really standard English, but that seems to be acceptable to students and faculty since the words seem to communicate. However, one does question if it is a good thing for the language that nineteen-year-olds go around saying things like, "I've got to recycle on my EOs."

One of the biggest problems during our first quarter was coordination. Teams were made up of from five to twelve faculty members; in some cases communication was difficult. At times students received different information from different professors and some rightfully became very upset. The students offered suggestions such as the necessity of having some central information place, and if more than one person was responsible for teaching a module, that one person be in charge and make decisions about due dates.

Because of the complexity of the program, we found it necessary to spend time going over the module outlines, making sure that students knew what they had to do, as well as where, when, and what their options were. It was imperative that the students understand the system because student self-management was necessary for the successful functioning of the program. As more and more of the modules become self-instructional and as students have more choices of instructional procedures, individualization demands that students regulate their own behavior, which requires a thorough understanding of the system. By simply going through the program, the undergraduates know more about CBTE than some of the graduate students who are studying about a systems approach to education.

As students and faculty understand more about CBTE and are able to do it, and as modules change to include more alternate instructional procedures and become more self-instructional, individualization becomes a reality and the early management problems lessen. Again, it is imperative that everyone understand what is going on and is able to operationalize CBTE. This can best occur by having input from *everyone* involved—faculty, administration, and students.

FACULTY REACTION TO STUDENT INPUT

When the implementation of the CBTE program began and there were some coordination difficulties, students were adamant about offering input. The faculty knew pretty much what the problems were and were working hard to overcome them. Listening patiently to students telling you what is wrong when you know very well what is wrong is sometimes difficult, especially when students are angry and are having difficulty pinpointing the exact problems. However, one of the best things was that faculty *did* listen patiently to students, which was effective in bringing about much better affect between faculty and students.

In most cases, faculty did find that students' input is very valuable, especially in maintaining open communications so that students' reactions can be heard and dealt with. The students are amazed when their input actually causes change, find this reinforcing, and continue to be interested in the decision-making function of the program. It is to be hoped that this practice in changing existing systems will result in a skill learned, and will transfer to the students' experiences in the public schools.

Students will learn to design and implement competency based education by being involved in decisions. The modules the students go through teach them skills in applying a systems approach to their own teaching, but by actually going through an existing program and seeing the problems that do occur and finding solutions, we hope that students will be more likely to implement these ideas in their own classrooms.

WAYS OF BRINGING ABOUT STUDENT INVOLVEMENT

We found that the one way to get students involved is to give them unclear objectives with vague criteria and to tell them that they will be evaluated at some tenuous date. However, general involvement is probably not going to help the students learn that much about CBTE. Attention must be paid to specific aspects of CBTE. Also, as many of the management problems were solved, students became less interested in becoming involved *unless* they could see that their input resulted in change. One group of students asked that its team of faculty members stay with it the following quarter. This was not in the organizational plan, which called for students to move to different teams each quarter. However, affect in this group was so good that, because of the students' request, faculty stayed with the students for the next quarter and for their next block of modules. These students saw that they could change the system, and now they seem more interested in giving input than any other students in the model.

Rather than suggest to students that whoever is interested should come to the team meetings whenever he wants, it is probably better to require more structure at the beginning. Students should be asked to select representatives to go to team meetings and act as liaisons between students and faculty. Classroom time should be allowed for students to meet with their representatives to make decisions on specific areas. Posting team meeting agendas before meetings could be useful in getting student interest. Students should know in advance what will be discussed, what will be voted on, and what are the alternative solutions to a problem. By being very structured at the beginning, students can more clearly learn the kinds of things that they could do if they become involved. As students get used to giving input and finding that their input has some effect, structure can be reduced and the students can start defining their own structure.

Another interesting way to get student involvement is to present the student with a blank module. Require the student to define an objective that he feels will help him become a better teacher, state some rationale, devise some measurement and appropriate procedures. Have the student go through his own module, evaluate his own performance, and also his entire module. This idea came from our doctoral program and is probably very good for an undergraduate student to go through; it should teach him some skills in CBTE and also teach him that he can change his own behavior.

STUDENTS' CRITICISM AND ANALYSIS OF CBTE

One of the main criticisms of CBTE by students is that it requires more work and more self-management than a non-CBTE program. In a traditional norm-referenced class with a midterm, final, and a paper, regardless of how good or bad his performance, the student is called on to perform only about three times. He does not necessarily have to go to class, interact with the professor, or do anything at any special time (except for that midterm, final, and paper). He can do the reading for the course in two massed sessions—the night before the midterm and the night before the final.

The self-management aspects of the program are probably most difficult for the student. He has to be aware of and attend classroom activities when they are scheduled because he will need that input (or must engage in those behaviors) in order to reach competency on a certain module. For self-instructional modules or for individually tested modules, he has to find out where and at what time assessment will occur. He has to coordinate his time to accommodate field experiences. He sometimes has to make decisions about preferred instructional procedures and types of assessment. In short, the student has changed from a passive receptacle who may or may not attend class and may or may not learn in class even if he does attend, to someone who must become involved in making decisions and taking responsibility for his own learning.

This can be difficult even for the highly motivated student, and can be a totally frustrating and unapproachable experience for the less motivated and/or less self-managed student. It is easier to sit in class for four hours a week, take a midterm and final on something that may or may not be related to what was done in class, and be done with it.

Being done with it is another problem for students. Recycling can be boring, especially if the recycling procedures are identical to the original instructional procedures. Some students in a non-CBTE program figure that it will be acceptable to get a D or two in classes they are simply not interested in. They will expose themselves as little as possible to the odious stimulus and take the D; their other grades can bring up their grade point average. However, in a CBTE program, the student not only is not permitted to make that decision, but he must encounter and reencounter the undesirable stimulus until he can perform the competency. A good program would not have too many modules that would be totally distasteful to students, but it is likely that this will occur to individual students. Alternate instructional procedures and assessment seem to be the best way out of this problem, along with a short delay until the student's avoidance gradient is lowered.

Another knotty problem that is more related to the philosophy of CBTE is the nonselectivity of criterion-reference grading. Students are generally happy with the idea that they can reach mastery and receive A's or Passes while they are involved in the program. However, students do express concern with what is going to happen to them if a number of people apply for the same job or same graduate school position. Since their grades are nondiscriminating, on what criteria will selection be made? Also, if a student from a CBTE program (with competencies listed on his transcript) competes for a position with a student from a non-CBTE program (with A's and B's listed on his transcript), might not the administrator who is making the selection favor the student with the A's and B's? The administrator may not understand CBTE, but he certainly knows what A's are.

Another question students have raised is whether CBTE is not encouraging mediocrity rather than excellence. The philosophy behind this is that not everyone can be excellent; therefore, criteria for competency are set lower and students who could successfully strive for excellence are pronounced competent in a certain situation when it may have been possible for them to do much more. Is this not a dangerous habit for students to learn?

As with many complex philosophical arguments, they become less complex and sometimes almost solvable when the situation is centered on a particular student dealing with a particular competency. The flexibility to deal with these kinds of problems can be built into more experienced and sophisticated programs by introducing individually tailored objectives, procedures, and assessment criteria, and by using optional modules.

The student criticism of too much work can change if students see that the work they put into learning actually pays off in greater learning by children in their own classrooms. The self-management problems lessen as students learn self-management skills. (Is this a valid reason for teaching self-management skills as part of the program?) Boredom with recycling (and even the necessity for recycling) can be decreased with more effective, and a greater choice of, instructional procedures. The problem of lack of selectivity is introduced because of criterion-referenced grading, which may be decreased by educating administrators in CBTE. One way to do this might be to include a simple explanation with examples along with a student's CBTE transcript. The student's interview might include work samples or tapes of in-class demonstrations of skills and competencies. The accusation that CBTE promotes mediocrity can be met with the opportunity for individual student selection of objectives, instructional procedures, and criteria for assessment.

These student criticisms of CBTE do not necessarily impugn CBTE as a concept, but may be an indication of how CBTE is being implemented.

Positive reactions to CBTE generally outnumber negative reactions. Students are most pleased with the stating of objectives and the objective assessment match. Students know what they are expected to be able to do and how they are going to be assessed. Students see the concept of recycling as sensible and fair and sometimes wonder why they never questioned nonrecycling systems before.

Another desirable aspect of CBTE is that students actually see it working at the same time they are learning about it. We sometimes wonder if the students do not learn more through modeling than through reading and discussing CBTE.

Probably the most positive aspect of CBTE is that students see it as relevant. Decisions about which competencies to master were based on a model of what teachers do in classrooms to promote student learning. Therefore anything that students learn in the program will in time be demonstrated by them in their own field experience. If relevancy means a match between what is learned by a student and what he will have to be able to do in a "real-life" situation, then CBTE is relevant.

SUMMARY

Student involvement in CBTE benefits both the student and the program. In order that a student can meaningfully contribute his ideas to a program, it is necessary that he first understand what is meant by CBTE, i.e., that he can discriminate among the components of objectives, assessment, procedures, program evaluation, and management and also that he can synthesize these concepts into modular form to express his ideas. Because students probably learn more about these concepts through modeling than through formal instruction, it is imperative that the faculty involved thoroughly understand the philosophy of CBTE and are able to implement the concept effectively.

The Last Relatively Complete Tentative Bibliography on Competency Based Education

Allen A. Schmieder

INTRODUCTION

The major purpose of this bibliography is to present, with one notable categorical exception,* a relatively complete listing of significant materials and publications on competency based education (CBE). The resource base for CBE is greater than is generally known and it is hoped that this comprehensive coverage will help lead program developers to many useful new sources.

---

*Because the number of modules now available for CBE programs number in the thousands, individual modules are included only if they relate specifically to the general nature of CBE; e.g., *Toward a Better Understanding of Performance Based Education or CBE: A Simulation.* For specific listings of modules that have been developed and that may be available for distribution write to one of the national materials centers listed at the end of the bibliography or write directly to individual CBE program locations. (For a listing of most of these programs, see Allen Schmieder, *Competency Based Education: The State of the Scene.* Washington, D.C.: American Association of Colleges for Teacher Education, 1972, pp. 12-17.)

The unusual title for this chapter is partly a reaction to the fact that bibliographies have had the same dull titles since the time of clay tablets, but it is mostly a tribute to the very rapid growth of the volume of materials now available and soon to be available on the subject. In late 1971, the author's first "complete" bibliography on the subject included twenty-two items (*Task Force 1972, Focus on Educational Reform—Accent on Involvement and Communication* (Washington, D.C.: United States Office of Education, 1971), pp. 11-22); this collection includes over 800 entries, and by the time this book is published, at least 800 more good pieces on CBE will have been generated. Any next "complete" bibliography on CBE will require many volumes—so I expect that future bibliographies on the subject will be specialized ones, e.g., "Competency Based Career Education," "Competency Based Programming in Special Education." (A specialized bibliography already exists for special education: Patricia M. Kay, Judy Kobarick, Marilyn Sevush, and Barbara Cohen, *Competency Based Teacher Education in Special Education: An Annotated Bibliography* (New York: City University of New York, 1973).)

Because of the rapid growth of CBE and the fact that it is still in the developmental stage, it was decided that it would be better to provide as complete a listing as possible of what is available rather than to construct what would necessarily be a much shorter annotated bibliography. (The National Committee on Performance Based Teacher Education of the American Association of Colleges for Teacher Education has already published an excellent annotated bibliography: *Performance Based Teacher Education: An Annotated Bibliography,* (Washington, D.C.: AACTE, 1972).) Because many of the publications cited cover more than one major CBE subject, it was also decided that to organize the items according to specific categories would require a large number of multiple listings, resulting in a bibliography that would be too lengthy for inclusion herein. Therefore, all entries are included in one alphabetical, numbered list. It is not expected (although it might provide some education, edification, and other important surprises), that the reader will peruse all citations from A to Z in search of the most promising sources. A topical index is provided at the end of this introductory section that provides cross-references for all bibliography items within fifty-seven specific subjects. Because there was not time to study and fully assess all the materials, many publications are not as fully cross-referenced as they might be, i.e., items are identified in the index as dealing with the general philosophy of the CBE concept but there are surely others which, although focusing on some more specific subject like assessment or evaluation, touch importantly on philosophy. We apologize both to those whom we have "under-indexed" and to those from whom we have wrung too much.

SUBJECT INDEX

Following are the subjects that were used for cross-referencing the bibliography in an attempt to provide the reader with some levers for sorting through this long listing of materials. Next to each are the numbers of some, not all, of the entries that touch on that subject. For those categories that include large numbers of entries (e.g., in assessment and evaluation), further sorting can occur in two ways: (1) Select only those references that deal *exclusively* with the index category (e.g., assessment and evaluation); (2) cross-reference categories (e.g., assessment and evaluation items that also treat the basic subjects). Most of the categories are self-explanatory but several require further elucidation: *General* items usually cover the CBE waterfront and make some reference to most of the subjects listed in the index; because so few general publications exist (there are many specific modules) on the basic subjects, the broad label of *subject area* as well as the particular specialty (i.e., mathematics) was used to better accommodate those who are interested in the general development of CBE within the basic studies fields.

B-28, B-33, B-36, B-37, B-39, B-41, B-42, B-44, B-45, B-49, B-54, B-55, B-57, B-58, B-66, B-67, B-70, B-71, B-76, B-84, B-87, B-91, B-94, B-99, C-4, C-9, C-10, C-11, C-13, C-18, C-28, C-35, C-36, C-40, C-48, C-52, C-53, C-66, D-5, D-15, D-27, D-29, D-31, D-33, D-36, E-1, E-8, E-9, E-18, E-19, F-1, F-5, F-10, F-11, F-12, F-13, F-14, F-16, F-21, F-36, G-1, G-20, G-23, G-24, G-26, G-27, H-3, H-6, H-8, H-9, H-10, H-13, H-17, H-20, H-28, H-29, H-32, H-37, H-52, H-55, H-56, H-57, I-1, I-4, J-1, J-2, J-3, J-12, J-14, J-19, J-28, J-31, K-13, K-15, L-4, L-8, L-9, L-23, M-2, M-6, M-7, M-8, M-9, M-12, M-13, M-14, M-15, M-19, M-20, M-21, M-24, M-29, M-31, M-33, M-40, M-41, M-42, M-44, M-47, M-48, M-49, M-50, M-51, M-52, M-54, M-58, M-60, M-62, M-63, M-65, M-66, N-6, N-7, N-16, N-18, O-1, O-12, O-13, O-15, P-3, P-7, P-16, P-18, P-22, P-33, P-34, P-35, P-36, P-37, P-38, P-40, P-41, P-43, P-55, Q-1, Q-2, Q-3, R-5, R-6, R-9, R-15, R-20, R-21, R-22, R-23, R-26, R-27, R-31, R-32, S-2, S-7, S-15, S-17, S-18, S-21, S-23, S-30, S-31, S-32, S-33, S-34, S-43, S-44, S-45, S-56, S-57, S-61, S-62, S-71, S-77, S-83, T-4, T-13, T-14, T-15, T-17, T-18, T-20, T-23, V-2, V-3, W-2, W-7, W-11, W-12, W-16, Y-5

Behavioral Objectives
A-7, A-26, A-27, A-29, A-49, A-50, A-51, A-52, B-7, B-8, B-9, B-20, B-38, B-48, B-85, B-86, B-87, B-88, B-89, B-90, B-91, B-92, B-98, C-7, C-17, C-35, C-40, C-44, C-53, C-67, D-25, D-26, H-38, J-7, J-12, J-14, J-19, K-1, K-2, K-7, K-9, K-19, K-20, L-12, M-1, M-2, M-13, M-19, M-31, M-46, M-47, O-6, P-27, P-35, P-37, P-39, P-40, S-30, S-31, S-32, S-33, U-1, U-2, Z-1

Bibliography
A-44, B-30, B-79, B-93, C-29, C-63, F-15, J-28, K-4, K-5, M-8, M-9, M-45, P-28, P-50, S-1, S-6, S-12, S-13, S-54, T-5, T-12

Certification
A-15, A-16, A-17, A-25, A-31, A-35, A-36, A-37, A-38, A-39, A-40, A-41, A-42, A-53, A-54, A-55, B-5, B-19, B-25, B-29, B-50, B-51, B-65, B-76, B-80, B-84, B-93, B-96, C-1, C-2, C-3, C-5, C-8, C-9, C-19, C-32, C-34, C-38, C-43, C-49, C-51, C-63, D-1, D-3, D-4, D-5, D-6, D-9, D-14, D-16, D-17, D-22, D-36, D-37, E-2, E-11, E-16, F-6, F-7, F-9, G-2, G-7, G-8, G-21, H-3, H-4, H-13, H-38, I-4, I-11, J-6, K-5, K-10, L-1, L-13, L-14, L-15, L-16, L-17, L-21, M-20, M-33,

M-34, M-38, M-54, M-61, M-64, N-12, N-13, N-16, N-17, O-10, O-13, P-4, P-7, P-8, P-11, P-13, P-14, P-16, P-17, P-22, P-24, P-26, P-29, P-30, P-35, P-45, P-46, P-48, P-49, P-53, P-54, R-1, R-3, R-5, R-7, R-11, R-12, R-18, S-7, S-12, S-20, S-24, S-34, S-37, S-38, S-42, S-45, S-46, S-57, S-60, S-63, S-64, S-65, S-66, S-67, S-68, S-69, S-76, S-78, S-79, S-80, T-3, T-5, T-7, T-8, T-9, T-10, T-11, V-1, V-4, Y-8

Competency Identification
A-50, A-57, B-11, B-22, B-39, B-57, B-62, B-71, B-86, B-94, C-11, C-13, C-40, D-13, D-26, D-27, D-29, F-3, F-25, G-11, G-26, H-6, H-36, H-40, H-56, J-7, J-11, J-14, J-15, K-7, L-2, L-4, L-19, L-23, M-4, M-10, M-12, M-21, M-23, M-33, M-44, M-49, M-53, M-63, N-6, N-7, O-7, O-8, O-9, O-12, P-7, P-9, P-27, P-31, P-43, S-47, T-20, V-3, W-6

Comprehensive
B-22, C-61, C-68, D-10, F-31, L-24

Cost
A-2, B-40, D-28, K-8, P-3, R-29, S-8, S-70, W-5

Differentiated Staffing
B-95, E-15, J-5, L-14, R-33

Educational Reform
A-8, A-12, A-13, A-30, A-38, A-39, A-55, B-1, B-27, B-50, B-51, B-52, B-70, B-78, B-95, C-1, C-14, C-22, C-30, C-50, C-56, C-60, C-64, D-16, E-3, E-5, E-15, F-4, F-30, H-7, H-9, H-20, H-23, H-26, I-5, I-8, J-25, K-8, L-10, L-22, M-50, N-12, N-13, N-14, O-2, O-10, O-11, P-25, P-32, P-43, R-3, R-8, R-11, R-33, S-5, S-15, S-26, S-41, S-49, S-53, T-19, W-13

Elementary Education
A-10, A-59, B-15, B-26, B-30, B-39, B-40, B-55, B-58, B-79, C-23, C-24, D-18, D-19, D-23, D-24, D-27, D-28, F-29, F-34, H-1, H-30, H-34, H-38, I-12, J-8, J-9, J-12, J-16, J-21, K-12, M-11, O-5, P-12, R-29, S-6, S-8, S-25, S-27, S-30, S-31, S-32, S-33, S-59, S-70, T-4, T-6, W-5, W-16

General
A-10, A-19, A-30, A-43, A-44, A-46, B-4, B-74, B-81, C-12, C-16, C-21, C-26, C-37, C-41, C-42, C-43, C-55, C-57, C-58, D-2, D-18, D-23, E-10, E-12, E-13, F-17, F-20, G-5, G-12, G-14, G-16, G-19, H-20, H-30, H-33, H-39, H-44, H-45, H-47, H-48, H-49, H-50, H-51, H-58, J-4, J-16, J-17, J-23, J-26, J-27, J-30, K-6, L-6, M-1, M-3, M-5, M-26, M-27, M-30, M-31, M-37, M-57, M-60, N-1, P-2, P-19, P-20, P-49, R-10, R-11, R-25, R-28, S-9, S-13, S-14, S-39, S-40, S-52, S-59, S-73, T-1, T-2, W-4, W-6, W-14, Y-3

Governance
C-60, I-5, K-11, O-2

History
A-58, C-9, C-24, C-32, E-2, F-23, F-28, J-23, L-1, P-4, S-27, S-55, S-80

Implementation Strategies
B-34, B-35, B-62, B-64, B-72, C-20, C-25, C-46, C-48, D-21, D-40, F-18, I-13, J-20, J-28, J-29, K-18, P-23, P-25, R-8, S-85, W-3

Individualized Instruction
A-18, B-32, B-45, B-82, B-99, C-59, C-65, D-30, D-35, E-7, F-29, G-3, G-4, G-7, G-18, H-41, I-2, I-7, J-18, K-3, M-18, M-36, P-5, P-21, Q-3, R-15, S-58, T-3, W-1, Y-7

Instructional Systems
A-5, A-6, A-32, A-33, A-34, A-49, A-56, B-6, B-12, B-13, B-19, B-23, B-24, B-35, B-46, B-47, B-59, B-73, B-75, B-77, B-83, B-90, B-95, C-23, C-27, C-31, C-44, C-54, C-56, C-59, C-62, C-64, C-69, C-70, D-17, D-30, D-35, E-7, F-29, G-3, G-4, G-10, G-18, G-21, H-14, H-35, I-9, J-5, K-3, K-9, K-17, K-21, L-2, L-3, L-7, M-10, M-17, M-22, M-36, M-39, M-41, M-43, M-46, N-10, N-19, O-1, O-16, P-9, P-23, P-28, P-39, P-42, S-1, S-3, S-19, S-48, S-51, S-54, S-74, S-84, T-1, T-21, W-2, W-3, W-15, Y-6, Y-7

Interaction Analysis
H-21, A-22, A-23, A-24, B-43, F-10, F-32, F-36, H-21, I-3, L-18, O-1, P-15, S-19

Management
B-18, C-46, C-48, D-11, D-39, F-8, H-23, H-53, J-13, L-9, L-22, M-1

Microteaching
A-11, A-14, B-45, B-47, C-27, C-54, G-4, L-19, M-9, P-9, P-50, W-15, Y-7

Module Development
A-49, B-16, H-33, H-46, I-9, J-2, J-18, J-28, K-3, M-24, M-36, N-6, N-7, P-21, P-47, P-56, S-29, W-1, Y-1

Modules
B-9, B-20, C-44, C-45, H-33, I-2, I-9, J-19, M-1, M-25, M-45, M-55, M-56, O-14

Newsletter
A-43, C-16, M-5, P-49

Parity
C-60, I-5, K-11, S-16, S-69

Philosophy
A-3, A-5, A-15, A-30, A-35, A-37, A-39, A-41, A-42, A-47, A-58, B-3, B-40, B-68, B-84, C-4, C-12, C-18, C-35, D-3, D-7, E-12, F-26, G-8, G-13, G-19, H-13, H-19, H-42, H-43, H-54, J-1, J-10, J-22, J-23, K-14, L-5, L-20, M-27, M-28, M-32, M-35, N-2, N-3, N-4, N-5, N-9, O-3, O-10, O-14, P-30, P-32, P-36, P-50, R-3, R-19, R-24, S-4, S-13, S-22, S-27, S-35, S-38, S-46, S-55, S-86, T-5, T-16, V-1, W-4, W-8, W-13, Y-8

Professional Associations
B-28, B-29, C-12, D-9, F-3, G-6, I-8, N-11, N-18, O-4, P-45

Program Design
A-2, A-4, A-5, A-10, A-29, A-50, B-18, B-23, B-40, B-45, B-46, B-49, B-59, B-64, B-83, B-85, B-97, C-25, C-28, C-46, C-48, C-54, C-58, C-60, C-69, D-11, D-20, D-21, D-28, D-39, E-3, E-5, F-7, H-30, H-34, H-35, H-36, H-44, H-50, H-53, J-2, J-7, J-9, J-13, J-15, J-22, J-25, K-15, K-18, M-17, M-19, M-22, M-24, M-31, M-52, M-59, O-5, P-5,

P-42, P-45, P-55, R-16, R-27, S-8, S-10, S-18, S-52, S-54, S-61, S-70, T-19, V-5, W-5, Y-2

Program Model
A-10, A-18, A-59, B-18, B-26, B-53, B-82, B-99, C-24, C-25, C-33, C-39, C-47, D-5, D-14, D-17, D-18, D-19, D-21, D-23, D-24, D-25, D-32, D-40, E-3, E-13, E-17, E-20, F-6, F-7, F-16, F-18, F-22, G-10, G-23, H-1, H-2, H-30, H-42, H-44, H-50, I-1, I-2, I-3, J-21, J-27, J-30, K-12, K-18, M-11, M-16, M-25, M-39, M-54, M-55, N-19, P-1, P-8, P-10, P-14, P-15, P-51, P-52, R-2, S-3, S-8, S-9, S-10, S-16, S-21, S-25, S-27, S-28, S-58, S-59, S-75, T-6, T-22, W-17, Y-4

Program Planning
A-1, B-3, B-40, B-44, B-65, B-75, C-14, C-20, C-46, C-48, C-68, D-21, D-28, F-24, F-33, H-23, H-25, H-27, H-34, H-38, J-9, K-16, L-22, M-39, M-60, M-61, O-5, P-21, P-25, P-26, P-55, R-8, S-8, S-10, S-16, S-36, S-74, W-5

Protocol and Training Materials
B-31, B-63, C-15, D-38, F-15, G-3, G-15, G-16, G-26, H-6, H-57, N-6, N-7, S-47, S-49

Research
A-3, A-26, A-31, A-60, B-6, B-11, B-21, B-33, B-37, B-41, B-42, B-47, B-57, B-59, B-60, B-61, B-80, C-6, C-19, C-52, C-53, C-54, D-12, D-33, F-5, F-12, F-21, F-32, F-35, G-1, G-27, H-8, H-16, H-55, K-7, K-19, M-6, M-7, M-9, M-15, M-50, M-53, M-63, O-15, P-6, P-31, P-45, Q-2, R-9, R-18, R-20, R-21, R-23, S-11, S-50, S-71, T-11, T-17, T-18

Secondary Education
B-55, B-95, D-12, D-38, I-9, P-41, S-3

Special Education
A-4, A-29, B-75, C-29, F-7, F-9, H-22, I-5, K-4, L-19, M-25, M-31, M-52, N-19, S-20, S-21, T-12, V-3

State Department of Education
A-15, A-16, A-17, A-25, A-35, A-36, A-38, A-40, A-41, A-42, A-43, A-53, A-54, A-55, B-44, B-50, B-51, B-65, B-76, B-80, B-96, C-1, C-5,

C-9, C-16, C-32, C-34, C-42, C-43, C-63, D-5, D-6, D-37, E-19, F-19, F-23, F-24, F-27, G-17, G-22, H-11, H-12, H-17, H-24, H-31, I-4, I-11, J-6, L-1, L-14, L-16, L-21, M-20, M-33, M-34, M-54, M-60, M-64, N-12, N-13, N-16, O-13, P-8, P-12, P-16, P-17, P-22, P-26, P-30, P-45, P-46, P-54, R-1, R-3, R-7, R-11, R-12, R-17, R-26, R-27, S-12, S-20, S-24, S-37, S-57, S-60, S-63, S-64, S-65, S-66, S-67, S-68, S-69, S-78, S-80, T-5, T-9, T-11, V-1, W-10, W-12, Y-4

State Education Agency
A-37, B-5, B-93, C-2, D-14, D-16, D-22, E-8, E-14, F-16, F-22, G-9, G-23, G-25, H-26, P-29, P-48, P-49, P-53, R-4, T-3, T-7, T-8, T-10

Subject
Business: N-8
English: C-15, F-1, N-8, R-31, Z-1
Educational Media: B-49, B-60, B-72, C-13, E-6, I-10, J-28, K-18, L-23, M-44, M-45, M-55, N-8, P-10, P-50, R-4
Health: G-3, S-18
History: S-84
Industrial Arts: M-21, P-41
Language Arts: C-15, K-7, R-29, S-33
Languages: D-26, D-31, N-8, P-31
Liberal Arts: C-39, S-30
Library: C-13, C-14, L-23, M-55, P-10, P-12, P-51, P-52, S-17
Mathematics: A-48, B-15, G-4, H-38, H-41
Music: B-15, S-30
Psychology: B-84, C-15
Reading: B-39, C-15, M-14, S-44, T-4
Science: B-58, B-99, E-11, H-3, N-8, R-13, R-14, S-30, W-16
Social Studies: A-59, C-15, H-22, H-44, H-50, J-24, N-8
Speech: C-15, N-8
Vocational Education: C-40, P-35

Supervision
B-56, C-48, J-1, P-47, Y-5

Teacher Aides
A-18, T-3

Teacher Education

A-3, A-4, A-5, A-9, A-10, A-11, A-13, A-14, A-16, A-23, A-39, A-41, A-48, A-49, A-50, A-55, A-57, B-1, B-2, B-3, B-5, B-8, B-9, B-14, B-19, B-20, B-22, B-25, B-26, B-28, B-31, B-32, B-36, B-37, B-45, B-46, B-47, B-48, B-49, B-50, B-51, B-55, B-56, B-58, B-66, B-67, B-68, B-69, B-71, B-73, B-75, B-76, B-78, B-84, B-85, B-86, B-94, C-2, C-3, C-4, C-6, C-11, C-15, C-18, C-19, C-24, C-25, C-26, C-33, C-35, C-36, C-37, C-38, C-40, C-44, C-45, C-47, C-49, C-50, C-51, C-52, C-53, C-54, C-56, C-57, C-59, C-60, C-61, C-69, C-70, D-6, D-9, D-12, D-14, D-21, D-22, D-23, D-24, D-27, D-29, D-30, D-33, D-38, E-1, E-4, E-8, E-17, E-19, E-20, F-2, F-4, F-7, F-9, F-10, F-16, F-19, F-21, F-22, F-28, F-31, F-34, F-35, G-1, G-5, G-6, G-7, G-8, G-10, G-11, G-13, G-14, G-15, G-18, G-22, G-24, G-26, H-2, H-3, H-5, H-6, H-7, H-10, H-14, H-15, H-18, H-22, H-26, H-27, H-30, H-38, H-41, H-44, H-50, I-1, I-2, I-3, I-7, I-9, I-12, J-1, J-7, J-8, J-13, J-22, J-25, J-29, K-4, K-6, K-11, K-15, L-3, L-17, L-19, M-3, M-4, M-11, M-18, M-20, M-27, M-29, M-31, M-33, M-38, M-41, M-52, M-57, M-64, N-6, N-7, N-12, N-13, N-14, N-15, N-19, O-1, O-3, O-4, O-7, O-10, O-13, O-14, P-6, P-8, P-15, P-16, P-22, P-25, P-29, P-31, P-35, P-47, P-48, P-53, R-3, R-7, R-8, R-12, R-28, R-29, R-30, R-31, R-33, S-2, S-3, S-7, S-10, S-21, S-22, S-27, S-28, S-35, S-47, S-48, S-50, S-57, S-58, S-60, S-62, S-64, S-66, S-69, S-72, S-75, S-77, S-81, S-82, S-86, T-2, T-4, T-5, T-6, T-7, T-8, T-9, T-11, T-12, T-17, T-19, W-9, W-12, W-13, W-17, Y-2, Y-3, Y-6, Y-7

As I have always found, all educators contacted were most helpful. Especially important contributions were made by Ted Andrews, Director of the Multi-State Consortium; Karl Massanari, Director of the National Committee on Performance Based Teacher Education of the American Association of Colleges for Teacher Education; Fred McDonald, Director of the National Commission on Performance Based Education; Joel Burdin and Lorraine Polliakof of the ERIC Center for Teacher Education; James Steffenson, Director of Planning and Development of the National Teacher Corps; Phyllis Hawthorne of the Wisconsin Center of the Seven States Project on Accountability; and William Israel of the Central Office of the Council of Chief State School Officers. Holly Reid, a student from Cleveland, helped gather raw materials, and Bob Houston, Sheila Ford, and the rest of the good members of the Houston crew generally did the hard and dirty work of refining the submitted goodies. But although all of the helpful folks listed did most of the important work, the author accepts full responsibility for any errors of judgment or representation regarding the content of the bibliography. But because I am not —and never want to be—a member of the 99.9 percent pure literature club,* I will not lose too much sleep over whatever possible injustices might have been unknowingly committed.

NATIONAL MATERIALS CENTERS/ACTIVITIES

Houston Module Bank, Wilford Weber, Director, College of Education, University of Houston, Houston, Texas

National Center for the Development of Training Materials in Teacher Education, David Gliessman, Director, College of Education, University of Indiana, Bloomington, Indiana

National Center for the Development of Protocol Materials in Teacher Education, B. Othanel Smith, Director, College of Education, University of South Florida, Tampa, Florida

Florida Center for (competency based) Teacher Training Materials, William Spino, Director, College of Education, University of Miami, Miami, Florida

(This list could be much longer, as it is becoming increasingly obvious that numerous places are developing CBE-related materials and that there is a rich "national storehouse" of materials and processes on which CBE program developers are able to build.)

NATIONAL COMPETENCY BASED EDUCATION CENTERS

Nine national centers have been established to provide developmental assistance and training services for those who are interested in installing competency based education programs.

---

*Educators numbering in the millions, with good intent and in pursuit of the goals of purity and protecting the ignorant consumer, continue to massage educational materials until years after the time for their maximum usefulness has passed.

CBE Center
College of Education
Florida State University
Tallahassee, Florida
904-599-2286

CBE Center
College of Education
University of Houston
Houston, Texas
713-749-3621

College of Education
CBE Center
University of Georgia
Athens, Georgia
404-542-4244

CBE Center
College of Education
University of Toledo
Toledo, Ohio
419-531-5711

CBE Center
College of Education
Teachers College,
    Columbia University
New York, New York
212-870-4160

CBE Center
College of Education
University of Wisconsin
Madison, Wisconsin
608-262-6152

CBE Center
College of Education
Michigan State University
East Lansing, Michigan
517-355-1903

CBE Center
Oregon State System of
    Higher Education
Monmouth, Oregon
503-838-1220

CBE Center
College of Education
Syracuse University
Syracuse, New York
315-476-5541

BIBLIOGRAPHIC LISTING

A

1. Abt, Clark C. "A Game for Planning Education." *Inventing Education for the Future.* Edited by Werner Z. Hirsh. San Francisco: Chandler, 1967, pp. 220-230.
2. ————. *Design for an Elementary and Secondary Education Cost Effectiveness Model.* Cambridge, Mass.: Abts Associates, 1967. Vol. 1, *Model Description.* ERIC ED 014 152.
3. *Accountability.* Parts 1, 2, and 3 of a four-part information package on ac-

countability. Washington, D.C.: NEA, Department of Instruction and Professional Development, 1972.

4. Adelman, H. S. *A Competency Based Model Training Program*. Riverside: University of California, College of Education, 1971.

5. —————. *Conceptualizing the Development of Instructional Content for Personnel Preparation Programs*. Riverside: University of California, College of Education, 1973.

6. Alder, Lee. "Systems Approach to Marketing." *Harvard Business Review* 45, no. 3 (May 1967), 105-118.

7. Allen, Dwight W. "Performance Criteria." Educational Cassette Series no. 106, 1970. ERIC ED 041 872.

8. —————. "Staff Attitudes toward Educational Change." Educational Cassette Series no. 102, 1970. ERIC ED 041 873.

9. —————. "Students as Teachers." Educational Cassette Series no. 116, 1970. ERIC ED 041 871.

10. Allen, Dwight W., and Cooper, James M. *A Proposed New Program for Elementary Teacher Education at the University of Massachusetts*. Amherst: University of Massachusetts, College of Education, 1968. ERIC ED 025 490. SP 002 136.

11. Allen, Dwight W., and Fortune, James C. "An Analysis of Microteaching: New Procedures in Teacher Education." *Microteaching: A Description*. Stanford, Calif.: Stanford University, School of Education, 1966.

12. Allen, Dwight W., and Krasno, Richard M. *New Perspectives in Teacher Education*. Washington, D.C.: NEA, n.d. ERIC ED 033 057.

13. Allen, Dwight W., and Mackin, Robert A. "Toward 76: A Revolution in Teacher Education." *Phi Delta Kappan* 9 (May 1970), 485-488.

14. Allen, Dwight W., and Ryan, Kevin. *Microteaching*. Reading, Mass.: Addison-Wesley, 1969.

15. Allen, Wendell C. "Accreditation of Teacher Education." Unpublished memorandum sent to members of the National Association of State Directors of Teacher Education and Certification. Olympia: Washington State Education Department, May 1, 1969.

16. —————. "A Different Role for the State Education Agency." *The Seattle Conference: The Role of the State Department of Education in Teacher Education*. Olympia, Wash.: State Superintendent of Public Instruction, 1967, pp. 76-83.

17. Allen, Wendell C., et al. "Performance Criteria for Educational Personnel Development: A State Approach to Standards." *Journal of Teacher Education* 20, no. 2 (summer 1969), 133-135.

18. Allen, William, ed. *Teacher Aides: A Process Description for an Individualized Competency Based Approach to Training for Instructional Roles*. Minneapolis: Minnesota State Education Department, 1972.

19. Altman, Burton, and Williams, Eugene. *Monday Morning*. St. Mary's College Press, 1973.

20. Amidon, Edmund. "Interaction Analysis and Its Application to Student Teaching." *Association of Student Teaching Yearbook* 44 (1965), 71-92.

21. ————. "Interaction Analysis and Microteaching Skill Development in Teaching." Paper presented at American Psychological Association meeting, Washington, D.C., 1969, 26 pp. ERIC ED 036 469.

22. Amidon, Edmund, and Hunter, Elizabeth. *Improving Teaching: The Analysis of Classroom Verbal Interaction.* New York: Holt, Rinehart & Winston, 1966.

23. Amidon, Edmund J., and Powell, Evan. *Interaction Analysis as a Feedback System in Teacher Preparation.* 1966. ERIC ED 013 798.

24. Amidon, Edmund J., and Hough, J. B., eds. *Interaction Analysis. Theory, Research, and Application.* Reading, Mass.: Addison-Wesley, 1967.

25. *Amendments to Education 540-551, Issuance and Renewal of Continuing Certificates.* St. Paul: Minnesota State Board of Education, 1971.

26. Ammerman, Harry L., and Melching, William H. "The Derivation Analysis and Classification of Instructional Objectives." Fort Bliss, Tex.: Human Resources Research Office (HUMRRO), 1966.

27. Ammons, M. "Definition, Function, and Use of Educational Objectives." *Elementary School Journal* 60, no. 8 (May 1962), 432-436.

28. Anderson, C. C., and Hunka, S. M. "Teacher Evaluation: Some Problems and a Proposal." *Harvard Educational Review* 33, no. 4 (winter 1963), 74-95.

29. Anderson, Daniel A., et al. *Behavior Modification Techniques for Teachers of the Developmentally Young.* Greeley: University of Northern Colorado, Instructional Materials Center, 1972.

30. Anderson, Daniel A., et al. *Competency Based Teacher Education: Problems and Prospects for the Decade Ahead.* Berkeley: McCutchan Publishing Corp., 1973.

31. Anderson, Earl W., and Rusher, Elfreda M. "Staff Certification." *Encyclopedia of Educational Research.* New York: Macmillan, 1960, pp. 1354-1357.

32. Anderson, G. E., Jr. "Are You Ready to Learn How Operations Analysis Works?" *Nation's Schools* 81, no. 4 (April 1968), 96.

33. ————. "Let's Look at the Instructional Systems Approach." *Business Education World* 47, no. 6 (February 1967), 19-20.

34. ————. "These Are the Trends to Watch in Data Processing." *Nation's Schools* 78, no. 4 (October 1966), 101-103.

35. Andrews, Theodore E. "Atlanta or Atlantis? Performance Based Teacher Education and State Implementation." *Journal of Teacher Education* 24, no. 3 (fall 1973), 232-237.

36. ————. "Certification." *Competency Based Teacher Education.* Palo Alto, Calif.: Science Research Associates, 1972.

37. ————. "Certification Issues in Competency Based Teacher Education." *Educational Technology* 12, no. 11 (November 1972).

38. ————. "Certification Reform: The Search for 'Better Folk.'" *New York State Education* 57, no. 5 (February 1970), 17-19.

39. ————. *Manchester Interview: Competency Based Teacher Education/Certification.* Washington, D.C.: AACTE, National Committee on Performance Based Teacher Education, April 1972.

40. ————. *New Directions in Certification.* Denver: Improving State Leadership in Education Project, September 1970. 79 pp. ERIC ED 043 796.

41. ————. "Performance Analogies, or Alice Chooses a Door." Paper presented at AERA, New Orleans, March 1973. Albany, New York: State Department of Education, Department of Teacher Education and Certification, 1973.

42. ————. "Performance Certification—No, Education for Competency—Yes." *Communicate* 1, no. 1 (November 1970), 1-5.

43. Andrews, Theodore E., ed. *The PBTE Newsletter.* A Publication of the Multi-State Consortium on PBTE. Albany: New York State Education Department, Division of Teacher Education and Certification, n.d.

44. *Annotated Listing of Competency Based Modules.* Coral Gables, Fla.: University of Miami, Center for Teacher Training Materials, 1972.

45. Anthony, Bobbie M. "A New Approach to Merit Rating of Teachers." *Administrator's Notebook,* September 1968. ERIC ED 027 627.

46. Arends, Robert L. *A Brief Summary of Competency Based Teacher Education.* Buffalo, N.Y.: State University College at Buffalo, 1972.

47. Arends, Robert L., et al. *Controversial Issues Concerning Competency Based Teacher Education.* Buffalo, N.Y.: State University College at Buffalo, 1972.

48. Arends, Robert L., et al. *Diagnosing in Mathematics Modules.* Buffalo, N.Y.: State University College at Buffalo, 1973.

49. Arends, Robert L., et al. *Handbook for the Development of Instructional Modules in Competency Based Teacher Education Programs.* Syracuse, New York: Center for the Study of Teaching, 1971. ERIC ED 050 009.

50. Arends, Robert L., et al. *Identification and Selection of Teacher Competencies.* Buffalo, N.Y.: State University College at Buffalo, 1972.

51. Armstrong, Robert J., et al. *Developing and Writing Behavioral Objectives.* Tucson, Ariz.: Educational Innovators Press, 1968.

52. Armstrong, Robert J., et al. *The Development and Evaluation of Behavioral Objectives.* Worthington, Ohio: Charles A. Jones Publishing Co., 1970.

53. Armstrong, W. Earl. "A Basis for Reciprocity in Teacher Certification." *Journal of Teacher Education* 11, no. 2 (June 1960), 217-223.

54. ————. "Summary on Certification Requirements in the United States." Unpublished paper. January 1968.

55. Armstrong, W. Earl, and Bosley, Howard E. "The State Education Agency in Teacher Education." *Teacher Education in Transition.* Baltimore, Md.: The Multi-State Teacher Education Project, 1969. Vol. 2, *Emerging Roles and Responsibilities,* pp. 1-19.

56. Arnstein, G. E. "Schoolmen: Don't Boggle at the Systems Concept; You've Probably Been Using It by a Different Name." *Nation's Schools* 80, no. 4 (October 1967), 76-77.

57. *Assessment of Teaching Competencies in Performance Based Teacher Education Programs.* Seattle: University of Washington, College of Education, 1972.

58. Aubertine, Horace E. "The Evolution of Performance Based Teacher Education Program." Paper presented at AERA, New Orleans, February 1973.

59. Aubertine, Horace E., et al. *A Model Elementary Teacher Education Program for Social Science Majors (An Interdisciplinary Approach).* 2 vols. Normal: Illinois State University, 1971, 1972. ERIC OGG 0 70 4050 725.

60. Averch, Harvey A., et al. *How Effective Is Schooling? A Critical Review and Synthesis of Research Findings.* Santa Monica, Calif.: Rand Corporation, 1972.

B

1. Bagley, Ayers, ed. *Making Teacher Education More Relevant.* Washington, D.C.: Society of Professors of Education, 1970. ERIC ED 049 170.

2. Baird, Hugh. *Evaluating Teacher Episodes.* Provo, Utah: Brigham Young University, n.d. ERIC ED 028 152.

3. ————. "The Institution: Building Bloc or Building Block." Paper presented at AERA, New Orleans, March 1973. Provo, Utah: Brigham Young University, College of Education, 1973.

4. Baird, Hugh, et al. *A Behavioral Approach to Teaching.* Dubuque, Ia.: William C. Brown Co., 1972.

5. Bakalis, Michael J. *Report of the Task Force on Certification.* Springfield, Ill.: Superintendent of Public Instruction, 1972.

6. Baker, Robert L., and Schutz, Richard E. *Instructional Product Development.* Southwest Regional Laboratory for Educational Research and Development. New York: Van Nostrand Reinhold, 1971.

7. Bandura, A. *Principles of Behavior Modification.* New York: Holt, Rinehart & Winston, 1969.

8. Baral, David P., et al. *A Taxonomy of Teaching Behaviors: Progress Report and Listing and Preliminary Classification of the Item Pool.* Research and Development Memorandum no. 36. Stanford, Calif.: Stanford University, School of Education, 1968. ERIC ED 049 157.

9. Barnes, Wanita F. *Behavioral Objectives.* (Module) Grambling, La.: Grambling College, 1973.

10. Barr, A. S. "Teaching Competencies." *Encyclopedia of Educational Research.* New York: Macmillan, 1956.

11. Barr, A. S., et al. "Supplement: Report of the Committee on the Criteria of Teacher Effectiveness." *Review of Educational Research* 22, no. 3 (June 1972), 238-264.

12. Barson, John. "Heuristics of Instructional Systems Development: A Team Report." *Audiovisual Instruction* 12, no. 6 (June 1967), 613-614.

13. Barson, John, et al. "Standard Operating Procedures for a Learning Resources Center: A System for Producing Systems." *Audiovisual Instruction* 10, no. 5 (May 1965), 378-379.

14. *Basic Teaching Tasks: A Teaching Laboratory Manual for Beginning Teacher Candidates.* Austin: University of Texas, September 1970.

15. Battle, Edwina. *Methods of Public School Music.* Madison: University of Wisconsin, Teacher Corps Associates Program, 1973.

16. Baush, Jerold P. *Program Module Evaluation Guidelines.* Athens: University of Georgia, College of Education, 1969. ERIC ED 040 921.
17. Beatty, Walcott H. *Improving Educational Assessment and an Inventory of Measures of Affective Behavior.* ERIC ED 034 730.
18. Beckhaud, Richard. *Organization Development: Strategies and Models.* Reading, Mass.: Addison-Wesley, 1969.
19. Beery, John R. *Professional Preparation and Effectiveness of Beginning Teachers.* Coral Gables, Fla.: University of Miami, College of Education, 1960. ERIC ED 052 156.
20. *Behavioral Objectives.* (Module) Toledo, Ohio: University of Toledo, College of Education, 1973.
21. Bellack, Arno A., et al. *The Language of the Classroom.* New York: Columbia University, Teachers College Press, 1966.
22. Bellflower Unified School District. *Identifying Strengths of Effective Teachers and Training Them to Share These Strengths with Other Teachers.* Washington, D.C.: U.S. Office of Education, Bureau of Educational Personnel Development, 1970. ERIC ED 041 845.
23. Benathy, Bela H. *Instructional Systems.* Palo Alto, Calif.: Fearon Press, 1968.
24. ————. "The Systems Approach." *Modern Language Journal* 52, no. 5 (May 1967), 281-289.
25. Benda, Nancy. *Florida Program for Improving the Training, Evaluation, and Licensure of Educational Personnel.* Tallahassee: Florida State Department of Education, 1971.
26. Benjamin, William, et al. *Specifications for a Comprehensive Undergraduate and Inservice Teacher Education Program for Elementary Teachers.* Washington, D.C.: Government Printing Office, 1969.
27. Benson, Charles S. *The School and the Economic System.* Chicago: Science Research Associates, 1966.
28. Bhaerman, Robert D. "A Paradigm for Accountability." *American Teacher* 55, no. 3 (November 1970), 18-19.
29. ————. "Which Way for Teacher Certification?" AFT Quest Paper no. 2. Washington, D.C.: American Federation of Teachers, 1969. (Reprint of article in *American Teacher,* February 1969.)
30. "Bibliography of Elementary Teacher Education Model Reports and Studies." *Journal of Research and Development in Teacher Education* 3, no. 3 (spring 1970), 120-123.
31. Bickimer, D. A., and Stone, J. C. *Protocols: A Continuum of Training and Retraining Formats.* 1970. ERIC ED 044 351.
32. Bicknell, John E., et al. *Summer Workshops in Individualization of Instruction, 1970.* Selected papers. Fredonia, New York: State University College at Fredonia, 1970. ERIC ED 049 163.
33. Biddle, Bruce J., and Allen, William S., eds. *Contemporary Research on Teacher Effectiveness.* New York: Holt, Rinehart & Winston, 1964.
34. *Bilingual Education: A Needs Assessment Case Study and Implementing Competency Based Educational Programs at Southern University.* Wash-

ington, D.C.: U.S. Office of Education, Teacher Corps Associates, spring 1973.

35. Bishop, Leslee J. "The Systems Concept." *Educational Leadership* 24, no. 8 (May 1967), 676.

36. Block, James H., ed. *Mastery Learning.* New York: Holt, Rinehart & Winston, 1971.

37. Bloom, Benjamin S., et al. *Handbook of Formative and Summative Evaluation of Student Learning.* New York: McGraw-Hill, 1971.

38. Bloom, Benjamin S., ed. *Taxonomy of Educational Objectives: The Classification of Educational Goals. Handbook I: Cognitive Domain.* New York: David McKay, 1965.

39. Blount, David. *Competencies Essential for Diagnosing Reading Difficulties.* Madison: University of Wisconsin, Teacher Corps Associates Program, 1973.

40. Boerrigter, Glenn C., advisory ed. "Beginning Programs for the Training of Elementary Teachers." *Journal of Research and Development in Education* 3, no. 3 (spring 1970), 1-7.

41. Bolton, Dale L. *Selection and Evaluation of Teachers: An Interpretive Study of Research and Development.* Seattle: University of Washington, College of Education, 1970. ERIC ED 054 088.

42. ————. *Teacher Evaluation.* PREP (Putting Research into Educational Practice) Kit no. 21. Washington, D.C.: U.S. Office of Education, 1971. ERIC ED 044 546

43. Bondi, Joseph C., Jr. "The Effects of Interaction Analysis Feedback on the Verbal Behavior of Student Teachers." *Educational Leadership* 26, no. 8 (May 1969), 794-799.

44. Boone, Shelly S. "Accountability: Planning for Action." Paper presented at AERA, New Orleans, March 1973. Tallahassee: Florida State Department of Education, 1973.

45. Borg, Walter R. "The Minicourse Instructional Model." Paper presented at AERA, Minneapolis, 1970.

46. ————. *The Minicourse as a Vehicle for Changing Teacher Behavior: The Research Evidence.* Berkeley: Far West Laboratory, 1969. ERIC ED 029 809.

47. Borg, Walter R., et al. *The Minicourse: A Microteaching Approach to Teacher Education.* Beverly Hills, Calif.: MacMillan Educational Services, 1970.

48. Borgers, Sherry B., and Ward, G. Robert. *Competency Based Teacher Education Affective Modules.* (14 modules) Houston, Tex.: University of Houston, College of Education, 1973.

49. Bosley, Howard E., et al. *Video Process in Teacher Education Programs: Scope, Techniques, and Assessment.* Monograph 3. Baltimore: Multi-State Teacher Education Project, 1968. ERIC ED 025 458.

50. Bosley, Howard E., ed. *Teacher Education in Transition.* Baltimore: Multi-State Teacher Education Project, 1969. Vol. 1, *An Experiment in Change.*

51. ————, ed. *Teacher Education in Transition.* Baltimore, Md.: Multi-State

Teacher Education Project, 1969. Vol. 2, *Emerging Roles and Responsibilities.*

52. Bottomly, Forbes. "How Seattle Gets Old Concepts Out of Its System." *Nation's Schools* 80, no. 4 (October 1967), 57-78.

53. Bowles, Douglas. "Competency Based Teacher Education: The Houston Story." *Educational Leadership* 30, no. 6 (March 1973), 510-512.

54. Brown, Oliver H. "The Brown Self-Report Inventory (SRI): A Quick Scanning Instrument for Mental Health Professionals." *Comprehensive Psychiatry* 8, no. 1 (1967), 45-52.

55. Bown, Oliver H., et al. "Comparison of Self-Perception of *Prospective* Elementary and Secondary School Teachers." *Psychology in the Schools* 4, no. 1 (1967), 21-24.

56. Boyan, Norman, et al. *A Program for Training Supervising Teachers in the Induction of New Professionals: Final Report for 1971-72,* vols. 1 and 2. Santa Barbara: University of California at Santa Barbara, School of Education, 1972.

57. Bradley, Ruth, et al. *Measuring Teacher Competence: Research Backgrounds and Current Practice.* Burlingame: California Teachers Association, 1967. ERIC ED 040 152.

58. Breit, Frank, and Butts, David P. "A Comparison of the Effectiveness of an Inservice Program and a Preservice Program in Developing Certain Teaching Competencies." Paper presented at National Association Research in Science Teaching, Pasadena, 1969. ERIC ED 028 069.

59. Briggs, Leslie J. *Handbook of Procedures for the Design of Instruction.* Pittsburgh: American Institute for Research, 1970.

60. ————. "Learner Variables and Educational Media." *Review of Educational Research* 38, no. 2 (April 1968), 160-176.

61. ————. "Review of Research in Adjunct Autoinstruction." (Mimeographed) Palo Alto, Calif.: Dymedia, Incorporated, 1967.

62. ————. *Sequencing of Instruction in Relation to Hierarchies of Competence.* Pittsburgh: American Institutes for Research, 1968.

63. ————. "Teaching Machines for Training of Military Personnel in Maintenance of Electronic Equipment." *Automatic Teaching: The State of the Art.* Edited by E. Galanter. New York: John Wiley & Sons, 1959, pp. 131-146.

64. Briggs, Leslie J., et al. *A Procedure for the Design for Multimedia Instruction.* Monograph no. 2. Pittsburgh: American Institute for Research, December 1966.

65. Brooks, Richard D. *Comprehensive Planning in State Educational Agencies: A Rationale and Discussion of the Planning Function and Structure within State Education Agencies.* Madison: Wisconsin State Department of Public Instruction, 1968.

66. Broudy, Harry S. "Can We Define Good Teaching?" *Teacher's College Record* 70, no. 7 (April 1969), 583-593.

67. ————. *The Continuing Search for Criteria.* Washington, D.C.: AACTE, 1967. ERIC ED 012 257.

68. —————. *A Critique of Performance Based Teacher Education.* Washington, D.C.: AACTE, Committee on Performance Based Teacher Education, May 1972.
69. Brown, Bob Burton, and Bane, Robert King. *Multidimensionality: A Technique for Studying the Classroom.* ERIC ED 091 171.
70. Brown, Bob Burton, and Soar, Robert S. *Available Tools and Techniques for Evaluating Innovations.* Gainesville: University of Florida, College of Education, 1971.
71. Brown, Jerry L., and Okey, James R. "Identifying and Classifying Competencies for Performance Based Teacher Training." Paper presented at AERA, New Orleans, March 1973. Bloomington: Indiana University, College of Education, 1973.
72. Brown, J. W. *Administering Educational Media.* New York: McGraw-Hill, 1965.
73. —————. "The Systems' Solution to College Problems." *Educational Screen and Audiovisual Guide* 45, no. 5 (May 1966), 34-36.
74. Bruner, Jerome S. *The Process of Education.* Cambridge: Harvard University Press, 1965.
75. Brunt, Vida Van. *Strategies for Introducing Skills in Effective Curriculum Planning for Teachers of the Highly Mobile "Troubled Youth" of the Inner-City.* Madison: University of Wisconsin, Teacher Corps Associates Program, 1973.
76. Buchmiller, Archie A. "The Legislative Mandates Contained in Various State Education Accountability Statutes." Paper presented at AERA, New Orleans, March 1973. Denver: Colorado Department of Education, 1973.
77. Buley, H. C. "Multimedia Systems of Instructions." *Audiovisual Instruction* 10, no. 5 (May 1965), 391-392.
78. Burdin, Joel L. *Futurism: A Needed Process in School Personnel Preparation.* ERIC ED 036 497.
79. Burdin, Joel L., and Lanzillotti, Kaliopee. *A Readers' Guide to the Comprehensive Models for Preparing Elementary Teachers.* Washington, D.C.: ERIC Clearinghouse on Teacher Education, December 1969. ERIC ED 034 076.
80. Burdin, Joel L., and Reagan, Margaret T., eds. *Accreditation and Research Problems.* Washington, D.C.: ERIC Clearinghouse on Teacher Education, 1971.
81. Burdin, Joel L., and Reagan, Margaret T., eds. *Performance Based Certification of School Personnel.* Washington, D.C.: ERIC Clearinghouse on Teacher Education and the Association of Teacher Educators, 1971. ERIC ED 049 152.
82. Burke, Caseel. *The Individualized, Competency Based System of Teacher Education at Weber State College.* Washington, D.C.: AACTE, Committee on Performance Based Teacher Education, March 1972. ERIC SP 005 754.
83. Burke, J. Bruce. "Curriculum Design." *Competency Based Teacher Education.* Palo Alto, Calif.: Science Research Associates, 1972.

84. Burkhart, Robert C., ed. *The Assessment Revolution: New Viewpoints for Teacher Evaluation.* National Symposium on Evaluation in Education. Albany: New York State Education Department and State University College at Buffalo, 1969. ERIC ED 036 485.

85. Burns, Richard B. "The Central Notion: Explicit Objectives." *Competency Based Teacher Education.* Palo Alto, Calif.: Science Research Associates, 1972.

86. ————. *New Approaches to Behavioral Objectives.* Dubuque, Ia.: William C. Brown, 1972.

87. Burns, Richard W. "Measuring Objectives and Grading." *Educational Technology* 8, no. 18 (September 30, 1968).

88. ————. "Objectives in Action." *Educational Technology* 7, no. 3 (February 15, 1968).

89. ————. "Objectives Involving Attitudes, Interests, and Appreciation." *Educational Technology* 7, no. 8 (April 30, 1968).

90. ————. "Objectives and Classroom Instruction." *Educational Technology* 7, no. 17 (September 15, 1967).

91. ————. "Objectives and Content Validity of Tests." *Educational Technology* 8, no. 23 (December 15, 1968).

92. ————. "The Theory of Expressing Objectives." *Educational Technology* 7, no. 20 (October 30, 1967).

93. Buser, Robert L., and Mumm, William L. *State Education Agencies: A Bibliography.* Carbondale: Southern Illinois University, July 1969. ERIC ED 034 297.

94. Bush, Robert. "A Definition of Professional Competence for Teaching." *Eighth Yearbook.* AACTE, 1955, pp. 128-140.

95. Bush, Robert N., and Allen, Dwight W. *A New Design for High School Education: Assuming a Flexible Schedule.* New York: McGraw-Hill, 1964.

96. Bush, Robert N., and Allen, Wendell C. "Certification and Professional Performance." *Journal of Teacher Education* 11, no. 2 (June 1960), 262-273.

97. Butts, David P. *The Classroom Experience Model.* Austin: University of Texas, R & D Research Monograph, 1969.

98. Butts, David P., and Montague, Earl J. "Behavioral Objectives." *The Science Teacher* 35, no. 3 (March 1968), 33-35.

99. Butts, David P., et al. *A Personalized Teacher Education Professional Program.* Austin: University of Texas, Research and Development Center for Teacher Education, 1970. ERIC ED 046 908.

C

1. Cahill, William. *First Annual [Governor's] Message.* Newark, N.J.: Office of the Governor, 1971.

2. *California Assembly Bill 293.* (The Stull Bill) Sacramento: California State Legislature, 1971.

3. *California Teachers' Reaction to Certification and Preservice Courses.* Sup-

plementary Research Report no. 58. Burlingame: California Teachers Association, 1966. ERIC ED 024 632.

4. Callahan, R. *Education and the Cult of Efficiency.* Chicago: University of Chicago Press, 1962.

5. Campbell, Ronald F., et al., eds. *Strengthening State Departments of Education.* Chicago: University of Chicago Press, 1967.

6. Campeau, P. L. "Test Anxiety and Feedback in Programmed Instruction." *Journal of Educational Psychology* 59, no. 3 (June 1958), 159-163.

7. Canfield, Albert A. "A Rationale for Performance Objectives." *Audiovisual Instruction* 13, no. 2 (February 1968), 127-129.

8. Cantor, Arnold. "Autonomy Is the Cure for Certification Woes." *New York State Education* 57, no. 5 (February 1970), 20-22.

9. Carman, Harry J. "The Historical Development of Licensing for the Professions." *The Journal of Teacher Education* 11, no. 2 (June 1960), 136-147.

10. Carrol, John B. "Words, Meanings, and Concepts." *Harvard Educational Review* 34, no. 3 (fall 1964), 178-202.

11. Carter, Heather L. *Assessing Student Behavior.* (Module) Austin: University of Texas, Research and Development Center for Teacher Education, 1973.

12. Cartright, Richard, and Pershing, Gerry. *Performance Based Teacher Education and Certification: Can Teachers Buy It?* Washington, D.C.: NEA, 1974.

13. Case, Robert N. "Criteria of Excellence Checklist." *School Libraries* 18, no. 3 (spring 1969), 43-46.

14. Case, Robert N., and Lowrey, Anna M. *School Manpower Project: A Report on Phase I.* Chicago: American Library Association, 1971.

15. *A Catalog of Protocol Materials in Teacher Education.* Tampa: University of South Florida, College of Education, 1972.

16. *CBE Newsletter* (Competency Based Certification). Albany: New York State Department of Education, Division of Teacher Education and Certification, n.d.

17. Chaney, Reece, and Passmore, J. Laurence. "Affective Education: Implications for Group Process." *Contemporary Education* 42, no. 5 (April 1971), 213-216.

18. Chavez, Simon I. "Performance Accountability in Teacher Education." *Audiovisual Instruction* 16, no. 3 (March 1971), 56-57.

19. Childress, Jack R. "Inservice Education of Teachers." *Encyclopedia of Educational Research.* New York: Macmillan, 1969, pp. 645-654.

20. Childs, J. W. "A Set of Procedures for the Planning of Instruction." *Educational Technology* (August 1968).

21. Chisholm, John. *Report to Faculty in Competency Based Teacher Education Symposium.* Asheville, N.C., April 17-18, 1973.

22. *A Citizens Action Program for Better Schools: Blueprint for the Possible.* Washington, D.C.: United States Chamber of Commerce, 1973.

23. Clark, E. M. "The Systems Approach—What It Is and How It Applies to Elementary Education." *Instructor* 75, no. 1 (August 1966), 74.

24. Clarke, S. C. "The Story of the Elementary Education Models." *Journal of Teacher Education* 20, no. 3 (fall 1969), 282-293.

25. Clegg, Ambrose A., and Ochoa, Anna. *Evaluation of a Performance Based Program in Teacher Education: Recommendations for Implementation.* Seattle, Wash.: University of Washington, College of Education, 1970. ERIC ED 057 017.

26. ————. "What Does Today's Teacher Need to Know and to Do?" *Educational Leadership* 27, no. 6 (March 1969), 568-572.

27. Codwell, John E. *A Demonstration of the Effect of an Adaption of Microteaching on the Instructional Behavior of Rural School Teachers.* Atlanta: Southern Association of Colleges and Schools, 1969. ERIC ED 034 620.

28. Cohen, Audrey C. *New Tests to Measure Job Skills and Determine Effective Performance.* New York: College for Human Services, 1970.

29. Cohen, Saul B. *A Selected Bibliography of Competency Based Teacher Education Literature.* New York: City University of New York at Hunter College, Regional Special Education Instructional Materials Center, April 1973.

30. Cohen, Saul B., and Lichtenberg, Mitchell P. *Ad Hoc National Advisory Committee on Training Complexes.* Worcester, Mass.: Clark University, 1970.

31. Cohodes, Aaron. "Using the Systems Approach Is Easier Than Defining It." *Nation's Schools* 81, no. 4 (August 1968), 16.

32. Collins, George J. "Constitutional and Legal Basis for State Action." *Education in the States: Nationwide Development Since 1900.* Washington, D.C.: NEA, 1969.

33. Collins, James, ed. *A Working Paper for a Personalized, Competency Based Teacher Education Program.* Syracuse, N.Y.: Syracuse University, College of Education, 1973.

34. Colton, David L. "State Power and Local Decision Making in Education." Paper presented at AERA, Los Angeles, February 8, 1969.

35. Combs, Arthur W. *Educational Accountability: Beyond Behavioral Objectives.* Washington, D.C.: Association for Supervision and Curriculum Development, 1972.

36. ————. "The Problem of Accountability from a Humanistic Perspective." Paper presented at AERA, New Orleans, March 1973. Gainesville: University of Florida, 1973.

37. ————. "Some Basic Concepts for Teacher Education." *Journal of Teacher Education* 23, no. 3 (fall 1972), 286-290.

38. *Commission for Teacher Preparation and Licensing. Annual Report.* Sacramento, Calif.: Commission for Teacher Preparation or Licensing, 1972.

39. *Commitment, Creativity, Challenge: We Are All Learning Together in the Process.* (PBTE in the arts) Atlanta: Clark College, 1972.

40. *Competencies and Performance Objectives.* Detroit: Wayne State University, College of Education, Department of Vocational and Applied Arts, 1973.

41. "Competency Based Education." (Entire issue) *Educational Technology* 12, no. 11 (November 1972).

42. *Competency Based Education Reaction Papers.* Series of reaction papers on major developmental issues of competency based education. Athens: Georgia State Department of Education, 1973.

43. "Competency Based Teacher Education and Certification." *Report of the Council of Chief State School Officer's Task Force on the Improvement of Educational Systems.* Washington, D.C.: U.S. Office of Education, National Center for the Improvement of Educational Systems, 1974, pp. 34-43.

44. *Competency Based Teacher Education Module Cluster on Instructional Objectives.* San Diego: California State University at San Diego, College of Education, 1973.

45. *Competency Based Teacher Education Modules.* Houston, Tex.: University of Houston, College of Education, n.d.

46. *Competency Based Teacher Education Organization, Operation, and Management.* Tallahassee: Florida A & M University, College of Education, 1973.

47. *Comprehensive Models on Teacher Education and Studies of the Models.* (A complete bibliography) Washington, D.C.: ERIC Clearinghouse on Teacher Education, 1971.

48. *Comprehensive Program Planning, Implementation, and Evaluation: A Systems Model for Problem Solving.* Jacksonville: University of North Florida, College of Education, 1973.

49. Conant, James B. "The Certification of Teachers: The Restricted State Approved Program Approach." *AACTE: A Decade of Thought on Teacher Education.* (The Charles W. Hunt Lectures) Washington, D.C.: AACTE, 1972.

50. ————. *The Education of American Teachers.* New York: McGraw-Hill, 1963.

51. *Connecticut Conferences: Teacher Evaluation in the Seventies.* Hartford: Commission for Higher Education, 1971.

52. Cook, Desmond L. *Program Evaluation and Review Technique: Applications in Education.* OE 12024. Washington, D.C.: U.S. Office of Education, 1966.

53. Cooper, James G., and Bemis, Katherine. *Teacher Personality, Teacher Behavior, and Their Effects upon Pupil Achievement.* Albuquerque: University of New Mexico, College of Education, 1967. ERIC ED 012 707.

54. Cooper, James M. "A Performance Curriculum for Teacher Education." Second annual Florence B. Stratemeyer Lecture presented at AERA, Chicago, February 1967. ERIC ED 030 590.

55. Cooper, James M., DeVault, M. Vere, et al. *Competency Based Teacher Education.* Berkeley: McCutchan Publishing Corporation, 1973. Vol. 1, *Problems and Prospects for the Decades Ahead.*

56. Cooper, James M., and Sadker, David. "Current Trends in Teacher Education Curriculum." *Journal of Teacher Education* 23, no. 3 (fall 1972), 312-317.

57. Cooper, James M., and Weber, Wilford. *Competency Based Teacher Education: A Scenario.* Washington, D.C.: AACTE, 1972.

58. Cooper, James M., et al. *Competency Based Teacher Education.* Berkeley: McCutchan Publishing Corporation, 1973. Vol. 2, *A Systems Approach to Program Design.*

59. Cooper, James M., et al. *Microteaching: Selected Papers.* Washington, D.C.: ERIC Clearinghouse on Teacher Education, Association of Teacher Educators, 1971. ERIC ED 055 960.

60. *Cooperation in Teacher Education: Report of the CITE Work Conference.* New York: Columbia University Teachers College, CITE Project, 1973.

61. Cormier, William H. *Effects of Approving Teaching Behaviors or Classroom Behaviors of Disadvantaged Adolescents.* Washington, D.C.: U.S. Office of Education, Bureau of Research, 1970. ERIC ED 040 974.

62. Cornell, Terry D. *A Systematic Approach to Needs Assessment.* Tucson, Ariz.: EPIC Evaluation Center, 1970.

63. Cottrell, Donald P. *Selected Bibliography on the Accreditation of Teacher Education.* Washington, D.C.: ERIC Clearinghouse on Teacher Education, 1970.

64. Coulson, John E. *Programmed Learning and Computer Based Instruction.* New York: J. Wiley & Sons, 1962.

65. ―――. *The Teacher's Role in Classes Using Self Study Materials.* Santa Monica, Calif.: Systems Development Corporation, 1967. ERIC ED 015 169.

66. Cox, Richard C. "Confusion Between Norm-Referenced and Criterion-Referenced Measurement." *Phi Delta Kappan* 55, no. 5 (January 1974), 319.

67. Craik, Mary B. "Writing Objectives for Programmed Instruction—Or Any Instruction." *Educational Technology* 6, no. 4 (February 28, 1966).

68. Crocker, W. A. "Ten Commandments for a PBTE Developer." *Phi Delta Kappan* 55, no. 5 (January 1974), 334.

69. Cruickshank, Donald R. "Conceptualizing a Process for Teacher Education Curriculum Development." *Journal of Teacher Education* 22, no. 1 (spring 1971), 73-82.

70. ―――. *Simulation as an Instructional Alternative in Teacher Education.* Washington, D.C.: Association of Teacher Educators, ERIC Clearinghouse on Teacher Education, 1971. ERIC ED 053 067.

D

1. Daly, Patrick L. "Certification by Performance." *Changing Education* 4, no. 4 (spring 1970), 23-24.

2. Daniel, K. Fred. *Performance Based Does Not Mean a Teacher Education Program Is Good—It Just Means It Is Easier to Tell.* Tallahassee: Florida State Department of Education, September 16, 1971.

3. ―――. "Performance Based Teacher Certification: What Is It and Why Do We Need It?" *Performance Based Certification of School Personnel.* Washington, D.C.: ERIC Clearinghouse on Teacher Education and the Association of Teacher Educators, 1971, pp. 3-9. ERIC ED 045 551.

4. ―――. "Managing Education: Educators Seeking Effective Techniques." *Florida Schools* 33, no. 5 (January-February 1971), 14-18.

5. ——————. *The Measurement and Evaluation of Teaching: A Conceptualization of a Plan for Use in State Educational Leadership.* Tallahassee: Florida State Department of Education, May 1969. ERIC ED 018 862.

6. ——————. "Whither Teacher Education?" *Teacher Education in Transition.* Baltimore: Multi-State Teacher Education Project, 1969. Vol. 2, *Emerging Roles and Responsibilities,* pp. 20-36.

7. Darcy, C. Michael. "Three Stages in the Development of CBTE." *Phi Delta Kappan* 55, no. 5 (January 1974), 325-327.

8. Darland, David D. "Profession's Quest for Responsibility and Accountability." *Phi Delta Kappan* 52, no. 1 (September 1970), 41-44.

9. ——————. "The Role of the Profession in Teacher Certification." *Journal of Teacher Education* 11, no. 2 (summer 1960), 201-206.

10. Darling, David W. "Why a Taxonomy of Affective Learning?" *Educational Leadership* 22, no. 7 (April 1965), 473-475.

11. Davis, Ivor K. *Competency Based Learning: Technology, Management, and Design.* New York: McGraw-Hill, 1973.

12. Davis, O. L., and Smoot, B. R. "Effects on the Verbal Teaching Behaviors of Beginning Secondary Teacher Candidates' Participation in a Program of Laboratory Teaching." *Educational Leadership* 28, no. 2 (November 1970), 165-169.

13. Dederick, Warren E. "Competencies of the School Administrator." *Phi Delta Kappan* 54, no. 5 (January 1973), 349-350.

14. DeLee, James, and Browning, Gilbert. *A Model for Competency Based Teacher Education.* Baton Rouge: Louisiana State Department of Education, 1973.

15. DeProposo, Ernest R. "Personal Evaluation As an Impetus to Growth." *Library Trends* 20, no. 1 (July 1971), 60-70.

16. *Designing Education for the Future: An Eight-State Project.* Santa Fe: New Mexico State Department of Education, 1969.

17. Dethy, Ray C. *Certification Alternative Project in Administration and Curriculum.* Jamaica, N.Y.: St. John's University, College of Education, 1973.

18. DeVault, M. Vere. *Wisconsin Elementary Teacher Education Project.* Madison: University of Wisconsin, College of Education, 1969.

19. DeVault, M. Vere, and Kean, John M. "An Economic Analysis of the Wisconsin Elementary Teacher Education Project: A Summary Statement." *Journal of Research and Development in Teacher Education* 3, no. 3 (spring 1970), 94-106.

20. DeVault, M. Vere, et al. *Organizing Resources for the Support of Competency Based Teacher Education.* Madison: University of Wisconsin, College of Education, 1972.

21. *Developing Competency in Teaching: A Professional Preparation Program.* Report to the California Commission for Teacher Preparation and Licensing. San Luis Obispo: California Polytechnic State University, 1973.

22. *Development of a Long Range Plan for Achieving Competency Based Education and Certification.* Athens: Georgia State Department of Education, 1973.

23. Dickson, George E. *Educational Specifications for a Comprehensive Elementary Teacher Education Program.* Toledo, Ohio: The University of Toledo, College of Education, 1968.

24. Dickson, George E., and Hinkle, Dennis E. "A Study of the Feasibility of the Ohio Teacher Education Model." *Journal of Research and Development in Teacher Education* 3, no. 3 (spring 1970), 56-67.

25. Dietz, Thomas S. *An Institute Program Designed to Train Vocational Education and Academic Teachers for the Development of Performance Objectives.* Willingboro, N.J.: Willingboro Public School District, 1971. ERIC ED 055 037.

26. Disick, Renee S. *Performance Objectives in Foreign Language Teaching.* New York: ERIC Clearinghouse on Languages and Linguistics, American Council on the Teaching of Foreign Languages, 1971. ERIC ED 055 522.

27. Dodl, Norman R. "Selecting Competency Outcomes for Teacher Education." *Journal of Teacher Education* 24, no. 3 (fall 1973), 194-199.

28. ————. "A Summary—Feasibility Study of the Florida State University Model for the Preparation of Elementary School Teachers." *Journal of Research and Development in Teacher Education* 3, no. 3 (spring 1970), 8-17.

29. Dodl, Norman R., et al. *The Florida Catalog of Teacher Competencies.* Tallahassee, Fla.: Florida State Department of Education, 1973. (Available from Panhandle Area Education Coop., Chipley, Fla., and from Multi-State Consortium, c/o James Collins, Syracuse University, New York.)

30. Doll, Ronald C., ed. *Individualizing Instruction, 1964 Yearbook.* Washington, D.C.: Association for Supervision and Curriculum Development, 1964.

31. Dominquez, Fernando. *Bilingual Education: A Needs Assessment Case Study.* Madison: University of Wisconsin, Teacher Corps Associates Program, 1973.

32. Doolittle, Lawrence W. "Harold's Report on 'The Lock Haven Experience': A CBTE Adventure." *Phi Delta Kappan* 55, no. 5 (January 1974), 327-329.

33. *Do Teachers Make a Difference? A Report on Recent Research on Pupil Achievement.* Washington, D.C.: U.S. Office of Education, National Center for the Improvement of Educational Systems, 1970. ERIC ED 037 396.

34. Dressel, Paul L. "Are Your Objectives Showing?" *National Education Association Journal* 44, no. 5 (May 1955), 297-298.

35. Drumheller, Sidney J. *Handbook of Curriculum Design for Individualized Instruction: A Systems Approach.* Englewood Cliffs, N.J.: Educational Technology Publications, 1971.

36. Drummond, William H. "The Meaning and Application of Performance Criteria in Staff Development." *Phi Delta Kappan* 52, no. 1 (September 1970), 32-35.

37. ————. "The Role of the State Education Agency in the Evolving Society." Speech presented at the Association for Student Teaching, Chicago, February 27, 1969. (Unpublished.) Gainesville: University of Florida.

38. Dulin, Kenneth L. "Skill Training for All Secondary Teachers." Speech presented at IRA, 1971. Madison: University of Wisconsin, School of Education, 1971.

39. Dunn, Thomas. "Monitoring and Management: Are New Strategies Needed?" Paper presented at AERA, New Orleans, March 1973. Toledo: University of Toledo, College of Education, 1973.

40. Dyer, James. *Consortium of Southern Colleges for Teacher Education.* Durham: North Carolina Central University, College of Education, 1973.

E

1. Ebel, R. L. "Relation of Testing Programs to Educational Goals." The 62d Yearbook of the National Society for the Study of Education: *The Impact and Improvement of School Testing of Programs.* Chicago: University of Chicago Press, 1963, pp. 38-44.

2. Edelfelt, Roy A. "Progress in Professional Practices Legislation." *NEA Journal* 57, no. 2 (February 1968), 64-65.

3. ―――――. "The Reform of Education and Teacher Education: A Complex Task." *Journal of Teacher Education* 23, no. 2 (summer 1972), 117-125.

4. Edelfelt, Roy A., et al. *Teacher Designed Reform in Teacher Education.* Washington, D.C.: U.S. Office of Education, 1972.

5. Edelfelt, Roy A., ed. *Innovative Programs in Student Teaching.* Baltimore: Maryland State Department of Education, 1969.

6. Edling, Jack V. "Educational Objectives and Educational Media." *Review of Educational Research* 38, no. 2 (April 1968), 177-189.

7. ―――――. *Individualized Instruction: A Manual for Administrators.* Corvallis, Ore.: OCE Publications, 1970.

8. *Educational Accountability.* Lansing: Michigan State Department of Education, 1971.

9. *Educational Accountability and Evaluation.* Washington, D.C.: Government Printing Office, PREP Report no. 35, n.d.

10. Edwards, Clifford H. *Competency Based Teacher Education: A Critique.* Normal: Illinois State University.

11. Eiss, Albert F., and Harbeck, Mary B. *Behavioral Objectives in the Affective Domain.* Washington, D.C.: National Science Teachers Association, 1969.

12. Elam, Stanley. *Performance Based Teacher Education: What Is the State of the Art?* Washington, D.C.: 1971.

13. Elfenbein, Iris M. *Performance Based Teacher Programs: A Comparative Description.* Washington, D.C.: AACTE, 1972.

14. *Emerging State Responsibilities for Education.* Denver: Improving State Leadership in Education Project, 1970.

15. English, Fenwick W., and Sharpes, Donald K. *Strategies for Differentiated Staffing.* Berkeley: McCutchan Publishing Corporation, 1972.

16. Engman, B. D. "Behavioral Objectives: Key to Planning." *The Science Teacher* 35, no. 7 (October 1968), 86-87.

17. Estes, Kenneth A. *Competency Based Education Development Project.*

Bowling Green: Western Kentucky State University, 1971. ERIC ED 065 483.

18. *Evaluation of Personnel—A Tentative Report*. Richmond: Virginia State Department of Education, 1972.
19. *Evaluation Report for the Commission for Teacher Preparation and Licensing*. Dominguez Hills: California State College at Dominguez Hills, 1973.
20. *Excellence in Teacher Education. Distinguished Achievement Awards Program*. 1971, 1972 editions. Washington, D.C.: AACTE, 1971. ERIC ED 051 095.

F

1. Fagan, Edward R. "Evaluating Tomorrow's English Teachers." *Journal of Secondary Education* 39, no. 7 (November 1964), 1321-1325. ERIC ED 034 748.
2. Falls, Charles. *Behaviors Knowledge and Basic Concepts Related to Teaching*. Buffalo, N.Y.: State University College at Buffalo, 1963.
3. Falls, Charles, and Blau, Guitta. *Teacher Competency and the Profession*. (Mimeographed) Albany: New York State TEPS Commission, 1969.
4. Fantini, Mario D. "The Reform of Teacher Education: A Proposal for New York State." *Phi Delta Kappan* 53, no. 8 (April 1972), 476-479.
5. Fattu, N. A. "Research on Teacher Evaluation." *National Elementary School Principal* 43, no. 2 (November 1963), 19-27.
6. *A Feasibility Study for a Comprehensive Competency Based Training and Certification System for Child Care Personnel in the Commonwealth of Pennsylvania*. Washington, D.C.: U.S. Office of Education, 1972.
7. Felfand, D. M. *A Training Program to Increase the Effectiveness of Personnel Teaching Retarded and Other Behaviorally Disadvantaged Children*. Salt Lake City: University of Utah, College of Education, 1970. ERIC ED 043 589.
8. Fink, A. H., and Semmel, M. I. *Indiana Behavior Management System II*. Bloomington: Indiana University, Center for Innovation in Teaching the Handicapped, 1972.
9. Flanagan, John C., et al. *Behavioral Objectives: A Guide for Individualizing Learning*. Palo Alto, Calif.: Westinghouse Learning Corporation.
10. Flanders, Ned A. *Analyzing Classroom Behavior*. Reading, Mass.: Addison-Wesley, 1971.
11. ————. *Analyzing Teaching Behavior*. Reading, Mass.: Addison-Wesley, 1970.
12. ————. "The Changing Base of Performance Based Teaching." *Phi Delta Kappan* 55, no. 5 (January 1974), 312-315.
13. ————. *Teacher Influence, Pupil Attitude, and Achievement*. Washington, D.C.: U.S. Office of Education, Cooperative Research Project no. 397, n.d.
14. Flanders, Ned A., and Simon A. "Teacher Effectiveness." *The Encyclopedia of Educational Research*, 4th ed. New York: Macmillan, 1969.

15. *Florida Catalog of Teacher Training Materials.* Tallahassee: Florida Department of Education, 1972. (See note D-29.)
16. *Florida Program for Improving the Training, Evaluation, and Licensure of Educational Personnel.* Tallahassee: Florida State Department of Education, 1971. ERIC ED 055 050.
17. *Florida State University Teacher Education Project (TEP) Materials.* Tallahassee: Florida State University, College of Education, 1973.
18. Fortenberry, James. *Implementing Competency Based Education Programs at Southern University.* Madison: University of Wisconsin, Teacher Corps Associates Program, 1973.
19. *Four Proposals Regarding the Certification and Professional Development of Michigan Teachers.* Lansing: Michigan State Department of Education, 1972.
20. Fraenkel, Jack R. *Evaluation of National Center for Educational Research and Development.* Washington, D.C.: National Teacher Corps, Teacher Corps Competency Based Education Development Project, 1972.
21. Franke, Eleanor. *Student Performance and Teacher Behavior: An Evaluation of a Developmental Teacher Education Project.* Ph.D. thesis, University of Nebraska, 1971.
22. Freeman, J. P. *Strategy for Improving Teacher Education in North Carolina.* Raleigh: North Carolina State Department of Education, 1971.
23. Frinks, Marshall Lee, Jr. *An Analytical Study of Teacher Certification Processes as Perceived by Leadership Personnel within the Teacher Education and Certification Sections of the Fifty State Education Agencies with Special Emphasis on the Development of the Performance Based Movement.* Ph.D. thesis, University of Massachusetts, 1971.
24. ————. *Emerging State Agency-Institutions of Higher Learning Relationships and Procedures in Planning and Effecting Improvements in the Preparation and Certification of Educators.* Denver: Improving State Leadership in Education Project, fall 1970.
25. Fritschell, Al L. "Minimum Standards for Teacher Competence." *Illinois Education* 55 (April 1967), 347-348.
26. Frymier, Jack. "Who Is Accountable to Whom and for What?" Paper presented at AERA, New Orleans, March 1973. Columbus: The Ohio State University, 1973.
27. Fuller, Edgar. "State School Systems." *Encyclopedia of Educational Research.* New York: Macmillan, 1960, pp. 1385-1397.
28. Fuller, Edgar, and Pearson, Jim B., eds. *Education in the State: Nationwide Development Since 1900.* Washington, D.C.: NEA, 1969.
29. Fuller, Frances F. *Personalized Education for Teacher Educators.* Austin: University of Texas, Research and Development Center for Teacher Education, 1970. ERIC ED 048 105.
30. Fuller, Frances F., and Bown, Oliver H. "Innovations in Counseling Teachers." *Innovations in Counseling.* Edited by R. E. Atta. Austin: University of Texas, 1968, pp. 41-47.
31. Fuller, Frances F., and Bown, Oliver H. "The Teacher's Emotional Develop-

ment." Austin: University of Texas, Hogg Foundation for Mental Health, 1968, pp. 17-24.

32. Fuller, Frances F., and White, Meda M. *Affective Interaction: The Sequence of Filmed Teacher-Pupil Behaviors.* Austin: University of Texas, Research and Development Center, 1967.

33. Fuller, Frances F., et al. "Creating Climates for Growth." Austin: University of Texas, Hogg Foundation for Mental Health, 1967.

34. Fuller, Frances F., et al. *Influences of Counseling and Film Feedback on Openness to Pupil Feedback in Elementary Teachers' Filmed Behavior.* Proceedings of the American Psychological Association, 1967, pp. 359-360.

35. Fuller, Frances F., et al. "Influences of Psychological Feedback of Empirically Derived Covert Concerns of Student Teachers." Paper presented to AERA (city unknown), 1967.

36. Furst, Norma, et al. *Interaction Analysis: Selected Papers.* Washington, D.C.: ERIC Clearinghouse on Teacher Education, Association of Teacher Educators, 1971.

G

1. Gage, N. L., ed. *Handbook of Research on Teaching.* Chicago: Rand McNally, 1973.

2. Gagné, Robert M. "Educational Objectives and Human Performance." *Learning and the Educational Process.* Edited by J. D. Krumboltz. Chicago: Rand McNally, 1965, pp. 1-24.

3. Gall, Meredith, et al. *Minicourse Five: Tutoring in Mathematics.* Paper presented at AERA, Minneapolis, March 1970.

4. Gall, Meredith, et al. *The Relationship between Personality and Teaching Behavior Before and After Inservice Microteaching Training.* Berkeley: Far West Laboratory for Educational Research and Development, 1969. ERIC ED 031 448.

5. Garrard, Judith. *Concerns of Student Teachers: A Review of the Literature.* Austin: University of Texas, Research and Development Center, 1966.

6. Garrard, Judith, and Fuller, Frances F. *Student Teachers' Perceptions of Their Professional Preparation during Depth Interviews.* Proceedings of APA, 1966, pp. 265-266.

7. Garrison, Harry. *Adjusting Objectives for Individual Learning.* (Module) Bellingham: Western Washington State College, 1973.

8. Garvey, James F. "What and Why Behavioral Objectives." *Instructor* 77, no. 8 (April 1968), 127.

9. Gay, Lorraine R., and Daniel, K. Fred. "Accreditation and Performance Based Teacher Education." *Educational Technology* 12, no. 11 (November 1972).

10. Gazda, George M. *A Design for an Inservice Program in Human Relations for Teacher Educators.* Athens: University of Georgia, College of Education, 1970.

11. *Generic Teaching Competencies: An Interim Inventory for Subsequent Independent Development by Pennsylvania Colleges and Universities.* Harrisburg: Office of the Secretary of Education, 1973.
12. Gerhand, Muriel. "Behavioral Outcomes: What the Child Is Able to Do and Does As a Result of the Teaching-Learning Experience." *Grade Teacher* 84, no. 8 (April 1967), 92-95.
13. Getz, Howard, et al. "From Traditional to Competency Based Teacher Education." *Phi Delta Kappan* 54, no. 5 (January 1973), 300-302.
14. Giles, Frederick T., and Foster, Clifford. *Changing Teacher Education in a Large Urban University.* Washington, D.C.: AACTE, 1972.
15. Gliessman, David. "An Introduction to Protocol and Training Materials." *Acquiring Teaching Competencies No. 1.* Bloomington: Indiana University, National Center for Training Materials in Teacher Education, 1972.
16. Gliessman, David, and Hudgins, Bryce. *Acquiring Teaching Competencies: Reports and Studies.* Bloomington: Indiana University, College of Education, National Center for the Development of Training Materials in Teacher Education, n.d.
17. Golden, William Cecil. "The Role of the State Department of Education in Managing Teacher Education and Certification." (Unpublished) Council of Chief State School Officers, San Diego, Calif., July 29, 1971.
18. Goodlad, John I. *School, Curriculum, and the Individual.* Waltham, Mass.: Blaisdell Press, 1966.
19. Grant, Carl, ed. *Resources for Competency Based Teacher Education.* A series of materials for the support of CBTE. Madison: University of Wisconsin, College of Education, Teacher Corps Associates Project, 1973.
20. Greene, Jay E. "Qualifying Examinations Plus Institutional Recommendations for Teacher Certification." *Journal of Teacher Education* 11, no. 2 (June 1960), 239-243.
21. Gronlund, Norman E. *Stating Behavioral Objectives for Classroom Instruction.* New York: Macmillan, 1970.
22. *Guidelines Established by the Commission for Teacher Preparation and Licensing.* Sacramento, Calif.: Commission for Teacher Preparation and Licensing, 1972.
23. *Guidelines for Local Performance Based Evaluation and State Certification of Professional School Personnel.* Hartford, Conn.: State Board of Education and the Commission for Higher Education, n.d.
24. *Guidelines for Professional Standards Boards.* Washington, D.C.: National Commission on Teacher Education and Professional Standards, January 1967.
25. *Guidelines and Standards for the Development and Approval of Preparation Leading to the Certification of School Professional Personnel.* Olympia, Wash.: State Superintendent of Public Instruction, 1971.
26. Gunderson, Doris. *Protocol Materials.* Washington, D.C.: U.S. Office of Education, National Center for the Improvement of Educational Systems, 1973.
27. Guthrie, James W., et al. *Schools and Inequality.* Boston: Massachusetts Institute of Technology Press, 1971.

H

1. Hafiz, M. Sharif. *Developing a Competency Based Elementary Teacher Education Program at Norfolk State College Based on the Implications Study of the Comprehensive Elementary Teacher Education Models.* 2 vols. Norfolk, Va.: Norfolk State College, 1972.
2. Haley, Frances, ed. *Colorado Innovates: A Directory of Alternative Teacher Education Programs.* Boulder, Colo.: Social Science Education Consortium, 1971. ERIC ED 055 027.
3. Hall, Gene E. *Analysis of Teaching Behavior.* (Module) Austin: Research and Development Center for Teacher Education, 1973.
4. Hall, R. V. *Managing Behavior.* Lawrence, Kan.: H. & H. Enterprises, 1971.
5. Hamachek, Don. "Characteristics of Good Teachers and Implications for Teacher Education." *Phi Delta Kappan* 50, no. 6 (February 1969), 341-344.
6. *Handbook on the Development and Use of Protocol Materials for Teacher Education.* Tampa: University of South Florida, College of Education, 1973.
7. Hansen, Kenneth H. "The Revolution in Teacher Education." *The School Administrator* 12 (August 1972), 9-12.
8. Hanushek, Eric. "The Production of Education, Teacher Quality, and Efficiency." *Do Teachers Make a Difference? A Report on Recent Research on Pupil Achievement.* Washington, D.C.: Government Printing Office, 1970, pp. 79-99. ERIC ED 037 396.
9. Harris, Chester W., ed. *Problems in Measuring Change.* Madison: University of Wisconsin Press, 1963.
10. Harrow, Arthur J. *Taxonomy of the Psychomotor Domain.* New York: David McKay, 1973.
11. Hartle, Helen W. "Mobility of Teachers Eased by Compact." *Compact.* Denver: Education Commission of the States, May-June 1973.
12. ————. *Progress Report for Interstate Certification Project.* Albany: New York State Department of Education, Interstate Certification Project, Division of Certification and Teacher Education, August 1973.
13. Haverman, Martin. "Behavioral Objectives: Bandwagon or Breakthrough." *Journal of Teacher Education* 19, no. 1 (spring 1968), 91-94.
14. ————. "Educating the Teachers: Changing Problems. Part Two: Elements of the System." *ASCD Yearbook,* 1971, pp. 110-126.
15. ————. "Teaching Behavior of Successful Interns." *Journal of Teacher Education* 16, no. 2 (June 1965), 215-20.
16. Havighurst, Robert J. "Research on the Developmental Task Concept." *School Review* 64, no. 5 (May 1956), 215-23.
17. Hawthorne, Phyllis. *Legislation by the States: Accountability and Assessment in Education.* Denver: State Educational Accountability Repository, Cooperative Accountability Project, 1972.
18. Haynes, Solon E., and Coyne, Charles E. "Accountability in Teacher Education." *NASSP Bulletin* 55, no. 359 (December 1971), 69-74.

19. Hechinger, F. "Tenure: The Case for—and Against." *New York Times,* September 24, 1972.

20. Hechinger, Grace. "Does Education for All Lead to Mediocrity?" Findings from the International Association for the Evaluation of Educational Achievement—a study of 9,700 schools in 19 countries. *Wall Street Journal,* July 25, 1973.

21. Heger, Herbert K. "Verbal and Nonverbal Classroom Communication: The Development of an Observational Instrument." Paper presented at AERA, Minneapolis, 1970. ERIC ED 040 957.

22. Henderson, Judith E. *A Summary of Initial Efforts in Developing Competency Based Teacher Training for Social-Emotional Education.* East Lansing: Michigan State University, College of Education, 1972.

23. Hersey, Paul, and Blanchard, Kenneth H. *Management of Organizational Behavior: Utilizing Human Resources.* Englewood Cliffs, N.J.: Prentice-Hall, 1969.

24. Hill, Warren G. "The Dynamic Duo." *The Seattle Conference: The Role of the State Department of Education in Teacher Education.* Olympia, Wash.: State Superintendent of Public Instruction, 1967, pp. 1-23.

25. Hite, Herbert. "Cost of Performance Based Teacher Education." *Journal of Teacher Education* 24, no. 3 (fall 1973), 21-24.

26. ————. "POINT—An Innovation in Teacher Education and State Leadership." *The Seattle Conference: The State Department of Education in Teacher Education.* Olympia, Wash.: State Superintendent of Public Instruction, 1967, pp. 51-61.

27. Hoehn, Lilburn P. *Teaching Behavior Improvement Program.* Washington, D.C.: U.S. Office of Education, Bureau of Research, 1969. ERIC ED 034 719.

28. Hood, Paul D., et al. *Development of Assessment Instruments for Competency Based Education.* San Francisco: Far West Laboratory, 1973.

29. Hough, John B., and Duncan, James K. *Teaching: Description and Analysis.* Reading, Mass.: Addison-Wesley, 1970.

30. Hough, John, et al. *Specification for a Comprehensive Undergraduate and Inservice Teacher Education Program for Elementary Teachers.* Syracuse, N.Y.: Syracuse University, College of Education, 1968.

31. *House Bill 2127, Chapter 270.* Salem: Oregon Legislative Assembly, 1973.

32. House, Ernest R., ed. *School Evaluation.* Berkeley: McCutchan Publishing Corporation, 1973.

33. Houston Module Bank. Houston, Tex: University of Houston, College of Education.

34. Houston, W. Robert. "Behavioral Science Teacher Education Programs—Feasibility Study Summary." *Journal of Research and Development in Teacher Education* 3, no. 3 (spring 1970), 45-55.

35. ————. "Designing Competency Based Instructional Systems." *Journal of Teacher Education* 24, no. 3 (fall 1973), 200-204.

36. ————. "Developing Competency Based Programs." Paper presented at AERA, New Orleans, March 1973. Houston, Tex.: University of Houston, College of Education, 1973.

37. ————. *HNAS, Houston Needs Assessment System—A Model for Assessing Educational Needs.* Houston, Tex.: University of Houston, Teacher Center, 1972.

38. ————. "Objectives for Prospective Elementary Teachers of Mathematics: A Developmental Process." *Journal of Teacher Education* 22, no. 3 (fall 1971), 326-30.

39. ————. *Strategies and Resources for Developing a Competency Based Teacher Education Program.* Albany: New York State Education Department, Division of Teacher Education and Certification, Multi-State Consortium on Performance Based Teacher Education, 1972.

40. ————. *Teacher Competency Inventory.* Houston, Tex.: University of Houston, College of Education, Houston Needs Assessment System, 1973.

41. Houston, W. Robert, and Hollis, Loye Y. "Personalizing Mathematics Teacher Education." *Educational Technology* 12, no. 3 (March 1972), 48-50.

42. Houston, W. Robert, and Howsam, Robert B. "CBTE: The Ayes of Texas." *Phi Delta Kappan* 55, no. 5 (January 1974), 299-303.

43. ————. "Change and Challenge." *Competency Based Teacher Education.* Palo Alto, Calif.: Science Research Associates, 1972.

44. Houston, W. Robert, et al. *Behavioral Science Teacher Education Program: Feasibility Study.* East Lansing: Michigan State University, College of Education, 1969.

45. Houston, W. Robert, et al. *Competency Based Teacher Education Program Design: A Simulation.* Westfield, Tex.: Competency Based Instructional Systems, 1973.

46. Houston, W. Robert, et al. *Developing Instructional Modules.* (Module, 4 slide/tapes) Houston, Tex.: University of Houston, College of Education, 1972.

47. Houston, W. Robert, et al. *Resources for Performance Based Education.* Albany: New York State Education Department, Division of Teacher Education and Certification, Multi-State Consortium on Performance Based Teacher Education, March 1973.

48. Houston, W. Robert, et al. *Resources for Performance Based Education. Supplement A.* Albany: New York State Education Department, Division of Teacher Education and Certification, Multi-State Consortium on Performance Based Teacher Education, January 1974.

49. Houston, W. Robert, et al. *Restructuring Teacher Education: A Report of the Rationale, Objectives, and Activities of the Houston Teacher Center, 1970-73.* Houston, Tex.: University of Houston, College of Education, 1973.

50. Houston, W. Robert, ed. *Behavioral Science Elementary Teacher Education Program,* vols. 1, 2, and 3. East Lansing: Michigan State University, College of Education, 1968.

51. Houston, W. Robert, and Howsam, Robert B., eds. *Competency Based Teacher Education: Progress, Problems, and Prospects.* Palo Alto, Calif.: Science Research Associates, 1972.

52. Howell, John J. *Performance Evaluation in Relation to Teacher Education and Teacher Certification.* April 1971. ERIC ED 055 974.
53. Howsam, Robert B. "Management of PBTE Programs." *Journal of Teacher Education* 24, no. 3 (fall 1973), 213-220.
54. ————. "Performance Based Instruction." *Today's Education* 61, no. 4 (April 1972), 33-40.
55. *How Teachers Make a Difference.* Washington, D.C.: U.S. Office of Education, 1970.
56. Hoyt, Donald P. *Identifying Effective Teaching Behaviors.* Manhattan: Kansas State University, 1969. ERIC ED 039 197.
57. Hudgins, Bryce B. "The Portrayal of Concepts: An Issue in the Development of Protocol Materials." *Acquiring Teaching Competencies No. 1.* Bloomington: Indiana University, National Center for the Development of Training Materials in Teacher Education, 1972.
58. Hughbanks, W. Monroe. *A Study of the Relationship between the Student Teaching Behavior of TEPS and the Teaching Skills Which They Have Been Taught in the NUSTEP Program.* Ph.D. thesis, University of Nebraska, 1971.

I

1. *An Illustrated Model for the Evaluation of Teacher Education Graduates.* Washington, D.C.: AACTE, Commission on Standards, n.d.
2. *ILM for Teachers, Supervisors, Principals, and Central Staff.* Salt Lake City, Utah: ILM Publishers, 1973.
3. *Implementation Project.* Mobile: University of South Alabama, School of Education, 1973.
4. *Implementation of the Stull Bill.* Hayward, Calif.: Alameda County School Department, 1972.
5. *Improvement and Reform for American Education: The Administration and Supervision Viewpoint.* Washington, D.C.: U.S. Office of Education, National Center for the Improvement of Educational Systems, 1973.
6. *The Informer* (newsletter of Teacher Education Section of State Education Department, Maryland) 2, no. 2 (January-February 1972).
7. *Individualized Inservice Teacher Education: A Performance Based Module.* Tallahassee: Florida State Department of Education, Department of Elementary and Secondary Education, 1971. ERIC ED 055 049.
8. *Inside-Out.* Washington, D.C.: U.S. Office of Education, National Center for the Improvement of Educational Systems, 1974.
9. *Instructional Modules: Professional Education—Secondary.* Emporia: Kansas State Teachers College, 1973.
10. *Instructional Technology in Teacher Education: Education-Industry Cooperation.* Washington, D.C.: Associated Organizations for Teacher Education, 1970. ERIC ED 054 050.
11. *Interim Report: Competency Based Certification.* Santa Fe: New Mexico State Department of Education, 1973.

12. Ivey, John, and Houston, W. Robert. "The Michigan State Behavioral Science Elementary Teacher Education Program." *Journal of Research and Development in Education* 2, no. 3 (spring 1969), 36-39.

J

1. Jackson, Andrew S. *Evaluation Procedures: A Position Paper for Competency Based Teacher Education.* Houston, Tex.: University of Houston, College of Education, 1971.
2. —————. *Module Evaluation Questionnaire.* Houston, Tex.: University of Houston, College of Education, 1972.
3. Jackson, Rex. *Developing Criterion-Referenced Tests.* Princeton, N.J.: ERIC Clearinghouse on Tests, Measurement, and Evaluation, 1970. ERIC ED 041 052.
4. James, Bernard J. "Can Needs Define Educational Goals?" *Adult Education* 7, no. 1 (autumn 1956), 19-26.
5. Jarolimek, J. "Taxonomy: Guide to Differentiated Instruction." *Social Education* 26 (December 1962), 445-447.
6. Johns, Roe L. "State Organization and Responsibility for Education." *Designing Education for the Future: An Eight-State Project.* New York: Citation Press, 1967.
7. Johnson, Charles E. *Competencies for Teachers: A Handbook for Specifying and Organizing Teaching Performances.* Athens: University of Georgia, College of Education, 1972.
8. —————. *Educational Specifications for a Comprehensive Elementary Teacher Education Program,* vols. 1 and 2. Washington, D.C.: Government Printing Office, 1969.
9. —————. "An Overview of the Georgia Feasibility Study." *Journal of Research and Development in Teacher Education* 3, no. 3 (spring 1970), 18-29.
10. —————. *Some Basic Principles Underlying Performance Based Programs for Higher Education and Competency Based vs. Common Educational Practices.* Athens: University of Georgia, College of Education, 1971.
11. —————. *Study Guide for Proficiency Module: Identifying Competencies.* Athens: University of Georgia, College of Education, 1972.
12. Johnson, Charles E., and Bauch, Jerold P. *Competency Based Teacher Evaluation Guide.* Athens: University of Georgia, College of Education, 1970. ERIC ED 042 698.
13. Johnson, Charles E., and Gentry, Castelle. *A Practical Management System for Performance Based Teacher Education.* Washington, D.C.: AACTE, 1973.
14. Johnson, Charles E., and Shearron, Gilbert F. *Selected Teacher Performance Specifications Generally Applicable to Teacher Education Curricula.* Athens: University of Georgia, College of Education, 1969. ERIC ED 040 924.
15. Johnson, Charles E., and Shearron, Gilbert F. *Specifying Assumptions, Goals, and Objectives for Teacher Education.* Athens: University of Georgia, College of Education, 1971.

16. Johnson, Charles E., et al. *Georgia Educational Model Specifications for the Preparation of Elementary Teachers.* Athens: University of Georgia, College of Education, 1968. ERIC ED 025 491.
17. Johnson, James, and Radebaugh, Byron F. "Excellent Teachers—What Makes Them Outstanding?" *The Clearinghouse* 44, no. 3 (November 1969), 152-156.
18. Johnson, Stuart and Rita. *Developing Individualized Instructional Material: A Self-Instructive Material in Itself.* Palo Alto, Calif.: Westinghouse Learning Press, 1971.
19. Jones, Howard L. *Accountability.* (Module) Houston, Tex.: University of Houston, College of Education, 1973.
20. ———. "Implementation of Programs." *Competency Based Teacher Education.* Palo Alto, Calif.: Science Research Associates, 1972.
21. Joyce, Bruce R. *Alternative Models for Elementary Education.* Boston: Blaisdell Press, 1968.
22. ———. *Performance Based Teacher Education Design Alternatives: The Concept of Unity.* Washington, D.C.: AACTE, 1973.
23. ———. *The Promise of Performance (Competency) Based Teacher Education: An Analytical Review of the Literature and Experience.* Washington, D.C.: ERIC Clearinghouse on Teacher Education. In press.
24. ———. *Social Studies Extension Service.* Chicago: Science Research Associates, 1968.
25. ———. *The Teacher-Innovator: A Program to Prepare Teachers.* Washington, D.C.: Government Printing Office, 1969.
26. Joyce, Bruce R., and Harootunian, Berj. *The Structure of Teaching.* Chicago: Science Research Associates, 1967.
27. Joyce, Bruce R., and Weil, Marsha. *Models of Teaching.* Englewood Cliffs, N.J.: Prentice-Hall, 1972.
28. Joyce, Bruce R., et al. *Materials for Modules.* New York: Columbia University, Teachers College, 1971. ERIC ED 057 016.
29. Joyce, Bruce R., et al. "Sensitivity Training for Teachers: An Experiment." *Journal of Teacher Education* 20, no. 1 (spring 1969), 75-83.
30. Joyce, Bruce R., ed. *Columbia University Model Program.* New York: Columbia University, Teachers College, 1968.
31. Justiz, Thomas B. "A Reliable Measure of Teacher Effectiveness." *Educational Leadership* 3, no. 1 (October 1969), 49-55.

K

1. Kapfer, Meriam B. "Behavioral Objectives and the Gifted." *Educational Technology* 8, no. 11 (June 15, 1968).
2. Kapfer, Philip G. "Behavioral Objectives in the Cognitive and Affective Domains." *Educational Technology* 8, no. 11 (June 15, 1968).
3. Kapfer, Philip, and Ovard, Glen F. *Preparing and Using Individualized Learning Packages for Ungraded, Continuous Progress Education.* Englewood Cliffs, N.J.: Educational Technology Publications, 1971.

4. Kay, Patricia M., et al. *Competency Based Education in Special Education: An Annotated Bibliography.* New York: City University of New York, Office of Teacher Education, 1973.

5. Kay, Patricia M., et al. *Performance Based Certification.* New York: City University of New York, Office of Teacher Education, 1971. ERIC ED 056 991.

6. Kelley, Edgar A., and Zininer, John W. *NUSTEP (Nebraska University Secondary Teacher Education Program), a Performance Based Teacher Education Program, the First Four Years, 1969-1973.* Lincoln: University of Nebraska, Teachers College, 1973.

7. Kelley, Marjorie L. "Teacher Behaviors That Improve the Pupils' Use of Language." Paper presented at AERA, Minneapolis, March 1970. ERIC ED 037 394.

8. Kelley, James A. "The Decade of Reform in Educational Finance." *The School Administrator* 10 (July 1972), 7-10.

9. Kibler, Robert, et al. *Behavioral Objectives and Instruction.* Boston: Allyn & Bacon, 1970.

10. Kinney, Lucien B. *Certification in Education.* Englewood Cliffs, N.J.: Prentice-Hall, 1964.

11. Kirst, Michael. *Issues in Governance for Performance Based Teacher Education.* Washington, D.C.: AACTE, 1973.

12. Klatt, J., and LeBaron, W. *A Short Summary of Ten Model Teacher Education Programs.* Washington, D.C.: Government Printing Office, 1970.

13. Klein, Stephen P. "The Uses and Limitations of Standardized Tests in Meeting Demands of Accountability." *Evaluation Comment* 2, no. 4 (January 1971).

14. Klingstedt, Joe Lars. "Philosophical Basis for Competency Based Education." *Educational Technology* 21, no. 11 (November 1972).

15. Klingstedt, Joe Lars, and Burns, Richard W. "Program Design for Performance Based Teacher Education." Paper presented at the Educational Technical Conference, 1972. ERIC ED 064 407.

16. Knezevich, Stephen J. *Program Budgeting (PPBS).* Berkeley: McCutchan Publishing Corporation, 1973.

17. Knirk, Fredrick G. "Analysis of Instructional Systems: A Reaction." *Audiovisual Instruction* 10, no. 8 (October 1965), 9.

18. Kozlowski, David, and Crane, Roger. "The Design and Implementation of a Performance Based Teacher Education Course in Instructional Technology." *Audiovisual Instruction* 17, no. 8 (October 1972), 30-33.

19. Krasner, Leonard, and Ullman, Leonard P. *Research in Behavior Modification.* New York: Holt, Rinehart & Winston, 1965.

20. Krathwohl, David R., et al. *Taxonomy of Educational Objectives. Handbook II: Affective Domain.* New York: David McKay, 1964.

21. Kristy, Norton F. "The Future of Educational Technology." *Phi Delta Kappan* 48, no. 5 (January 1967), 240-243.

L

1. LaBue, Anthony C. "Teacher Certification in the United States: A Brief History." *Journal of Teacher Education* 11, no. 2 (June 1960), 147-173.

2. Langer, Philip. "The Range of Teaching Skills That Can Be Changed by the Minicourse Model." Paper presented at the American Psychological Association, Washington, D.C., 1969. ERIC ED 032 293.

3. Langer, Philip, and Allen, Edward G. "The Minicourse as a Tool for Training Teachers in Interaction Analysis." Paper presented at AERA, Minneapolis, March 1970. ERIC ED 037 393.

4. Lawson, Gene R. "Indicators of Teacher Ability to Relate to Students." Paper presented at AERA, New York, 1971. ERIC ED 050 008.

5. Leake, Horace. *A Seminar on Competency Based Teacher Education for University Personnel.* Madison: University of Wisconsin, Teacher Corps Associates Program, 1973.

6. Leavitt, H. B. "Dichotomy between Ends and Means in American Education." *Journal of Education* 141, no. 1 (October 1958), 14-16.

7. Lefforge, Orland S. *Inservice Training as an Instrument for Change.* Gainesville: University of Florida, Institute for Higher Education, 1971. ERIC ED 055 577.

8. Lessinger, Leon M. *Every Kid a Winner: Accountability in Education.* Palo Alto, Calif.: Science Research Associates, 1970.

9. Lessinger, Leon M., et al. *Accountability: Policies and Procedures.* 4 vols. New London, Conn.: Croft Educational Services, 1972.

10. Lessinger, Leon M., and Tyler, Ralph W., eds. *Accountability in Education.* Worthington, Ohio: Charles A. Jones Publishing Co., 1971.

11. Levin, Henry M. *Report to the National Academy of Education Task Force on Accountability.* Stanford, Calif.: Stanford University, 1972.

12. Lewey, Arieh. "Empirical Validity of Major Properties of a Taxonomy of Affective Educational Objectives." *Journal of Experimental Education* 36, no. 3 (spring 1968), 70-77.

13. Lieberman, Myron. "Considerations Favoring National Certification of Teachers." *Journal of Teacher Education* 11, no. 2 (June 1960), 191-201.

14. Lierheimer, Alvin P. *An Anchor to Windward: A Framework of State Certification to Accommodate Current Development in Differentiating Staff Roles.* Washington, D.C.: National Commission on Teacher Education and Professional Standards, 1969.

15. ———. "Changing the Palace Guard." *Phi Delta Kappan* 52, no. 1 (September 1970), 20-25.

16. ———. "Give Up the Ship: A New Basis for State Certification." *The English Record* 20, no. 1 (October 1969), 64-70. ERIC ED 035 646.

17. ———. *Parsing the Paradox: Assuring Quality in School Personnel Preparation.* Washington, D.C.: ERIC Clearinghouse on Teacher Education, 1971.

18. Ligons, Claudette M. *Nonverbal Communication and the Affective Domain.* Madison: University of Wisconsin, Teacher Corps Associates Program, 1973.
19. Lillie, L. *Information on T.E.E.C.H.—Training in Early Education of Children with Handicaps.* Chapel Hill: University of North Carolina, 1972.
20. Lindsey, Margaret. "Performance Based Teacher Education: Examination of a Slogan." *Journal of Teacher Education* 24, no. 3 (fall 1973), 180-186.
21. *Linking Schools to State Education Departments.* Eugene, Ore.: ERIC Clearinghouse on Educational Administration, September 1970. ERIC ED 043 117.
·22. Lippitt, Gordon L. *Organizational Renewal: Achieving Viability in a Changing World.* New York: Appleton-Century-Crofts, 1969.
23. Lowrey, Anna M. "School Library Manpower Project Launches Phase II." *Audiovisual Instruction* 17, no. 1 (January 1972), 26-28.
24. Lutonsky, Linda. *Portal Schools.* Washington, D.C.: Council of the Great City Schools, 1972.

M

1. McAshan, H. H. *The Goals Approach to Writing and Using Performance Objectives: Cognitive Domain, Affective Domain, Management by Objectives.* Philadelphia: W. B. Saunders Co., 1974.
2. ———. *Writing Behavioral Objectives: A New Approach.* New York: Harper & Row, 1970.
3. McAvoy, Roger, and Carter, Alvin R. *A Performance Curriculum in Undergraduate Teacher Education.* ERIC ED 039 174.
4. McCleary, Lloyd, and McIntyre, Kenneth. "Competency Development and University Methodology." *National Association of Secondary School Principals Bulletin* 56, no. 362 (March 1972), 53-68.
5. McCleary, Lloyd, ed. *The Competency Based Curriculum Notebook.* (Newsletter) Salt Lake City: University of Utah, College of Education, n.d.
6. McDonald, Frederick J. "Evaluation of Teaching Behavior." *Competency Based Teacher Education.* Palo Alto, Calif.: Science Research Associates, 1972.
7. ———. "The National Commission on Performance Based Education." *Phi Delta Kappan* 55, no. 5 (January 1974), 296-298.
8. McKenna, Bernard H., et al. *Teacher Evaluation: An Annotated Bibliography.* Washington, D.C.: ERIC Clearinghouse on Teacher Education, 1971. ERIC SP 005 351.
9. McKnight, Philip C., and Baral, David P., eds. *Microteaching and the Technical Skills of Teaching: A Bibliography of Research and Development at Stanford University, 1963-69.* Stanford, Calif.: Stanford University, School of Education, 1969. ERIC ED 030 621.
10. McMahan, M. "A Challenge: The Systems Approach in Development of Media Competencies." *Audiovisual Instruction* 12, no. 10 (December 1967), 1060-1063.

11. McMillan, N. M. *A Model for a Performance Based Elementary Education Program at Shaw University*. Raleigh, N.C.: Shaw University, 1971. ERIC ED 056 974.

12. McNally, Harold I. "Teacher Evaluation That Makes a Difference." *Educational Leadership* 29, no. 4 (January 1972), 353-357.

13. McNeil, John D. "Concomitants of Using Behavioral Objectives in the Assessment of Teacher Effectiveness." *Journal of Experimental Education* 36, no. 1 (fall 1967), 69-74.

14. ————. "Performance Tests: Assessing Teachers of Reading." Paper presented at California Educational Research Association, San Diego, 1971.

15. McNeil, John D., and Popham, W. J. "The Assessment of Teacher Competency." *Second Handbook of Research on Teaching*. In press. ERIC ED 054 200.

16. Maddox, Kathryn. *In West Virginia, It Is Working: One Teacher Education Center in Action*. Washington, D.C.: AACTE, 1972.

17. Maddox, Kathryn, et al. *New Dimensions in Teacher Education Inservice*. Charleston, W. Va.: Kanawha County Teacher Center, 1970.

18. Mager, Robert F. *Developing Attitudes toward Learning*. Palo Alto, Calif.: Fearon Publishers, 1968.

19. Mager, Robert F., and Pipe, Peter. *Analyzing Performance Problems or You Really Oughta Wanna*. Palo Alto, Calif.: Fearon Publishers, 1971.

20. *Manual for Developing, Evaluating, and Approving Teacher Preparation Program Plans, 1972-73*. Sacramento, Calif.: Commission for Teacher Preparation and Licensing, 1972.

21. Margules, Morton, and Keith, Virginia M. "A Study of Supervisors' Ratings of Most Effective and Least Effective Industrial Arts Teachers on Three Competency Dimensions." *Journal of Experimental Education* 37, no. 4 (summer 1969), 37-44.

22. Markel, D. G. *The Development of the Bell System First Aid and Personal Safety Course: An Exercise in the Application of Empirical Methods to Instructional System Design*. Palo Alto, Calif.: American Institutes for Research, 1967.

23. Marsh, David, and McDonald, Lynn. "Developing a Teacher Competency: A Case Study." (Slide/tape) Monmouth, Ore.: Teaching Research, 1972.

24. Martin, G. N., and Clark, M. C. *Developing a Modular Teacher Education Program for an R and D Center*. Austin: University of Texas, Research and Development Center for Teacher Education, 1970. ERIC ED 055 983.

25. Martin, M., and Yates, J. *Special Education Administration Simulation Project*. Columbus: Ohio State University, University Council for Educational Administration, 1971.

26. *Massachusetts Study of 1969*. Boston: State Department of Education, Massachusetts Advisory Council on Education, 1969.

27. Massanari, Karl. "CBTE's Potential for Improving Educational Personnel Development." *Journal of Teacher Education* 24, no. 3 (fall 1973), 244-249.

28. ————. *Performance Based Teacher Education: What's It All About?* Washington, D.C.: AACTE, 1971. ERIC ED 055 972.
29. Massanari, Karl, ed. *Evaluation Criteria for Accrediting Teacher Education.* Washington, D.C.: AACTE, 1967.
30. ————. "Symposium on Performance Based Teacher Education." *Journal of Teacher Education* 24, no. 3 (fall 1973), 179-249.
31. *Materials Information Briefs.* New York: City University at Hunter College, Regional Special Education Instructional Materials Center, 1973.
32. Maucker, J. W. "Performance Based Teacher Education." *AACTE Yearbook, 1972.* Washington, D.C.: AACTE, 1972, pp. 75-77.
33. Maurer, Wallace M., et al. *Generic Teaching Competencies: An Interior Inventory for Subsequent Independent Development by Pennsylvania Colleges and Universities.* Harrisburg: Pennsylvania State Department of Education, 1973.
34. Maurer, Wallace M., ed. "Competency Based Teacher Certification in the United States." A working paper of the Pennsylvania Competency Assessment Certification Program. Harrisburg: Pennsylvania State Department of Education, 1973.
35. Maxwell, W. David. "A Case of the Emperor's New Clothes." *Phi Delta Kappan* 55, no. 5 (January 1974), 305-311.
36. May, Frank B. "Some Practical Suggestions for Developing Competency Based, Independent Study Modules for Teacher Education." *Journal of Teacher Education* 23, no. 2 (summer 1972), 155-160.
37. Mayer, Frederick. "Aims of Education." *Education* 76, no. 10 (June 1956), 630-638.
38. Mayor, John R. *Accreditation in Teacher Education, Its Influence on Higher Education.* Washington, D.C.: National Commission on Accrediting, 1965.
39. Meals, Donald W. "Heuristic Models for Systems Planning." *Phi Delta Kappan* 48, no. 5 (January 1967), 199-203.
40. Medley, Donald M. *Specifications for a New Teacher Examination: A First Approximation.* Princeton, N.J.: Educational Testing Service, 1970. ERIC ED 055 094.
41. ————. "The Language of Teacher Behavior: Communicating the Results of Structured Observations to Teachers." *Journal of Teacher Education* 22, no. 2 (summer 1971), 157-165.
42. Medley, Donald M., and Mitzel, Harold E. "Measuring Classroom Behavior by Systematic Observation." *Handbook of Research on Teaching.* Chicago: Rand McNally, 1963, pp. 247-328.
43. Meierhenry, W. C. "Analyzing Instructional Problems." *Audiovisual Instruction* 10, no. 6 (June 1965), 64.
44. ————. *Media Competencies for Teachers, A Project to Identify Competencies Needed by Teachers in the Uses of the Newer Media and Various Approaches to Achieving Them.* Lincoln: University of Nebraska, College of Education, 1966.
45. Meierhenry, W. C., ed. *Mediated Teacher Education Resources.* Washington, D.C.: AACTE, 1970.

46. Melching, William H., et al. *Introducing Innovation in Instruction: Inservice Teacher Workshops in Classroom Management.* Alexandria, Va.: Human Resources Research Organization, 1970. ERIC ED 048 098.

47. Merrill, M. David. "A Better Way to Cut the Pie: Instructional Behaviors and Instructional Materials Characteristics." Paper presented at AERA, New Orleans, March 1973. Salt Lake City: University of Utah, 1973.

48. Merritt, Daniel L. "Performance Objectives: A Beginning, Not an End." *Contemporary Education* 43, no. 5 (April 1971), 209-212.

49. Merwin, Jack C. *Performance Based Teacher Education, Some Measurement and Decision Making Considerations.* Washington, D.C.: AACTE, 1973.

50. Messick, S. J. *Research Methods for Educational Change.* Princeton, N. J.: Educational Testing Service, 1971.

51. Metzner, Seymour. "The Teacher as Viewed by His Principal." *Changing Education* 4, no. 4 (winter 1969), 25.

52. Meyeh, E. W., et al. *The SECTRAC Program: Prototype Training Program for the Preparation of Curriculum Consultants for Exceptional Children.* Columbia: University of Missouri, Department of Special Education, 1972.

53. Mitzel, Harold E., and Gross, Cecily F. "The Development of Pupil-Growth Criteria in Studies of Teacher Effectiveness." *Educational Research Bulletin* 37 (October-November 1958), 205-215.

54. *A Model Plan for Evaluation of Certified Staff in the Management of Learning.* Hayward, Calif.: Alameda County School Department, 1972. 20 pp.

55. *A Modular Curriculum for the Education of School Library Media Specialists.* Tempe: Arizona State University, Department of Library Science, 1970.

56. *Module Clusters.* Buffalo, N.Y.: State University College at Buffalo, 1972.

57. Mohr, Paul. *Competency Based Teacher Education.* Tallahassee: Florida A & M University, College of Education, 1973.

58. Mood, Alexander M., et al. *How Teachers Make a Difference.* Washington, D.C.: Government Printing Office, 1971. Order number: 1780 0813.

59. Morphet, Edgar L., et al. *Educational Organization and Administration—Concepts, Practices, and Issues.* Englewood Cliffs, N.J.: Prentice-Hall, 1967.

60. Morphet, Edgar L., et al. *Planning and Providing Excellence in Education.* Denver: Improving State Leadership in Education Project, 1971.

61. Morphet, Edgar L., and Jesser, David L., eds. *Planning and Effecting Improvements in the Preparation and Certification of Educators: Emerging State Relationships and Procedures.* Denver: Improving State Leadership in Education, n.d.

62. Mosier, Earl E. "Proficiency Examinations—A Wise or Unwise Policy?" *Journal of Teacher Education* 11, no. 2 (June 1960), 223-231.

63. Morsh, Joseph E., and Wilder, Eleanor W. *Identifying the Effective Instructor: A Review of the Quantitative Studies, 1900-1952.* Chanute Air Force Base, Ill.: Air Force Personnel and Training Research Center, 1954.

64. Mouritsen, Roger C. *The Impact of Competency Based Teacher Education and Certification Programs in Utah.* Salt Lake City: Utah State Board of Education, 1972.
65. Mueller, Dorothy G. "How to Evaluate Teaching." *Journal of Teacher Education* 22, no. 2 (summer 1971), 229-244.
66. Musella, Donald. "Improving Teacher Education." *Journal of Teacher Education* 21, no. 1 (spring 1970), 15-21.

N

1. Nagle, Thomas S., and Richman, Paul T. *Competency Based Education.* Columbus, Ohio: Charles E. Merrill Publishing Co., 1972.
2. Nash, Paul. *A Humanistic Approach to Performance Based Teacher Education.* Washington, D.C.: AACTE, 1973.
3. ————. *The Major Purposes of the Humanistic Behavioral Studies in Teacher Education.* Washington, D.C.: AACTE, 1971.
4. Nash, Robert J. "Commitment to Competency: The New Fetishism in Teacher Education." *Phi Delta Kappan* 52, no. 4 (December 1970), 240-243.
5. Nash, Robert J., and Agne, Russell M. "Competency in Teacher Education: A Prop for the Status Quo?" *Journal of Teacher Education* 22, no. 2 (summer 1971), 147-156.
6. National Center for the Development of Protocol Materials in Teacher Education. Tampa: University of South Florida, College of Education.
7. National Center for the Development of Training Materials in Teacher Education. Bloomington: University of Indiana, College of Education.
8. Nebraska University Secondary Teacher Education Program (NUSTEP) Task Kits. Lincoln: University of Nebraska, NUSTEP, 1973.
9. Neff, Frederick C. "Competency Based Teaching and Trained Fleas." *Phi Delta Kappan* 53, no. 8 (April 1972), 480-482.
10. Neff, Monroe C. "Materials Systems for Basic Adult Education." *Audiovisual Instruction* 11, no. 4 (April 1966), 246-248.
11. *Negotiating Professional Standards.* Burlingame: California Teachers Association, 1970. ERIC ED 045 565.
12. *A New Approach to Teacher Education and Teacher Certification.* Olympia, Wash.: State Superintendent of Public Instruction, 1972.
13. *New Developments in Teacher Education and Certification Aimed at Improvement.* Trenton: New Jersey State Education Department, 1971.
14. *New Directions in Teacher Education.* Seattle: University of Washington, College of Education, 1970. ERIC ED 045 547.
15. *A New Order in Student Teaching: Fixing Responsibilities for Student Teaching.* Washington, D.C.: NEA, National Commission on Teacher Education and Professional Standards, 1967.
16. *A New Style of Certification.* Albany: New York State Education Department, Department of Teacher Education and Certification, 1972.
17. *New Style of Certification.* Albany: New York State Department of Education, March 15, 1971.

18. "NJEA Speaks Out on . . . Teacher Education." Policy statement adopted by the NJEA Delegate Assembly, November 5, 1970. Trenton: New Jersey Education Association, 1970. ERIC ED 045 600.
19. Norman, O. W. *A Multi-Dimensional Field Centered Training Model.* Eugene: University of Oregon, College of Education, 1972.

O

1. Ober, Richard L., et al. *Systematic Observation of Teaching: An Interaction Analysis Approach.* Englewood Cliffs, N.J.: Prentice-Hall, 1971.
2. *Obligation for Reform.* Washington, D.C.: U.S. Office of Education, National Center for the Improvement of Educational Systems, 1974.
3. Ochoa, Alberto. *A Module for Understanding the Characteristics of Competency Based Education.* Madison: University of Wisconsin, Teacher Corps Associates Program, 1973.
4. Oestreich, Arthur H. "The Professional Growth of the Student Teacher." *Phi Delta Kappan* 55, no. 5 (January 1974), 319.
5. Ojala, Milton H., and Cooper, James M. "A Feasibility Study of the Massachusetts Model Elementary Teacher Education Program." *Journal of Research and Development in Education* 3, no. 3 (spring 1970), 30-44.
6. Ojemann, R. H. "Should Educational Objectives Be Stated in Behavioral Terms?" *Elementary School Journal* 68, no. 5 (February 1968), 223-231.
7. Okey, James R., and Brown, Jerry L. "Competencies for Performance Based Teacher Training." *Acquiring Teacher Competencies: Reports and Studies No. 4.* Bloomington: Indiana University, National Center for the Development of Training Materials in Teacher Education, 1973.
8. O'Leary, K. D., and O'Leary, S. G. *Classroom Management.* New York: Pergamon Press, 1972.
9. Olmsted, Ann G., et al. "Stances Teachers Take: A Basis for Selective Admission." *Phi Delta Kappan* 55, no. 5 (January 1974), 330-334.
10. Olson, Paul, et al. *Education for 1984 and After.* Lincoln: University of Nebraska, 1972.
11. Olson, Paul, et al. *The University Can't Train Teachers.* Lincoln: University of Nebraska, 1972.
12. Openshaw, M. Karl, et al. *Development of a Taxonomy for the Classification of Teacher Classroom Behavior.* Columbus: The Ohio State University, 1966. ERIC ED 010 067.
13. *Oregon State Board of Education Rules for Certification of Teachers, Specialists, and Administrators.* Salem, Ore.: State Superintendent of Public Instruction, 1972.
14. *Orientation to Teaching.* (Module cluster) Yorktown Heights, New York: CITE, Putnam County BOCES, 1973.
15. Ornstein, Allan C. "Teacher Behavior Research: Approaches, Limitations, and Recommendations." Based on chapters 1, 5, and 8 of "Selected Teacher Behavior Attributes Rated as Desirable by Ninth-Grade Disad-

vantaged Students and Ninth-Grade Teachers of the Disadvantaged."
Ph.D. thesis, New York University, 1970. ERIC ED 046 862.

16. Oxhandler, Eugene K. "Afterthoughts on a Systems Conference." *Audio-visual Instruction* 10, no. 5 (May 1965), 395-397.

P

1. Parker, Reese. "Weber State College Evaluates IPTE after Three Years." *Phi Delta Kappan* 55, no. 5 (January 1974), 320-324.

2. Pate, R. T., and Bremer, N. H. "Guiding Learning through Skillful Questioning." *Elementary School Journal* 67, no. 8 (May 1967), 417-422.

3. Payne, David A. *Estimating Cost for Development of Candidate Performance Evaluation Procedures.* Athens: University of Georgia, College of Education, 1969.

4. Pearson, Jim B., and Fuller, Edgar, eds. *Education in the States: Historical Development and Outlook.* Washington, D.C.: NEA, 1969.

5. Peck, Robert F. *Personalized Education: An Attainable Goal in the Seventies.* Austin: University of Texas, Research and Development Center for Teacher Education, 1970. ERIC ED 051 137.

6. Peck, Robert F., and Tucker, James A. "Research on Teacher Education." *Handbook of Research in Teaching.* 2d ed. Chicago: Rand McNally, 1973.

7. Pendergraft, Daryl. "The Process versus the Product Issue in the Accreditation of Teacher Education." *Evaluative Criteria for Accrediting Teacher Education.* Washington, D.C.: AACTE, 1967, pp. 84-89.

8. *Pennsylvania's Competency Based Teacher Education Program.* Harrisburg: Pennsylvania State Department of Education, Bureau of Teacher Education and Certification, 1973.

9. Pereira, Peter, and Guelcher, William. *The Skills of Teaching: A Dynamic Approach.* TEC Occasional Paper no. 2. Chicago: University of Chicago, Teacher Education Center, 1970. ERIC ED 049 162.

10. *Performance Based Curriculum Library Science K-12.* Millersville, Pa.: Millersville State College, Department of Educational Media, 1972.

11. *Performance Based Education and Certification.* Denver: Department of Education, Regional Interstate Project Program, 1973.

12. *Performance Based Inservice Instruction for the Preparation of Teacher and Library Aides in Elementary Schools.* Dover: Delaware State Department of Instruction, 1972.

13. *Performance Based Teacher Certification.* Denver: Department of Education, Regional Interstate Project, 1972.

14. *Performance Based Teacher Certification: Florida's Project Program.* Tallahassee: Florida State Department of Education, 1972.

15. *Performance Based Teacher Training Interactive Skills, A Demonstration Project.* Emporia: Kansas State Teachers College, 1973.

16. *Performance Recertification—Field Test Guidelines.* Phoenix: Arizona State Department of Education, 1972.

17. *Performance Recertification—What Is It?* Phoenix: Arizona State Department of Education, 1972.
18. Perry, Richard R. "Evaluation of Teaching Behavior Seeks to Measure Effectiveness." *College and University Business* 47, no. 4 (October 1969), 18-22.
19. Peter, Laurence J. *Prescriptive Teaching.* New York: McGraw-Hill, 1965.
20. ————. *Prescriptive Teaching, Instructor's Manual.* New York: McGraw-Hill, 1966.
21. Petrequin, Gaynor. *Individualizing Learning through Modular-Flexible Programming.* New York: McGraw-Hill, 1968.
22. Pfau, Edward. *Competent Performance in Teacher Education.* Lansing: Michigan State Department of Education, 1970.
23. Phillips, M. G. "Learning Materials and Their Implementation." *Review of Educational Research* 36, no. 4 (June 1966), 373-379.
24. Pierce, Truman M. *Federal, State, and Local Government in Education.* Washington, D.C.: Center for Applied Research in Education, 1964.
25. *Planned Change in a Developing Institution.* Marshall: Southwest Minnesota State College, Division of Education, 1973.
26. *Planning for Competency Based Teacher Education and Certification.* (Report of workshop) Salem: Oregon State Board of Education, Western Region, Interstate Planning Project, 1972.
27. Plowman, Paul. *Behavioral Objectives: Teacher Success through Student Performance.* Chicago: Science Research Associates, 1971.
28. Poliakoff, Lorraine. *Teacher Centers: An Outline of Current Information.* Washington, D.C.: ERIC Clearinghouse on Teacher Education, 1972. ERIC SP 005 685.
29. *Policies, Procedures, and Standards for Certification of Professional School Personnel.* Harrisburg: Pennsylvania State Department of Education, 1970.
30. *Policies and Resolutions of the Council of Chief State School Officers.* Adopted at the annual business meeting of the Council of Chief State School Officers, San Francisco, November 15, 1972.
31. Politzer, Robert L. *Performance Criteria for the Foreign Language Teacher.* Stanford, Calif.: Stanford University, Stanford Center for Research and Development, 1967. ERIC ED 034 73.
32. Pomeroy, Edward C. *Beyond the Upheaval.* Washington, D.C.: AACTE, 1972.
33. Popham, W. James. *Development of a Performance Test of Teaching Proficiency.* Los Angeles: University of California, 1967. ERIC ED 013 224.
34. ————. "Evaluation." (Filmstrip) Los Angeles: VIMCET Association, 1971.
35. ————. *Performance Tests of Instructor Competency for Trade and Technical Education.* Los Angeles: University of California, 1968. ERIC ED 027 418.
36. ————. "Performance Tests of Teaching Proficiency: Rationale, Development, and Validation." *American Educational Research Journal* 8, no. 1 (January 1971), 105-117.

37. ————. "Probing the Validity of Arguments on Behavioral Goals." A symposium presentation at AERA, Chicago, 1968.
38. ————. "Teaching Skill under Scrutiny." *Phi Delta Kappan* 52, no. 10 (June 1971), 599-602.
39. Popham, W. James, and Baker, Eva L. *Establishing Instructional Goals.* Englewood Cliffs, N.J.: Prentice-Hall, 1969.
40. ————. "Measuring Teachers' Attitudes toward Behavioral Objectives." *Journal of Educational Research* 60, no. 4 (July 1967), 453-455.
41. ————. "A Performance Test of Teaching Effectiveness." Paper presented at AERA, Chicago, 1966. ERIC ED 015 144.
42. ————. *Systematic Instruction.* Englewood Cliffs, N.J.: Prentice-Hall, 1970.
43. Popham, W. James, ed. *Criterion Referenced Measurement: An Introduction.* Englewood Cliffs, N.J.: Educational Technology Publications, 1971. ERIC ED 053 200.
44. Postlethwait, S. N., et al. *The Audio-Tutorial Approach to Learning.* Minneapolis: Burgess Publishing Co., 1969.
45. Potter, David A., ed. *Research Memorandum—Performance Based Education—Position Papers.* Papers presented at AERA, New Orleans, March 1973. Princeton, N.J.: Educational Testing Service, 1973.
46. *In the Preparation and Practice of Professionals for Elementary and Secondary Education.* Unit of the New York Regents Statewide Plan for the Development of Post Secondary Education. Albany: New York State Department of Education, 1972.
47. *Preparing Performance Based Competency Modules.* Jacksonville: University of North Florida, College of Education, 1973.
48. *Process Standards and Guidelines for Competency Based Educational Personnel Development Programs.* Salem: Oregon State Board of Education, 1972.
49. *Professional Development Newsletter.* Minneapolis: Minnesota State Department of Education, n.d.
50. *Professional Teacher Education II: A Programmed Design, Developed by the American Association of Colleges for Teacher Education and Media Project.* Washington, D.C.: AACTE, 1968. ERIC ED 026 294.
51. *Project Libra, A Competency Based, Field Centered Approach to the Preparation of Library Media Specialists.* Auburn, Ala.: Auburn University, Department of Educational Media, 1970.
52. *Proposal Format and Guidelines for Experimental Programs in School Library Media Education.* Chicago: American Library Association, School Library Manpower Project, 1970.
53. *Proposed Modifications to Existing Teacher Education Regulations.* Little Rock: Arkansas State Board of Education, 1972.
54. *Proposed Standards for State Approval of Teacher Education.* Salt Lake City: Utah State Board of Education, Division of Teacher Personnel, 1968.
55. Provus, Malcolm. *Discrepancy Evaluation.* Berkeley: McCutchan Publishing Corporation, 1971.

56. Pyatte, Jeff A. "The Effectiveness of Performance Training Modules on Planning and Presenting." Paper presented at AERA, Chicago, 1972. ERIC ED 062 299.

Q

1. Queer, Glenn. *An Analysis of Teacher Rating Scales: A National Survey.* Pittsburgh, Pa.: Pittsburgh Public Schools, Office of Research, 1969. ERIC ED 030 968.
2. Quirk, Thomas J. "Some Measurement Issues in Competency Based Teacher Education." *Phi Delta Kappan* 55, no. 5 (January 1974), 316-319.
3. Quirk, Thomas J., et al. "Comparison of Teacher Behavior at Different Grade Levels within Project PLAN: A Program of Individualized Education." Paper presented at AERA, Minneapolis, March 1970. ERIC ED 039 185.

R

1. Rackley, J. R., and Miller, Norman A. "Broad Policy Concerns and Directions for a State Department of Education in Teacher Education." *The Seattle Conference: The Role of the State Department of Education in Teacher Education.* Olympia, Wash.: State Superintendent of Public Instruction, 1967, pp. 14-23.
2. Ramp, Wayne, and Anderson, Edward. *A Competency Based Model Graduate Program in Occupational Education Administration.* Normal: Illinois State University, College of Education, 1972.
3. *Recommendations of the Designing Education for the Future Committee.* Salt Lake City: Utah State Department of Education, 1971.
4. *Recommended Proficiency Guidelines for Media Endorsements.* Salt Lake City: Utah State Department of Education, 1972.
5. *Recommended Standards for Teacher Education.* Washington, D.C.: AACTE, March 1970.
6. Redfern, G. B. *How to Appraise Teaching Performance.* Columbus, Ohio: School Management Institute, 1965.
7. *Regulations Governing the Certification of Educational Personnel.* Montpelier: Vermont State Department of Education, 1971.
8. *Related Problems and Strategies for the Development and Implementation of Competency Based Teacher Education Programs.* Buffalo, N.Y.: State University College at Buffalo, 1973.
9. Remmers, H. H. "Rating Methods in Research in Teaching." *Handbook of Research on Teaching.* Chicago: Rand McNally, 1963, pp. 329-378.
10. *Report of the Council of Chief State School Officer's Task Force on the Improvement of Educational Systems.* Washington, D.C.: U.S. Office of Education, National Center for the Improvement of Educational Systems, 1974.
11. *Report on the 1970 Workshop of the Organization of State TEPS Chairmen and Consultants, NEA.* Washington, D.C.: NEA, 1970.

12. *Responsibilities of State Departments of Education for Teacher Education.* Washington, D.C.: Council of Chief State School Officers, 1954.
13. Ricker, Kenneth S., and Hawkins, Michael L. *Reactions of College Students to a Science Education Proficiency Module.* Athens: University of Georgia, College of Education, 1969. ERIC ED 040 928.
14. ─────. *Testing a Science Education Proficiency Module with College Students.* Athens: University of Georgia, College of Education, 1970. ERIC ED 042 695.
15. Roberson, E. Wayne. *Teacher Self-Appraisal Source Book.* Tucson, Ariz.: Educational Innovators Press, 1970. ERIC ED 041 864.
16. Roberts, W. Glyn. "How to Apply a Systems Analysis Approach to Education." *Education Canada* 10, no. 7 (September 1970), 9-13.
17. Roe, William H. "Organizational Patterns: State and Federal." *Review of Educational Research* 31, no. 4 (October 1961), 368-379.
18. ─────. "State Regulations of Education." *Encyclopedia of Educational Research.* New York: Macmillan, 1969, pp. 1299-1307.
19. Rosenshine, Barak. *Critique of the Model Teacher Elementary Education Programs.* Washington, D.C.: ERIC Clearinghouse on Teacher Education, 1971. ERIC ED 055 976.
20. ─────. "Enthusiastic Teaching: A Research Review." *School Review* 77, no. 8 (August 1970), 499-514.
21. ─────. *Interpretation Study of Teacher Behaviors Related to Student Achievement.* Philadelphia: Temple University, 1970.
22. ─────. "The Stability of Teacher Effects upon Student Achievement." *Review of Educational Research* 40, no. 5 (December 1970), 647-662.
23. ─────. "To Explain: A Review of Research." *Educational Leadership* 26, no. 3 (December 1968), 303-309.
24. Rosner, Benjamin, and Kay, Patricia M. "Will the Promise of C/PBTE Be Fulfilled?" *Phi Delta Kappan* 55, no. 5 (January 1974), 290-295.
25. Rosner, Benjamin, ed. *The Power of Competency Based Teacher Education.* Final report of the "Outside Track" of Task Force '72, USOE. Boston: Allyn & Bacon, 1972.
26. Roth, Robert. *Performance Based Teacher Certification: A Survey of the States.* Trenton: New Jersey State Department of Education, December 1972.
27. ─────. *Performance Evaluation Project.* Trenton: New Jersey State Department of Education, 1971.
28. Roush, Robert E., and Holcomb, J. David. "Teaching Improvements in Higher Education: Medical Education May Be the Leader." *Phi Delta Kappan* 55, no. 5 (January 1974), 338-340.
29. Rudman, Marsha K. *Feasibility Study of a Performance Based Teacher Education Curriculum in Language Arts.* Ann Arbor: University of Michigan, University of Michigan, University Microfilms, 1970.
30. ─────. "A Performance Based Teacher Education Curriculum in Language Arts." *Elementary English* 49, no. 2 (February 1972), 197-201.
31. Ruth, Leo. *Accountability and the Teaching of English.* Urbana, Ill.: National Council of Teachers of English, 1972.

32. Ryan, David G. *Characteristics of Teachers: Their Description, Comparison, and Appraisal—A Research Study.* Washington, D.C.: American Council on Education, 1960.

33. Ryan, Kevin A. *A Plan for a New Type of Professional Training for a New Type of Teaching Staff.* Washington, D.C.: NEA, National Commission on Teacher Education and Professional Standards, 1968.

S

1. Sandefur, J. R., and Bressier, Alex A. *Classroom Observation Systems in Preparing School Personnel.* Washington, D.C.: ERIC Clearinghouse on Teacher Education, 1970. ERIC ED 036 483.

2. Sandefur, J. T. *An Illustrated Model for the Evaluation of Teacher Education Graduates.* Washington, D.C.: AACTE, 1970.

3. Sandefur, J. T., et al. *An Experimental Study of Professional Education for Secondary Teachers.* Emporia: Kansas State Teachers College, 1967. ERIC ED 022 724.

4. Sandoz, Ellis. "CBTE: The Nays of Texas." *Phi Delta Kappan* 55, no. 5 (January 1974), 304-306.

5. Savason, Seymour B. *The Culture of the Public School and the Problem of Change.* Boston: Allyn & Bacon, 1971.

6. Schaefer, J. *A Biliography of References Used in the Preparation of Nine Model Teacher Education Programs.* Washington, D.C.: ERIC Clearinghouse on Teacher Education, 1969. ERIC ED 031 460.

7. Schalock, H. Del. "The Focus of Performance Based Certification: Knowledge, Teaching Behavior, or the Products?" *Performance Based Certification of School Personnel.* Washington, D.C.: ERIC Clearinghouse on Teacher Education and the Association of Teacher Educators, 1971, pp. 41-49. ERIC ED 045 550.

8. ————. "An Overview of the Oregon Elementary Teacher Education Program and Feasibility of Its Implementation." *Journal of Research and Development in Teacher Education* 3, no. 3 (spring 1970), 68-79.

9. Schalock, H. Del, et al. *A Competency Based, Field Centered Systems Approach to Elementary Teacher Education.* Portland, Ore.: Northwest Regional Laboratory, 1968.

10. Schalock, H. Del, et al. *A Plan for Managing the Development, Implementation, and Operation of a Model Elementary Teacher Education Program.* Monmouth: Oregon College of Education, 1969.

11. Schmidtlein, F. "The Program of the Fifteen Regional Educational Laboratories." *Journal of Research and Development in Education* 3, no. 2 (winter 1970).

12. Schmieder, Allen A. "Competency Based Education, A Profile of the States." Washington, D.C.: U.S. Office of Education, Commissioner's Annual Report to the Congress, 1973.

13. ————. *Competency Based Education: The State of the Scene.* Washington, D.C.: AACTE, 1973.

14. ————. *A Glossary for Competency Based Education.* Washington, D.C.: U.S. Office of Education, National Center for the Improvement of Educational Systems, 1973.

15. ————. *Reformese Jargon: The Language and Literature of Educational Reform.* Washington, D.C.: U.S. Office of Education, National Center for the Improvement of Educational Systems, ERIC Clearinghouse on Teacher Education, 1973.

16. Schmieder, Allen A., and Holwenzak, Stephen. "Consortia." *Competency Based Teacher Education.* Palo Alto, Calif.: Science Research Associates, 1972.

17. *School Library Personnel: Task Analysis Survey.* Chicago: American Library Association, School Library Manpower Project, 1969.

18. Schulberg, H. G., et al., eds. *Program Evaluation in the Health Fields.* New York: Behavioral Publications, 1969.

19. Schure, Alex. "Educational Escalation Through Systems Analysis—Project ULTRA at New York Institute of Technology." *Audiovisual Instruction* 10, no. 5 (May 1965), 371-377.

20. Schwartz, L. "Survey of Certification Requirements for Teachers of Children with Learning Disabilities." Paper presented at the Conference of the Association for Children with Learning Disabilities, Fort Worth, Texas, 1969. ERIC ED 032 999.

21. Schwartz, L., et al. *Innovative Noncategorical and Interrelated Projects in the Education of the Handicapped.* Tallahassee: Florida State University, College of Education, 1972.

22. Searle, William, ed. *Teacher Education—Still an Urgent Matter.* Durham, N.H.: New England Program in Teacher Education, 1972.

23. Selden, David. "Evaluate Teachers?" AFT QUEST Paper no. 4. Washington, D.C.: American Federation of Teachers, 1969.

24. *Senate Bill 8.* Austin: Texas State Legislature, 1972.

25. Shaftel, Fannie R. *The Stanford Evaluation of Nine Elementary Teacher Training Models.* Washington, D.C.: U.S. Office of Education, Bureau of Research, 1969. ERIC ED 037 395.

26. Shane, Harold G. *The Educational Significance of the Future.* Washington, D.C.: U.S. Office of Education, World Future Society, 1972.

27. Shearron, Gilbert F. "Some Contributions to Competency Based Teacher Education Made by the 'Elementary Models.' " Address to the Association for Teacher Education, Chicago, 1973. Athens: University of Georgia, College of Education, 1973.

28. Shearron, Gilbert F., and Johnson, Charles E. "A Competency Based Teacher Education Program in Action: University of Georgia." *Journal of Teacher Education* 24, no. 3 (fall 1973), 187-193.

29. ————. *A Prototype for a Competency Based Proficiency Module.* Athens: University of Georgia, College of Education, 1969.

30. Shearron, Gilbert F., and Johnson, Charles E., eds. *Specification Worksheets for Behaviors in the Arts and Sciences.* Athens: University of Georgia, College of Education, 1969. ERIC ED 040 935.

31. ————. Specification Worksheets for Behaviors Drawn from Educational Principles. Athens: University of Georgia, College of Education, 1969. ERIC ED 040 934.

32. ————. Specification Worksheets for Cognitive Processes and Affective Behaviors. Athens: University of Georgia, College of Education, 1969. ERIC ED 040 933.

33. ————. Specification Worksheets for Language Arts Behavior. Athens: University of Georgia, College of Education, 1969. ERIC ED 040 936.

34. Shearouse, H. S. "Planned Programs of Teacher Education versus Evaluation." Journal of Teacher Education 11, no. 2 (June 1970), 285-291.

35. Shepardson, Richard D. "A Survey (Utilizing the Delphi Method) to Assess and Objectively Display the Arguments for and against Developing a Performance Based Teacher Education Program." Journal of Teacher Education 13, no. 2 (summer 1972), 166-168.

36. Shmuck, Richard A., and Runkel, Philip J. Handbook of Organization Development in Schools. Palo Alto, Calif.: National Press Books, 1972.

37. Shofstall, W. P. Accountability and Certification. Phoenix: Arizona State Department of Education, 1972.

38. ————. Ten Assumptions about Performance Based Recertification. Phoenix: Arizona State Department of Education, 1972.

39. Shugrue, Michael F. Performance Based Teacher Education and the Subject Matter Fields. Washington, D.C.: AACTE, 1973.

40. Siegel, Laurence, ed. Instruction: Some Contemporary Viewpoints. San Francisco: Chandler, 1967.

41. Silberman, Charles. Crisis in the Classroom. New York: Random House, 1970.

42. Simandle, Sidney. "Certification across State Lines." NEA Journal 55, no. 9 (December 1965), 56-58.

43. Simpson, R. H. Teacher Self-Evaluation. New York: Macmillan, 1966.

44. Skager, Rodney. "The System for Objectives Based Evaluation—Reading." Center for the Study of Evaluation 3 (September 1971), 6-11.

45. Slaughter, Eugene E. "The Use of Examinations for State Certification of Teachers." Journal of Teacher Education 11, no. 2 (June 1960), 231-239.

46. Smith, B. Othanel. "Certification of Educational Personnel." Paper read to the Council of Chief State School Officers, San Diego, 1971.

47. Smith, B. Othanel, and Orlosky, Donald. "The Development of Protocol Materials." Acquiring Teaching Competencies: Reports and Studies. Report no. 3. Bloomington: Indiana University, School of Education, National Center for the Development of Training Materials in Teacher Education, 1973.

48. Smith, B. Othanel, et al. Strategies of Teaching. Urbana: University of Illinois, Bureau of Educational Research, 1967.

49. Smith, B. Othanel, et al. Teachers for the Real World. Washington, D.C.: AACTE, 1969.

50. Smith, B. Othanel, ed. Research in Teacher Education: A Symposium. Washington, D.C.: AACTE, 1971. ERIC ED 049 193.

51. Smith, E. Brooks. *Needed: A New Order in Student Teaching That Brings Joint Accountability for Professional Development.* 1968. ERIC ED 023 624.
52. Smith, Karl. *Cybernetic Principles of Learning and Educational Design.* New York: Holt, Rinehart & Winston, 1966.
53. Smith, Luis M., and Keith, Pat M. *Anatomy of Educational Innovation.* New York: John Wiley & Sons, 1971.
54. Smith, Robert G. *An Annotated Bibliography on the Design of Instructional Systems.* Alexandria, Va.: George Washington University, Human Resources Research Office, 1967.
55. Smith, William L. "First Steps First." *Competency Based Teacher Education.* Palo Alto, Calif.: Science Research Associates, 1972.
56. Soar, Robert. "Accountability: Assessment Problems and Possibilities." *Journal of Teacher Education* 24, no. 3 (fall 1973), 205-212.
57. *South Dakota Certification Advisory Committee Position Paper* (on Competency Based Certification of Educational Personnel). Pierre: South Dakota State Department of Public Instruction, 1972.
58. Southworth, Horton C. *A Model for Teacher Training for the Individualization of Instruction.* Pittsburgh: University of Pittsburgh, 1968.
59. Sowards, G. Wesley. *A Model for the Preparation of Elementary School Teachers.* Tallahassee: Florida State University, College of Education, 1968.
60. *Staff Development for Educational Personnel—Guideline Requirements in Preparation of Local Master Plans.* Concord: New Hampshire State Department of Education, 1971.
61. Stake, Robert E. *School Accountability Laws.* Los Angeles: University of California at Los Angeles, Center for the Study of Education, 1973.
62. *Standards for Accreditation of Teacher Education.* Washington, D.C.: National Council for Accreditation of Teacher Education, 1970.
63. *Standards of Competent and Ethical Professional Performance for Oregon's Certificated Educators.* Salem: Oregon State Department of Education, Teachers Standards and Practices Commission, 1970.
64. *Standards and Guidelines for the Approval of Institutions and Programs for Teacher Education—"Competency Based Program."* Raleigh: North Carolina State Department of Public Instruction, 1971.
65. *Standards for the Preparation and Certification of School Professional Personnel, 1971.* Olympia: Washington State Department of Public Instruction, 1971.
66. *Standards for State Approval of Teacher Education.* Lincoln: Nebraska State Department of Education, 1965.
67. *State Goals for Elementary and Secondary Education.* Denver: Cooperative Accountability Project, 1972.
68. *State and Local Responsibilities for Education.* Washington, D.C.: Council of Chief State School Officers, 1968.
69. *Statement regarding Consortium Developed, Competency Based, and Individualized Teacher Education Programs.* Olympia: Washington State Superintendent of Public Instruction, 1972.

70. Steffenson, James P., and Ingve, Cheryl. "Feasibility of the Elementary Teacher Education Model in Developing Institutions." *Journal of Research and Development in Teacher Education* 3, no. 3 (spring 1970), 107-119.

71. Stemnock, Suzanne K. *Evaluating Teaching Performance.* Washington, D.C.: NEA, Educational Research Service, 1969. ERIC ED 033 488.

72. Stendler, Celia B. "Aspects of Piaget's Theory That Have Implications for Teacher Education." *Journal of Teacher Education* 16, no. 3 (spring 1965), 329-35.

73. Stevens, John M. "Competency Based Education and Its Enemies." *Phi Delta Kappan* 55, no. 5 (January 1974), back cover.

74. Stewart, D. K. "The Articulated Instructional Media Program at the University of Wisconsin." *Audiovisual Instruction* 10, no. 5 (May 1965), 380-382.

75. Stiles, Lindley J. "Teacher Education Programs." *Encyclopedia of Educational Research.* New York: Macmillan, 1969, pp. 1414-1423.

76. Stiles, Lindley J., et al. *Teacher Certification and Preparation in Massachusetts.* Boston: Massachusetts Advisory Council on Education, 1968.

77. Stimson, James. "The Educational Sociologist's Role in Competency Based Teacher Education." Paper presented at AERA, New Orleans, March 1973. New York: City University of New York, City College, 1973.

78. Stinnett, T. M. *A Manual on Certification Requirements for School Personnel in the United States, 1970 Edition.* Washington, D.C.: NEA, 1970.

79. ———. "Teacher Certification." *Encyclopedia of Educational Research.* New York: Macmillan, 1969, pp. 1410-1414.

80. ———. "Teacher Education, Certification, and Accreditation." *Education in the States: Nationwide Development Since 1900.* Washington, D.C.: NEA, 1969, pp. 381-437.

81. Stone, James C. "The Future of Teacher Education: Implications for a State Department of Education." *The Seattle Conference: The Role of the State Department of Education in Teacher Education.* Olympia, Wash.: State Superintendent of Public Instruction, 1967, pp. 23-24.

82. Strong, William. "A Switchboard Metaphor for Teacher Education." *Phi Delta Kappan* 55, no. 5 (January 1974), 341-343.

83. Stufflebeam, D. L., et al. *Educational Evaluation and Decision Making.* Itasca, Ill.: Peacock Publishers, 1971.

84. *Suggestions for Curriculum Content within Major Areas of Competencies.* Chicago: American Library Association, School Library Manpower Project, 1970.

85. Swineford, Edwin J. "Critical Teaching Strategies." *Journal of Teacher Education* 22, no. 1 (spring 1971), 29-36.

86. Sybouts, Ward. "Competency Based Teacher Education: Does It Make a Difference?" *Phi Delta Kappan* 54, no. 5 (January 1973), 303-304.

T

1. Tallmadge, G. Kasten, and Shearer, James W. "Relationships among Learning Styles, Instructional Methods, and the Nature of Learning Experiences." *Journal of Educational Psychology* 60, no. 3 (June 1969), 222-230.

2. Tanruther, E. M. *Clinical Experiences in Teaching for the Student Teacher or Intern.* New York: Dodd Mead, 1967.

3. *Teacher Aides, A Process Description for an Individualized Competency Based Approach to Training for Instructional Roles.* Minneapolis: Minnesota State Department of Education, 1972.

4. *Teacher Competency and Indicators Overarching Affective Reading.* New Paltz, N.Y.: State University College at New Paltz, CITE Project Workshop, 1973.

5. *Teacher Education Memoranda.* A series of memoranda on competency based education. Harrisburg, Pa.: Office of the Secretary of Education, Bureau of Teacher Education and Certification, 1972-73.

6. *Teacher Education at Southwest Minnesota State College.* Marshall: Southwest Minnesota State College, School of Education, 1973.

7. *Texas Standards for Teacher Education and Certification.* Austin: Texas State Education Agency, 1972.

8. *The Role of the State Department in Managing Teacher Education and Certification.* Tallahassee: Florida State Department of Education, 1971.

9. *The State Department of Education.* Washington, D.C.: Council of Chief State School Officers, 1952.

10. *The State of State Departments of Education.* Fourth Annual Report of the Advisory Council on State Departments of Education. Washington, D.C.: Government Printing Office, 1969.

11. *There's a New School Coming.* Tallahassee: Florida State Department of Education, 1972.

12. Thiagarjan, S., et al. *Sourcebook on Instructional Development for Training Teachers of Exceptional Children.* Bloomington: Indiana University, Center for Innovation in Teaching the Handicapped, 1973.

13. Thomas, Thomas C., and McKinney, Dorothy. *Accountability in Education.* Menlo Park, Calif.: Stanford Research Institute, 1972.

14. Thomson, J. "A Note on the Evaluation of Teaching Performance." *Journal of Educational Administration* 9 (May 1971), 74-78.

15. Tittle, Carol K. "Assessment and Context: The Case for Assessing the Environment as Well as Teacher Competency." Paper presented at AERA, New Orleans, March 1973. New York: City University of New York, Office of Teacher Education, 1973.

16. ————. "Program Priorities in Teacher Education." Paper presented at AERA, Chicago, 1972.

17. Travers, R. "A Study of the Relationship of Psychological Research to Educational Practice." *Training Research and Education.* Pittsburgh: University of Pittsburgh Press, 1962.

18. Travers, R. M., ed. *Second Handbook of Research on Teaching.* Chicago: Rand McNally, 1973.
19. Trow, William C. *Teacher and Technology—New Design for Learning.* New York: Meredith Publishing Co., 1963.
20. Turner, Richard L., "Levels of Criteria." *The Power of Competency Based Teacher Education.* Edited by Benjamin Rosner. Boston: Allyn & Bacon, 1972.
21. Twelker, Paul A. "Classroom Simulation and Teacher Preparation." *School Review* 75 (summer 1967), 197-204.
22. *Two Vocational and Applied Arts Education Systems Models.* Detroit: Wayne State University, Department of Vocational and Applied Arts Education, 1973.
23. Tyler, Ralph W. *Educational Evaluation: New Roles, New Means.* Sixty-eight Yearbook, Part II, of the National Society for the Study of Education. Chicago: University of Chicago Press, 1969.

U

1. Ullmann, Leonard P., and Krasner, Leonard. *Case Studies in Behavior Modification.* New York: Holt, Rinehart & Winston, 1965.
2. Ulrich, R. E., et al. *Control of Human Behavior.* 3 vols. Glenview, Ill.: Scott, Foresman & Co., vol. 1, 1966; vol. 2, 1970; vol. 3, 1974.

V

1. Vail, Robert B., et al. *Questions and Answers about Local Certificates.* Montpelier, Vt.: State Department of Education, Division of Teacher and Continuing Education, 1973.
2. Veldman, Donald J. *Student Evaluation of Teaching.* Research Methodology Monograph no. 10. Austin: University of Texas at Austin, Research and Development Center of Teacher Education, 1970.
3. Verner, Zenobia, et al. *Generic Competencies for Secondary School Teachers.* Houston, Tex.: University of Houston, College of Education, 1973.
4. Viall, William P. "The NASDTEC—AAAS Teacher Preparation Certification Study." *Journal of Teacher Education* 11, no. 2 (June 1960), 273-276.
5. Voelker, Alan M. "Competencies Approach to Teacher Education." *The Science Teacher* 37, no. 6 (September 1970), 37-39.
6. Von Meter, Eddy, and Leftoff, Marty. *A Competency Based Training Package for Educational Building Administrators.* In cooperation with Kansas Conclave of Professors of Educational Administrators. Manhattan: Kansas State University, 1972.

W

1. Walter, Kenneth A. *Authoring Individualized Learning Modules: A Teacher Training Manual.* Rockville, Md.: Montgomery County Public Schools;

Washington, D.C.: National Center for Educational Research and Development, 1970. ERIC ED 047 529.

2. Watson, Joseph. *Curriculum Specialist's Role in Enabling Interns to Acquire and Demonstrate Mastery of Teaching Competencies.* Madison: University of Wisconsin, Teacher Corps Associates Program, 1973.

3. Watson, Paul G. "Instructional Strategies and Learning Systems." *Audiovisual Instruction* 13, no. 8 (October 1968), 842-846.

4. Weber, Wilford A., and Cooper, James M. *Competency Based Teacher Education: A Scenario.* Washington, D.C.: AACTE, 1972.

5. Weber, Wilford, and Rathbone, Charles. "A Study of the Feasibility of the Syracuse University Model for the Preservice and Inservice Education of Elementary School Teachers—A Summary." *Journal of Research and Development in Teacher Education* 3, no. 3 (spring 1970), 80-93.

6. Weigand, James, ed. *Developing Teacher Competencies.* Englewood Cliffs, N.J.: Prentice-Hall, 1971.

7. Werdell, Philip R. *Courses and Teacher Evaluation.* Washington, D.C.: National Student Education Association, 1967. ERIC ED 050 693.

8. White, Louise R. "Performance Based Teacher Education in a Multi-cultural Society." *Journal of Teacher Education* 24, no. 3 (fall 1973), 225-231.

9. *Who's in Charge Here?: Fixing Responsibilities for Student Teaching.* Washington, D.C.: NEA, National Commission on Teacher Education and Professional Standards, 1966.

10. Winget, Lerue W., et al. "State Departments of Education within State Governments." *Education in the States: Nationwide Development Since 1900.* Washington, D.C.: NEA, 1969, pp. 1354-1357.

11. Wittrock, M. C., and Wiley, David E. *The Evaluation of Instruction: Issues and Problems.* New York: Holt, Rinehart & Winston, 1970.

12. Woodington, Donald D. "The Challenge of Accountability for Effective SEA Administration." Paper presented at AERA, New Orleans, March 1973. Denver: Colorado Department of Education, 1973.

13. Woodruff, Asahel D. "Performance Based Teacher Education 10 Years Hence." *Journal of Teacher Education* 24, no. 3 (fall 1973), 238-243.

14. Woodruff, Asahel D., and Taylor, Janyce L. *A Teaching Behavior Code.* Salt Lake City: Utah State Board of Education, 1970.

15. Woolman, Lorraine. *The Effect of Video-Taped Single Concept Demonstrations in an Inservice Program for Improving Instruction.* Houston, Tex.: University of Houston, College of Education, Bureau of Education Research and Services, 1969. ERIC ED 032 771.

16. Wright, Clifford J., and Nuthall, Graham. "Relationships between Teacher Behaviors and Pupil Achievement in Three Experimental Elementary Science Lessons." *American Educational Research Journal* 7, no. 4 (November 1970), 477-491.

17. Wright, J. Zeb, ed. *Models for Revising Teacher Education.* Charleston, W. Va.: State Department of Education, 1971. ERIC ED 054 081.

Y

1. Yarger, Samuel J., and Mallan, John T. *Instructional Modules: The Corner-stone of Competency Based Education.* Syracuse, N.Y.: Syracuse University, College of Education, 1973.
2. Yarington, David J. "A Performance Curriculum for Training Reading Teachers." *Journal of Reading* 13, no. 1 (October 1969), 21-24.
3. Yarington, David J., and Boffey, Barnes. "Report on a Performance Curriculum for Teacher Training." *Journal of Reading* 15, no. 2 (November 1971), 115-118.
4. *Year End Status Report, Competency Based Teacher Preparation in Michigan.* Lansing: Michigan State Department of Education, 1973.
5. Yevish, Irving A. "The Observation Fallacy." *Educational Forum* 32, no. 2 (January 1968), 171-175.
6. Young, David B. "Teacher Education Centers Make a Difference." Paper presented at AERA, Minneapolis, March 1970. ERIC ED 044 356.
7. Young, Dorothy A., and Young, David B. "The Effectiveness of Individually Prescribed Microteaching Training Modules on an Intern's Subsequent Classroom Performance." Paper presented at AERA, Los Angeles, February 1969. ERIC ED 030 586.
8. Young, James. "Confusion Is Certification by Performance." *New York State Education* 57 (February 1970), 20-23.

Z

1. Zoellner, Robert. "Behavioral Objectives for English." *College English* 33, no. 4 (January 1972), 418-432.